THE COOL WEB

The Pattern of
Children's Reading

MARGARET MEEK
AIDAN WARLOW
GRISELDA BARTON

THE BODLEY HEAD
LONDON   SYDNEY
TORONTO

For Denys Harding and James Britton
in gratitude and admiration

Editors' note

The text of this book was prepared in 1974, in
anticipation of the Bullock Report, *A Language
for Life,* published by HMSO in 1975. It shares
with that publication contemporary references
to recurrent interests in offering a contribution
to the theoretical study of the place of literature in literacy. *The Cool Web* was planned for
publication by the Oxford University Press in
1975, but production was interrupted at proof
stage and the book was subsequently transferred to the imprint of the Bodley Head.

critical commentary © Margaret Meek,
Aidan Warlow and Griselda Barton 1977
ISBN 0 370 10863 9
Printed and bound in Great Britain for
The Bodley Head Ltd
9 Bow Street, London WC2E 7AL
by Redwood Burn Ltd,
Trowbridge & Esher
First published 1977

Contents

Contents

Contents

SECTION THREE **Approaches to criticism**

Contents

Introduction

In 1969 a collection of essays about books and writing for children appeared in Canada under the Oxford University Press imprint with the title *Only Connect*. The essays were chosen by Canadian teachers who studied and taught literature for children and whose concern was to show that, if the author's art is good enough, books for children are 'an essential part of the whole realm of literary activity, to be discussed in the same terms and judged by the same standards as would apply to any other branch of writing.' They continue by saying 'We do not subscribe to the view that criticism of children's books calls for the adoption of a special scale of values.' By including in the book the now classic pieces by T. S. Eliot, Graham Greene, J. R. R. Tolkien, C. S. Lewis, and others, the editors summed up the claims that were being made for children's books at that time by authors, critics, librarians, and publishers (but, in England, less by teachers): that writing and reading stories for children was an activity of creative significance which adults could take seriously. They suggested that literature, however defined, began with Beatrix Potter and stretched in a developmental line to the *Portrait of the Artist as a Young Man*; that myth, legend, and fairy tales are archetypal forms which engage the imagination at an early age, and that children's literature has its own genres, comparable with those in adult literature, to be delineated and studied.

S. Egoff *et al.*
Only Connect
OUP Toronto
1969

   This is an important thesis, built up from the statements of those whose contribution to children's literature is outstanding. It has a counterpart in the wider realm of certain kinds of literary criticism which maintains that literature is a vehicle for learning to mature, where 'mature' means putting away or growing out of childish things, and these things might even include fairy-stories, science fiction, and formula novels.

   While *Only Connect* and a more recent collection, *Children and Literature*, confirmed the belief of its editors and readers in the importance of adult standards and judgements of children's literature, it left essential questions unexamined. What do children actually get out of reading? Do all children profit equally? Do we really 'grow out of' fairy stories? Can we be so sure about what a good book is without reference to the reader? How can we form judgements when the reader cannot be

V. Haviland (editor)
Children and Literature
Scott, Foresman
1973
English edition
The Bodley Head
1974

explicit about his own judgement or response ? How does the author who writes the books children read see his audience ? What do the mediators think: the editors who choose the books, the teachers who put them in the classrooms, and the librarians ? What about the comics that millions of children read ? Is it helpful to 'worry about the rubbish', in Aidan Chambers' words, or can we be reassured ? All of these questions have had an airing, and the provision of books for children has gone ahead on a vast scale, accompanied by bibliophilic criticism on the one hand – a new scrutiny of minor works of art – and on the other, a preoccupation both with the teaching of reading and with topic and non-fiction books.

A. Chambers
Introducing Books to Children
Heinemann, 1973

But if the focus of attention moves to the reader of the book rather than to the author or the topic, there has to be a comparable shift of emphasis in other quarters, and this has happened since the first appearance of *Only Connect*. Critical studies of adult books have changed, have become more socially aware, less coterie-centred, and more international. It is no longer enough to press for 'adult standards' in children's books in general. The notion has to be particularized. The insights of authors and critics of children's books continue to develop, and many of their writings deserve a wider audience and a longer home than their first appearance offered them. It would be difficult to justify another collection of essays such as this, unless it opened up a way forward from the minority cult which children's literature can so easily become if the authors and the critics, mutually sustaining as they are, lose sight of the readers. The adult's response and the child's cannot be the same; the former has a memory of childhood and categories for delineating experience and judging it. The latter has childhood itself, passing every day, and memory is one of the things that a reading experience creates.

Teachers have discovered that, in coming to terms with the challenge of teaching children to read, they find themselves asking over and over again 'What is reading *for* ?' They have had lots of help in choosing books: the reviewing media have increased so that *Watership Down* found its niche and its audience with great speed compared with *Swallows and Amazons*. Consequently, teachers are tackling with new zest questions which ask about the relationship of literature to life, looking even beyond the authors and critics for insights to help them. Next, professional educators, compensating for what they once ignored, have moved into the world of children's books and made it a kind of growth industry in researches and studies embracing psychology, sociology, linguistics, and librarianship. The Schools Council has inaugurated two projects, one on what boys and girls read and the other on children as readers. All these concerns, and the studies that link language and learning, children's understanding and children's writing, show that the thesis that literature is a special vehicle for the growth of special human beings who are learning to value their cultural heritage is too restrictive. Similarly, how a 'good' book for children is judged becomes less obvious and has to be redefined, and the once popular 'genre' theories of children's books – fables, fairy-stories, fantasy, realism – taken from models in adult literature are no longer found to be as helpful as once they were.

These speculations have to be seen against a background both wider and more specific. It is wider in that we need to begin by examining what the reader has to learn in relation to *narrative*, and how he uses this convention to organize his experience – including his dreams and his fantasies – into a conception of the world. The background is more specific when set against the art form we call 'story'. What is the nature of the experience which gives a young reader a memory and a past not his own, or projects him into a future he might never have anticipated? How is reading related to our experience of the outer workaday world and to the inner world of feeling and to the growth of personality?

It is the responsibility of all those who play a part in teaching children to read to examine the nature of certain specific aspects of the reading experience, notably those concerned with narrative, story, or fiction. We have therefore collected these essays and joined them loosely by a running commentary in order to bring together what Piaget calls 'a rich exchange of values'. Our examination of experiences generally found in stories called fiction will, we hope, encourage others to make their own.

The writings are collected under these headings:
The reader: which defines the realm and the modes of experience.
The authors: which looks at how those who write for children see their role.
Approaches to criticism: which collects the writings of those concerned with the application of critical ideas to children's books.
Ways forward: which suggests the kinds of study which are relevant as our knowledge increases.
The *Bibliography* contains a list of sources that have contributed to the central ideas of the book and a list of relevant reading so that the ideas contained in the essays can be pursued further.

The reader

Introduction

'Imaginary gardens with real toads in them'

We begin with the young reader and the book. We look at them together and are
disposed to believe that we understand what is the traffic between them, the
operation of the one on the other. Although he moves scarcely at all, the reader
may be in rapid flight across time and space, or deep in some exploration of
himself. Silent as he is to the onlooker, the author speaks to his reader as clearly as
if he were present. The relationship between them is made and sustained by a
mutual agreement that the one should tell and the other should interpret the
telling in a way that seems like listening.

By learning to read, the child satisfies the adults around him that he now
has access to one of the ways by which his society organizes itself. He satisfies
himself that, having mastered a complicated learning task, he can take on others
like it, and that he now has the means of deriving meaning from print so that
he scarcely even sees the words. The worry that surrounds illiterates focuses on
the fact that they become social cripples, as that aspect of their lack is easiest to
define. But they are also shut out from a way of looking at the world which
other people habitually use as if it were an extension of their perceptions. Unable
to read, a child or an adult is cut off from a way of entering into the experiences
of other people the better to understand his own.

This access to experience by means of reading is the central theme of this
collection of essays. For all our preoccupation with children learning to read, we
have not fully accepted the implications of the fact that the real book for our
children is the story book. Offering stories to be read is the way our print-
dominated society carries on a habit even older than writing and as common as
bread – telling stories and listening to them.

Almost too readily we believe that, in our electronic age, the habit of storytelling has been lost so that we have stopped expecting it to operate. But it is
still powerfully there, behind the news bulletin, the strip cartoon, the sports
report. Ask a friend about his holidays, how he moved house, what happened to

J. N. Britton
Language and Learning
Allen Lane
1970

his car, wife, sweetheart, dog, and the result will be a narrative. We sort out our sense impressions into storying. Indeed, as James Britton says, 'We so readily construct stories out of past experience that it is difficult to perceive that anything has been constructed at all.' We usually call it memory, and leave it there. But man makes an autobiography of his past that is the parallel of history; thus *Akenfield* is both chronicle and personal narrative embalmed in print. Storying is the most significant way we explain how we came to be where we are, and a universal language habit that transcends all cultural barriers. We are cut off from its origins by the device of writing.

For an extensive
discussion of this
topic see J. Goody
and I. Watt 'The
Consequences of
Literacy' (1963)
reprinted in
P. P. Gigliogli
(editor)
*Language and Social
Context*
Penguin Books, 1972

For children, narrative or storying operates in a way that is both like and unlike its function for adults. The similarity of organization sometimes obscures the difference of significance. In cognitive development, in categorizing information, in progressing to abstract thought from concrete actions, the role of narrative is crucial. This is how James Moffett explains it:

'Whereas adults differentiate their thought with specialized kinds of discourse such as narrative, generalization, and theory, children must, for a long time, make narrative do for all. They utter themselves almost entirely through stories – real or invented – and they apprehend what others say through story. The young learner, that is, does not talk and read explicitly about categories and theories of experience, he talks and reads about characters, events, and settings [which are] charged with symbolic meaning because they are tokens standing for unconscious classes and postulations of experience, the sort we can infer from regularities in their behaviour ...

James Moffett
*Teaching the Universe
of Discourse*
Houghton Mifflin
1968

Children must represent in one mode of discourse – the narrative level of abstraction – several kinds of conception that in the adult world would be variously represented at several layers of abstraction.'

The child's conception of the world is rooted in this narrative organization. He uses it to draw a boundary between himself and what is outside himself. Both are distinctively 'real' to him, but until he is able to know himself as a thinking being, his thought 'is a prey to perpetual confusion between objective and subjective, between the real and the ostensible.' The crucial question is to make sense of the world and to be at home in it. The child's distinctive mode of action for doing this is *play*, the symbolic representation of what has happened or what he hopes to bring about. The essential quality of play is that of *trying out*, what Piaget calls 'assimilation without the need for accommodation'. Language is an essential part of the organization of play, and also a plaything. Parents offer children stories and nursery rhymes as they give them toys: *Hey Diddle Diddle, Little Miss Muffet*,

cf. Jean Piaget
*The Child's
Conception of the
World*
Routledge and
Kegan Paul, 1929
(Paladin edition
1973 is source
of quotations). Here,
as elsewhere, the
juxtaposition of
ideas owes much to
the bedrock of
Piagetian studies

The House that Jack Built. Long before they make their contribution to the conversation of mankind, children learn that language represents both what *is*, and *is not*, and they discover the enabling power of the image. They can understand eyes as big as saucers, boots that march seven leagues, a wardrobe that opens into fairyland. Thus, when they are organizing the world into 'inner' and 'outer', they are also exploiting the gap between what *is*, and what language *says*. Between the ages of about six and twelve, the child becomes aware of thought, of dreams, and above all, of his emotions and feelings, all in the form of narrative. As he becomes aware of Story he organizes a series of secondary worlds which operate according to rules he comes to recognize.

In listening to stories or reading them, the child moves outwards from himself into a world of action, or inwards into his thoughts and feelings. Because the limits he draws between himself and the outside world are less rigid than in later life, he construes experience gained in stories both as memory (that is, backwards) and as an anticipation of events, real or imagined (that is, forwards). This is possible because the storyteller makes a whole world self-contained and self-consistent, just as a child makes a whole world from his experience, real or imaginary, relating everything he knows to everything else. He and the author have a social bond which operates in place of logic. The author offers the child a kind of world which the child enters and surveys from the inside; 'getting lost in a story' is a more distinctive characteristic of a child's reading than an adult's, although there is enough evidence that this does not fade with age. This theme is taken up in Section one.

Most of the ideas in this introduction recur in the essays that follow. Our chief intention in introducing them is to show the nature of the insights which are available and which, as far as we know, are not generally applied to books written for children nor readily accessible to those whose concern is to teach children to read. We should be less than honest if we did not admit to certain perplexities about the way children *understand* stories. The whole topic of response is fraught with indecision. We see characters and events from books reappearing in children's play, in their writing, and in what at first sight look like 'original' stories made up by children. We know very little about obvious obstacles – how children understand narrated time sequences, or the eliptical structure of a ballad or narrative poem. What clues do they follow to construe a narrative, other than the 'rule of three' for the fairy-story, for example?

Because of their connection with children learning to read, we seem to mention stories mostly in the context of young children. But there is another great storying

cf. A. R. Luria and O. S. Vinogradova *Speech and the Development of Mental Processes in the Child* 1959 Penguin Books 1971 edition

This point is dealt with in detail in K. Chukovsky *From Two to Five* University of California Press 1963

J. Piaget and
B. Inhelder
*The Growth of Logical
Thinking from
Childhood to
Adolescence*
Routledge and
Kegan Paul, 1958

burst at adolescence where the connection with development is again crucial. As Piaget demonstrates, when the making of new worlds in terms of ideas becomes an adolescent preoccupation, narrative or storying is again the chief method of describing a desired experience, helping to project 'the world as I would like it to be' and 'the adult role I should like to play in it'.

The loss of literary innocence comes when the reader stands outside and looks in on the storyteller's world from the adult's viewpoint. At the same time he discovers that in adult stories – in novels – the ending is not always happy, the issues are ambiguous, the characters are mixed in motive and feeling. This is where the authors who have made their distinctive contribution to storying like best to dwell. This is where Alan Garner's readers become the readers of Henry James.

But adult literary taste and discernment do not just happen. They are developed and refined from the earlier forms of response to stories at each stage of growth.

The growth is cognitive, affective, moral. Cognitive in that, for a considerable time, the subject matter of history and geography, religious education, and some sciences are forms of fiction. 'A child approaches the facts of history,' says James Britton 'by involving himself in the lives of people of past ages ... It is by sharing their experiences that he moves towards an impersonal appreciation of historical issues.'

The phrase and
concept were first
used by R. Jones in
*Fantasy and Feeling
in Education*
Penguin Books, 1972

E. Cook
*The Ordinary and
the Fabulous*
CUP, 1969

Affective and moral development are notoriously under-researched, but story is at the heart. Where our authors examine the child's notions of fear, for example, the issue becomes one of 'imagining reality the better to test it'. There is no doubt that myths, legends, and fairy tales are archetypal symbols of feeling ... 'a world of fighting, of sudden reversals of fortune, of promises kept and broken, of commands delayed, of wanderings, of quests, of testing and judgement, gratitude and ingratitude, and light and darkness. It is clearly impressed with patterns that anyone can trace, more uncertainly, in his own experience of the primary worlds.'

Anyone who would know more about the affective development of children must draw on evidence offered by children's responses to stories. Such evidence as we have is notoriously 'soft', but we would argue that, besides the material gathered in surveys of children's tastes and choices (governed as these are by fashion and local availability) we need insights such as are contained in James Britton's paper on 'The Role of Fantasy' and Aidan Warlow's analysis of 'Alternative Worlds Available'. A theory of emotional development begins, like that of Sartre, by sketching the way the child sees the requirements the world makes of him. His response to an author is a measure of his willingness to concede the

J. P. Sartre
*Sketch for the Theory
of the Emotions*
1939
(trans. Philip Mairet)
Methuen, 1962

author's demands. In the same way, we should be looking at the child's moral judgement in terms of the kind of universe he can tolerate. In a London school with a high proportion of immigrant children, *The Eagle of the Ninth*, a story of Roman Britain, is accepted by the pupils of West Indian origin better than many a cruder attempt to depict their lot in 'realistic' stories. The truth to feeling is more important than a simple transcription of surface actuality. In Rosemary Sutcliff's novel there is a chapter in which a British girl tells the Roman centurion about how her aunt wants her to conform to Roman ways. The pupils see this as symbolic of their predicament and respond accordingly.

The testimony comes from our colleague Mrs Joan Goody

For the last twenty years or so, strong claims have been made by adults for the artistic validity of stories written for children. These claims have now been conceded. By the very quality of their work, children's authors are accepted as artists in their own right, and splendid books abound. Our chief concern here is to focus on the reader and to ask about the nature of his experience in the development of his thinking and feeling. We have emphasized the point that, although it is possible to judge books for children by what are called 'adult standards' and regard them as part of literature, the young reader carries a different world in his head, no less complex than an adult's but differently organized. He needs his stories in a different way, his experience of reading must be different. When discussing stories for children, to lose sight of the reader is too dangerous to contemplate.

Narrative as a primary act of mind

The main theme of the book begins with a statement that narrative is a basic way of organizing human experience. Barbara Hardy, Professor of English Literature in the University of London, argues that the act of the storyteller, the author, the novelist arises from what we all do all the time, in remembering, dreaming, planning. To extend the insights of this essay to the whole realm of stories and books for children would increase our awareness of how the stories we tell or read to children are related to those they tell themselves.

Towards a poetics of fiction: an approach through narrative

Barbara Hardy

My approach through *narrative* is set forward neither as primary nor comprehensive but as locally illuminating. My argument is that narrative, like lyric or dance, is not to be regarded as an aesthetic invention used by artists to control, manipulate, and order experience, but as a primary act of mind transferred to art from life. The novel merely heightens, isolates, and analyses the narrative motions of human consciousness. One might say that the novelists have been more concerned with this element of fiction than the critics, and indeed the main point of this essay is to suggest that we go to novels to find out about narrative. Novelists have for a long time known enough about the narrative mode to be able to work in it, criticize it, and even play with it. Sterne juggles, shows off, and teases us in a form which draws special attention to its own nature – and ever since, novelists have been dislocating, inverting, attenuating, and analysing narrative. The uses and dislocations exist in a pre-aesthetic state in routine acts of human consciousness, and the 'analysis' is not narrowly literary but extends to the whole range of physic narratives.

I take for granted the ways in which storytelling engages our interest, curiosity,

fear, tensions, expectation, and sense of order. What concern me here are the
qualities which fictional narrative shares with that inner and outer storytelling that
plays a major role in our sleeping and waking lives. For we dream in narrative,
daydream in narrative, remember, anticipate, hope, despair, believe, doubt, plan,
revise, criticize, construct, gossip, learn, hate, and love by narrative. In order really
to live, we make up stories about ourselves and others, about the personal as well
as the social past and future.

I set out this long, incomplete, and highly obvious list not simply to point to
the narrative structure of acts of mind but to suggest the deficiency of our commonly
posited antagonism between dream and realistic vision. Educationalists still suggest
that the process of maturation involves a movement out of the fantasy-life into a
vision of life 'as it is'. Teachers have even constructed syllabuses on the assumption
that we begin with fairy tales and daydreams and work gradually into realistic
modes. John Stuart Mill, with his feelings restored by the poetry of Wordsworth,
took the love of narrative to be characteristic of the infancy of men and societies.
F. R. Leavis and his followers are stern about immature and indulgent fantasy in
literature. There is a widespread and, I suggest, dubious but understandable
assumption on the part of wishful believers in life-enhancement that human beings
begin by telling themselves fairy tales and end by telling truths.

If we apply some introspection it looks rather more as if we go on oscillating
between fairy tale and truth, dream and waking. Fantasy-life does not come to an
end at eighteen but goes on working together with the more life-orientated modes
of planning, faithful remembering, and rational appraisal. We can distinguish the
extremes of cut-off indulgent fantasy and faithful document, but the many intermediate states blur the distinction and are compounded of fantasy and realism.
The element of dream can be sterile and dangerously in-turned; it can also penetrate
deeply and accept a wide range of disturbing and irrational experience that cannot
easily, if at all, be accepted, ordered, understood, or reconstructed coherently and
dispassionately. Dream can debilitate, but its subversive discontents are vital for
personal and social development. It can provide escape or a look at the unwished-
for worst. It lends imagination to the otherwise limited motions of faithful memory
and rational planning. It acts on future, joining it with past. It creates, maintains,
and transforms our relationships: we come to know each other by telling, untelling,
believing, and disbelieving stories about each other's pasts, futures, and identities.
Dream probes and questions what can be the static and overly rational stories about
past, future, and identity, and is in the process itself steadied and rationally eroded.
We tell stories in order to escape from the stubbornness of identity, as Randall

Jarrell reminds us:

> What some escape to, some escape: if we find Swann's
> Way better than our own, and trudge on at the back
> Of the north wind to – to – somewhere east
> Of the sun, west of the moon, it is because we live
>
> By trading another's sorrow for our own; another's
> Impossibilities, still unbelieved in, for our own …
> 'I am myself still ?' For a little while, forget:
> The world's selves cure that short disease, myself,
> And we see bending to us, dewy-eyed, the great
> CHANGE, dear to all things not to themselves endeared.

Here, in *Children Selecting Books in a Library*, he argues the paradox that to be mature involves escape, or rehearses a non-attachment to self which is perfected in death. Thus we may be engaged in telling ourselves stories in a constant attempt to exchange identity and history, though many of us stay in love with ourselves, sufficiently self-attached to rewrite the other stories for our own purposes. But 'escaping' and 'escaping to' form only a part of narrative activity and function. We tell stories in order to change, remaking the past in a constant and not always barren *esprit d'escalier*. The polarity between fantasy and reality is another instance of convenient fiction: we look back to go forward or to stay in a past-centred obsession. Like most works of fiction, personal history is made up of fantasy and realism, production and idling.

We often tend to see the novel as competing with the world of happenings. I should prefer to see it as the continuation, in disguising and isolating art, of the remembering, dreaming, and planning that is in life imposed on the uncertain, attenuated, interrupted, and unpredictable or meaningless flow of happenings. Real life may have the disjointedness of a series of short stories, told by someone like Katherine Mansfield, but seldom has the continuity of a novel. Recollection of happenings, which removes certain parts for various conscious and unconscious motives, is the best life-model for the novel. We do not grow out of telling stories.

What consequences are involved in seeing fictional narrative as continuous with narrative action and reaction ? One might be the erosion of our favourite distinction between fantasy and reality. The best fantasists, as we know from introspection or from *Emma*, work in starkly realistic terms, staying in the drawing-room, using the minutiae of everyday dress and dialogue. Another consequence would be an increased attentiveness to the combination of reminiscence and anticipation, inter-penetrating each other and complicating the temporal relations of beginning, middle, and end as they do indeed in our play of consciousness, which is more like the loose-leaf novel than the Aristotelian progress. Another consequence would be the recognition that while twentieth-century interior monologues are more realistic in form than their Victorian predecessors, earlier novelists represent or symbolize the inner narrative in indirect and less mimetically accurate modes. Joyce and Proust and Beckett use the stream of consciousness in ways which force us to acknowledge the continuities of narrative I have spoken of, but eighteenth and nineteenth-century novelists use the multiple plot, the shifting point of view, the combined impersonal and personal narrative, the person-centred third-person novel, and so on, to represent the same confused and complex fluency of recording. Such earlier novels mime the sheer variety of mental narration, often most explicitly.

Children's novelists who use some of these rhetorical devices interestingly include George MacDonald (*At the Back of the North Wind*, 1871), A. A. Milne (*Winnie the Pooh*, 1926), Mary Norton (*The Borrowers*, 1952), and Alan Garner (*Red Shift*, 1973)

Out of many such interests, I take the self-conscious representation of narrative as a starting-point. Art-forms frequently and unsurprisingly discuss and explore the subject of their own mode. Narratives and dramas are often *about* making up stories and playing roles. The novel is introverted in this sense, not because novels tend to be about novels, but because they tend to be about the larger narrative structure of consciousness, and the value and dangers involved in narrative modes of invention, dream, casual projection, and so on. Sterne shows this introversion in a highly literary way, and his play, like most, is based on certainties, or at all events starts off from theories which are locally or temporarily entertained as exploratory hypotheses. When in *Tristram Shandy* he plays with the complexities of authorial voice, generality, omniscience, completion, chronological order, and biography, he reveals the complexities of such conventions by exaggeration, distortion, suspension, and isolation. Our attention is engaged with such narrative means in a play which temporarily and wittily presents them as ends. In order to perform such virtuoso acts of distortion and separation Sterne has had to identify, judge, and analyse as persistently and closely as any Hypercritic. Narrative – analysed and judged in the chronological displacements – is revealed as a coherence and a solicitation of curiosity, a movement towards completion. The very incoherence, the tantalizing, and the incompleteness unbare characteristics of narrative and also mime the complexity of the process in the primary act of consciousness. Tristram is both a novelist and an informal presenter, his medium close to the medium of interior monologue. He 'unrealistically' interrupts his story over

and over again, refuses to let us read straight through, frustrates and plays with
our desire to learn, know, keep to the point, and come to a conclusion. The form
is only unrealistic or artificial when contrasted with other narratives; set beside
the multiplicity and complexity of psychic narration it is close to life. Unrealistic,
rather, is the story that has its say for good long stretches, the story that is isolated,
the story that gets finished. One characteristic of most novels is the sheer number
of narratives they contain, and *Tristram Shandy's* many anecdotes, stories, tall
tales, travelogues, and so forth are small and artificial conventional stories that
draw attention to the fidelity of the main wayward stream.

    Beckett is perhaps the novelist closest to Sterne in his marvellous combination
of anecdote with discontinuous, self-defeating story. Joyce seems to me to mime
the life-narrative much less well, and to impose too great a control on fluency and
incompleteness, though I know this is open to argument. But all three provide us
with lucid criticism of narrative as well as with great narratives. They have
analysed well enough to play. Less realistic novelists, like the Victorians, seem to be
caught between the assured conventionality of an earlier age of fiction and the
assured brave dislocations of the next. They too are sufficiently in touch with the
forms of narrative in consciousness, using them implicitly and analysing them
explicitly, to be worth a look in this context. Fielding and Sterne, in their individual
ways, contrast the neatness of artistic narrative with the flux and fits and starts,
the untidiness and incompleteness of inner action. The Brontës, Thackeray, early
Dickens, George Eliot, and even Henry James, tend to divide action evenly
between many stories, and to avoid an encapsulated model of artificial narrative like
Sterne's anecdotes or the comic epic or the inset story. Their interest in narrative
tends to show itself in discussion. But there may be less obvious connections
between their narrative forms and narrative acts of mind. Charlotte and Emily
Brontë sometimes drive a lyric wedge between the narrative parts of their novels,
and their use of different narrators or points of view shows some reflection of the
tension between dream and actual vision, between wishing or praying, and
accepting events. The socially directed novels of Thackeray, Mrs Gaskell, and
Dickens show an insistence on the connections and collisions between separate
stories, though this is sometimes blurred by the Providential pattern. George Eliot
and Henry James, for all their differences in intensity, can combine a deep central
core of complex inner narrative – Dorothea's or Rowland Mallett's – with a briefer
treatment of another opposing or antagonistic story. James of course differs from
all the others I have mentioned in the way he centres the narrative on one register
of consciousness while avoiding a first-person novel. Charlotte Brontë and Dickens

are especially attached to narrative based on memory; George Eliot and Henry
James to the reports of immediate apprehension. Taking in the present might be
said to be the basic stance in their major novels. But all the novelists I have
mentioned not only reflect narrative forms but also discuss them.

James likes to show the working of sensibility and intelligence in the present
happening, but as he so often centres the interest in a spectator, he can show and
exploit a slight but subtle and important gap between happening and interpretation:
the narrative contains a narrative of what happens counterpointed on a narrative
of what seems to be happening, or what the spectator tells himself is happening.
The gap is also present but on an enormous scale and with vast irony in *Tom
Jones* and *Wuthering Heights*. One of James's great achievements is to narrow
the gap so that many readers never see it at all, and all readers have to work uncomfortably hard to see it. One of his major themes is the relation between what
happened and what was reported, expected, believed, dreamed, and falsified. The
self-contemplating narrative of fiction is nowhere subtler and more explicit than
in *The Ambassadors*.

Let us begin with the *locus classicus*, Strether by the river:
'What he saw was exactly the right thing – a boat advancing round the bend·
and containing a man who held the paddles and a lady, at the stern, with a pink
parasol. It was suddenly as if these figures, or something like them, had been
wanted in the picture, had been wanted more or less all day, and had now
drifted into sight, with the slow current, on purpose to fill up the measure.
They came down slowly, floating down, evidently directed to the landing-
place near their spectator and presenting themselves to him not less clearly as
the two persons for whom his hostess was already preparing a meal. For two
very happy persons he found himself straightway taking them – a young man
in shirtsleeves, a young woman easy and fair, who had pulled pleasantly
up from some other place, and being acquainted with the neighbourhood,
had known what this particular retreat could offer them. The air quite
thickened, at their approach, with further intimations; the intimation that they
were expert, familiar, frequent–that this wouldn't at all events be the first time.'
David Lodge, in *Language of Fiction*, quotes Wittgenstein's saying, 'The limits
of my language are the limits of my world.' Mediated through the limits of
James's language are the limits of his narrative, but he is explicitly aware of such
limitations, and they form at least a major part of his subject. Our narratives are
of course limited by our sensibility, inhibitions, language; history, intelligence,
inclinations to wish, hope, believe, dream. *The Ambassadors*, like most great

novels, is concerned with the powers and limitations of narrative, and so Strether is shown here, as elsewhere, as seeing and telling. He has been seeing these same characters and telling himself stories about them for a long time, and here he is, seeing them for the first time with the truly alienated vision of the stranger. He is therefore made to show his sensibilities as narrator. We are about to see – not for the last time, indeed, in this novel that goes on moving – a climactic collision between what he wants to tell and what he has to see. We see his impulse to order and his impulse to praise, first in the pure form of a vision of people who mean nothing to him. The imagery is pictorial and even impressionistic, deriving as it does from the generalized imagery of painters, painting, and aesthetic vision, and from the localized context of the remembered unbought Lambinet. But this is the kind of picture the impressionists did not paint, the kind that tells a story. James, like Lawrence, seems often to write about artists so that he may and yet need not be writing about novelists. Here the implications, for all the trembling visual delicacy and radiance, are plainly narrative. The figures are 'as if' wanted in the picture but they come to break down the picture's static composition, do not stay, like figures cut through by the frame, on the edge of the impressionist landscape. They continue to move, to come nearer and loom larger, they cease to be compositionally appropriate to the picture and become people. The stories Strether tells are elegant configurations, and who should know more than Strether's creator about the special temptations of aesthetic arrangement in narrative ? But Strether is also moved to tell stories out of curiosity: he does not know enough, he is kept guessing, there are secrets and mysteries. He is lied to by Little Bilham and left by Maria Gostrey, who runs away rather than lie or stop telling the story. Maria says at the end that Strether has been vague. He has also, of course, been benevolent. He is more like a Dickens than a James, trying to see the best in people, wanting his characters to be moral as well as dashing. James's method is to show the special bent of Strether's vague and curious benevolence almost unobtrusively set in a routine process of consciousness. What is there in this passage that is coloured by the viewpoint of Strether and his storytelling ? He straightway takes the couple for 'very happy persons' on the pretty slight evidence of their dress, their youth, the day, the boating, and nothing else. He sees them as having pulled 'pleasantly' from somewhere else. But much of what he says and thinks is rightly inferred from what is before him. Strether is not a narrator like Emma, who projects her wishful fantasies and interpretations on to highly intransigent materials. Strether needs more malleable stuff to work in. Just as Jane Austen tells us, as well as shows us, that Emma is an imaginist, so James gives us many explicit clues, long after we might have ceased to need them. Here he tells us that Strether's inventiveness is active: 'the air quite thickened, at their approach, with further intimations.' The scene is of course created for a narrator by a narrator and the last stroke of irony is that the air was indeed quite right to thicken.

Strether is not the only narrator, only the chief one. Most novels concerned with the nature of narrative – that is, most novels – create tensions between narrators. In *To the Lighthouse* we have Mr Ramsay, the realist who will not use fantasy and lies even to comfort a child, and Mrs Ramsay, who will, but who also tells James the terrible fairy story of *The Fisherman's Wife*, thus making it clear that she is no mere sentimental protector of the child. In *The Mill on the Floss* we have the narrow moralizing realism of Tom Tulliver, the narrow, powerful fantasy of Stephen's desire, and the strengths and weaknesses of dream, moral scheme, and emotional continuity, in Maggie. In *The Ambassadors* Strether's benevolently coloured vagueness is contrasted with Marie's truthtelling, Little Bilham's kind lies, and Chad's dazzling evasions and omissions, which show him a master of the kind of narrative that will make him succeed in advertising. We also have within single characters the attempt to attend to what really happens and the desire to change by the pressure of wish and faith. This often takes the most subtle form of the benevolent story: Strether, Isabel Archer, and Dorothea Brooke do not move from selfish fantasies towards life as it really is but from self-abnegatory fantasies towards a different story. There is a conflict between the story they tell themselves – about marrying Casaubon, helping society, marrying Gilbert Osmond, not marrying Lord Warburton, living hard no matter how, and so forth – and the harder, more realistic story their author has written for them. Yet in a sense the story these heroic characters try to live does shape their lives too. The ironies are blurred and complex. Dreams are productive when they lead to productive conflicts. Stories need not be just lies.

But there are novelists who show a larger discrepancy between the inner narrative and the novel. Gissing and Hardy write about characters very like the heroic figures in James and George Eliot – but characters who do not succeed in making their fantasy in any sense productive, who indeed fail most bitterly by the imaginative energy involved in telling the story of life as they wish to lead it. Tess is a passive instance, involved and manipulated by her family's narrative, in all its socially significant and pathetic crudeness, rather than by her own energies. Jude is the classical instance of failure of imagination, since the tale he tells himself can have no substance and would have been better untold. Gissing's heroes are often like Hardy's. In *Born in Exile* the hero creates an enterprising narrative and role, explicitly and intelligently attempting to give society what it wants in order to take what he wants. Gissing shows the social impulse to lie, in the extreme inventiveness of the man who is essentially a novelist's creation, who researches for his lie, dresses for it, moves into the right environment, and acts it out, right to the point of collapse. He shows here, as in *New Grub Street*, the failure to impose and sustain a certain kind of story, though in *Born in Exile* the breakdown is weak, coming out of accidental, though probable, discovery, rather than out of socially and psychologically expressive action. Gissing diverts the interest and misses a fine opportunity, failing to finish his story properly, like his hero. Indeed, the two failures may be related. Gissing may fail because he cannot carry through a story about a man who lives a lie – or rather, about a man of such imagination and humanity. His novels are indeed full of more simplified minor characters, like some of the successful writers in *New Grub Street*, who lie successfully by finding the right formula and telling the right story to themselves and others in the right place at the right time and in the right style.

There are also novelists and novels who are more optimistic about the stories people tell, who show the productiveness of fantasy. In Joyce and Beckett we see the healing power or the sheer survival of mythmaking, of telling stories about past and future and identity, even in the face of a dislocation of time and identity. The nostalgias and unrealities and comfort of the dream of youth, love, and past happiness, for instance, are set against Molly Bloom's sexually obsessed repetitions – another narrative novelists did not invent – and against the harshness of infidelity and impotence and the grander nostalgias of the *Odyssey*. In Beckett the human beings tell stories in the least promising circumstances, in the mud, dragging the sacks, jabbed and jabbing: they tell the incoherent story of life as they feel its pressures, with the odd sweet flash of what seems to be memory. The novels of Beckett are about the incorrigibility of narrative, and indeed the pessimistic novelist who wrote a story in which narrative as an act of mind had collapsed would clearly be telling lies about the relation of his own creativity to his own pessimism. Novelists are expected to show the story going on. But in Beckett the productiveness of story, joke, memory, or dream is rudimentary, spasmodic, often absurd. Narrative survives, no more.

There are novelists who are less clearly in command of the relation between the storytelling of their characters and the novel in which the stories are told and discussed. Jane Austen creates novels in which characters learn to imagine scrupulously, and feel correctly, in response to the sense of probability. Her novels might be said to describe the difference between writing a Gothic novel and a novel by Jane Austen, to reveal the assimilation of so much parody and criticism of the wrong kind of story. But Mrs Gaskell, Dickens, and George Eliot write novels which set out to show a similar process of learning how to dispense with fantasy but which in the end succumb to fantasy after all. And here too, as in Gissing, is a kind of understandable inconsistency: they are attempting what they know, even if they fail.

In *North and South* we have a *Bildungsroman* in which Margaret Hale tells herself a story, a fable about North and South. The novel tests, corrects, and dispels this story and others. The narrative is full of supporting cases, not just of blatant and apparently deliberate instances of differences between North and South, but of people telling stories. Bessy Higgins tells the common story of Heaven, which her father sees as the sustaining fantasy she needs. Mr Hale tells himself a story about leading a new life in the North. Mrs Thornton tells a story about North and South too, and a more interesting and personally coloured story about her son and the marriage he may make. Margaret also tells other stories. One is about saving her brother's reputation and bringing about a family reunion. Whenever character comes up against character there is an immediate narrative reaction, and the marked social and regional contrast encourages social fable, though the significant narratives that are tried and dispelled are moral and psychological. Mrs Gaskell is often said to be a rather mechanical and sensational plot-maker, but I have been struck by the way the heavily plotted parts of this novel (almost like sensation-novels in capsule form) eventually have the effect of showing up the falsity and sensationalism of the stories the characters tell. The story about Margaret's brother brings out not only her fantasy of rescue and reunion but also the lie that she has told herself about her own moral principles and the lie that Thornton has told himself about her moral nature. Mrs Gaskell was clearly interested in the way we tell high moral tales about ourselves and each other. This novel takes us and the characters through the complex process of adjusting and rejecting untrue and unreal stories.

Yet it ends with the reconciliation of Margaret and Thornton which subsidizes his new liberalized attitudes and activities, with the fabulous story of the financial failure and the legacy. The novel which criticizes sensational narrative ends with the plotting of the sensation novel, and we run up against a concluding fable after all, one which resembles the stories that have been tested and found wanting, in its falsity and its ready usableness.

Such a self-division is not a weakness peculiar to Mrs Gaskell. We find it in Dickens and George Eliot too. They write novels about growing away from the romantic daydream into a realistic acceptance, but most of their novels – except perhaps *Middlemarch* – end with the dream-conclusion and wish-fulfillment. *David Copperfield* tells the story of a novelist who learns to discipline his heart, and though there is an interesting lack of connection between his development as a novelist and his development as a man, he certainly thinks he learns to stop dreaming by hearing other people's stories and finding the traps and dangers of his own. This is to express the course of the novel too simply and lucidly. The brilliant parodies of calf-love are anticipations, both literary and psychological, of David's blindness, and we follow him into the 'real' world. Unfortunately, neither the Wordsworthian imitation of natural sublimities in Switzerland nor the saintly and rocklike qualities of Agnes act convincingly to clear the heady air, and the final harmony of financial, professional, moral, and domestic successes seems more dreamlike and unreal than anything that has gone before. Not only do we move towards a concluding dream after criticizing the dangers of dreaming, but we move further and further away from the real world, while more and more is salvaged by plot and idealized invocation. *David Copperfield* is Dickens's most divided novel, I believe, but a similar self-destructiveness and contradiction exists in most of his other books.

Dickens's attempt to criticize fantasy may often fail because of his personal dependence on sexual fantasy, and because he seems to have been caught between a fairly common Victorian antagonism between faith in the individual and despair about society. Almost the reverse might be said of George Eliot, but she too illustrates the attempt to supplant fantasy by realism, and an interestingly uncontrolled reversion to fantasy. As in Dickens, her characters tell stories to each other, to themselves, try to impose the stories, try to live by them, try to 'escape or escape to'. She puts an enormous energy of imagination and intelligence into a critical analysis of the stories we tell about life. There is no doubt about the life-enhancing realism she sees as her end: it is unfantastic and realistic. She speaks of gradually losing poetry and accepting prose, and all her novels explore the moral consequences of sterile dreaming and productive realism. She shows the interpenetration of many narrative modes that do not come into earlier English novels: the social myth, the literary fantasy, the sustained and culture-fed fantasy, the imaginative fantasy (Maggie's), the ethically noble fantasy (Dorothea's), and the feeble but still potent fantasy (Hetty's), and the tempting nightmare (Gwendolen's). As an analyst of narrative she stands with Stendhal and Flaubert. But in one novel she too succumbs as Mrs Gaskell and Dickens succumb.

I neither want nor need to follow Maggie Tulliver's story through in order to bring out the clash between analysis and dénouement. We follow Maggie's progress through the dreamworld of a child's fantasy-life, responding to varied deprivations, sufficiently individualized and sufficiently common. We follow her through the solicitations and failure of the fantasies of literature, myth, music, religion, and sexual desire. George Eliot not only analyses the individual qualities of the different stories Maggie listens to and tells herself, she most subtly shows their mutual influence, correction, tension, and interpenetration. Maggie's fantasies are not knocked down like ninepins, but leave their traces even when they have been explicitly discarded: we see her giving up the nourishing fantasies of wishfulfilling childish story, Romantic poetry and Scott, and Thomas à Kempis, but eventually each is shown to be a remaining influence, both for good and evil. But at the end, after such a searching and scrupulous analysis, and after taking her heroine into a solitude few Victorian fictional characters ever know, she too falls back into fantasy: the answer to prayer, the healing flood, the return to the past, forgiveness, the brother's embrace, and – most subtle illusion – forgiveness and understanding newborn in Tom's eyes. The novel refuses the prose realities, and saves its heroine from the pains of fresh starts and conflicts by invoking the very narrative consolation it has been concerned to analyse and deny.

Are such failures Victorian weaknesses? The proximity of Providence? We might perhaps look again at Proust, Forster, Virginia Woolf, and even Joyce, and find something like the narrative solution which retreats into fantasy. How often do we as students of politics, self, or literature, make the move from realism back to fantasy again, and translate the despair and pain as stoicism, the madness as aesthetic eloquence, the disorder as a new order? It is hard to stop telling stories.

From *Novel: A forum on fiction*, Brown University, Fall 1968

Forms of storying: the inner and outer worlds

Drawing on the theme of Barbara Hardy's paper, the author of this essay, an English schoolteacher, takes a special case from a book which, though dated, is still enjoyed by many girls. He shows that 'storying' goes on at many levels inside the main narratives and that these ways of fictionalizing events relate directly to real life but with 'the kind of distancing we require of art'. In so doing he shows that successful books for children have a complexity and particularity which are linked to the author's visions of the primary worlds they live in and the secondary worlds they create.

Uses of narrative   Dick Cate

I want to take a fairly close look at *A Little Princess* by Frances Hodgson Burnett. My thirteen-year-old daughter has said of this book: 'I think it and *The Secret Garden* are the best books I've ever read – they're really real, you know.' That is one good reason for taking a close look at it. Another is the fact that the heroine of *A Little Princess* is herself a maker of stories. A third reason is that whatever her short-comings may have been as a fiction writer, Mrs Burnett was very alert to the overlapping of fiction and reality, our everyday habit of make-believe, and the ebb and flow relationship that exists between fantasy and the world of reality as we perceive it.

Firstly let us look at what is perhaps Sara's most obvious use of fictionalizing – the way in which she projects an image, a personality on to her doll. I say 'obvious' not only because little girls who talk to their dolls must be pretty universal, but also because the very act of creating a doll, making an image, a reflection of oneself, is in itself if not an act of narration then at least the providing of the medium for narration and the overt acceptance of the need, the almost compulsive need for make-believe, for trying out, for rehearsing those contingencies, those relation-ships, that will occur and which *are occurring simultaneously* in what we refer to as 'real life'. Sara does not so much *buy* Emily as recognize her: ' "Oh, papa!" she

cried. "There is Emily!" ' And, as we might expect, Emily is named and conceived
of before she is actually purchased. And, to some extent, she serves as a substitution:
' " … She is going to be my friend when papa is gone. I want her to talk to about
him." ' But there is a healthy ring to Sara's relationship with her doll. When her
little friend Ermengarde asks if Emily can walk, Sara says: ' "Yes. At least I think
she can. At least I *pretend* I believe she can. And that makes it seem as if it were true." '

There is a kind of detachment in this make-believe which is correlative, I
think, with the kind of distancing we require of art. And Sara seems always to
have her fantasy under control. Maggie Tulliver, too, has a doll. But Maggie,
from the start, seems to run *to* her doll and *away from* life, whereas for Sara the
doll leads *out* to Ermengarde and Becky. Sara uses her doll to grow outwards
into life, not in order to retreat from it. And as she says in her letter to her father,
Emily is to be her last doll: for the fact is that she has Lottie and Becky and
Ermengarde to look after.

Malone, on his death-bed, unsure about how long he will manage to 'pant
on' for, persists in telling tales without reason, certainly without an audience.
It is a habit that seems as integral a part of our nature as breathing and sleeping.
And as with sleeping and breathing, we are more often than not unconscious of
our storytelling, taking it so much for granted that we rarely notice its presence.

Take, for example, the stories we tell about animals. Barbara Hardy has
stated how relatively easy it is to spot the polaric extremities of fantasy and
'faithful document', and how correspondingly difficult it is to define those
in-between stages where blurring takes place. On which side of the line do we lie
when we say, 'Poor little sparrow!'? How accurate are dog owners who say their
dog understands every word they say? Whatever the answers to these questions,
I think it is certainly true that fictionalizing about animals is a fairly widespread
phenomenon.

Here is Sara, relegated to the attic, confronted by the rat who is to become
known as Melchisedec:

' "I dare say it is rather hard to be a rat," she mused. "Nobody likes you.
People jump and run away and scream out: 'Oh, a horrid rat!' I shouldn't
like people to scream and jump and say 'Oh, a horrid Sara!' the moment
they saw me, and set traps for me, and pretend they were dinner. It's so
different to be a sparrow. But nobody asked this rat if he wanted to be a rat
when he was made." '

A fairly common kind of empathizing, I would have thought, but one which
should make quite clear that fantasy and narration *can* lead to the kind of imaginative

understanding necessary for the solving of social difficulties at any level. Of course, fantasy, like all aspects of the mind, is two-edged, and can be made use of to our detriment, as well as to our advantage. Sara uses her insight to the *rat's* advantage, not as a means to her own ends.

Sara not only invents a family life for the attic rat, but she also, with more attention to detail, invents a 'life' for a family who live in the same square as she lives in. It is a happy, warm, domesticated life – the sort that she appears to have lost for ever. And she even gives them names. She calls them the Large Family and surnames them The Montmorencys. It is obviously a reflection – in opposite terms – of her own situation. She gives them suitably romantic Christian names – a point that is humorously touched on when she meets them:

> 'Her voice was so unlike an ordinary street child's voice, and her manner was so like the manner of a well-bred little person that Veronica Eustacia (whose real name was Janet) and Rosalind Gladys (who was really called Nora) leaned forward to listen.'

And before she ever meets him, in fact on the moment of first seeing him, Sara 'makes up' the story of Ram Dass:

> 'As Sara looked toward him he looked toward her. The first thing she thought was that his dark face looked sorrowful and homesick. She felt absolutely sure he had come up to look at the sun, because he had seen it so seldom in England that he longed for a sight of it. She looked at him interestedly for a second, and then smiled across the slates. She had learned to know how comforting a smile, even from a stranger, may be.'

Here, what begins as an imaginative narrative, ends as an establishing of a relationship. It is difficult to say where Sara's invention ends and actuality begins: or, to refer again to Barbara Hardy, there is a 'blurring'.

One scene in particular demonstrates the interrelation between imagination and actuality, the mutually affecting aspects of fantasy and reality. It is a rainy, depressing day, and Sara is busy doing the errands for Miss Minchin. She is cold and hungry and depressed – but she knows how to cope:

> ' … She hurried on, trying to make her mind think of something else. It was really very necessary. Her way of doing it was to "pretend" and "suppose" with all the strength that was left in her.'

She 'supposes' that she is wearing warm clothes, that she has an umbrella, that she has found a sixpence, that she has gone into a baker's and bought some buns. This is fantasy, daydreaming, granting in a fantasy form the wishes that she has in actuality.

Then she *does* see some money: a silver fourpenny piece. Unrealistic? Yes.
But there is a grain of truth in even this obvious fiction: I do believe that if you
look for a thing you are more likely to see it than you would be if you didn't
bother to look. I mean, look for depressing evidence to confirm your suspicion
that the world is a depressing place and you will not have to look far to find it.
Believe that you can find a sixpence and you will be more likely to find one than
you would be if you were to start with the assumption that such a find would be
out of the question.

Then, just as she is about to enter the baker's, Sara sees a beggar-girl:

'Sara knew they were hungry eyes the moment she saw them, and she felt
a sudden sympathy.'

She knows that they are 'hungry eyes' because she has imaginative insight.

'Just to look at her made Sara more hungry and faint. But those queer little
thoughts were at work in her brain …

"If I'm a princess", she was saying – "If I'm a princess – when they were
poor or driven from their thrones – they always shared – with the populace
– if they met one poorer and hungrier than themselves. They always shared.
Buns are a penny each …" '

And so we move from a story read, a fictional example set, to an act of imaginative
identification which decides Sara's action in the world of actuality. When Sara
goes into the shop, the baker woman *reads* her face just as Sara had previously read
the beggar-girl's look – and gives her six penny-buns instead of four. Sara returns
to the beggar-girl and gives her five of the six buns. But her kindness is not un-
observed: the baker woman has seen her and, affected by the example set by Sara,
she invites the beggar-girl into her shop:

' "Get yourself warm", said the woman, pointing to a fire in the tiny
back-room. "And look here; when you are hard up for a bit of bread, you
can come in here and ask for it. I'm blest if I won't give it to you for that
young one's sake." '

Of course, there is a lot of unlikelihood in this scene – though baker-women *do*
sometimes give away the extra bun, and sixpences *are* found in the streets. But
even accepting the unlikely aspects as being sugary and far-fetched, it still seems
to me that there is a core of truth in the way that Sara is able to 'take her mind
off things' by supposing things to be different; in the way that she makes up a
story for herself about the beggar-girl; in the way that Sara, after imagining that
she is a princess, acts in the way that she imagines (from her reading) that a princess
would act; and in the way in which actuality and suppositions (based on

imaginative insights, past experience, stories, etc.) are intermingled inextricably in the thoughts of the baker-woman and Sara.

Since 1905 when *A Little Princess* was first published, our definition of the word 'realistic' has come to be made in blacker and harsher terms, and from today's standpoint the book must appear, on the whole, unrealistic and sentimental. But it has its moments of darker revelations. The way, for instance, in which parents have a habit of deciding – sometimes in direct contradiction of the facts – the attributes and abilities that their children will have. We are told in Chapter Three with some irony that Ermengarde's chief trouble in life is that she has the misfortune to have a clever father:

> ' ... Sometimes this seemed to her a dreadful calamity. If you have a father who knows everything, who speaks seven or eight languages, and has thousands of volumes which he has apparently learnt by heart, he frequently expects you to be familiar with the contents of your lesson-books at least; and it is not improbable that he will feel you ought to be able to remember a few incidents of history, and to write a French exercise. Ermengarde was a severe trial to Mr St. John. He could not understand how a child of his could be a notably and unmistakably dull creature who never shone in anything.'

I'm afraid that this is a little fiction that 'clever' parents still tell themselves, and still force upon the Ermengardes of this world. And then, if the child refuses to live up to the standards prescribed for her, some parents (not us, of course!) sometimes have a nasty Procrustean habit of demanding that she constrain herself to fit the cap:

> ' " She must be *made* to learn", her father said to Miss Minchin.'

And Miss Minchin herself is not above telling herself stories that suit her purpose. If Sara can use story as a road to empathy and understanding and relationship, then Miss Minchin is capable of telling and believing that other kind of story, the one about *other* people, *other* races, *other* anything-you-like, so long as it's *other* something:

> ' "My dear Sara", she said, "Becky is the scullery-maid. Scullery-maids – er – are not little girls."
>
> It really had not occurred to her to think of them in that light. Scullery-maids were machines who carried coal-scuttles and made fires.'

And Miss Minchin is also aware of the value of acting out a role suitable to her position as the head of a private school. We are told that when she thought of Sara 'she disliked her', but that 'she was far too worldly a woman to do or say anything which might make such a desirable pupil leave her school'. And so, until Sara is dispossessed, Miss Minchin keeps up a pretence of affection and interest that is appropriate to her position. Perhaps she over-acts her part: certainly there is an air of predictability about her treatment of Sara that causes Jessie to say, ' "It's disgusting, the way Miss Minchin shows her off when parents come!" ', and which stirs Lavinia into mimicry:

> ' "Dear Sara must come into the drawing-room and talk to Mrs. Musgrave about India" mimicked Lavinia, in her most highly flavoured imitation of Miss Minchin. "Dear Sara must speak French to Lady Pitkin. Her accent is so perfect." '

The more closely we identify ourselves with a role, an act, the more easy does it become to imitate and mock us. For playing a role too closely enforces a kind of rigidity in us which leads to stereotype and ossification.

It is a fate that teachers in general fall easy prey to. One reason for this is that role-playing can often seem to be an escape, a refuge from the attrition of day-to-day face-to-face encounter with children. Another reason is that the profession by tradition demands a kind of duality of the teacher: at home he may very well swear, read *The Morning Star* or *Playboy*, and spend more money weekly on alcohol than on books, but it would be considered unsuitable and unprofessional of him to advertise such facts in his classroom. A good public image has for long been regarded as a necessary accoutrement of the teacher (could it possibly be that some would consider it more primary in importance than say intelligence, ability, experience?), and Mr Barrow the solicitor, as a perspicacious member of the general public, knows this very well. When he first tells Miss Minchin that Sara has become a penniless orphan, her immediate thought is to turn the girl out on to the streets, but Mr Barrow turns as he is about to leave and says:

> ' "I wouldn't do that, madam, ... it wouldn't look well. Unpleasant story to get about in connexion with the establishment. Pupil bundled out penniless and without friends." '

One feels that Mr Barrow has in him the makings of a good P.R.O. If he has, then he will most surely be well aware of the subtly interlocking relationship between fiction and 'faithful document'.

But it is not only the adults who abuse their imagination in their use of fiction. Lottie and Ermengarde, because they are both under pressures, resort to fiction as a kind of pain-killer. Like Mr Tulliver, they feel that the world has been one too many for them. One feels that sooner or later they will retreat from it. But, at least for the moment, Sara is able to carry them along with her own peculiar brand of strength, born itself – paradoxically enough – of her own ability to tell stories.

Of the two of them, Lottie is headed in the more dangerous direction when Sara finds her. Sara provides the quiet strong directing push that perhaps Maggie Tulliver lacked. Lottie has lost her mother and has a 'rather flighty papa'. and Lottie 'had found out that a very small girl who had lost her mother was a person who ought to be pitied', and so she invents and acts out a system of behaviour which accords not so much with her own feelings as with the expectations of those she has heard discussing little girls in her situation. One morning both Miss Minchin and Miss Amelia are unable to suppress her wailing tantrum. Miss Minchin eventually resorts to violent shouting and says that she ought to be whipped. When she emerges from Miss Amelia's classroom she is a little disconcerted to discover that Sara has overheard her in this kind of role:

'When Sara entered the room, Lottie was lying upon the floor, screaming and kicking her small fat legs violently, and Miss Amelia was bending over her in consternation and despair, looking quite red and damp with heat. Lottie had always found, when in her own nursery at home, that kicking and screaming would always be quieted by any means she insisted on.
Poor plump Miss Amelia was trying first one method, and then another.'
But whichever act poor Miss Amelia puts on she cannot penetrate into Lottie's:
' "Poor darling!" she said one moment, "I know you haven't any mamma, poor –" Then in quite another tone: "If you don't stop, Lottie, I will shake you. Poor little angel! There – there! You wicked, bad, detestable child, I will smack you! I will!" '
Of course one should set a thief to catch a thief, and perhaps Miss Amelia isn't quite storyteller enough to deal with this situation. But Sara knows all about stories and she knows just how to deal with the situation:
' "I haven't – any – ma – ma – ma-a!" she announced; but her voice was not so strong.
Sara looked at her still more steadily, but with a sort of understanding in her eyes.
"Neither have I," she said.'
And having knocked Lottie over with a truth, she begins to build her up again with the help of fiction.

Sara uses story for all kinds of purposes. Sometimes to amuse herself, but more often to amuse others. To sugar the pill for Lottie and for Becky. To enrich life with stories of the exotic and perilous. To help others to escape for a moment from the unbearable nature of their real lives. And sometimes to escape herself.

But more often than not, Sara uses fiction to strengthen and sustain. She uses it not so that she can close her eyes and forget, but so that she has the courage (from example) to keep her eyes open, to go on, to reverse her position from that of being a person in need of help to that of being a person able to give help to others. The pervading 'story' of this book is the one that Sara tells herself: that she is a little princess. It is not a self-pitying role but one which demands of her responsibilities and sacrifices. When despair threatens to overcome her, she remembers who she is – a princess. And fortified by that, she sets to and makes the best circumstances will allow. When, at the beginning, she *is* rich and privileged, she exacts of herself that generosity and sense of responsibility towards others that her fictional encounters have taught her to expect of princesses. And when she is poor, she continues to set herself these standards. She sees that being 'a princess' is a matter of comparison and that one is always better off than some others.

In Sara fiction and actual experience are inextricably intermingled. She says that she can't help making up things and adds: ' "If I didn't, I don't think I could live" '. And I don't think this means only that fiction allows her to escape – though she means that in part. What she means is that there is no hard and fast boundary between the one and the other. When consigned to the attic she thinks of the Count of Monte Cristo in the dungeons of the Chateau d'If and of the prisoners in the Bastille. It is a natural step to think of Becky who now lives in the adjoining room as 'the prisoner in the next cell'. And, of course, they soon evolve a system of communication based on the sequencing of taps on the wall which both divides and joins them. The interdependence of fiction and actual experience is as real as that.

' "Oh, Sara", Ermengarde whispered joyfully, "it is like a story!"

"It is a story", said Sara. "*Everything's a story* – I am a story. Miss Minchin is a story." '

From *English in Education*, volume 5, number 3, 1971

Growing outwards into life

In his essay Dick Cate refers to an incident in 'A Little Princess' concerning a doll. He says that the heroine 'projects an image, a personality on to her doll' and uses it 'to grow outwards into life, not in order to retreat from it'. In this chapter from her autobiography, published in 1893, Frances Hodgson Burnett shows how the projection of that image was in its turn something she learned to do from stories read in early childhood. She considered her dolls as 'only things' until they became, in her imaginative play, the characters she had met in books. This is a clear example of the trying out of fictive possibilities with the doll as the symbolic central figure. It is a significant testimony from a less self-conscious age of what seems to us a universal tendency. As the statement comes from an expansive time, we have chosen only the first half of a very long chapter.

Literature and the doll   Frances Hodgson Burnett

Whether as impression-creating and mind-moulding influences, Literature or the Doll came first into her life it would be most difficult to decide. But remembering the role the Doll played, and wherein its fascination lay, I see that its way must have been paved for it in some rudimentary manner by Literature, though their clearly remembered existences seem to have begun at one and the same time. Before the advent of literary influence I remember no Doll, and curiously enough, there is, before the advent of the Doll, a memory of something like stories – imperfect, unsatisfactory, filling her with vague, restless craving for greater completeness of form, but still creating images for her, and setting her small mind at work.

It is not in the least likely she did not own dolls before she owned books, but it is certain that until literature assisted imagination and gave them character, they seemed only things stuffed with sawdust and made no special impression.

It is also certain that she cannot have been told stories as a rule. I should say that she did not hear them even as the exception. I am sure of this because I so well recollect her desperate efforts to wring detail of any sort from her Nurses.

The 'Slaughter of the Innocents' seems to me to have been the first story impression in her life. A little illustrated scripture history afforded a picture of Jewish mothers rushing madly down broad stone stairways clasping babies to their breasts, of others huddling under the shadow of high walls clutching their little ones, and of fierce armed men slashing with swords.

This was the work of Herod the King. And 'In Rama was there a voice heard, lamentation and weeping, and great mourning. Rachel weeping for her children, and would not be comforted, because they were not.'

This was the first story, and it was a tragedy – only made endurable by that story of the Star in the East which led the way to the Manger where the little Child lay sleeping with a light about his head – the little Child before whom the wise men bent, worshipping and offering gifts of frankincense and myrrh. She wondered greatly what frankincense and myrrh were, but the wise men were beautiful to her, and she could see quite clearly the high deep dome of blue which vaulted the still plain where the Shepherds watched their flocks at night, when the Angel of the Lord came to them and glory shone round about and they were 'sore afraid', until the angel said unto them, 'Fear not, for behold, I bring you good tidings of great joy.'

This part of the story was strange and majestic and lovely and almost consoled her for Herod the King.

The Nurse who was the unconscious means of suggesting to her the first romance of her life, must have been a dull person. Even at this distance I find myself looking back at her vague, stupid personality with a sense of impatience.

How could a person learn a couple of verses of a song suggesting a story, and not only neglect to learn more, but neglect to inquire about the story itself.

And oh, the helpless torture of hearing those odd verses and standing by that phlegmatic person's knee with one's yearning eyes fixed on her incomprehensible countenance, finding one's self unable to extort from her by any cross-examination the details!

Even the stray verses had such wonderful suggestion in them. They opened up such vistas. At that time the Small Person faithfully believed the song to be called 'Sweet Alice Benbolt' – Miss Alice Benbolt being, as she supposed, the name of the young lady described in the lines. She was a very sensitive young lady, it appeared, from the description given in the first verse:

Ah, don't you remember Sweet Alice Benbolt,
Sweet Alice with hair so brown;
How she wept with delight when you gave her a smile,
And trembled with fear at your frown?

It did not then occur to the Small Person that Miss Benbolt must have been trying in the domestic circle; she was so moved by the tender image of a brown-haired girl who was called 'Sweet Alice' and set to plaintive music. Somehow there was something touching in the way she was spoken of – as if people had loved her and were sorry about her for some reason – the boys had gone to the school-house 'under the hill,' connected with which there seemed to be such pathetic memories, though the Small Person could not comprehend why they were pathetic. But there was a pathos in one verse which broke her heart when she understood it, which she scarcely did at first:

In the little churchyard in the valley Benbolt,
In a corner obscure and alone,
They have fitted a slab of the granite so grey,
And sweet Alice lies under the stone

'Why does she lie there?' she asked, with both hands on the Nurse's knee. 'Why does Sweet Alice lie under the stone?'

'Because she died,' said the Nurse, without emotional compunctions, 'and was buried there.'

The Small Person clung rather helplessly to her apron.

'Sweet Alice,' she said, 'Sweet Alice with hair so brown?'

(Why was the brown hair pathetic as well as the name? I don't know. But it was.)

'Why did she die?' she asked. 'What did she die for?'

'I don't know,' said the Nurse.

'But – but – tell me some more,' the Small Person gasped. 'Sing some more.'

'I don't know any more.'

'But where did the boys go?'

'I don't know.'

'What did the schoolmaster do?'

'The song doesn't tell.'

'Why was he grim?'

'It doesn't tell that either.'

'Did Sweet Alice go to school to him?'

'I dare say.'

'Was he sorry when she died?'

'It does not say.'

'Are there no more verses?'

'I can't remember any more.'

Questioning was of no use. She did not know any more and she did not
care. One might implore and try to suggest, but she was not an imaginative
character, and so the Small Person was left to gaze at her with hungry eyes and a
sense of despair before this stolid being, who *might* have known the rest and would
not. She probably made the woman's life a burden to her by imploring her to
sing again and again the stray verses, and I have no doubt that at each repetition
she invented new questions.

'Sweet Alice Benbolt,' she used to say to herself. 'Sweet Alice with hair so
brown.' And the words always called up in her mind a picture which is as clear
today as it was then.

It is a queer little picture, but it seemed very touching at that time. She
saw a hillside covered with soft green. It was not a high hill and its slope was
gentle. Why the 'school-house under the hill' was placed on the top of it, would
be difficult to explain. But there it was, and it seemed to look down on and watch
benignly over something in a corner at the foot of it. The something was a slab
of the granite so grey lying among the soft greenness of the grass.

'And sweet Alice lay under the stone.'
She was not a shadow – Sweet Alice. She is something far more than a shadow
even now, in a mind through which thousands of shadows have passed. She was
a tender thing – and she had brown hair – and somehow people loved her – and
she died.

It was not until Literature in the form of story, romance, tragedy, and
adventure had quickened her imagination that the figure of the Doll loomed up
in the character of an absorbing interest, but once having appeared it never retired
from the scene until advancing years forced the curtain to fall upon the exciting
scenes of which it was always the heroine.

That was the truth of the matter – it was not a Doll, but a Heroine.

And some imagination was required to make it one. The Doll of that day
was not the dimpled star-eyed creature of today, who can stand on her own firm
little feet, whose plump legs and arms can be placed in any position, whose
attitudes may be made to express emotions in accordance with the Delsarte

system, and who has parted lips and pearly teeth, and indulges in features. Not at all.

The natural advantages of a doll of that period confined themselves to size, hair which was sewn on a little black skull-cap – if it was not plastered on with mucilage – and eyes which could be jerked open if one pulled a wire which stuck out of her side. The most expensive and magnificent doll you could have was merely a big wax one, whose hair could be combed and whose eyes would open and shut. Otherwise they were all the same. Only the face and neck were of wax, and features were not studied by the manufacturers. All the faces were exactly the same shape, or rather the same shapelessness. Expression and outline would have been considered wanton waste of material. To-day dolls have cheeks and noses and lips and brows, they look smiling or pensive, childlike or sophisticated. At that time no doll was guilty of looking anything at all. In the middle of her smooth round face was a blunt excrescence which was called a nose, beneath it was a line of red paint which was meant for a mouth, on each side of it was a tight-looking black or blue glass eye as totally devoid of expression and as far removed from any resemblance to a real eye as the combined talents of ages of doll manufacturers could make it. It had no pupil and no meaning, it stared, it glared, and was only a little more awful when one pulled the wax lid over it than it was when it was fixed and open. Two arches of brown paint above it were its eyebrows, and all this beauty was surmounted with the small black cap on the summit of which was stretched a row of dangling curls of black or brown. Its body was stuffed with sawdust, which had a tragic tendency to burst forth and run out through any hole in the white calico which was its skin. The arms and legs were like sawdust-stuffed sausages, its arms were covered with pink or blue or yellow or green kid, there being no prejudice caused by the fact that arms were not usually of any of these shades; its legs dangled painfully and presented no haughty contours, and its toes invariably turned in.

How an imagination, of the most fervid, could transform this thing into a creature resembling anything human one cannot explain. But nature is very good – sometimes – to little children. One day, in a squalid London street, I drove by a dirty mite sitting upon a step, cuddling warmly a little bundle of hay tied round the middle with a string. It was her baby. It probably was lily fair and had eyes as blue as heaven, and cooed and kissed her again – but grown-up people could not see.

When I recall the adventures through which the Dolls of the Small Person passed, the tragedies of emotion, the scenes of battle, murder, and sudden death,

I do not wonder that at times the sawdust burst forth from their calico cuticle in streams, and the Nursery floor was deluged with it. Was it a thing to cause surprise that they wore out and only lasted from one birthday to another? Their span of life was short, but they could not complain that existence had not been full for them. The Doll who, on November 24th, begins a chequered career by mounting an untamed and untamable, fiercely prancing and snorting steed, which, while it strikes sparks from the earth it spurns with its disdainful hoofs, wears to the outward gaze the aspect of the mere arm of a Nursery Sofa covered with green baize – the Doll who begins life by mounting this steed, and so conquering its spirit that it responds to her touch and leaps the most appalling hedges and abysses, and leaves the lightning itself behind in its career; and having done this on the 24th, is executed in black velvet on the 25th as Mary Queen of Scots, besides being imprisoned in the Tower of London as someone else, and threatened with the rack and the stake because she will not 'recant' and become a Roman Catholic – a Doll with a career like this cannot be dull, though she may at periods be exhausted. While the two little sisters of the Small Person arranged their doll's house prettily and had tea-parties out of miniature cups and saucers, and visited each other's corners of the Nursery, in *her* corner the Small Person entertained herself with wildly thrilling histories, which she related to herself in an undertone, while she acted them with the assistance of her Doll.

She was all the characters but the heroine – the Doll was that. She was the hero, the villain, the banditti, the pirates, the executioner, the weeping maids of honour, the touchingly benevolent old gentleman, the courtiers, the explorers, the king.

She always spoke in a whisper or an undertone, unless she was quite alone, because she was shy of being heard. This was probably an instinct at first, but it was a feeling intensified early by finding out that her habit of 'talking to herself', as others called it, was considered a joke. The servants used to listen to her behind doors and giggle when they caught her, her brothers regarded her as a ridiculous little object. They were cricket-playing boys, who possibly wondered in private if she was slightly cracked, but would have soundly thumped and belaboured any other boy who had dared to suggest the same thing.

The time came when she heard it said that she was 'romantic'. It was the most crushing thing she had ever experienced. She was quite sure that she was not romantic. She could not bear the ignominy of the suggestion. She did not know *what* she was, but she was *sure* she was not romantic. So she was very cautious in the matter of keeping to her own corner of the Nursery and putting

an immediate stop to her performance the instant she observed a silence, as if
any one was listening. But her most delightful life concentrated itself in those
dramatized stories through which she 'talked to herself'.

At the end of the entrance hall of the house in which she lived was a tall
stand for a candelabra. It was of worked iron and its standard was ornamented
with certain decorative supports to the upper part.

What were the emotions of the Small Person's Mamma, who was the
gentlest and kindest of her sex, on coming upon her offspring one day, on
descending the staircase, to find her apparently furious with insensate rage,
muttering to herself as she brutally lashed with one of her brother's toy whips, a
cheerfully hideous black gutta-percha doll who was tied to the candelabra stand
and appeared to be enjoying the situation.

'My dear, my dear!' exclaimed the alarmed little lady, 'what *are* you doing?'

The Small Person gave a little jump and dropped at her side the stalwart
right arm which had been wielding the whip. She looked as if she would have
turned very red, if it had been possible for her to become redder than her
exertions had made her.

'I – I was only playing,' she faltered, sheepishly.

'Playing!' echoed her Mamma. 'What *were* you playing?'

The Small Person hung her head and answered, with downcast
countenance, greatly abashed, –

'I was – only just – *pretending* something,' she said.

'It really quite distressed me,' her Mamma said, in discussing the matter
afterward with a friend. 'I don't think she is really a *cruel* child. I always thought
her rather kind-hearted, but she was lashing that poor black doll and talking
to herself like a little fury. She looked quite wicked. She said she was "pretending"
something. You know that is her way of playing. She does not play as Edith
and Edwina do. She "pretends" her doll is somebody out of a story and she is
somebody else. She is very romantic. It made me rather nervous the other day
when she dressed a baby-doll in white and put it into a box and covered it with
flowers and buried it in the front garden. She was so absorbed in it, and she
hasn't dug it up. She goes and strews flowers over the grave. I should like to
know what she was "pretending" when she was beating the black doll.'

Not until the Small Person had outgrown all dolls, and her mother
reminded her of this incident, did that innocent lady know that the black doll's
name was Topsy, but that on this occasion it had been transformed into poor
Uncle Tom, and that the little fury with the flying hair was the wicked Legree.

She had been reading *Uncle Tom's Cabin*. What an era it was in her existence! The cheerful black doll was procured immediately and called Topsy; her 'best doll', which fortunately had brown hair in its wig, was Eva, and was kept actively employed slowly fading away and dying, while she talked about the New Jerusalem, with a hectic flush on her cheeks. She converted Topsy, and totally changed her gutta-percha nature, though it was impossible to alter her gutta-percha grin. She conversed with Uncle Tom (then the Small Person was Uncle Tom), she cut off 'her long golden-brown curls' (not literally; that was only 'pretended': the wig had not ringlets enough on it), and presented them to the weeping slaves. (Then the Small Person was all the weeping slaves at once.) It is true that her blunt-nosed wax countenance remained perfectly unmoved throughout all this emotion, and it must be confessed that at times the Small Person felt a lack in her, but an ability to 'pretend' ardently was her consolation and support.

It surely must be true that all children possess this right of entry into the fairyland where *anything* can be 'pretended'. I feel quite sure they do, and that if one could follow them in the 'pretendings', one would make many discoveries about them.

From *The One I knew the Best of All*, (1893) Warne, 1975

The third area where we are more ourselves

The ideas contained in this essay take our concern with children and the worlds they make in narrative into the areas where these things are linked with play on the one hand and ideas on the other. Here James Britton draws on the work of the psycho-analyst, D. W. Winnicott, in suggesting that fantasy occurs in an area of free activity lying between the world of shared and verifiable activity and the world of inner necessity. Besides developing its own powerful thesis, which owes something to Jean Piaget's 'Play, Dreams, and Imitation', this essay shows the organizing function of fantasy in children to which narrative stories and reading contribute.

The role of fantasy   James Britton

Sometimes, as I am on the point of going to sleep, the image of a hideous face comes to float above my pillow. It may be a face that threatens hideously or one that is itself hideously mutilated – but I suspect there is, deep enough within me, a common origin for the two versions. Usually – or perhaps I should say in the cases that I can recall – I am enough awake to have to deal with this apparition: and I do that best by wakening further to summon the image of some other face, a familiar and benign one. These two acts of my imagination have a good deal in common, no doubt, yet originate quite differently, for one is voluntary, the other involuntary. In our waking hours, up and about, the bidden and the unbidden images are likely, I believe, to be less clearly differentiated since they will arise, directly or indirectly, in closer association with whatever occupies our attention.

Both deliberately and despite ourselves, then, we are proliferators of images. Even in the process of attending to what is before our eyes, we generate images of what we expect to see. As, for example, we try to 'make out' a mysterious object in the distance, we are likely to perceive it as more like the object we took it for than its actual features might justify: thus, at times, we shall change our 'recognition' – what we took to be a bear we shall now recognize as a bush, what we took to be a mountain peak we shall now recognize as a cloud formation. Though we have taken a special case as illustration, it is likely that all perceiving involves the generating of visual expectations and their matching with what our sight indicates. In other words, it requires an act of the imagination to construct any situation in which we actually find ourselves. A. A. Milne has illustrated this unfamiliar truth in his poem 'Nursery Chairs' from *When We Were Very Young*. In each of the first three stanzas, he has the three-year-old imagining (with the aid of a chair) that he is an Amazonian explorer, or a lion in a cage, or a sailor on the high seas; and for the final stanza:

> Whenever I sit in a high chair
> For breakfast or dinner or tea
> I try to pretend that it's *my* chair,
> And that I am a baby of three.

Nowadays, when I dream in my sleep, I usually dream of people talking, and often remember what they have said. It is all very reasonable. Very occasionally, however, silent images build up into a frightening situation, sometimes of falling or leaping into space, but more often of having to get somewhere on foot, knowing that I am under dire threat if I am not there in time, and experiencing (as Beckett's old men do) extraordinary physical difficulty in making any progress at all. Obviously I cannot generalize from this difference between the commonplace and wordy and the silent and frightening among dreams: but it is true of my own experience and illustrates a point I want to make.

Our concern here is with fantasy themes in children's reading. It was important therefore to remember at the outset that language is only one way of representing to ourselves both the actual world and unreal, fantastic worlds; and that other means, such as the visual image, antedate the use of words and continue to operate both in association with words and independently. Putting experiences into words is a process of *ordering* them in a particular way, imposing on the data, in fact, some effects of the organization inherent in language itself. (Language, as the linguists tell us, is *rule-governed* behaviour.) My description, for example, of the kind of walking paralysis that afflicts me in my dreams is a far more orderly expression of a state of affairs than anything that enters the dream.

To speak is to 'articulate', over a wide range of that word's meanings; both

to joint and to join; to provide with a framework; to knit, perhaps, or to weave –
and the web, as Robert Graves has suggested, is a *cool* one – a means of
lessening the intensity of experience:

> Children are dumb to say how hot the day is,
> How hot the scent is of the summer rose,
> How dreadful the black wastes of evening sky,
> How dreadful the tall soldiers drumming by.
>
> But we have speech to chill the angry day,
> And speech, to dull the rose's cruel scent.
> We spell away the overhanging night,
> We spell away the soldiers and the fright.
>
> There's a cool web of language winds us in ...

It has often enough been claimed, with justification, that by the use of language
we construct the world of ideas. We need to note for our present purposes
that as soon as we bring words into our reflection of experience, the *image* takes
one step towards the *idea*.

Let us begin to define the area of our concern here by saying that we shall
take fantasy to mean the handling of images *as play* – a statement that will need
to be explained, extended, perhaps modified in the course of our consideration.
As human beings we proliferate images; and to varying degrees, by various
means and to various ends, we work upon them, manipulate them further. How
for our present purpose do we sort these many variables? To begin with the very
broad distinctions, adaptive behaviour – recognized throughout the evolutionary
scale as the purposive activity by which organisms survive and prosper in
relation to their environment – may in human beings be distinguished from
behaviour which supersedes the demands of the here and now, the immediate
environment. Certainly a young child's curiosity may seem to direct him into
activities in which he seeks to use and control the objects around him – adaptive
behaviour – but then to go a stage further where he seems to explore *for the sake
of finding out*, for the sake of *knowing*. One cannot divorce this function of the
human mind from the existence of language; language which so manifestly assists
adaptive behaviour brings also this new possibility, that of storing the outcomes
of experience and of other people's experience with scant regard for their

immediate adaptive value. To adaptive behaviour, then, we add this that has been called 'reflective behaviour'. The small boy whose chances of controlling an automobile are still at least a dozen years away may nevertheless treasure a great deal of knowledge about how automobiles work.

The organization to which images are submitted for reflective purposes – to arrive in other words at knowledge – is the kind of organization that psychologists and philosophers are most familiar with. We have already referred to it in speaking of language, of 'articulation', of 'ideas', though of course a great deal more could be said. Words provide us with the means of classifying phenomena at different levels of generality; and of abstracting aspects of phenomena and creating superordinate abstract categories; and of systematically relating those abstractions into theories about the universe or any part of our experience of it. All these processes continue, of course, to be capable of serving practical ends, capable of entering into adaptive behaviour (as witness the technical devices in daily use whose origins lie in a scientific curiosity about the nature of matter); but they are by no means restricted to such purposes, and that being so they account for a wide range of human preoccupations we can roughly call 'reflective'.

So much has been known for so long about the laws of knowing, about the cognitive mode of organization, that it has sometimes been taken as the only form of organization that images (or whatever else we might decide to call the fundamental acts of the human mind) could enter into. Let us clear our ground by agreeing, in crude terms, that from *images* by organization of this cognitive kind come *ideas:* and that language in its characteristic and ordinary uses is the principal means by which the organizing is carried out. But is that the whole story?

Susan Isaacs, in writing of the intellectual development of young children, seems inclined to accept the view that order comes out of *disorder* as a child comes to master cognitive processes:

> 'I consider it very important that we should not blur the distinction between thought and fantasy in our theories of intellectual growth ... The egocentrism of the little child is strictly an affair of feeling and fantasy, not of thought. He is egocentric in so far as he has not yet learned to think. But as experience comes to him, and noetic synthesis grows, true relational thought emerges more and more out of the matrix of feeling and fantasy. ... But the essential characteristic of egocentric ways of dealing with reality is surely that they *have* no "structure". It is not that one kind of

Susan Isaacs
Intellectual Growth in Young Children
Routledge and Kegan Paul, 1930
(page 107)

structure gives place to another; it is rather that there is a progressive penetration of feeling and fantasy by experience, a progressive ordering by relational thought of the child's responses to the world.'

What we are asking here is whether feeling and fantasy, at the stage of a child's development Susan Isaacs is describing, may not in fact represent, at least in embryonic form, some other kind of organization of his mental activity, an organization on a different principle from that of the cognitive; secondly, whether such an organization, if it exists, could appropriately be associated with 'play' in the way we have suggested; and finally how activities in play would relate to the two broad categories we have referred to, adaptive and reflective.

Play, as we mean it, is a voluntary activity: it occupies because in itself it *preoccupies*, and not for any reason outside itself – not, for example, as the direct legacy of any other kind of activity. Secondly, in so far as play takes up images of the actual world, it does so in a context and a mode of organization which indicates a comparatively low level of concern for their verisimilitude, their resemblance to things in the actual world. For this reason simulation exercises and the 'games' currently popular as a mode of teaching are not in our sense play activities. Putting this more generally, to the images we generate we attach varying degrees of credence: in our attempts to make out whether what we are looking at is a mountain peak or a cloud formation we shall generate visual expectations in close relation to what we believe to exist; in play we abandon such claims: the credibility of what we pretend in make-believe play is not likely to be a determining criterion: in our ordinary daydreaming (and we count this as a kind of play) we are not primarily concerned with the likelihood of fulfilment.

To say this is to draw a distinction between, on the one hand, play and on the other, the adaptive and reflective activities that create for each of us a shared world – the 'actual' world as we know it, that is to say, as we have represented it to ourselves in the course of such adaptive and reflective activities. In play we improvise upon the representation for reasons other than that of improving its truth to the facts of our experience. And freed from this necessity, we seem able in some sense to *be more ourselves*. This general distinction between the familiar kind of organization that belongs to adaptive and reflective behaviour (cognitive organization) and the postulated other kind of organization we are now looking for in play activities is one that has already been made elsewhere in terms of 'participant' and 'spectator' roles. (See D. W. Harding's 'The Role of the Onlooker' and my own *Language and Learning*.) Here I must take that as read, and yet rely on it to support two points I need to make. First, to suggest that the arts (including literature) represent a highly organized activity within the general area of 'play': all we have said earlier about playing might be applied to the practice of the arts, and the alternative kind of organization we are looking for is 'art-like' – occurs indeed in its most perfected version in a work of art. (To say that is of course merely to *begin* to understand the nature of the organization.) The claim is important in our present context, for, if it is true, a child's daydreaming and the stories he reads – stories such as *Alice in Wonderland* – are birds of a feather.

The second claim that arises from previous thinking about participant and spectator roles is the claim that spectator role activity is primarily *assimilative* in function. Freed from the demands made upon us as participants in the world's affairs, we are able to take more fully into account *our experience as a whole*. To put the same point rather differently, even where a poet may focus narrowly upon some tiny particular such as a snow flake, yet it is with the *whole of himself* that he looks. This item of his experience becomes as it were a small peephole through which we can see a great deal of his personality. A concern with the world-as-I-have-known-it, with my total world representation, is essentially an assimilative activity – a digestive activity, if the crude figure can be accepted. Play, then, is an activity which is not adaptive or reflective in function, but assimilative.

Daydreams, make-believe play, a child's storytelling, *Alice in Wonderland*, *Treasure Island*, and the rest – these are all play activities just as they are all activities in the spectator role. Seeing them as play, however, makes it possible, I believe, to move on to a further important distinction. We have suggested that play loses its essential characteristic when it submits the necessity of truth to the facts of experience. But we must note now that there is another necessity that may encroach upon it, one that I can only call an inner necessity. What was idle daydreaming on the part of a given individual may, from inner need, become obsessional: the images of play may be called upon to meet inner demands which become so urgent that those images are no longer freely manipulated, or a matter of choice. 'Escapism' is a word I have always found it difficult to use or understand: it must be a part of the assimilative function of play that we are able, in play, to improvise freely upon events in the actual world and in doing so enable ourselves to go back and meet the demands of real life more adequately: here is a kind of escape, but a fruitful one. On the other hand, the play images of a Walter Mitty may become a systematic means of avoiding the demands of

D. W. Harding
'The Role of the
Onlooker',
Scrutiny, volume VI
number 3, 1937

James Britton
Language and Learning
Allen Lane, 1970
(Chapter 3)

real life and lessening the possibility of adequate response: and this perhaps is what 'escapism' should mean. When this happens we can only infer the existence of inner psychic demands powerful enough to rob play-like activities of the freedom that makes them genuinely 'playful'.

I heard in New England, only a week ago, of an eighteen-year-old girl who is wandering alone from picnic-site to picnic-site in the woods of Vermont, and calling herself 'the White Rabbit'. When my friend's young children asked what her 'real name' was, and why she had taken this other name, she grew very distressed. The experience of *Alice in Wonderland* must for that girl be very different from the eagerly appropriate delights and horrors, loves and fears, that generations of children have moved freely into and out of in reading the book.

I want to see play, then, as an area of free activity lying between the world of shared and verifiable experience and the world of inner necessity – a 'third area', as Donald Winnicott has called it. The essential purpose of activity in this area for the individual will be to relate for himself inner necessity with the demands of the external world. The more the images that clothe inner instinctual needs enter into the play activity, directly or indirectly, and the more they engage and relate to images from the world of shared experience, the more effectively, it seems to me, is the activity achieving its assimilative function. In the range of activities that come into the category of play as we have defined it, some will take up more of the demands of the inner world and are likely for that reason to include features that are inconsistent with our everyday notions of reality. It is activities towards that end of the scale that we shall most readily, and rightly, call 'fantasy', whether they are children's own creations or the stories they read.

My intention in this exploratory article has been to link ideas already familiar to me with the suggestions put forward by Donald Winnicott in his recent book *Playing and Reality*, published soon after he died. That my task (like so many others in this area of thinking) is far from complete will be clear from a reading of the following brief quotations from that book:

'I have tried to draw attention to the importance both in theory and in practice of a third area, that of play, which expands into creative living and into the whole cultural life of man. This third area has been contrasted with inner or personal psychic reality and with the actual world in which the individual lives, which can be objectively perceived. I have located this important area of *experience* in the potential space between the individual

D. W. Winnicott
Playing and Reality
Tavistock
Publications, 1971

Derived in the main
from Ernst Cassirer
Susanne Langer and
D. W. Harding

and the environment, that which initially both joins and separates the baby
and the mother when the mother's love, displayed or made manifest as
human reliability, does in fact give the baby a sense of trust or of confidence in the environmental factor.

Attention is drawn to the fact that this potential space is a highly variable
factor (from individual to individual) whereas the two other locations –
personal or psychic reality and the actual world – are relatively constant, *Playing and Reality*
one being biologically determined and the other being common property.' (pages 102–3)

'Cultural experience begins with creative living first manifested in play.' ibid. page 100

'In using the word culture I am thinking of the inherited tradition. I am
thinking of something that is in the common pool of humanity, into which
individuals and groups of people may contribute, and from which we may
all draw if we have somewhere to put what we find.' ibid. page 99

Culture, the common pool of humanity, offers the young child witches and
fairy godmothers, symbols which may embody and work upon the hate and love
that are part of a close, dependent relationship: he will read of witches and tell
stories of his own that arise directly from his needs. In doing so, he performs an
assimilative task, working towards a more harmonious relationship between
inner needs and external demands. Culture offers him, at a later stage perhaps,
Alice in Wonderland, which among many other matters must certainly be concerned, if covertly, with *scale* – with bigness and littleness – and so with the
difficulties a small comparatively powerless creature may feel in facing the
demands of a world of full-grown, powerful adults.

If the Freudian view is right, there will be children whose ability to operate
in the 'third area' has been so severely restricted in infancy that we as teachers
can do little to help them. For the rest, it is important that we should recognize
their need to 'play', understand as fully as we can the nature and the value of
such activity, and provide the cultural material on which it may flourish.

From *English in Education*, volume 5, number 3, 1971

The inevitability of storying

In his remarkable book 'From Two to Five' Chukovsky examines what happened when a culture rich in myth, legend, and fairy tales, tried to establish a total social realism. The stories simply reappeared in other forms. The straightforwardness of this account should not lead us to underestimate the immense importance of the point he is making.

There is no such thing as a shark   K. Chukovsky

Once upon a time there lived in Moscow a pedologist by the name of Stanchinskaia. And a very strange thing happened to this pedologist.

She was also a mother, and she did everything in her power to protect her son from fairy tales. Even when she talked to him about animals she made sure to mention only those he had seen with his own eyes. After all, he had to grow up a realist! The fewer harmful fantasies the better! She considered especially harmful fairy tales that told about supernatural transformations – werewolves, Baba-Yagas, and others.

This ardent foe of the fairy tale even published an article in a Moscow magazine in which she wrote:

'We propose to replace the unrealistic folk tales and fantasies with simple realistic stories taken from the world of reality and from nature.'

No compromises, no weakening! Let us get rid of all fairy tales, epic tales, the entire folklore of Russia and of the rest of the world – without any exception! And everything would have been just fine, but, unfortunately, as a loving mother she began to keep a most detailed diary about her little son. Without being aware of it, she contradicted, in her entries, all her favourite arguments about the harmful influences of fantastic tales and destroyed with her own pen, so to speak, her formidable theories.

She wrote in this diary – and it has been published – that her boy, as if to make up for the fairy tales of which he had been deprived, began to spin from morning till night the wildest fantasies. He pretended that a red elephant came to live in his room; he invented a friend – a bear whom he named Cora; and he would often say, 'Please, don't sit on the chair next to mine because – can't you see? – the she-bear is sitting on it.' And, 'Mother, why are you walking right on top of the wolves? Can't you see the wolves standing there?'

And with the first snow he became a reindeer, a little reindeer in a Siberian forest. And if he sat on a rug, the rug would immediately be transformed into a ship. At any time, with the power of his childish fantasy, he could draw any animal out of the air. His mother wrote in the diary:

'Today he returned home carrying something very carefully:

"Mommie, I brought you a little tiger," and he extended to me his empty hand. "Do you like my baby tiger?"

"Yes, yes, my little one!"

"Let him stay with us," he pleaded.

Before sitting down to dinner he placed next to his plate a smaller one, and when his food was brought to him he said:

"And for the baby tiger?"

Once he recounted in a lively manner:

"I went down into the sea and splashed about for a while. Then, suddenly, a big tiger came. I hid myself under the shore, then I threw out a net and caught a fish."

"Where is the fish?"

"I ate it up – raw!"

Most of his days were spent this way. Every minute he made up some fairy tale for himself:

"Mother, I'm a little bird and you're a bird too. Yes?"

"Mother, a bug came to visit me. He wanted to shake hands with me and put out his little paw …"

And although his mother observed that he literally bathed in fantasies as in a river, she continued to 'protect' him from the ill effects of books of fairy tales.

As if there were a basic difference between the fairy tale that a child made up himself and one that was created for him (as a folk tale) by imaginative folk or by a good writer.

It makes no difference whether or not the child is offered fairy tales for, if he is not, he becomes his own Andersen, Grimm, Ershov. Moreover, all his

E. I. Stanchinskaia *Dnevnik materi. Istoria razvitia sovremionnova rebionka ot rozhdeniia do 7 let* (A Mother's Diary. The History of the Development of a Child from Birth to the Age of Seven), (Moscow 1924)

ibid. page 66

ibid. page 92

ibid. page 48

playing is a dramatization of a fairy tale which he creates on the spot, animating, according to his fancy, all objects – converting any stool into a train, into a house, into an airplane, or into a camel.

From *From Two to Five*, University of California Press, 1963 (pages 118–20)

What are stories? The children tell us

In the course of an important investigation into the nature of what Britton and Harding call 'the role of the spectator', Arthur Applebee asked a number of children where stories come from, what is a good story and what happens in a story. In this article he records their replies and comments on them. In this short extract we can already see some signs of how their sense of a story is developing.

A. Applebee
The Spectator Role
(unpublished PhD
thesis, University of
London, 1974)

Where does Cinderella live? Arthur Applebee

'Where does Cinderella live? – *In a little house.* – Do you know where that is? – *In the woods.* – Where are the woods? – ... – Do you think you could go to the woods to visit her? – (no) – Why not? – *There might be a wolf there.*' (Paul, 5 years 6 months.)

We tell stories and children listen. But do we know what they are hearing, how our simple tales of fairies and elves, ghosts and goblins, or little engines-that-think-they-can are assimilated by the child to his rather different world? The idea of a story is not as simple a thing as it may seem to us, who long ago have established a 'spectator role' for ourselves with literature. (See James Britton's *Language and Learning*, 1970.) We know where Cinderella lives, or rather that she doesn't, but Paul and his friends are not quite so sure.

The comments which follow are based on some informal discussions with a class of 5, 6 and 7 year olds in south-east London. (The author's thanks are due to Mrs P. Ryalls, Head, John Stainer Infant School, and to Mrs Marcia Applebee, who cheerfully tolerated the disruption which even a well-intentioned visitor inevitably brings to a classroom.) The sampling cannot claim to be systematic, the questions were constantly changing, and the number of subjects was limited. None the less the comments that were recorded were vivid and seem worth sharing; if nothing else the mosaic they provide may serve to stimulate others, as it has me, to look more carefully at children and stories.

Where do stories come from?

Questions of origin are often confusing to children, but by school age, at least in the mix of 5, 6 and 7 year olds studied here, there is a general acceptance that stories are 'made up', the product of men. Most also have quite firm expectations about where they come from. Stephen (6 years 9 months) gives an answer that is very close to one Piaget heard from a young Swiss girl: Kauf, 8 years 8 months, imagines that memory is a little square of skin in the head, written on in pencil.

Jean Piaget
*The Child's
Conception of the
World*
Paladin, 1973
(page 52)

> 'Where does a story come from? – *A book*. – How does it get in the book? – *A man or a lady tells it*. – Where did they get the story from? – *Nowhere*. – How do they get it then? – *They just write a story*. – Where is it before they write it? – *In their brain*. – If you could take a look inside their head, what would it look like? – *Three little pigs or* ... – What would it look like though? – *Piece of paper*. – In their head? – (yes)'

Lisa (5 years 2 months) is more typical, sure of the general procedure but not willing to be so venturesome about the details:

> 'Where does a story come from? – *From a book*. – Where does the book come from? – *Library*. – Who made it in the first place? – *Factories*. – Where did they get the story? – *They get a little piece of paper and they do writings*. – How do they know what to write on it? – *I don't know but they learn it*.'

Stories, then, are first of all books, a point which Kevin (5 years 6 months) unwittingly emphasizes when, in the course of another series of questions, he refuses to tell me a story because he is too little to read me a book yet! As a manufactured article, there is no question about the 'life' or 'animism' of the story itself. Even the most immature of the children readily assert that stories cannot think, cannot get cold, and cannot be strong. In fact most intimate by their tone of incredulity that it is rather silly to ask such questions at all.

The very fact that a story has been inscribed in a book seems to give it a permanence and immutability that it might not otherwise have. Stephen, confronted with a story he does not like and asked what we could do to make it better, is also incredulous:

> 'If you were telling "Sleeping Beauty", could you change it so that you would like it? – *No*. – Why not? – ... – Is it all right to make changes in stories? – *No*. – Why not? – ... – Do you think you could tell it better? – *No*. – Why not? – *Because you can't rub out the words*.'

He at least seems to know what we were pushing towards, even if not willing to accept it. Many of his classmates simply decided that the only way to improve a story they do not like is to pick another one instead!

What is a good story?

The whole problem of what makes a story good or bad, why it is liked or disliked, is a perplexing one for students at this unselfconscious age. They like it because they like it, of course. When they have reasons to offer, they centre on the content of the book, or occasionally, like Jack's (5 years 8 months), on its cover:

'Why don't you like some stories? – *Because they don't look good.* – Why does that matter? – *Because they're ugly.*'

Jacqueline (6 years 1 month), more typical of the group, turns when pushed to the actions of the characters for a basis for her judgements:

'What things make you like a story? – ... – What kinds of stories do you like? – *I don't know.* – What story do you like? – *Peter Pan.* – Why do you like it? – *Because he's a nice story.* – Why is he a nice story? – *Because he can fly.* – Which story don't you like? – *Seven Wolves.* – Why don't you like it? – *Because they were bad.*'

Many of the children generalize similarly from the characters to a global impression of the story as a whole. A bad story, according to Stephen, is one about jails and hospitals; according to Ernest (7 years 10 months), it is one about witches. Harold (6 years 7 months) arrives at much the same point:

'What things happen in stories? – *Sad things and happy things and wicked things.* – What is a wicked story? – *When you kill someone for nothing.*'

Time and again, *Sleeping Beauty* becomes a 'sleepy story' (or even one to read 'when you are sleepy'); *Beauty and the Beast* a sad story (because she marries the beast); and the stories with witches are wicked, though we read them anyhow. Such 'wicked' stories put Charles (5 years 9 months) in a corner he has difficulty getting out of:

'Which rhymes don't you like? – *The sad ones. We've got sad and a happy one.* – What sad ones don't you like? – *About people who are wicked.* – Who do you know who would like those kinds of poems? – *People who are wicked.* – Do you think good people ever like poems about wicked things? – ... – Do you like "The Snaggle-Toothed Beast"? – *Yes.* – Does that mean you are

wicked? – *I'm not!* – But he is wicked isn't he? – *No he isn't, and I just
listen to it.'*
Though children are very firm in their judgements about poems and stories,
even if hard pushed to defend them, they are aware that the judgement about
which stories are 'good' and which 'bad' is a purely personal decision.
Surprisingly, there is little hesitation in responding when children are asked who
might like a story which they have just declared a poor one. Each seems aware
of his friends' idiosyncrasies, tolerant of differences of opinion even if quite
sure that his own is more reasonable. Listen to Stephen again:

'What stories have you heard that you do not like? – *"The Little Red Hen"*.
Why don't you like it? – ... – What's wrong with it? – ... – Who do you
think would like it? – ... – Who do you know that would like it? –
Michael. – Why would Michael like it if you don't? – *Because I don't like
hens*. – What other stories are there that you do not like? – *"Sleeping
Beauty"*. – Why don't you like "Sleeping Beauty"? – *Because it's old,
in the old times*. – Who do you know that might like "Sleeping Beauty"? –
Ayemen. – Why? – *Because she liked the prince and the king.'*

What happens in a story?

What is the nature of this world of stories, stories that are made by men and
put into books that are wicked or sleepy or ugly? Children have firm ideas
about what they expect to find, just as they have firm judgements after they have
found it. 'What happens in stories?' we asked Ernest:

'*They live happily ever after*. – Who does? – *Poor people.'*
The patterns of the stories are quickly sensed by children, just as they are by
adults; even the characters have their appointed roles:

'If you are reading a story about a rabbit, what is the rabbit usually like? –
Fast. – What about a fox? – *Fast. He wants to eat someone*. – What about a
witch? – *Cook someone*. – What about fairies? – *Fairies? They don't do nothing*. –
What are they usually like? – *Flying.'* (Stephen)
And Charles in a similar vein:

'What does a lion do in a story? – *Kills people*. – What about an elephant? –
He drinks water. He don't kill people. He just runs about.'
Such answers repeat back to us the symbols and images that we have built
our myths and fairy tales around; they bear little relation to the real nature of the

animals involved, but then they were never intended to.

Children have great difficulty in summarizing a story, responding to questions asking what stories are about with short lists of characters. (This is true whether we ask about stories in general or offer specific titles for summation.) Lisa knows stories are about 'Cinderella, Humpty Dumpty, and Jack and Jill.' Stephen, a bit older, thinks the three little pigs or the little red hen more appropriate. And Ernest answers in the same vein:

> 'If you were feeling sad, what kind of story would you like? – *Bears, The Three Bears.* – Why? – *Because, that makes me happy.* – What is it about? – *Three Bears, and Goldilocks, and her mother.*'

Yet if there is difficulty in summarizing, there is none at all in reciting. When Ernest is next pressed to *tell* the three bears story, he launches into a long, detailed, and accurate account. A few bits of his recitation will give a sense of the whole:

> 'She knocked on the door and nobody answered. And so, she pushed the door open and she saw three bowls. She tasted one bowl, but it was too lumpy. She tasted the second one and it was too cold. She tasted the little one and it was just right. And she ate it all up.'

Later the bears return home:

> 'Daddy Bear said, [In a deep voice:] "Someone has been sitting in my … eating in my . . . eating out of my porridge."
> [In a higher voice:] "Someone has been eating out of my porridge."
> [And higher still:] "Someone has been eating out of my porridge, and they have eaten it all up." And he began to cry.'

Such detail is very typical in stories retold by children at this age – they may have difficulty telling us 'what happens in a story', but one would be hard pressed to argue that they do not none the less know.

Where does Cinderella live?

Finally we have the question with which we opened our discussion – how much do children accept of the story-world, how real is it to them? Notions here were approached by asking the children where various storybook characters lived, and whether or not we could go along for a visit. The younger children are quite sure we could, though usually a bit awed at the prospect of the journey. Paul's opening comments on the wolf in his path implicitly accept that there *is* a path, somewhere, to follow. Lisa is equally sure, though she has clearly assimilated Cinderella more closely to her own life:

> 'Where does Cinderella live? – *With her family*. – And where is that? – *She lives a long way*. – Do you think you could go visit her? – *Yes*. – What do you think she is doing right now? – *I think she is going on holiday*. – Why? – *I think she is*. – Do you like holidays? – *We went on one a long time ago*.'

Age, however, is not the determiner here; responses seem controlled by the *kind* of experience of stories a child has had, rather than the *amount* of his contact with them. Thus some five-year olds are quite emphatic that Cinderella is 'just a story', while Ernest, one of the more capable and sophisticated of the older children, still cannot handle the question well:

> 'Where do you think that Goldilocks lives? – *In the woods*. – Where are the woods? – … – Where do you think she really lives? – *I don't know*. – Do you think you could go visit her? *No!* – Why not? – *Because I don't know where she lives*. – [Later:] Have you ever seen fairies? *No*. – How come? – *Because, I'm already asleep*. – Where do you think fairies live? – *In the sky*.'

Jackie (7 years 1 month) is more clearly in a period of transition, aware on the one hand that a story is 'just a story', but on the other more or less sure that stories are about real things. She is pushed into contradiction, tries a reconciliation and finally just accepts the conflict:

> 'Is Cinderella a real person? – *Yes!* – Could you go visit her? – *No*. – Why not? – … *I don't know where she lives*. – If you knew where she lived could you go talk with her? – *Yes*. – Are the three little pigs real pigs? – *Yes*.– Do you think you could go talk with them? – … – Have you ever seen pigs that could talk? – *No*. – Why do you think you haven't? – *Pigs can't talk*. – But you just told me that the three little pigs were real, and they talk, don't they? – *Well, the three little pigs, that's a story*. – But you told me they were real. – *Pigs are real*. – Are those pigs real though? – (Shrug of shoulders.)'

The progression seems to be from total acceptance of story characters, to a stage at which they are real but very far away, to an awareness of insurmountable contradictions between what story characters do and the child's knowledge of the possible. At this last stage, story characters become 'just a story', often being assimilated to puppets and other active but clearly 'made up' characters. Thus Patricia (6 years 3 months), after stoutly declaring that Cinderella certainly is 'just a story', equally stoutly maintains we could go visit her – 'to the pictures'. And in Charles' answer we can almost feel his opinion shifting back and forth as he considers one side of the problem and then another:

> 'Could you visit the three pigs, could you go see them? – *In real life? I can't*. –

Why? – *You could only see them in pictures, but you can't see them in real life.* –
Why not? – *Cause they're just puppets, if you see them in real life.*'
He is not quite willing to assert that they are 'just puppets' everywhere and
always, though he is convinced enough that that is all he will ever see. They have
begun to move to a special place, the place of stories, and there, with Cinderella,
they will remain.

From *The Use of English*, volume 25, number 2, 1973, (pages 136–46)

What happens when we read? (1)

Most of the themes taken up in this section impinge on the ideas contained in this essay. D. W. Harding sees the interested reader of a story as an onlooker, but in a different way from a participant. This spectator role 'may in certain ways be even more formative than events in which we take part.' The reader of a story is like a man listening to gossip or a good tale. He has a pact with the storyteller to agree that what he has to say deserves a listener. Fiction is a convention of storytelling which children have to learn. Harding says, 'little seems to be known about the way they reach it', but we think we can be more enlightening (cf. Aidan Warlow 'What the reader has to do'). Two further points to note: Harding's claim that fiction helps to define the spectator's sense of values; and his notion of 'experience as insight' as a clearer description of what, especially in writing about children's books, is usually called 'identification'.

Psychological processes in the reading of fiction   D. W. Harding

One of the unsatisfactory features of psychology at the present time (1961) is the contrast between an attempt at very exact definition of concepts and terms in some directions and a toleration of extreme vagueness and woolliness in others. The effort after precision is seen mostly in the planning and interpreting of experiments that lead farther and farther back into the recesses of methodology and abstract theory; the very high toleration of ambiguity occurs in discussing problems of complex behaviour in civilized societies. If we want to say how a rat learns a maze, we know by now that we shall have to come to grips with exactly defined terms and a meticulously scrutinized conceptual framework. If we are invited to consider the psychological processes that occur in reading a novel, we probably expect some rather vague waffle compounded of psycho-analysis, sociology and literary criticism. If I provide that, I shall have failed in my aim. Although real precision may at present be far out of reach, an effort in that direction is incumbent on anyone who believes that psychology as a science can have something useful to say about fiction.

An initial question is whether we should try to discuss fiction within a framework of general aesthetics. I agree with those who maintain that the numerous and extremely dissimilar activities conventionally grouped together as the arts don't form a separate psychological category. Very few literal statements that apply to a novel, a landscape painting, a porcelain dish and a piece of music will be at all illuminating about any one of those things. A novel is so distantly related to many other sorts of art, and so closely related to activities that are not included among the arts, that an approach through aesthetic generalizations would be restricting and misleading. It may seem, perhaps, that the form of a novel and the style of a novelist can be discussed in terms equally applicable to other arts, but I suspect that it can be done only by substituting metaphor and analogy for literal statement.

Much more important aspects of fiction are illuminated if the reader of a novel is compared with the man who hears about other people and their doings in the course of ordinary gossip. And to give an account of gossip we have to go a step or two farther back and consider the position of the person who looks on at actual events. As a framework, then, within which to discuss fiction, I want to offer some statement of the psychological position of the onlooker (of which I attempted a fuller discussion in 'The Role of the Onlooker', *Scrutiny*, VI, 3, December, 1937), and then to view the reading of a novel as a process of looking on at a representation of imagined events or, rather, of listening to a description of them. This involves examining carefully – and I believe discarding – psychological assumptions about some of the processes, such as identification and vicarious satisfaction, that have been supposed to occur in the reader. ·

Part of everyone's time is spent in looking on at events, not primarily in order to understand them (though that may come in) and not in preparation for doing something about them, but in a non-participant relation which yet includes an active evaluative attitude. We can say two things of the onlooker: first, that he attends, whether his attention amounts to a passing glance or fascinated absorption; and second, that he evaluates, whether his attitude is one of faint liking or disliking, hardly above indifference, or strong, perhaps intensely emotional, and perhaps differentiated into pity, horror, contempt, respect, amusement, or any other of the shades and kinds of evaluation, most of them unlabelled even in our richly differentiated language. Attentiveness on any particular occasion implies the existence of an interest, if we take that to mean an enduring disposition to respond, in whatever way, to some class of objects or events. The response almost instantaneously becomes (or is from the start) evaluative, welcoming or aversive. And in a complex, experienced organism, an evaluative attitude is usually one expression of a sentiment, if we take that to mean an enduring disposition to evaluate some object or class of objects in a particular way; an event or situation is then assessed in the light of its cognized significance for the object of a sentiment.

To take an example, for most of us a human being is interesting, and conflict is interesting, and a struggle between two groups of people is extremely likely to command our attention. When we observe one of the groups to be policemen a system of sentiments will be activated; according to the way we identify the other group, as men or women, drunk or sober, strike pickets, rowdy students, smash-and-grab thieves, political demonstrators, or what not, so other sentiments will be activated; the apparent brutality or good humour of the contestants will stir yet others; and whether we want to boo or cheer or shrug when the Black Maria eventually drives off will be the outcome of a complex interaction among many mutually entangled systems of sentiment.

The idea – still occasionally held – that the spectator's link with the scene consists mainly in his recognition that similar things might have happened to him – 'There, but for the grace of God, go I' – depends on far too limited a view of the human mind. Admittedly the man watching a ship-wreck from the safety of the shore may realize thankfully that he might have been in it and isn't, or more subtly that it symbolizes something that might happen to him; but to suppose that this is his chief link with the scene would be a crude piece of unpsychological rationalism. By far the likeliest response, and one that almost certainly accompanies any others, is simple horror and distress that this thing is happening to living people, whom he values as fellow-beings and whose sufferings he can imagine. We have a vivid description by William Hickey of what he felt when he was actually in the traditional role of watching a shipwreck from the shore:

> 'At half-past five nine ships that had parted from their anchors drove on shore between Deal and Sandwich, a distance of only eight miles; others, having drifted foul of each other, were obliged to cut away rigging and masts to prevent the dire alternative of going to the bottom together; two were seen actually to founder. A more horrid spectacle I never beheld, yet so interested did I feel on account of the unhappy people on board the different vessels that neither wet nor cold nor want

of rest could induce me to quit the beach whilst a ray of light remained ...

At eight o'clock I followed the advice of the hostess by drinking some excellent hot punch, and going directly afterwards to bed, where, although anxiety for the sufferings of the many poor drowning wretches kept me awake some time, fatigue at last got the better, and I fell into a profound and deep sleep, which continued uninterrupted for full twelve hours.'

It was only by chance that Hickey himself was not in one of the ships, and yet it seems clear that any relief he felt on his own account was a small part of his total state of mind compared with his concern for the victims.

Memoirs of William Hickey (editor Alfred Spencer) Hurst, 1949 volume 2, (pages 5–6)

Although the disclosure or reminder of environmental possibilities in a merely cognitive mode is a minor matter, it remains true that the experience of looking on at events does extend and modify, besides reflecting, the spectator's systems of interest and sentiment. A girl who watches a mother caring for an infant is not just reminded of one of the possibilities of her own life; she may also be extending her insight into the sort of satisfaction that a mother gets, perhaps correcting sentimental preconceptions or seeing compensations where she would have anticipated only trouble. In the same way we may learn as onlookers from the panic or the calmness of people faced with a threatening situation, or from the courage or the blind hope with which they meet serious illness, or from the sort of pleasure they show on achieving a success. In ways of this kind the events at which we are 'mere onlookers' come to have, cumulatively, a deep and extensive influence on our systems of value. They may in certain ways be even more formative than events in which we take part. Detached and distanced evaluation is sometimes sharper for avoiding the blurrings and bufferings that participant action brings, and the spectator often sees the event in a broader context than the participant can tolerate. To obliterate the effects on a man of the occasions on which he was only an onlooker would be profoundly to change his outlook and values.

Besides looking on at events in progress we can be spectators in memory or imagination of things past and things anticipated; further, we can release our imaginings from practical limitations and consider what might have been and what might be if the restrictions of reality were suspended. Even in looking on at actual happenings the spectator often grossly distorts what occurs, misleading himself by a variety of unconscious mechanisms; in memory and anticipation the unwitting distortion of fact and probability is even greater; and in fantasy even the intention to control thought by the measure of possibility is largely relinquished. In all the forms of fantasy, whether dreams, daydreams, private musings or make-believe play, we give expression to perfectly real preoccupations, fears and desires, however bizarre or impossible the imagined events embodying them.

The imaginary spectatorship of fantasy and make-believe play has the special feature of allowing us to look on at ourselves, ourselves as participants in the imagined events – the hero in the rescue fantasy, the victim of the assault, the defendant rebutting unjust accusations, the apparent nonentity suddenly called to national responsibility. In spite, however, of seeing himself as a participant in the story, the daydreamer or the child engaged in make-believe remains an onlooker, too; in all his waking fantasy he normally fills the dual role of participant and spectator, and as spectator he can when need be turn away from the fantasy events and attend again to the demands of real life. But although in waking experience we normally never quite lose grip on the role of onlooker, it remains true that every degree of abandonment to the invented occurrences may occur. We may at times give them, as it were, no more than a sceptical glance, perhaps contrasting them immediately with our present situation; we may let them develop very great vividness although we still remain only onlookers, never letting our real situation be far beyond the margins of attention and always being able at the least necessity to switch back to where we really are; or they may reach the extreme vividness, obliterating everything else, that the night dream possesses, and then, whether as daydreamers or psychotics, we have abandoned the role of onlooker and given ourselves up to delusional and perhaps hallucinated participation.

The solitary onlooker and the man engaged in private fantasy are, of course, members of a highly social species and their apparent isolation is unreal; what they see and invent, and what they feel, must be strongly influenced by their culture. In an environment which is highly saturated socially, our experience as spectators forms an important part of our cultural moulding. Everything we look on is tacitly and unintentionally treated as an object lesson by our fellow-spectators; speech and gesture or the mere intake of breath, smiles, pauses, clucks, tuts and glances are constantly at work to sanction or challenge the feelings we have as spectators. Needless to say, we can at least to some extent resist our fellow-onlookers' influence; and we in our turn, of course, are sanctioning and challenging and suggesting modifications of viewpoint to them.

The influence of our fellow-onlookers draws our attention to one aspect of events rather than another, changing the emphasis or bringing to mind what we might have overlooked. From this it is only a step – but a very important step –

to telling us about events we missed seeing, as in a vast amount of gossip and narrative. Instead of literally looking on, we now listen to representations of events; and the social influence of our companion is greater than ever because he not only reports selectively but also conveys what he regards as an appropriate attitude to what he saw. The gossip implicitly invites us to agree that what he reports is interesting enough to deserve reporting and that the attitude he adopts, openly or tacitly, is an acceptable evaluation of the events.

From giving an account of what has happened the next step is to suggest things that *might* happen, a process seen at its simplest in the child's 'Suppose ...' technique: 'Suppose that lion got out ...' 'Wouldn't it be fun if we found a secret cave?' 'Suppose that man was a spy ...' Here at one step we pass into the area of make-believe, whether it takes the form of play with companions, of drama, or of fiction. Imaginary spectatorship now occurs in a social setting. The result is a vast extension of the range of possible human experience that can be offered socially for contemplation and assessment. The ends achieved by fiction and drama are not fundamentally different from those of a great deal of gossip and everyday narrative. Between true narrative and fiction there exist, in fact, transitional techniques such as the traveller's tale and the funny anecdote in which the audience's tacit permission is assumed for embellishments and simplifications that enhance the effectiveness of the story. True or fictional, all these forms of narrative invite us to be onlookers joining in the evaluation of some possibility of experience.

Here I must make two digressions. The first is that the possibilities of experience include grief and disaster. Onlookers gather round accidents and funerals, gossips converse about disease, conflict and misery, newspaper readers want to hear of crime and calamity, the daydream is by no means always an invention of pleasures and children's make-believe includes its quota of illness, injury and punishment. In all these simpler forms of onlooking we are familiar with the fact that the unhappy chances of life are at least as interesting as the happy ones. It is not surprising, therefore, to find the same thing when we come to fiction and drama; the fact that tragic events are of intense human interest should not lead us into formulating pseudo-problems as to how the contemplation of something painful can be pleasurable. If there is a problem here, it is not confined to tragedy. The spectator, whether of actual events or representations, is interested in any of the possibilities of human experience, not merely its pleasures.

My second digression is that in saying that fiction represents possibilities of human experience we have to notice that it may be doing so through the medium of physical impossibilities. Tales that deal in the impossible are of two kinds. On the one hand there are tales of wonder which claim that the wonders are real possibilities – like the 'very true' account Autolycus was selling, of 'how a usurer's wife was brought to bed of twenty money-bags at a burthen'. Some of our contemporary tales of ghosts and the supernatural, whether offered as fiction or as true report, come into this category, as do some forms of science fiction. But on the other hand physical impossibilities may be used, both in fairy tales and in some sophisticated fiction, as vehicles for presenting realities of experience. In many fairy tales the wonders are of importance chiefly as providing the least laborious, most compressed and vivid means of representing some quite possible human experience. Everyone longs from time to time to have his own way, untrammelled by reality; the three miraculous wishes offer a dramatic compression of that possibility and allow the consequences to be discussed. Any of us might feel downtrodden and hope to have the tables turned by a benign authority who recognized our merit; a fairy godmother is a brief and vivid way of saying how delightful that would be.

In sophisticated fiction it is a question of the author's technique of presentation whether he aims at verisimilitude or avowed fantasy. When he chooses to depart from real possibilities we might say with Coleridge that the reader is called on for a 'willing suspension of disbelief'. But it makes less of a mystery of the process if we say that he is willing to participate in a recognized mode of communication, an accepted technique for discussing the chances of life. Basically we are engaged in the 'Suppose ...' technique of children's conversation.

Moreover in this respect – to return to the main theme – fantasy only highlights what is true of all fiction, that it is a convention of communication. The full grasp of fiction as fiction is a sophisticated achievement. Children come to it gradually, and although little seems to be known about the steps by which they reach it, we can plausibly suppose that the phase of 'lying' fantasy that many children go through is one stage of the process. There is good reason to think that the less-sophisticated adult often has only a precarious hold on the distinction between fiction and narrative; so some of the reactions to popular series in broadcasting have suggested, though here again full investigation seems to be lacking. It would appear, too, that some primitive peoples, though they enjoy storytelling as a pastime, regard all the stories as true narrative (perhaps of a remote ancestral past) and have little conception of avowed fiction. The Samoans of R. L. Stevenson's time, having read a missionary translation of his story *The Bottle Imp*, assumed that his wealth really came from his command of a magic bottle, and after a convivial evening with him would sometimes feel sufficiently in his confidence to ask if they might see 'the bottle'. Fiction has to be seen, then, as a convention, a convention for enlarging the scope of the discussions we have with each other about what may befall.

The 'discussion' may seem a one-sided affair since the reader is unable to answer back. But he is none the less active in accepting or rejecting what the author asserts. In the first place, the author offers what he claims to be a possibility of experience; the reader may in effect say 'No: that action of the hero is inconsistent with what he has said or done before; that monster of iniquity isn't humanly possible; that sudden repentance could never have happened ...' Secondly, the author conveys what he regards as appropriate attitudes towards events, characters and actions. He is constantly – but of course tacitly – saying: 'Isn't this exciting. ... He's attractive, isn't he. ... Wasn't that tragic. ... Isn't this moving ... ?' Again the reader accepts or rejects the implied assessments.

He may not consciously formulate his agreement and disagreement, but these are the underlying processes that show themselves eventually in enthusiasm for an author's work or disappointment with it. The reader discriminates; and this is true even at the low levels of trivial fiction, though there the discriminations may depend on criteria that better-educated or more practised readers have discarded.

The view I have been offering of the reader's active part at the receiving end of a conventional mode of communication contrasts with a good deal of pseudo-psychologizing that sees the process of novel-reading as one of identification and vicarious experience. Those ideas, vague and loose as they have always been, have had such currency that they have to be seriously examined.

We may once more begin with the man looking on at actual events. Unless he deliberately adopts the discipline of detached observation for the purposes of science or painting, he soon in some sense 'enters into' the experience of one or more of the participants.

The basic process connecting the onlooker with any event, real or fictional, involving living things, is that of imagining. The fundamental fact is that we can imagine ourselves in a situation very different from the one we are in, we can create images of the sensations we should have, we can become aware, in part, of the meanings we should see in it, what our intentions, attitudes and emotions would be, what satisfactions and frustrations we should experience. Suppose you are looking out of the window at torrents of rain lashing down in the street: you can imagine yourself out in it, rain beating on your face, your shoes squelching, your legs wet below the mackintosh, rain getting down inside your collar, hands in your pockets, shoulders hunched – and you can imagine the emotions you might experience out there. Suppose a man is in the street, the same process can occur, perhaps facilitated by the sight of him; and because you assume a fundamental likeness between yourself and him you take it that you have imaginative or empathic insight into his experience. Suppose that you watch a film of a man walking through pouring rain, or read of him in a book, or dream of him at night, the same basic process of imagining is at work. To say that this process has long been understood in psychology would be to claim too much, but it has long been recognized; and to what extent more recent ideas of identification and vicarious experience really advance our understanding is a matter for cautious discussion.

The great difficulty about the term 'identification' is to know which one of several different processes it refers to. The reader may see resemblances between himself and a fictional *persona* only to regret them (and perhaps hope to become different); is this recognition of resemblances 'identification'? He may long enviously to be like a fictional character so different from himself that he discounts all possibility of approximating to him; is this admiration 'identification'? He may adopt the character as a model for imitation, more or less close and successful, and it may be this process to which 'identification' refers. Or he may be given up, for the duration of the novel or film, to absorbed empathy with one of the characters. The fact is that we can avoid all this uncertainty and describe each of the processes accurately by speaking explicitly of empathy, imitation, admiration, or recognition of similarities. We sacrifice little more with the term 'identification' than a bogus technicality.

With this pseudo-technicality we discard the idea that there is something pathological about the processes we describe, or something to be better understood by examining pathological exaggerations of them. It may well be true that a continuity can be detected between absorbed empathy with a character and – at the pathological extreme – a psychotic delusion of identity with a great man, Napoleon, St. Peter, the President of the U.S.A. There may also be a continuum between the everyday imitation of some feature of an admired person (the handwriting of a favourite teacher or the hairstyle of a film star) and the pathological forms of imitation in which, for instance, psychosomatic processes produce symptoms similar to those of the illness from which a close relative has just died (though in this case devotion is often fused with fear and self-reproach). Even latah may claim to be on the same continuum. But we have not illuminated the ordinary processes by showing that they pass by gradual stages into the pathological and by giving to them all, healthy and morbid, the term 'identification'. We are still left with the perfectly usual and healthy processes of having empathic insight into other people (or representations of them) and of imitating features of their behaviour that we admire. To suppose that these processes are explained by being called identification is to be taken in by verbal magic.

The onlooker's observation of other people or of *personae* in fiction and drama may be accompanied by a preference for some, by specially sensitive or full insight into some, by awareness of likenesses between himself and some (not necessarily those he admires), and by a wish that he resembled some. These processes, occurring with all degrees of clear awareness or obscurity, form part of the tissue of ordinary social intercourse as well as entering into the enjoyment of fiction. An adequate account of a reader's attitude to a fictional *persona* may have to include a reference to them all, as well as to the subtler shades and complexities of these broad types of response. No good purpose is served by blanketing them all with a term like 'identification'.

The spectator who gives himself up to absorbed sympathy with some character of a novel or play is sometimes said to experience vicariously whatever the character undergoes. Among those who want a simple but psychological-sounding explanation for the enjoyment of fiction this idea of vicarious experience or vicarious satisfaction has long been popular. But it stands up poorly to serious examination.

Jung expressed the prevailing view when he said: 'The cinema ..., like the detective story, makes it possible to experience without danger all the excitement, passion and desirousness which must be repressed in the humanitarian ordering of life.' Notice that he says 'possible to *experience*', not possible to 'contemplate' or 'imagine'. On this formulation depends any exact meaning that the notion of vicarious experience possesses. Other writers, over a wide range of criticism and journalism, have popularized the idea. It was used, for instance, by the Lynds in *Middletown* and by Q. D. Leavis in *Fiction and the Reading Public*, where she took 'Living at the Novelist's Expense' as one of her leading themes and interpreted much novel-reading as the indulgence of wish-fulfilment fantasies. A contributor to *The Adelphi* (March 1934), wrote: 'With the lovely heroine, the laundry worker dons silk underwear ... an evening cloak with soft furry collar. During the day she had stood with damp feet in badly fitting high-

C. G. Jung
Modern Man in Search of a Soul
Routledge and Kegan Paul, 1970

heeled shoes which took two weeks' savings. But now her well-shaped leg is enclosed in stockings of finest silk, and shod by shoes from the Rue de la Paix. For an hour!' And Rebecca West wrote in *Nash's Pall Mall Magazine* (February 1934): 'George was glad to earn two pounds a week by tedious toil, and for relaxation ... indulge in remote concupiscence with unknowing film-stars.' (The quotations date from a period when the cultivated could pity wage-earners.)

What can be meant literally by these views? The desires are not in fact satisfied, of course. The implied suggestion is apparently that viewing a film or reading a novel approximates to having a wish-fulfilment dream – as hungry explorers are reported to dream of good meals – and that the spectator temporarily gets a delusive satisfaction through what amounts to hallucination while he reads or watches. That something approaching this may possibly happen to a few rather unusual people would be difficult to prove or disprove. But that it can be at all a usual mechanism is unbelievable. We may in moments of bitterness speak of the cinema or television as a dope, but we don't seriously believe that the spectators are sitting there in the same psychological condition as opium smokers in a dream, supposing themselves actually to be in some world of their fantasy. (They can pass each other sandwiches or stand up to let somebody else get to a seat, all in the real world, though they watch the screen.) It seems to be a case where a vivid metaphor has been taken literally without realization of the extent of pathological disorientation that the supposed psychological process would imply.

We get nearer the truth by starting from the fact that the 'wish-fulfilment' dream is also a *statement* of a pressing need or desire, defining the desire at the same time as it offers hallucinated satisfaction. In expressing interests and affirming desires for which ordinary life provides small scope, fiction and drama may indeed have something a little in common with dreams. They may, for instance, give expression to interests and attitudes that are partially checked (perhaps even repressed) in ordinary social intercourse, such as sexuality, cruelty, arrogance and violence. But it is very doubtful whether plays or novels that do this can rightly be said to give *substitute* satisfaction to the spectators' desires. They give perfectly real, direct satisfaction, but to a muted and incomplete version of the desires. The parallel is with the person who exclaims of someone annoying: 'I'd like to knock his block off' or 'He deserves to be horsewhipped'; exclamations like this offer no vicarious satisfaction for impulses to homicide or assault, but they constitute a real social attack and give direct satisfaction to a permissible degree of hostility (and may thereby

give very incomplete but still direct satisfaction to a more immoderate degree
of hidden rage). They may, if the anger grows or the countervailing impulses
weaken, lead on towards actual physical attack, but more commonly they serve
in themselves as a safety-valve. So with novels, plays and films, the represented
expression of interests and desires usually held in check may in some spectators
precipitate overt action to satisfy the desire (for instance, sexual activity or
some form of violence), but in other cases the fiction itself will be a sufficient
and a direct satisfaction of the slight degree of interest and desire that it elicits or
releases.

Interests and attitudes that are repressed or condemned, however, form only
a small part of the material of fiction and drama. Entirely acceptable values, too,
receive definition and affirmation. The desire for affection (prominent among the
desires represented in the films analysed for the Payne fund studies of the cinema),
the desire for advertising, for achievement, for the courage of one's convictions,
for prestige, for cheerful companionship and for endless other things may all be
stimulated, defined more concretely and vividly, revived after waning or confirmed
after doubt. Although these desires, perhaps thwarted in real life, will not be
satisfied in drama or fiction (or through contemplating real people more happily
circumstanced), there may still be a highly important gain in having joined with
the novelist or dramatist in the psychological act of giving them statement in a
social setting. What, after all, is the alternative to defining and expressing our
unattained and perhaps unattainable desires ? It is to acquiesce in the deprivation
and submit to the belief that with our personality or in our circumstances we
ought not even to desire such things; and to forfeit the right to the desire is even
worse than to be denied the satisfaction.

What is sometimes called wish-fulfilment in novels and plays can, therefore,
more plausibly be described as wish-formulation or the definition of desires.
The cultural levels at which it works may vary widely; the process is the same.
It is the social act of affirming with the author a set of values. They may centre
round marble bathrooms, mink coats and big cars, or they may be embodied in
the social milieu and *personae* of novels by Jane Austen or Henry James; Cadillacs
and their occupants at Las Vegas or carriages and theirs at Pemberley and Poynton.
We may lament the values implied in some popular forms of fiction and drama,
but we cannot condemn them on the ground of the psychological processes they
employ. The finer kinds of literature require the same psychological processes,
though putting them to the service of other values.

It seems nearer the truth, therefore, to say that fictions contribute to defining the reader's or spectator's values, and perhaps stimulating his desires, rather than to suppose that they gratify desire by some mechanism of vicarious experience. In this respect they follow the pattern, not of the dream with its hallucinated experiencing, but of waking supposition and imagination – 'Wouldn't it be wonderful if ...' 'Wouldn't it be sad if ...'

Empathic insight allows the spectator to view ways of life beyond his own range. Contemplating exceptional people, he can achieve an imaginary development of human potentialities that have remained rudimentary in himself or been truncated after brief growth; he can believe that he enters into some part of the experience of the interplanetary explorer, the ballerina, the great scientist, the musician or the master-spy, and again this applies at every level from popular entertainment to serious literature. The spectator enters imaginatively, with more or less accuracy and fullness, into some of the multifarious possibilities of life that he has not himself been able to achieve. One of the bonds between ourselves and others, one among our reasons for interest in them, is that they have done things that we have not. A great deal of gossip, newspaper reports, memoirs, fiction and drama, serves to remind us of the human potentialities that for one reason or another we have left to others, but the knowledge of which, in a diversified group with highly developed modes of communication, forms one of our social possessions.

A related source of satisfaction in entering imaginatively into activities far beyond our own range lies in the fact that we can see in very diverse ways of life certain broad types of experience that we know in our own: we view familiar experiences of struggle, disappointment, excitement, moral challenge, companionship, in the heightening context (biographical or fictional) of a more remarkable way of life, and the ordinary possibilities of our own lives may gain an enhanced significance as a result – whether the Saturday night dance takes on a Ruritanian glamour, or the determination of a Pasteur or Cézanne redeems our everyday persistence in face of the usual setbacks, or the commonplace failure of courage reveals the Lord Jim in our own personality.

In all these ways the process of looking on at and entering into other people's activity, or representations of it, does enlarge the range, not of the onlooker's experience but of his quasi-experience and partial understanding. For it has to be remembered that the subtlest and most intense empathic insight into the experience of another person is something far different from having the experience oneself.

I have suggested that the processes that are sometimes labelled 'identification'

and 'vicarious experience' need to be described more carefully and in more detail
for psychological purposes. But we have to go further. For even when these
processes have been accurately defined they are totally insufficient as an account
of the reader's response to fiction. An account based on them alone neglects the
fact that the onlooker not only enters into the experience of the participants but
also contemplates them as fellow-beings. It is an elementary form of onlooking
merely to imagine what the situation must seem like and to react *with* the
participant. The more complex observer imagines something of what the participant is experiencing and then reacts *to* him, for instance with pity or joy on his
account. The spectators who watch Othello as he kills his wife are not feeling
simply what they imagine him to be feeling, they are also feeling, as onlookers,
pity *for* him.

Nor is this part of the onlooker's role confined to the upper levels of fiction
and drama. It figures prominently in the response of the most naïve spectator
watching, say, one of the old films of the hero tearing along a dangerous road in
a car, to the rescue of the heroine on whom disaster is closing in. Do the spectators
experience imaginatively only what the hero is supposed to be experiencing – his
determination, his anxiety and hope, his concentration on the road, his exaspera-
tion at the fallen tree, his conflict before taking a hair's-breadth chance on the edge
of the precipice? Some part of this comes across but the spectators are in addition
responding to the situation as a whole: they are hoping *for* the hero as well as
with him, they assess his chances in the light of what they see of the heroine's
position, they have ups and downs of hope and anxiety as the situation alters
(often in ways that the hero knows nothing about), they may think more of the
heroine and her danger than of the hero's supposed feelings, and their taking
sides with both of them against the villains introduces another social element
that forms no part of the supposed experience of any of the participants.

The onlooker's response to the events as a whole goes much beyond
identification with any one of the characters, a point so obvious that one would
apologize for making it were it not regularly ignored by those who psychologize
about fiction and drama. A clear example of response to the situation as a whole
is given by K. O. Newman, who describes '... the climax of the last act [of the
war play that he saw repeatedly], when a stage-character, believed missing or
dead, reappears bodily, hale and hearty, though somewhat tired and bedraggled.
The delight of the audience at this auspicious dispensation knew no bounds,
night after night, matinée after matinée. His appearance, behind the back of the
hero and heroine, engaged in conversation, invariably evoked an excited mutter

K. O. Newman
*Two Hundred and
Fifty Times I Saw
a Play*
Pelagos Press
Oxford, 1944

in the audience, which, at some performances, went as far as an outburst of rapturous applause from the more naïve and impressionable playgoers.' The impulse to applaud was clearly not the outcome of feeling what any one of the characters on the stage was feeling. In viewing a situation like this, commonplace enough, the spectator is contemplating the whole social situation, perhaps anticipating what the characters will soon be feeling, but primarily adopting an attitude *towards* them. His attitude is that of a well-wisher who is not merely anticipating the joy that they will feel but enjoys the fact that they will be feeling joy. He feels pleased *for* them as well as *with* them. For the reader to know more about the events than the characters are shown as knowing is a normal and frequent feature of novels and plays. Dramatic irony is entirely dependent on it. And, of course, rereading or rewitnessing a novel or play extends and emphasizes the audience's superior knowledge of events and outcomes. Whenever the reader or spectator is in this position it becomes still more evidently a mistake to describe his response as 'identification' and 'vicarious experiencing'.

Let me recapitulate my main points. The mode of response made by the reader of a novel can be regarded as an extension of the mode of response made by an onlooker at actual events. One process on which the response depends – apart from the elementary perception and comprehension of the scene – is that of imaginative or empathic insight into other living things, mainly other people. But this would give only imaginative *sharing* of the participants' experience. At least equally important is the onlooker's, or the reader's, evaluation of the participants and what they do and suffer, an evaluation that I would relate in further analysis to his structure of interests and sentiments. But there is a third aspect of the process: the reader knows that the characters of the novel are not real people but only *personae* created by the author for the purpose of communication. Many readers, even educated readers, fail to hold this fact clearly in mind and they retain traces of the naïve view of the *personae* as real people, wanting to speculate for instance about the influences that made them what they are when the story opens or what will become of them after it ends. The more sophisticated reader knows that he is in social communication of a special sort with the author, and he bears in mind that the represented participants are only part of a convention by which the author discusses, and proposes an evaluation of, possible human experience.

From *British Journal of Aesthetics*, volume 2, number 2, 1962

Interchapter

At this point we divide narrative, the 'primary act of mind', the habit we have
called 'storying', from Story, the form we give to fiction and call art – in Susanne
Langer's term 'the mode of completed experience'.

Our contributors have said that we use narrative to make sense of the
world and to feel at home in it, compensating in dreams for what we are denied,
putting to rights what we feel is crooked, re-ordering experience the better to
accommodate it. We edit our memories into the kind of personal history we can
bear to live with and we entertain possibilities, both probable and improbable;
in all of this we rely on the distinctly human device of language which can utter
with equal conviction what is and is not the case. 'I am the queen' announces
the child in the nursery school, and no one contradicts her.

With great willingness we enter into the narratives of others when they want
us to listen, especially if there is a space in the occupations of the workaday
world. We enjoy a well-told anecdote, especially if the climax is subtly timed;
we savour domestic drama when the crisis is past. A widespread addiction to
fiction is evident from television, radio, magazines, and comic strips in newspapers.
Thirty seconds of television advertising time, at vast cost, is all the promoters of
a product need to create a drama of thirst quenched, love quickened, or disaster
averted by timely investment. Our inner fictions and our approval and enjoyment
of the stories people tell us march together, and allow us to be diverted, moved,
persuaded, and worked on emotionally in a way we recognize as legitimate.

This recognition of story as a form is based on certain recurrent features
which we become familiar with quite early in our experience of them: anticipation
of climax, expectation of judgement and, as Frank Kermode calls it, 'the sense of
an ending'. These distinguish story from narrative, art from life. In life there are
recurrent crises, temporary judgements, and only one final end. When we invent
fictions in dreams and make-believe we meet ourselves in them and the end is
delayed. When we tell stories for others, we draw to a close, a pay-off time, and
part of the pleasure is the form as the box-lid snaps shut. When we read a story
we both experience events as we read (in Harding's and Britton's 'spectator role')

Frank Kermode
*The Sense of an
Ending: Studies in the
Theory of Fiction*
OUP New York,
1967
OUP London, 1969

and we also remember the story as a story when we have read it. As a memory it is what Aristotle calls 'a completed action' to be contemplated in a way that life cannot be.

The climax, judgement, ending are all crucial in the separation of story from narrative. We learn the pattern as we learn to talk:

> Ring-a-ring o' roses
> A pocket full of posies
> Atisshoo, atisshoo
> We all fall down.

and recognize it in 'Once upon a time' and 'happily ever after'. Stories told and read to children give them both the age-old inheritance of their culture – whatever they make of it – and the templates, patterns, and symbolic outlines for their personal storymaking. They learn from the shape of anecdotes, the punch line in jokes, the timing of a climax, how a written story emerges from a 'yarn' and what conventions it adheres to so that they have the rules as part of their expectation when they read stories on their own. Gradually they learn to shape written stories for themselves. One of the recurrent handicaps of illiterate adults is their inability to anticipate what may happen in a story they are learning to read because they have never learned how the rules of the story game are transferred to the print on a page. Most of them were never read to as children.

In stories for children, both short and long, there is a special sense of an ending, closely bound up with the role of fantasy and symbolic play. Tolkien says children need the 'eucatastrophe', the 'consolation of the Happy Ending'. He believes it is a special feature of fairy stories.

J. R. R. Tolkien
Tree and Leaf
Allen and Unwin
1964

We are the more likely to rejoice in the eucatastrophe if we have acquiesced in the justice of the solution to the problem posed at the outset. Novelists can then be expected to mete out fair play to their characters in proportion to their deserts. Although in life we know that good men die, scoundrels flourish, and true love often does not run smooth, we do not, as children, tolerate this rough justice. Instead we prefer the small courageous serf to outwit the bullying land-lord, the thoughtful younger son to marry the princess, not only because he deserves to, but because in a universe of our making that is how we should order things.

So the author, his inner narrative wrested from him and shaped into Story, offers his reader a 'secondary world' as Tolkien says, or Winnicott's 'third area' if his art is good enough, where 'literary belief' offers possibilities that life cannot, and the ending is a guarantee that the Story will order its events aright. As the reader grows older, he can, with practice, relinquish the stock conventions of the popular tale and take on the novels called 'great' where the authors vary these patterns more and more. But while they are young, readers becoming acquainted with Story make considerable imaginative investments in coherent patterns, and, as Frank Kermode says, the author 'by the provision of an end makes possible a satisfying consonance with the origins and with the middle'.

The reader and all kinds of stories

Reprinted in
Only Connect
OUP Toronto, 1969

As the author of the Narnia books and a well-known essay on 'Three ways of writing for children', C. S. Lewis needs no introduction. In this piece Lewis examines the universal features of Story and the continuity of certain kinds of pleasure from childhood to adulthood, Hiawatha to Homer. His examination of the nature of 'excitement', the kinds of world stories present, and the means of access to these worlds available to the inexperienced reader, shows the range and depth of his insight.

On Stories   C. S. Lewis

It is astonishing how little attention critics have paid to Story considered in itself. Granted the story, the style in which it should be told, the order in which it should be disposed, and (above all) the delineation of the characters, have been abundantly discussed. But the Story itself, the series of imagined events, is nearly always passed over in silence, or else treated exclusively as affording opportunities for the delineation of character. There are indeed three notable exceptions. Aristotle in the *Poetics* constructed a theory of Greek tragedy which puts Story in the centre and relegates character to a strictly subordinate place. In the Middle Ages and the early Renaissance, Boccaccio and others developed an allegorical theory of Story to explain the ancient myths. And in our own time Jung and his followers have produced their doctrine of Archtypes. Apart from these three attempts the subject has been left almost untouched, and this has had a curious result. Those forms of literature in which Story exists merely as a means to something else – for example, the novel of manners where the story is there for the sake of the characters, or the criticism of social conditions – have had full justice done to them; but those forms in which everything else is there for the sake of the story have been given little serious attention. Not only have they been despised, as if they were fit only for children, but even the kind of pleasure they give has, in my opinion, been misunderstood. It is the second injustice which I am most anxious to remedy. Perhaps the pleasure of Story comes as low in the scale as modern criticism puts it. I do not think so myself, but on that point we may agree to differ. Let us, however, try to see clearly what kind of pleasure it is: or rather, what different kinds of pleasure it may be. For I suspect that a very hasty assumption has been made on this subject. I think that books which are read merely 'for the story' may be enjoyed in two very different ways. It is partly a division of books (some stories can be read only in the one spirit and some only in the other) and partly a division of readers (the same story can be read in different ways).

What finally convinced me of this distinction was a conversation which I had a few years ago with an intelligent American pupil. We were talking about the books which had delighted our boyhood. His favourite had been Fenimore Cooper whom (as it happens) I have never read. My friend described one particular scene in which the hero was half-sleeping by his bivouac fire in the woods while a Redskin with a tomahawk was silently creeping on him from behind. He remembered the breathless excitement with which he had read the passage, the agonized suspense with which he wondered whether the hero would wake up in time or not. But I, remembering the great moments in my own early reading, felt quite sure that my friend was misrepresenting his experience, and indeed leaving out the real point. Surely, surely, I thought, the sheer excitement, the suspense, was not what had kept him going back and back to Fenimore Cooper. If that were what he wanted any other 'boy's blood' would have done as well. I tried to put my thought into words. I asked him whether he were sure that he was not over-emphasizing and falsely isolating the importance of the danger simply as danger. For though I had never read Fenimore Cooper I had enjoyed other books about 'Red Indians'. And I knew that what I wanted from them was not simply 'excitement'. Dangers, of course, there must be: how else can you keep a story going? But they must (in the mood which led one to such a book) be Redskin dangers. The 'Redskinnery' was what really mattered. In such a scene as my friend had described, take away the feathers, the high cheek-bones, the whiskered trousers, substitute a pistol for a tomahawk, and what would be left? For I wanted not the momentary suspense but that whole world to which it belonged – the snow and the snow-shoes, beavers and canoes, war-paths and wigwams, and Hiawatha names. Thus I; and then came the shock. My pupil is a very clear-headed man and he saw at once what I meant and also saw how totally his imaginative life as a boy had differed from mine. He replied that he was perfectly certain that 'all that' had made no part of his pleasure. He had never cared one brass farthing for it. Indeed – and this really made me feel as if I were talking to a visitor from another planet – in so far as he had been dimly aware of 'all that', he had resented it as a distraction from the main issue. He would, if anything, have preferred to the Redskin some more ordinary danger such as a crook with a revolver.

To those whose literary experiences are at all like my own the distinction which I am trying to make between two kinds of pleasure will probably be clear enough from this one example. But to make it doubly clear I will add another. I was once taken to see a film version of *King Solomon's Mines*. Of its many sins – not least the introduction of a totally irrelevant young woman in shorts who accompanied the three adventurers wherever they went – only one here concerns us. At the end of Haggard's book, as everyone remembers, the heroes are awaiting death entombed in a rock chamber and surrounded by the mummified kings of that land. The maker of the film version, however, apparently thought this tame. He substituted a subterranean volcanic eruption, and then went one better by adding an earthquake. Perhaps we should not blame him. Perhaps the scene in the original was not 'cinematic' and the man was right, by the canons of his own art, in altering it. But it would have been better not to have chosen in the first place a story which could be adapted to the screen only by being ruined. Ruined, at least, for me. No doubt if sheer excitement is all you want from a story, and if increase of dangers increases excitement, then a rapidly changing series of two risks (that of being burned alive and that of being crushed to bits) would be better than the single prolonged danger of starving to death in a cave. But that is just the point. There must be a pleasure in such stories distinct from mere excitement or I should not feel that I had been cheated in being given the earthquake instead of Haggard's actual scene. What I lose is the whole sense of the deathly (quite a different thing from simple danger of death) – the cold, the silence, and the surrounding faces of the ancient, the crowned and sceptred, dead. You may, if you please, say that Rider Haggard's effect is quite as 'crude' or 'vulgar' or 'sensational' as that which the film substituted for it. I am not at present discussing that. The point is that it is extremely different. The one lays a hushing spell on the imagination; the other excites a rapid flutter of the nerves. In reading that chapter of the book curiosity or suspense about the escape of the heroes from their death-trap makes a very minor part of one's experience. The trap I remember for ever: how they got out I have long since forgotten.

It seems to me that in talking of books which are 'mere stories' – books, that is, which concern themselves principally with the imagined event and not with character or society – nearly everyone makes the assumption that 'excitement' is the only pleasure they ever give or are intended to give. *Excitement*, in this sense, may be defined as the alternate tension and appeasement of imagined anxiety. This is what I think untrue. In some such books, and for some readers, another factor comes in.

To put it at the very lowest, I know that something else comes in for at least one reader – myself. I must here be autobiographical for the sake of being evidential. Here is a man who has spent more hours than he cares to remember in reading romances, and received from them more pleasure perhaps than he should. I know the geography of Tormance better than that of Tellus. I have been more curious about travels from Uplands to Utterbol and from Morna Moruna to Koshtra Belorn than about those recorded in Hakluyt. Though I saw the trenches before Arras I could not now lecture on them so tactically as on the Greek wall, and Scamander and the Scaean Gate. As a social historian I am sounder on Toad Hall and the Wild Wood or the cave-dwelling Selenites or Hrothgar's court or Vortigern's than on London, Oxford, and Belfast. If to love Story is to love excitement then I ought to be the greatest lover of excitement alive. But the fact is that what is said to be the most 'exciting' novel in the world, *The Three Musketeers*, makes no appeal to me at all. The total lack of atmosphere repels me. There is no country in the book – save as a storehouse of inns and ambushes. There is no weather. When they cross to London there is no feeling that London differs from Paris. There is not a moment's rest from the 'adventures': one's nose is kept ruthlessly to the grindstone. It all means nothing to me. If that is what is meant by Romance, then Romance is my aversion and I greatly prefer George Eliot or Trollope. In saying this I am not attempting to criticize *The Three Musketeers*. I believe on the testimony of others that it is a capital story. I am sure that my own inability to like it is in me a defect and a misfortune. But that mis- fortune is evidence. If a man sensitive and perhaps over-sensitive to Romance likes least that Romance which is, by common consent, the most 'exciting' of all, then it follows that 'excitement' is not the only kind of pleasure to be got out of Romance. If a man loves wine and yet hates one of the strongest wines, then surely the sole source of pleasure in wine cannot be the alcohol?

If I am alone in this experience then, to be sure, the present essay is of merely autobiographical interest. But I am pretty sure that I am not absolutely alone. I write on the chance that some others may feel the same and in the hope that I may help them to clarify their own sensations.

In the example of *King Solomon's Mines* the producer of the film substituted at the climax one kind of danger for another and thereby, for me, ruined the story.

But where excitement is the only thing that matters kinds of danger must be irrelevant. Only degrees of danger will matter. The greater the danger and the narrower the hero's escape from it, the more exciting the story will be. But when we are concerned with the 'something else' this is not so. Different kinds of danger strike different chords from the imagination. Even in real life different kinds of danger produce different kinds of fear. There may come a point at which fear is so great that such distinctions vanish, but that is another matter. There is a fear which is twin sister to awe, such as a man in war-time feels when he first comes within sound of the guns; there is a fear which is twin sister to disgust, such as a man feels on finding a snake or scorpion in his bedroom. There are taut, quivering fears (for one split second hardly distinguishable from a kind of pleasurable thrill) that a man may feel on a dangerous horse or a dangerous sea; and again, dead, squashed, flattened, numbing fears, as when we think we have cancer or cholera. There are also fears which are not of *danger* at all: like the fear of some large and hideous, though innocuous, insect or the fear of a ghost. All this, even in real life. But in imagination, where the fear does not rise to abject terror and is not discharged in action, the qualitative difference is much stronger.

I can never remember a time when it was not, however vaguely, present to my consciousness. *Jack the Giant-Killer* is not, in essence, simply the story of a clever hero surmounting danger. It is in essence the story of such a hero surmounting *danger from giants*. It is quite easy to contrive a story in which, though the enemies are of normal size, the odds against Jack are equally great. But it will be quite a different story. The whole quality of the imaginative response is determined by the fact that the enemies are giants. That heaviness, that monstrosity, that uncouthness, hangs over the whole thing. Turn it into music and you will feel the difference at once. If your villain is a giant your orchestra will proclaim his entrance in one way: if he is any other kind of villain, in another. I have seen landscapes (notably in the Mourne Mountains) which, under a particular light, made me feel that at any moment a giant might raise his head over the next ridge. Nature has that in her which compels us to invent giants: and only giants will do. (Notice that Gawain was in the north-west corner of England when 'etins aneleden him', giants came *blowing* after him on the high fells. Can it be an accident that Wordsworth was in the same places when he heard 'low breathings coming after him'?) The dangerousness of the giants is, though important, secondary. In some folk tales we meet giants who are not dangerous. But they still affect us in much the same way. A *good* giant is legitimate: but he would be twenty tons of living, earth-shaking oxymoron. The intolerable pressure, the sense of something older, wilder, and more earthy than humanity, would still cleave to him.

But let us descend to a lower instance. Are pirates, any more than giants, merely a machine for threatening the hero? That sail which is rapidly overhauling us may be an ordinary enemy: a Don or a Frenchman. The ordinary enemy may easily be made just as lethal as the pirate. At the moment when she runs up the Jolly Roger, what exactly does this do to the imagination? It means, I grant you, that if we are beaten there will be no quarter. But that could be contrived without piracy. It is not the mere increase of danger that does the trick. It is the whole image of the utterly lawless enemy, the men who have cut adrift from all human society and become, as it were, a species of their own – men strangely clad, dark men with earrings, men with a history which they know and we don't, lords of unspecified treasure buried in undiscovered islands. They are, in fact, to the young reader almost as mythological as the giants. It does not cross his mind that a man – a mere man like the rest of us – might be a pirate at one time of his life and not at another, or that there is any smudgy frontier between piracy and privateering. A pirate is a pirate, just as a giant is a giant.

Consider, again, the enormous difference between being shut out and being shut in: if you like between agoraphobia and claustrophobia. In *King Solomon's Mines* the heroes were shut in: so, more terribly, the narrator imagined himself to be in Poe's *Premature Burial*. Your breath shortens while you read it. Now remember the chapter called 'Mr Bedford Alone' in H. G. Wells's *First Men in the Moon*. There Bedford finds himself shut out on the surface of the Moon just as the long lunar day is drawing to its close – and with the day go the air and all heat. Read it from the terrible moment when the first tiny snowflake startles him into a realization of his position down to the point at which he reaches the 'sphere' and is saved. Then ask yourself whether what you have been feeling is simply suspense. 'Over me, around me, closing in on me, embracing me ever nearer was the Eternal … the infinite and final Night of space.' That is the idea which has kept you enthralled. But if we were concerned only with the question whether Mr Bedford will live or freeze, that idea is quite beside the purpose. You can die of cold between Russian Poland and new Poland, just as well as by going to the Moon, and the pain will be equal. For the purpose of killing Mr Bedford 'the infinite and final Night of space' is almost entirely otiose: what is by cosmic standards an infinitesimal change of temperature is sufficient to kill a man and absolute zero can do no more. That airless outer darkness is important not for what it can do to Bedford but for what it does to us: to trouble us with Pascal's old fear of those eternal silences which have gnawed at so much religious faith and shattered so many humanistic hopes: to evoke with them and through them all our racial and childish memories of exclusion and desolation: to present, in fact, as an intuition one permanent aspect of human experience.

And here, I expect, we come to one of the differences between life and art. A man really in Bedford's position would probably not feel very acutely that sidereal loneliness. The immediate issue of death would drive the contemplative object out of his mind: he would have no interest in the many degrees of increasing cold lower than the one which made his survival impossible. That is one of the functions of art: to present what the narrow and desperately practical perspectives of real life exclude.

I have sometimes wondered whether the 'excitement' may not be an element actually hostile to the deeper imagination. In inferior romances, such as the American magazines of 'scientifiction' supply, we often come across a really suggestive idea. But the author has no expedient for keeping the story on the move except that of putting his hero into violent danger. In the hurry and scurry of his escapes the poetry of the basic idea is lost. In a much milder degree I think this has happened to Wells himself in the *War of the Worlds*. What really matters in this story is the idea of being attacked by something utterly 'outside'. As in *Piers Plowman* destruction has come upon us 'from the planets'. If the Martian invaders are merely dangerous – if we once become mainly concerned with the fact that they can *kill* us – why, then, a burglar or a bacillus can do as much. The real nerve of the romance is laid bare when the hero first goes to look at the newly fallen projectile on Horsell Common. 'The yellowish-white metal that gleamed in the crack between the lid and the cylinder had an unfamiliar hue. *Extra-terrestrial* had no meaning for most of the onlookers.' But *extra-terrestrial* is the key word of the whole story. And in the later horrors, excellently as they are done, we lose the feeling of it. Similarly in the Poet Laureate's *Sard Harker* it is the journey across the Sierras that really matters. That the man who has heard that noise in the cañon – 'He could not think what it was. It was not sorrowful nor joyful nor terrible. It was great and strange. It was like the rock speaking' – that this man should be later in danger of mere murder is almost an impertinence.

It is here that Homer shows his supreme excellence. The landing on Circe's island, the sight of the smoke going up from amidst those unexplored woods, the god meeting us ('the messenger, the slayer of Argus') – what an anti-climax if all these had been the prelude only to some ordinary risk of life and limb! But the peril that lurks here, the silent, painless, unendurable change into brutality, is worthy of the setting. Mr de la Mare too has surmounted the difficulty. The threat launched in the opening paragraphs of his best stories is seldom fulfilled in any identifiable event: still less is it dissipated. Our fears are never, in one sense, realized: yet we lay down the story feeling that they, and far more, were justified. But perhaps the most remarkable achievement in this kind is that of Mr David Lindsay's *Voyage to Arcturus*. The experienced reader, noting the threats and promises of the opening chapter, even while he gratefully enjoys them, feels sure that they cannot be carried out. He reflects that in stories of this kind the first chapter is nearly always the best and reconciles himself to disappointment; Tormance, when we reach it, he forbodes, will be less interesting than Tormance seen from the Earth. But never will he have been more mistaken. Unaided by any special skill or even any sound taste in language, the author leads us up a stair of unpredictables. In each chapter we think we have found his final position: each time we are utterly mistaken. He builds whole worlds of imagery and passion, any one of which would have served another writer for a whole book, only to pull each of them to pieces and pour scorn on it. The physical dangers, which are plentiful, here count for nothing: it is we ourselves and the author who walk through a world of spiritual dangers which makes them seem trivial. There is no recipe for writing of this kind. But part of the secret is that the author (like Kafka) is recording a lived dialectic. His Tormance is a region of the spirit. He is the first writer to discover what 'other planets' are really good for in fiction. No merely physical strangeness or merely spatial distance will realize that idea of other-ness which is what we are always trying to grasp in a story about voyaging through space: you must go into another dimension. To construct plausible and moving 'other worlds' you must draw on the only real 'other world' we know, that of the spirit.

Notice here the corollary. If some fatal progress of applied science ever enables us in fact to reach the Moon, that real journey will not at all satisfy the impulse which we now seek to gratify by writing such stories. The real Moon, if you could reach it and survive, would in a deep and deadly sense be just like anywhere else. You would find cold, hunger, hardship, and danger; and after the first few hours they would be *simply* cold, hunger, hardship, and danger as you might have met them on Earth. And death would be simply death among those bleached craters as it is simply death in a nursing home at Sheffield. No man would find an abiding strangeness on the Moon unless he were the sort of man who could find it in his own back garden. 'He who would bring home the wealth of the Indies must carry the wealth of the Indies with him.'

Good stories often introduce the marvellous or supernatural, and nothing about Story has been so often misunderstood as this. Thus, for example, Dr Johnson, if I remember rightly, thought that children liked stories of the marvellous because they were too ignorant to know that they were impossible. But children do not always like them, nor are those who like them always children; and to enjoy reading about fairies – much more about giants and dragons – it is not necessary to believe in them. Belief is at best irrelevant; it may be a positive disadvantage. Nor are the marvels in good Story ever mere arbitrary fictions stuck on to make the narrative more sensational. I happened to remark to a man who was sitting beside me at dinner the other night that I was reading Grimm in German of an evening but never bothered to look up a word I didn't know, 'so that it is often great fun' (I added) 'guessing what it was that the old woman gave to the prince which he afterwards lost in the wood'. 'And specially difficult in a fairy tale,' said he, 'where everything is arbitrary and therefore the object might be anything at all.' His error was profound. The logic of a fairy tale is as strict as that of a realistic novel, though different.

Does anyone believe that Kenneth Grahame made an arbitrary choice when he gave his principal character the form of a toad, or that a stag, a pigeon, a lion would have done as well? The choice is based on the fact that the real toad's face has a grotesque resemblance to a certain kind of human face – a rather apoplectic face with a fatuous grin on it. This is, no doubt, an accident in the sense that all the lines which suggest the resemblance are really there for quite different bio-logical reasons. The ludicrous quasi-human expression is therefore changeless: the toad cannot stop grinning because its 'grin' is not really a grin at all. Looking at the creature we thus see, isolated and fixed, an aspect of human vanity in its funniest and most pardonable form; following that hint Grahame creates Mr Toad – an ultra-Jonsonian 'humour'. And we bring back the wealth of the Indies; we have henceforward more amusement in, and kindness towards, a certain kind of vanity in real life.

But why should the characters be disguised as animals at all? The disguise is very thin, so thin that Grahame makes Mr Toad on one occasion 'comb the dry leaves out of his *hair*'. Yet it is quite indispensable. If you try to rewrite the book with all the characters humanized you are faced at the outset with a dilemma. Are they to be adults or children? You will find that they can be neither. They are like children in so far as they have no responsibilities, no struggle for existence, no domestic cares. Meals turn up; one does not even ask who cooked them. In Mr Badger's kitchen 'plates on the dresser grinned at pots on the shelf'. Who kept them clean? Where were they bought? How were they delivered in the Wild

Wood? Mole is very snug in his subterranean home, but what was he living *on*? If he is a *rentier* where is the bank, what are his investments? The tables in his forecourt were 'marked with rings that hinted at beer mugs'. But where did he get the beer? In that way the life of all the characters is that of children for whom everything is provided and who take everything for granted. But in other ways it is the life of adults. They go where they like and do what they please, they arrange their own lives.

To that extent the book is a specimen of the most scandalous escapism: it paints a happiness under incompatible conditions – the sort of freedom we can have only in childhood and the sort we can have only in maturity – and conceals the contradiction by the further pretence that the characters are not human beings at all. The one absurdity helps to hide the other. It might be expected that such a book would unfit us for the harshness of reality and send us back to our daily lives unsettled and discontented. I do not find that it does so. The happiness which it presents to us is in fact full of the simplest and most attainable things – food, sleep, exercise, friendship, the face of nature, even (in a sense) religion. That 'simple but sustaining meal' of 'bacon and broad beans and a macaroni pudding' which Rat gave to his friends has, I doubt not, helped down many a real nursery dinner. And in the same way the whole story, paradoxically enough, strengthens our relish for real life. This excursion into the preposterous sends us back with renewed pleasure to the actual.

It is usual to speak in a playfully apologetic tone about one's adult enjoyment of what are called 'children's books'. I think the convention a silly one. No book is really worth reading at the age of ten which is not equally (and often far more) worth reading at the age of fifty – except, of course, books of information. The only imaginative works we ought to grow out of are those which it would have been better not to have read at all. A mature palate will probably not much care for *crême de menthe*: but it ought still to enjoy bread and butter and honey.

Another very large class of stories turns on fulfilled prophecies – the story of Oedipus, or *The Man who would be King*, or *The Hobbit*. In most of them the very steps taken to prevent the fulfilment of the prophecy actually bring it about. It is foretold that Oedipus will kill his father and marry his mother. In order to prevent this from happening he is exposed on the mountain: and that exposure, by leading to his rescue and thus to his life among strangers in ignorance of his real parentage, renders possible both the disasters. Such stories produce (at least in me) a feeling of awe, coupled with a certain sort of bewilderment such as one often feels in looking at a complex pattern of lines that pass over and under one another. One sees, yet does not quite see, the regularity. And is there not good occasion both for awe and bewilderment? We have just had set before our imagination something that has always baffled the intellect: we have *seen* how destiny and free will can be combined, even how free will is the *modus operandi* of destiny. The story does what no theorem can quite do. It may not be 'like real life' in the superficial sense: but it sets before us an image of what reality may well be like at some more central region.

It will be seen that throughout this essay I have taken my examples indiscriminately from books which critics would (quite rightly) place in very different categories – from American 'scientifiction' and Homer, from Sophocles and *Märchen*, from children's stories and the intensely sophisticated art of Mr de la Mare. This does not mean that I think them of equal literary merit. But if I am right in thinking that there is another enjoyment in Story besides the excitement, then popular romance even on the lowest level becomes rather more important than we had supposed. When you see an immature or uneducated person devouring what seem to you merely sensational stories, can you be sure what kind of pleasure he is enjoying? It is, of course, no good asking *him*. If he were capable of analysing his own experience as the question requires him to do, he would be neither uneducated nor immature. But because he is inarticulate we must not give judgement against him. He may be seeking only the recurring tension of imagined anxiety. But he may also, I believe, be receiving certain profound experiences, which are, for him, not acceptable in any other form.

Mr Roger Green, writing in *English* not long ago, remarked that the reading of Rider Haggard had been to many a sort of religious experience. To some people this will have seemed simply grotesque. I myself would strongly disagree with it if 'religious' is taken to mean 'Christian'. And even if we take it in a sub-Christian sense, it would have been safer to say that such people had first met in Haggard's romances elements which they would meet again in religious experience if they ever came to have any. But I think Mr Green is very much nearer the mark than those who assume that no one has ever read the romances except in order to be thrilled by hair-breadth escapes. If he had said simply that something which the educated receive from poetry can reach the masses through stories of adventure, and almost in no other way, then I think he would have been right. If so, nothing can be more disastrous than the view that the cinema can and should replace popular written fiction. The elements which it excludes are precisely those which give the untrained mind its only access to the imaginative world. There is death in the camera.

As I have admitted, it is very difficult to tell in any given case whether a story is piercing to the unliterary reader's deeper imagination or only exciting his emotions. You cannot tell even by reading the story for yourself. Its badness proves very little. The more imagination the reader has, being an untrained reader, the more he will do for himself. He will, at a mere hint from the author, flood wretched material with suggestion and never guess that he is himself chiefly making what he enjoys. The nearest we can come to a test is by asking whether he often *re-reads* the same story.

It is, of course, a good test for every reader of every kind of book. An unliterary man may be defined as one who reads books once only. There is hope for a man who has never read Malory or Boswell or *Tristram Shandy* or Shake-speare's *Sonnets*: but what can you do with a man who says he 'has read' them, meaning he has read them once, and thinks that this settles the matter? Yet I think the test has a special application to the matter in hand. For excitement, in the sense defined above, is just what must disappear from a second reading. You cannot, except at the first reading, be really curious about what happened. If you find that the reader of popular romance – however uneducated a reader, however bad the romances – goes back to his old favourites again and again, then you have pretty good evidence that they are to him a sort of poetry.

The re-reader is looking not for actual surprises (which can come only once) but for a certain ideal surprisingness. The point has often been misunderstood. The man in Peacock thought that he had disposed of 'surprise' as an element in landscape gardening when he asked what happened if you walked through the garden for the second time. Wiseacre! In the only sense that matters the surprise works as well the twentieth time as the first. It is the *quality* of unexpectedness, not the *fact* that delights us. It is even better the second time. Knowing that the 'surprise' is coming we can now fully relish the fact that this path through the shrubbery doesn't *look* as if it were suddenly going to bring us out on the edge of the cliff. So in literature. We do not enjoy a story fully at the first reading. Not till the curiosity, the sheer narrative lust, has been given its sop and laid asleep, are we at leisure to savour the real beauties. Till then, it is like wasting great wine on a ravenous natural thirst which merely wants cold wetness. The children understand this well when they ask for the same story over and over again, and in the same words. They want to have again the 'surprise' of discovering that what seemed Little-Red-Riding-Hood's grandmother is really the wolf. It is better when you know it is coming: free from the shock of actual surprise you can attend better to the intrinsic surprisingness of the *peripeteia*.

I should like to be able to believe that I am here in a very small way contributing (for criticism does not always come later than practice) to the encouragement of a better school of prose story in England: of story that can mediate imaginative life to the masses while not being contemptible to the few. But perhaps this is not very likely. It must be admitted that the art of Story as I see it is a very difficult one. What its central difficulty is I have already hinted when I complained that in the *War of the Worlds* the idea that really matters becomes lost or blunted as the story gets underway. I must now add that there is a perpetual danger of this happening in all stories. To be stories at all they must be series of events: but it must be understood that this series – the *plot*, as we call it – is only really a net whereby to catch something else. The real theme may be, and perhaps usually is, something that has no sequence in it, something other than a process and much more like a state or quality. Giantship, otherness, the desolation of space, are examples that have crossed our path. The titles of some stories illustrate the point very well. *The Well at the World's End* – can a man write a story to that title? Can he find a series of events following one another in time which will really catch and fix and bring home to us all that we grasp at on merely hearing the six words? Can a man write a story on Atlantis – or is it better to leave the word to work on its own? And I must confess that the net very seldom does succeed in catching the bird. Morris in the *Well at the World's End* came near to success – quite near enough to make the book worth many readings. Yet, after all, the best moments of it come in the first half.

But it does sometimes succeed. In the works of the late E. R. Eddison it succeeds completely. You may like or dislike his invented worlds (I myself like that of *The Worm Ouroboros* and strongly dislike that of *Mistress of Mistresses*) but there is here no quarrel between the theme and the articulation of the story. Every episode, every speech, helps to incarnate what the author is imagining. You could spare none of them. It takes the whole story to build up that strange blend of renaissance luxury and northern hardness. The secret here is largely the style, and especially the style of the dialogue. These proud, reckless, amorous people create themselves and the whole atmosphere of their world chiefly by talking. Mr de la Mare also succeeds, partly by style and partly by never laying the cards on the table. Mr David Lindsay, however, succeeds while writing a style which is at times (to be frank) abominable. He succeeds because his real theme is, like the plot, sequential, a thing in time, or quasi-time: a passionate spiritual journey. Charles Williams had the same advantage, but I do not mention his stories much here because they are hardly pure story in the sense we are now considering. They are, despite their free use of the supernatural, much closer to the novel; a believed religion, detailed character drawing, and even social satire all come in. *The Hobbit* escapes the danger of degenerating into mere plot and excitement by a very curious shift of tone. As the humour and homeliness of the early chapters, the sheer 'Hobbitry', dies away we pass insensibly into the world of epic. It is as if the battle of Toad Hall had become a serious *heimsókn* and Badger had begun to talk like Njal. Thus we lose one theme but find another. We kill – but not the same fox.

It may be asked why anyone should be encouraged to write a form in which the means are apparently so often at war with the end. But I am hardly suggesting that anyone who can write great poetry should write stories instead. I am rather suggesting what those whose work will in any case be a romance should aim at. And I do not think it unimportant that good work in this kind, even work less than perfectly good, can come where poetry will never come.

Shall I be thought whimsical if, in conclusion, I suggest that this internal tension in the heart of every story between the theme and the plot constitutes, after all, its chief resemblance to life? If story fails in that way does not life commit the same blunder? In real life, as in a story, something must happen. That is just the trouble. We grasp at a state and find only a succession of events in which the state is never quite embodied. The grand idea of finding Atlantis which stirs us in the first chapter of the adventure story is apt to be frittered away in mere excitement when the journey has once been begun. But so, in real life, the idea of adventure fades when the day-to-day details begin to happen. Nor is this merely because actual hardship and danger shoulder it aside. Other grand ideas – home-coming, reunion with a beloved – similarly elude our grasp. Suppose there is no disappointment; even so – well, you are here. But now, something must happen, and after that something else. All that happens may be delightful: but can any such series quite embody the sheer state of being which was what we wanted? If the author's plot is only a net, and usually an imperfect one, a net of time and event for catching what is not really a process at all, is life much more? I am not sure, on second thoughts, that the slow fading of the magic in *The Well at the World's End* is, after all, a blemish. It is an image of the truth. Art, indeed, may be expected to do what life cannot do: but so it has done. The bird has escaped us. But it was at least entangled in the net for several chapters. We saw it close and enjoyed the plumage. How many 'real lives' have nets that can do as much?

In life and art both, as it seems to me, we are always trying to catch in our net of successive moments something that is not successive. Whether in real life there is any doctor who can teach us how to do it, so that at last either the meshes will become fine enough to hold the bird, or we be so changed that we can throw our nets away and follow the bird to its own country, is not a question for this essay. But I think it is sometimes done – or very, very nearly done – in stories. I believe the effort to be well worth making.

From *Essays presented to Charles Williams*, OUP, 1947

What happens when we read (2)

This article attempts to summarize as concisely as possible what we know about the nature of the task confronting the reader of a book. The psychologists have supplied us with great quantities of information about our visual perception of the print, the linguists have enabled us to describe the lexical and syntactic demands of the text, and the psycholinguists have researched the problems of assimilating meaning. But the most interesting stage in the process – 'getting lost in the story' – is not amenable to direct observation and we must rely on introspection to tell us what happens. This is why Coleridge is so helpful.·

What the reader has to do   Aidan Warlow

'Getting into the story' is a very expressive phrase, much used by young readers. We all know *roughly* what it means. At first you're not in the story, then you are. It is a strange and complex process and well worth trying to describe in greater detail. This is what seems to happen:

The child (we are discussing children but all this applies to adults as well) picks a book from the shelf, or unpacks it on Christmas morning, or has it dumped on his desk by a teacher. And then he asks the crucial question 'Will it be any good?' His answer will depend largely on the matching of his personal needs with the expectations that he forms of the book after a rapid examination of the title, format, illustrations, and typography, reinforced perhaps by the comments on the dust-jacket and the opening sentences of the story. Drawing on his previous experience of comparable books, he has to decide whether the anticipated satisfactions are likely to outweigh the effort required to read it.

If these expectations prove favourable, he starts his reading. The early part of the story is the difficulty. At first, perhaps only for a sentence, perhaps for several pages, the reader is in a confused position. He does not know the location, characters, or situation of the novel (though the pictures, blurb, and his previous expectations may have helped). Then it all gradually becomes clear. This ambivalent period before 'getting into the story' is critical in deciding whether to go on or put the book aside.

Clearly the period of confusion is very brief in stories which conform to familiar and predictable conventions, for example the traditional fairy story or the fourteenth Enid Blyton book. And some novelists make sure that we have all the essential data as early as possible. E. B. White opens *Charlotte's Web* with the words: ' "Where's Papa going with that axe?" said Fern to her mother as they were laying the table for breakfast', which, with maximum economy of words, tells us the heroine's name, her family relationships and what she is doing at a particular time in the morning as well as alerting us to the rather ominous idea of a father wandering around with an axe. Other novelists keep us waiting longer. In *The Owl Service*, for example, Alan Garner keeps the reader confused as to who the characters *are* for several pages and it is not until the second chapter that we really grasp who is whose brother and which is the father. Meanwhile the reader is distracted by essential information being withheld.

It is the real test of the maturity of the reader to see how long he can tolerate this ambivalent period of doubt. If the fantasy experience is not forthcoming quite soon he may lose faith in the novel. The inexperienced reader cannot defer his gratification for long. The expectation of pleasure has to outweigh present dissatisfaction.

If he is reasonably competent, the reader will be able to adapt his technique to the difficulty of the text and the degree of accuracy with which he wishes to achieve understanding. An easily predicted narrative, such as one of Enid Blyton's, will require very few eye-fixations on each line. The mind of the reader is merely registering the main action-events. He will cease to be aware of the *sound* of the words (though some traces of auditory and vocal processes may never be entirely eliminated). He will associate the printed symbols directly with what the psycholinguists refer to as the 'deep structure' of meaning. What the rapid reader is doing is utilizing his knowledge of the context which he is storing at a 'deep' semantic level and supplementing this by additional visual cues from the text. To quote the current psycholinguistic jargon, 'Because the fluent reader operates simultaneously at the surface and deep structure level – discriminating visual features and using his knowledge of grammar to associate them with the developing semantic interpretation – he is able to read with the minimum of visual information.'

On the other hand, the delicately paced account of Mary's encounter with

F. Smith
Understanding Reading
Holt Rinehart, 1971

the robin in chapter 7 of *The Secret Garden* may force the child to reduce the speed of his reading to match the tentative movements and hushed expectancy of the situation. And the opening page of Ted Hughes' *The Iron Man* cannot be read rapidly even when one tries; the sentence structures force us to pause and 'vocalize' as we read – as when we read poetry. (We are reminded of C. S. Lewis's suggestion that we evaluate a book by the way in which it needs to be read.)

C. S. Lewis
An Experiment in Criticism
CUP, 1961

Whether he 'vocalizes' or not, the reader fuses groups of words and sentences into larger units of meaning. He is converting perceived verbal symbols into a personal awareness of factual (material), cognitive (theoretical, assertive) or expressive (betraying state of writer) information; it is a perceptual identification that locates the event in the entire structure of knowledge of the perceiver.

Much of the essential 'context support' is brought to the reading from outside the text. In particular the reader brings:

1. Past literary experience which has familiarized him with the language and conventions of fictional narrative and provided him with an extensive knowledge of the sort of thing one can meet with in these sorts of stories.
2. Past life experience which has taught him, through personal memory and observation of others, how human beings behave and feel in various situations.

The proportions of each can of course vary enormously. (It is interesting to see which emphasis the standard 'reading schemes' give: *Breakthrough to Literacy* and the *Nippers* series rely heavily on the second; the early *Ladybird* readers use neither; the Macmillan *Language in Action* scheme makes an effort to draw on both.)

Provided he has the necessary skills, experience, and stamina to comprehend and orientate himself, the reader is able finally to 'get into the story'. Tolkien explains:

J. R. R. Tolkien
Tree and Leaf
Allen and Unwin
1964

'What really happens is that the storymaker proves a successful "sub-creator". He makes a Secondary World which your mind can enter. Inside it, what he relates is "true": it accords with the laws of the world. You therefore believe it, while you are, as it were, inside. The moment disbelief arises, the spell is broken; the magic, or rather art, has failed.'

This is an advance on Coleridge's marvellous but essentially negative description of 'that willing suspension of disbelief for the moment which constitutes poetic faith', since it emphasizes the *increased* area of belief. It is summed up in the phrase 'the world of make-believe'. But Coleridge's account is still extraordinarily helpful as far as children's fiction is concerned. It is worth reminding ourselves

S. T. Coleridge
Biographia Literaria
(chapter 14) 1817

The reader

of his words:

> 'The mind of the spectator, or the reader, therefore is not to be deceived
> into any idea of reality …; neither, on the other hand, is it to retain a perfect
> consciousness of the falsehood of the presentation. There is a state of mind
> between the two, which may properly be called illusion, of which the
> comparative powers of the mind are completely suspended; as in a dream,
> the judgement is neither beguiled, nor conscious of the fraud, but remains
> passive.'

Coleridge's analogy between literary illusion and dream takes us straight back to
Freud, Winnicott, and Britton (see page 40). And the importance of this insight,
together with Tolkien's point about the spell being broken if disbelief arises, lies
in the realization that there is an *all-or-nothing commitment by the reader*; either he is
'in' the Secondary World or 'out' of it. If the reader is 'in', then, as Coleridge said,
the comparative powers of the mind are completely suspended.

W. H. Auden
describes this on
page 103

However, the total commitment to a fantasy must not be regarded as being
in conflict with 'critical reading'. The really important point is that *the two
activities cannot take place simultaneously*. It is a commonplace of modern psychology
that the human mind is only capable of attending to one object, idea, or activity
at a time. One cannot contemplate the voice of the narrator while one's consciousness is in the fantasy, though the adult reader may come close to doing so.
Professor Lovell (1971) explains the focus of attention thus:

K. Lovell
*Educational
Psychology and
Children*
University of
London Press, 1971
(pages 92–3)

> 'While we can only attend to one main thing at a time, that is, we are more
> conscious of it than of anything else at the given moment, we are often
> dimly aware of other objects, scenes, sensations, and thoughts to which we
> are not actually attending. Thus a person may be attending to a television
> programme and be vaguely aware that he feels cold or hears the ticking of
> the clock. In addition, various psychological processes such as heart beat
> and breathing are taking place of which he might not be aware at all. At any
> given time, then, there is usually a definite focus of attention, a near margin
> of attention, and subconscious activity.'

Really there appear to be two methods of reading fiction. Either the attention of
the reader, particularly if a child, is focused exclusively on the Secondary World
of the novel, his eyes are glued to the rapidly turning pages, his critical faculties
are entirely suspended and he does not notice his mother yelling to him to come
down to dinner; or else he reads more carefully, pausing to think, making mental
notes of interesting points and considering whether the book is good or not.

The latter technique, what is normally meant by 'critical' reading, involves a form of mental 'flickering' between a commitment to the Secondary World and critical evaluation of it. In other words, fantasy experience and critical evaluation are rapidly exchanging roles as the 'definite focus' and the 'near margin' of attention. Hence the importance of Coleridge's emphasis on the very temporary nature of suspended disbelief – 'for the moment'.

For the young reader, lost in the world of Narnia or jungle warfare, that 'moment' will last a long time, perhaps until the book is completely read, unless forcibly interrupted by his parents to turn the lights out and go to sleep. At the opposite extreme is the 'A' level candidate revising *Joseph Andrews* for the fifteenth time before the exam, so completely familiar with the plot that his curiosity about its development has been quite lost, his attention now alerted to the discovery of new critical comments to make on each episode, character, and stylistic device. He is not believing the story, merely reflecting on it.

Traditionally, English teachers have concentrated on training the latter type of reader; promoting thought about the text at the expense of the free encounter and involvement with the Secondary World. It is therefore worth enquiring whether in fact the frequently interrupted critical reading – 'flickering' in and out of the illusion – is the most effective means of understanding a novel and preparing to make an evaluation of it. James Squire (1964) carried out experiments with a group of adolescents reading four short stories and found that those most involved in the fantasy were also those who were *retrospectively* able to make the most perceptive critical comments:

J. R. Squire
The response of adolescents while reading four short stories
NCTE, Champaign, Illinois, 1964

> 'When involved, as during the reading of the central portions of these stories, the subjects made fewer literary judgements. This apparent inverse relationship does not conflict with the earlier finding through partial correlation technique of a high positive relationship between the total response in these categories (literary judgements and statements of self-involvement). *The two types of responses seem to reinforce one another, with readers who are emotionally involved formulating more literary judgements* even though the responses occur at different times. Many of the evaluations of the story as literature occur either before the reader has become involved or after an extended period during which the subject seems considerably involved in the central experience or the character whom he is interpreting or identifying with or rejecting. Only when the reading of a story is completed do literary judgements become a major concern.'

Only by committing himself unreservedly and uninterruptedly to the hypotheses of the author has the reader been able to feel the impact of a 'virtual experience' in literature. Children, even more than adults, share D. H. Lawrence's view that 'We judge a work of art by its effect on our sincere and vital emotion, and nothing else.' And so we are led to the question of *response*.

There has been a great deal of bad research on 'response'. The pitfall is to assume an identity between the inner response of the reader and the public critical utterance. We must somehow study 'response' as a highly elaborate and *mostly unarticulated* element in the kinetic process of reading, which takes place both while one reads and, in modified forms, when one has raised one's eyes from the page or closed the book altogether. It is of course essentially affective, what D. W. Harding calls 'the outcome of the complex interaction among mutually entangled systems of sentiment.' Sometimes it may find expression in a long critical essay, at other times in a flood of bitter tears.

Kinds of fiction: a hierarchy of veracity

The core of this article is the chart which accompanies it. Taking as his starting point Tolkien's assertion that the great question children ask is 'Is it true?' Aidan Warlow has constructed a 'hierarchy of veracity' to introduce a new categorization of children's books according to the similarity or dissimilarity of the stories to the world as it is usually seen to be. The reader then knows the kind of world he is taking on and the conventions by which the story operates. A fruitful follow-up of this essay for anyone interested in this new analysis would be to allot the books one knows to the categories on the chart.

The chart is on page 100

Alternative worlds available   Aidan Warlow

Children create alternative selves, alternative lives, and alternative worlds, in play and in storymaking, modifying and supplementing their everyday experience – making it better and more interesting. The great Soviet writer Kornei Chukovsky realized that a child does this not in order to evade reality, but in order to confirm his knowledge of it. 'When we notice that a child has started to play with some newly acquired component of understanding, we may definitely conclude that he has become full master of this item of his understanding; only those ideas can become toys for him whose proper relation to reality is fully known to him.'

K. Chukovsky
From Two to Five
Moscow, 1925
(trans. Miriam Morton)
University of California Press
1963
(page 163)

However, the recognition of the 'proper relation to reality' of *other people's* alternative worlds is less clearly known to a young reader. When he enters someone else's alternative world through literature he sometimes needs to check what sort of world he is going into. According to Tolkien: ' "Is it true?" is the great question children ask ... They do ask that question I know ... Most often it proceeds from the child's desire to know what kind of literature he is faced with. Children's knowledge of the world is often so small that they cannot judge off-hand and without help between the fantastic, the strange (that is rare and remote facts), the nonsensical, and the merely "grown up" ... But they recognize the

J. R. R. Tolkien
Tree and Leaf
Allen and Unwin
1964

different classes ...'

And then, gradually and intuitively, the child seems to learn that there is
what might be called a 'hierarchy of veracity'. Some classes of fiction are 'truer'
than others. Some narrators are more honest and better informed than others
(Booth 1961). Some types of story allow people to travel on magic carpets and
animals to talk, while others do not. Some stories invite (quoting a distinction
made by I. A. Richards) 'verifiable belief' while others require 'imaginative
assent'. The conventions of one class of story do not apply to others. Different
sorts of fiction bear different relationships to life as he knows it.

W. C. Booth
The Rhetoric of Fiction
University of
Chicago Press, 1961

On the accompanying chart I have attempted to grade works according to
their similarity and dissimilarity to the external world as we see it and generally
understand it. I have 'reality-tested' a selection of works commonly read by
children, in terms of the prevailing rules that govern the setting and plot. This has
produced two main categories. The first consists of works that bear only a limited
mimetic resemblance to life as we normally observe it; the physical laws of nature,
as a phenomenologist might see them, have been suspended or amended, as in
myths, legends, fairy tales, and their modern derivatives. The familiar typologies
of connection, causality, and explanation that we expect, for example, in the
study of history and science, are absent. The second main category consists of
works in which the normal laws of nature have been maintained and supernatural
phenomena have been excluded. The movement from left to right on the chart
represents a progression in realism from highly allegorical myth towards psychologically accurate and explicit contemporary fiction.

There are a number of advantages in grading material like this. The first is
that, at present, all serious discussion of children's reading has been hopelessly
confused by the lack of mutually exclusive categories. Conventional phrases such
as 'adventure story' (most stories surely consist of some sort of adventure),
'fantasy' (any fiction is in some sense a fantasy), 'animal story' (what have
Aesop's Fables, *Black Beauty*, *Tarka the Otter*, and *Rupert Bear* in common save
the number of their characters' legs?) offer no basis for analysis.

A second advantage is that attention focuses on the narrative content and
not the medium of publication, so that we can examine, for example, television
programmes and comics on the same bases as novels.

It will be noticed that the chart in fact represents a cyclic continuum, since
certain contemporary writers, notably Catherine Storr and Alan Garner, have
designed novels with a firm background of psychological and sociological realism
and then examined the imaginative lives of the protagonists, giving the novel a

sort of fourth dimension of fantasy that links directly with the mythic tales of
the left-hand side of the chart. Such writers have abandoned the traditional
assumption that underlies most children's fiction that there is a state of stability
existing between objective reality and our perception of it. Books such as *Alice's
Adventures in Wonderland* and Sendak's *Where the Wild Things Are*, which explicitly
describe a dream, as opposed to drawing on dream's imagery, might also be said
to link the two ends of the chart. (Northrop Frye notes a similar continuum in
adult literature – the return to what he calls the 'mythic mode' in Kafka, Joyce,
and science fiction.)

N. Frye
Anatomy of Criticism
Princeton University
Press, 1957

It will also be noticed that the chart reflects very broadly the historical
development of storytelling and we can see in the passage from left to right a
reflection of man's shift from the ancient view of himself as a participant in a
holistic universality to a modern egocentric sense of his individuality. It will be
interesting to see to what extent the child's evolving literary taste recapitulates
the history of the species in this respect.

But what we would most like to do with the thirteen types of story that I
have identified is see *to what extent they each maintain consistent and distinctive
conventions*. If we can describe their conventions in terms of:

1. the sort of events that can take place,
2. the legitimate modes of behaviour and motivational patterns of the
   characters,
3. the moral system by which we are to evaluate this behaviour,
4. the appropriate narrative style and vocabulary that regulates meaning,

then we might see that the *combination of these elements represents a characteristic code –*
patterns of thought that represent a consistency.

Then I think we will be able to say more clearly that *this* sort of book
operates a code that makes particular demands on the experiential and intellectual
resources of the reader and *that* sort makes other types of demand. It will
perhaps lead us back to the work of Frank Smith and the psycholinguists who
have shown us that it is not so much the surface structure of the text that enables
the reader to assimilate meaning, as the accessibility of the deep structures at a
semantic cognitive level. The child does not merely have to identify the superficial
word meanings; he must also have access to the value systems and behavioural
characteristics of the protagonists and the physical and metaphysical characteristics
of the Secondary World in order to predict and therefore comprehend the
narrative.

F. Smith
*Understanding
Reading*
Holt Rinehart, 1971

A few cursory references to the conventions of one particular group on the

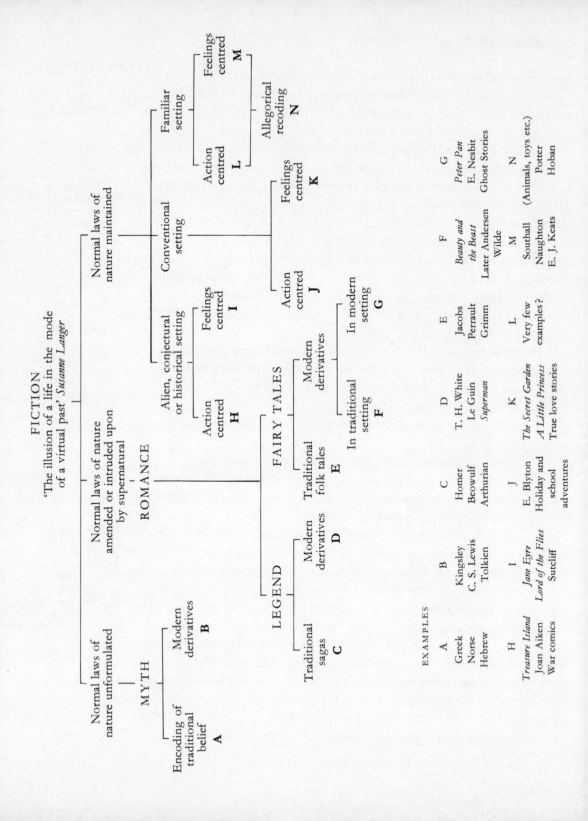

chart, the traditional European folk tale (normal laws of nature operating but intruded upon by the supernatural) will indicate the sort of analysis that we need to make if we are to describe what kind of world the reader is taking on. First, in contrast to saga and myth, folk tales contain supernatural transformations but no gods; the practitioner of sympathetic magic, Frazer tells us in *The Golden Bough*, 'supplicates no higher power; he sues the favour of no fickle and wayward being; he abuses himself before no awful deity.' It is only in the modern derivatives of the folk tale such as those of Andersen and Wilde that an omnipotent god appears. Second, a person's status (princess, woodcutter, widow) is an indication of moral as well as social worth; the hierarchy is structured so that the third son of a poor widow is worth a dozen lords and is fully entitled to the princess's hand in marriage. (In legend, with its great respect for social status, the hero would have to discover that actually he was the long lost son of a king.) But, as Susanne Langer explains, the hero is not the saviour or helper of mankind as in saga. 'If he is good, his goodness is a private asset, for which he is richly rewarded ... The beneficiary of his clever acts, his prowess, or his virtue is he himself, not mankind for ever after.' Third, the dramatis personae are limited to a small number of stereotypes – what George Kelly refers to as 'constellatory' or 'pre-emptive' constructs – whose behaviour and personal qualities are entirely predicatable; our whole understanding of the story would be destroyed if the elder sister turned out to be wiser than the younger or the princess turned out to have another secret lover on the side. Finally, the Rule of Three is the dominant structure – third son succeeds at third attempt – but a splendid alternative structure is the cumulative tale such as *The Old Woman and her Pig* and *The House that Jack Built*; here the notion of causality takes precedence over mere temporal sequence in the narrative. And all these conventions, and many others that I have not referred to, are immediately and unquestioningly assumed by us the moment we see the words 'Once upon a time ...'

S. Langer
Philosophy in a New Key
Harvard University Press, 1944

G. Kelly
The Psychology of Personal Constructs
2 volumes
Norton, 1955

Such stories were, as Tolkien emphasizes to us, originally told by adults for adults, affording them the satisfactions of 'Fantasy, Recovery, Escape, Consolation, all things of which children have, as a rule, less need than older people.' But in fact we know that nowadays they have a special appeal for children between the ages of about five and eight, roughly corresponding to Piaget's stage of intuitive pre-operational thought. This phase is characterized by naïve typological thinking. Children interpret morality in terms of stern retributive justice, rigid hierarchical privilege and rules that transcend human motives and needs – what Piaget (1932) calls the 'transcendental' stage in moral development. In *The Child's Conception of*

J. Piaget
*The Moral Develop-
ment of the Child*
Routledge and
Kegan Paul, 1932

J. Piaget
*The Child's Con-
ception of the World*
Routledge and
Kegan Paul, 1929
Paladin, 1973

the World Piaget also describes processes that relate to fairy tale, though they may be more closely associated with mythic thought: an 'artificialist' tendency – the sun and moon have been made by man whose actions, such as striking a match, provoke the same sort of activity in the sun and moon; an 'animist' tendency – the sun and moon are alive and conscious of their activities; and a tendency to establish 'participation' between natural phenomena and ourselves – the moon came into being 'because we began to live' and 'that made the moon grow bigger'. A reading of Piaget's works offers us many opportunities to compare the child's early thought processes with the systems that prevail in mankind's collective thinking as recorded in folklore.

If we attempt to identify the 'proper relation to reality' of other types of story and describe their conventions along the lines that I have so briefly suggested above, then we will be getting very much closer to an understanding of the notion of 'readability'. Up to now, elaborate and costly research has been applied to texts in order to describe 'readability' in terms of typography, vocabulary, and syntax. Very little thought has been devoted to the question of whether one *story* can be read more easily than another. We know that children will overcome all sorts of linguistic obstacles (usually by simply ignoring them) if the alternative world of the story is one that is desirable and comprehensive. Future research might more usefully be applied not to how a text is written but to what sort of a world the storyteller is inviting the reader to enter.

The fairy tale: the reader in the Secondary World

Still pursuing our theme of what the reader has to do, we come to his involvement in the Secondary World, an involvement that Tolkien calls 'literary belief' and which, according to Auden, demands 'total surrender of the reader'. An additional virtue of this piece is the use it makes of quotations of other writers who have spoken with equal conviction on this theme.

Afterword – George MacDonald   W. H. Auden

Every normal human being is interested in two kinds of worlds: the Primary, everyday, world which he knows through his senses and a Secondary World or worlds which he not only can create in his imagination, but also cannot stop himself creating.

A person incapable of imagining another world than that given him by his senses would be subhuman, and a person who identifies his imaginary world with the world of sensory fact has become insane.

Stories about the Primary World may be called Feigned Histories; stories about a Secondary World, myths or fairy tales. A story about the Primary World, that is to say, may be fiction – the characters in it and the events may have been 'made up' by the writer – but the story must affect the reader in the same way that an historical narrative does: the reader must be able to say to himself, 'Yes, I have met people like that, and that is how, I know from experience, such people talk and act.'

The Secondary Worlds of myth and fairy tale, however different from the Primary World, presuppose its reality. As Professor Tolkien has said: 'If men could not distinguish between men and frogs, stories about frog kings would not have arisen.' A Secondary World may be full of extraordinary beings (fairies, giants, dwarfs, dragons, magicians, talking animals) and extraordinary objects (glass mountains and enchanted castles), and extraordinary events may occur in it, like a live man being turned to stone or a dead man restored to life, but, like the Primary World, it must, if it is to carry conviction, seem to be a world governed by laws, not by pure chance. Its creator, like the inventor of a game, is at liberty to decide what the laws shall be but, once he has decided, his story must obey them.

Most fairy tales and myths have come down to us from a prehistoric past, anonymous stories which cannot be attributed to the conscious invention of any individual author. Every now and again, however, within historical memory, writers whose names we know have appeared who can invent such a story: Kafka, for example, in this century, and George MacDonald, the author of this tale, in the last. The gift for such mythical creation is difficult to define, and the satisfaction that works of this genre give us is equally difficult to describe. As C. S. Lewis has said:

> 'To call it literary genius seems unsatisfactory since it can co-exist with great inferiority in the art of words – nay, since its connection with words at all turns out to be merely external and, in a sense, accidental. Nor can it be fitted into any of the other arts ... It produces works which give us (at the first meeting) as much delight and (on prolonged acquaintance) as much wisdom and strength as the works of the greatest poets ... It goes beyond the expression of things we have already felt. It arouses in us sensations we have never had before, never anticipated having ... hits us at a level deeper than our thoughts or even our passions ... and in general shocks us more fully awake than we are for most of our lives.'

History, actual or feigned, demands that the reader be at one and the same time inside the story, sharing in the feelings and events narrated, and outside it, checking these against his own experiences. A fairy tale like *The Golden Key*, on the other hand, demands of the reader total surrender; so long as he is in its world, there must for him be no other.

In recent times, under the influence of modern psychology, critics have acquired a habit of 'symbol hunting'. Though, in my opinion, the rewards for such a hunt can never be more than meagre, in the case of feigned histories about the Primary World, it can do no harm and may even, on occasion, be illuminating.

But to hunt for symbols in a fairy tale is absolutely fatal. In *The Golden Key*, for example, any attempt to 'interpret' the Grandmother or the air-fish or the Old Man of the Sea is futile: they mean what they are. The way, the only way, to read a fairy tale is the same as that prescribed for Tangle at one stage of her journey.

'Then the Old Man of the Earth stooped over the floor of the cave, raised
a huge stone from it, and left it leaning. It disclosed a great hole that went
plumb-down.

"That is the way," he said.

"But there are no stairs."

"You must throw yourself in. There is no other way." '

To me, George MacDonald's most extraordinary, and precious, gift is his ability,
in all his stories, to create an atmosphere of goodness about which there is nothing
phony or moralistic. Nothing is rarer in literature. As Simone Weil observed:

'Imaginary evil is romantic and varied; real evil is gloomy, monotonous,
barren, boring. Imaginary good is boring; real good is always new,
marvellous, intoxicating. "Imaginative literature", therefore, is either
boring or immoral or a mixture of both.'

George MacDonald's tales are a proof that this is not necessarily the case. That is
why, though there are many writers far greater than he, his permanent importance
in literature is assured.

From *Forewords and Afterwords*, Faber, 1973

The nature of the reader's satisfaction

In discussing response, James Britton pushes back the confines of 'literary experience' to begin from 'responses the children are already making – to fairy stories, folk songs, pop songs, television serials, their own game rhymes, and so on'. The medium of storying is largely irrelevant at the level of narrative. Development comes from 'a sense of the pattern of events' which we call Story. He examines the development of the sense of form and the satisfactions it brings at different stages. This essay contains many things which educators still neglect and which offer a way forward for those concerned about children and adolescents who have not been 'hooked on books'. It is equally at home in Section four of this collection.

Response to literature   James Britton

Men make some things to serve a purpose, other things simply to please themselves. Literature is a construct of the latter kind, and the proper response to it is therefore (in D. W. Harding's words) to 'share in the author's satisfaction that it was as it was and not otherwise'. Literature is a construct in language, and language is of all the symbolic systems or modes of representation the most *explicit*, the best fitted, for example, to present a running commentary upon experience. It follows that much of the satisfaction in most literature comes from a contemplation of the form given to events, a characteristic that distinguishes a work of literature from a sculpture or piece of music, where other forms are contemplated. A novel, in Susanne Langer's terms, is 'a virtual experience'. The satisfaction in which a reader shares, therefore, must have something in common with the satisfaction he feels, not so much in having an experience as in looking back at an experience he has had; it is as though he were to look back at an experience he has *not* had.

Clearly a naïve writer and a naïve reader may share a satisfaction in circumstances which would only infuriate or at least disappoint a more sophisticated reader. Is this naïve response different in kind from that we desire for literature, or merely different in intensity of feeling or complexity or comprehensiveness or verisimilitude? In other words, are such responses (and children must make many of them) the bad currency we seek to drive out, or are they the tender shoots that must be fostered if there is to be a flower at all? Kate Friedlander, a Freudian psychologist, noticed the tremendous satisfaction young children derive from reading stories related to an Oedipus situation (the fatherless boy proves his manhood in *Treasure Island*, the orphan girl has a series of substitute mothers in *Heidi*, and so on), but she sharply distinguishes this satisfaction from 'a literary response', which she seems to feel must somehow have to do with art rather than life. I am sure she is wrong; these responses are unsophisticated in the sense that they might be equally as appropriate to a story of less merit as to *Treasure Island*, but they are the stuff from which, with refinement and development, literary responses are made. Again, at quite a different level, teachers using the 'practical criticism' method sometimes introduced passages of literature paired with senti-mental or otherwise second-rate writing, inviting comment leading to a verdict. Is not this an attempt to drive out bad currency? If, as I believe, satisfaction with the second-rate differs in degree but not in kind from the higher satisfaction, teachers should surely be concerned to *open* doors; as the pupils advance, other doors will close behind them with no need for the teacher to intervene.

Kate Friedlander 'Children's books and their function in latency and puberty' *New Era* volume 39, 1958

Our aim, then, should be to refine and develop responses the children are already making – to fairy stories, folk songs, pop songs, television serials, their own game-rhymes, and so on. Development can best be described as an increasing sense of form. In literature, I have suggested, this means principally a sense of the pattern of events, and this, however rudimentarily, children certainly feel in the stories that satisfy them. (A three-year-old referred to Cinderella as, 'A big sad book about two ugly sisters and a girl they were ugly to.') Progress lies in per-ceiving gradually more complex patterns of events, in picking up clues more widely separated and more diverse in character, and in finding satisfaction in patterns of events less directly related to their expectations and, more particularly, their desires; at the same time, it lies in also perceiving the form of the varying relationships between elements in the story and reality, as increasingly they come to know that commodity.

But the forms of language itself – its words with their meanings and associations, its syntax, its sounds and rhythms, its images – these contribute to the total form, not as fringe benefits but as inseparable elements of a single effect. 'An increasing sense of form' must be taken to mean an extension of responses to include these forms, or perhaps an integration of earlier responses to some of them into a total and inclusive response.

Our sense of literary form increases as we find satisfaction in a greater range and diversity of works, and particularly as we find satisfaction in works which, by their complexity or the subtlety of their distinctions, their scope or their unexpectedness, make greater and greater demands upon us. Our sense of form increases as our frame of reference of reality grows with experience, primary and secondary, of the world we live in. A sense of literary form must grow thus, from within; it is the legacy of past satisfactions. It may become articulate, finding expression in comment and criticism, but equally it may not; and this, as pedants, we find very difficult to admit. There are certainly situations in the classroom where receptive listening and a following silence are more eloquent testimony of satisfaction than any comment could be.

It is probably true that the responses of most adult readers are sharpened (and perhaps more fully integrated with their previous experiences) if they are in some measure formulated, so that they become aware of the nature of the processes that have led to satisfaction. But it is certainly not true for children under the age of eleven or so, children who have not yet passed through what Piaget has called the stage of 'concrete operations'. Here their responses to literature may indeed be lively, discriminating, and complex, but it will be no help to them to attempt to formulate those responses. There is ample scope for talk, of course, and value in it; but it will be talk about the people and events of literature and not about forms, conventions, devices, techniques. We should be more afraid of introducing such matters too early than too late.

It is equally clear that to be made aware of the processes that have led to the satisfaction of *another* reader – a teacher, say, or a critic – can have value only in so far as the knowledge helps us formulate our own processes, helps us, that is, become aware of the form of a response we have already made or are capable of making. A critical statement is a discursive form and quite different in organization from the 'presentational symbols' or 'expressive forms' of literature; an understanding of the one cannot substitute for a response to the other. I take this to be the reader's counterpart of what Robert Frost said of the writer: 'You cannot worry a poem into existence, though you may work upon it once it is in being.' The author's satisfaction in his work is something he *feels* and not something that can be *proved* right or wrong. The principle of organization of a critical statement is cognitive; that of a work of literature is, in the final analysis, affective.

The point at which critical statements can be of help to a student is therefore a difficult one to determine. It is even more important, however, to consider the manner in which such help is offered. The voice of the critic must not be allowed to seem the voice of authority; more harm has probably been done to the cause of literature by this means than by any other. It is all too easy for the immature student, feeling that his own responses are unacceptable, to disown them and profess instead the opinions of respected critics. And to many teachers, with their eyes on what may rightly go on in other parts of the curriculum, this looks like good teaching. It may of course be the best kind of preparation for an ill-conceived examination, and this may be the real root of the trouble.

To have children take over from their teachers an analysis of a work of literature which their teachers in turn have taken over from the critics or their English professors – this is not a short cut to literary sophistication; it is a short circuit that destroys the whole system. A response to a work of literature is, after all, an interaction between the work and the reader – not a free interaction, of course, but even the most disciplined responses of two different persons must reflect something of their individual differences. Further, while Shakespeare may continue supreme and Samuel Rogers forgotten, some very general differences of opinion must be expected even among the initiated: there will probably always be respected critics who judge *Silas Marner* to be a bad novel and other critics, equally respected, who regard it highly.

Perhaps the meaning of a work of literature may be compared (as most other things have been) to the ripples that move out from a stone thrown into water; what happens to them depends to some extent upon the configuration of the pond. To me, Blake's poem 'Never Seek to Tell Thy Love' has some relevance to the arguments I put forward earlier concerning the difference between a critical statement and a response; I do not expect the poem to suggest that to another reader, unless perhaps his interest in language resembles my own.

How then do we encourage the improved response, the developed sense of form?

A girl of eight was asked what sort of things she liked reading. 'Well,' she said, 'there's *Treasure Island* – that's a bloody one for when I'm feeling boyish. And there's *Little Men* – a sort of half-way·one.' 'Don't you ever feel girlish?' she was asked. 'Yes, when I'm tired. Then I read *The Smallest Dormouse*.'

We must expect, and encourage, reading to go on for various purposes at various levels and not concern ourselves solely with performance at maximum effort. 'Reading for enjoyment' (to pick up an ancient controversy) will certainly be an apt description of the lower levels of effort but is probably misleading when applied to the most demanding kind of reading. Satisfaction, however, the appropriate satisfaction we have repeatedly referred to, must be there in the end, and no examination or other external incentive can take its place; reading without satisfaction is like the desperate attempts we make to keep a car going when it has run out of petrol.

That a student should read *more books* with satisfaction may be set down as one objective; as a second, he should read books with *more satisfaction*. We need to foster, in other words, wide reading side by side with close reading. The importance of freedom of choice is obvious enough in the first situation, less recognized in the second, since close reading is usually taken to mean class teaching. But choice is no less desirable in the classroom, and students should whenever possible choose what is studied by the class as a whole or, better still, by groups on their own with occasional help from the teacher.

The problems lie, then, not in knowing what to do but in getting enough suitable books sufficiently accessible. Paperbacks have made things much easier; local prescriptions and proscriptions that have militated against spending money in this way are on the decline in some areas, still need vigorous attack in others. When other attempts have failed, boys and girls themselves have sometimes provided a class library by pooling paperbacks, say for a term at a stretch. Such a collection may need supplementing to meet the needs of the best readers, who are likely to contribute the most rewarding books and find few of comparable value in return.

Close reading and wide reading should not be thought of as quite separate activities. Active response to a work of literature invokes what might be called an unspoken monologue of responses – a fabric of comment, speculation, relevant autobiography. It is natural for something which one member of the class has read to be brought before the rest of them at his suggestion as the object of a closer scrutiny. (It is always preferable of course that a passage studied should in some way be related to the whole book.) Talk in class should arise from, and further stimulate, the individual monologues of response.

It is in the context of this talk that views of the critic or teacher can best be handled if they are to be useful at all. Clearly, for advanced college-preparatory pupils they can be valuable. As part of the to and fro of discussion critical judgements may be accepted for the help they offer; if the discussion is as open as it should be, they will frequently be disputed and sometimes rejected by individual students. The attitudes engendered by the mode and tone of discussion carry forward and influence the reading of both literature and criticism.

In all I have said so far I have accepted the terms of my commission as they would be generally understood. By 'literature' I have therefore meant the body of works represented in literature syllabuses, studied in university schools of English, and the like. However, before finishing my task I should like very briefly to point to an unorthodox way of defining literature which has the advantage of placing it among linguistic activities generally.

I would go back to my opening paragraph and define literature as a particular kind of utterance – an utterance that a writer has 'constructed' not for use but for his own satisfaction.

Sapir pointed out long ago that man, unlike the zoological animals, does not handle reality by direct and *ad hoc* means but via a symbolic representation of the world as he has experienced it. Given this, two courses are open to a man: he may operate in the real world by means of his representation, or he may operate *directly upon the representation itself* – improvising upon it in any way that pleases him (that allays his anxieties, for example, or sweetens his disappointments, or whets his appetite, or flatters his ego).

Edward Sapir
Language
Harcourt Brace
1921

We all use language in both these ways, to get things done in the outer world and to manipulate the inner world. Action and decision belong to the former use; freedom from them in the latter enables us to attend to other things – to the forms of language, the patterns of events, the feelings. We take up as it were the role of spectators: spectators of our own past lives, our imagined futures, other men's lives, impossible events. When we *speak* this language, the nearest name I can give it is 'gossip'; when we *write* it, it is literature.

By this definition, then, literature is not simply something that other people have done. What a child writes is of the same order as what the poet or novelist writes and valid for the same reasons. What are the reasons? Why do men improvise upon their representations of the world? Basically because we never cease to long for more lives than the one we have; in the role of spectator we can participate in an infinite number.

From *Response to Literature*, NCTE, Champaign, Illinois, 1968

Virtual experience: the darker side

If reading is to offer children modes of experience in a Secondary World, does this include the darker side of life, fear, tragedy, and horror ? Are they to examine these within themselves and outside in the world ? In the next two articles the authors discuss the inevitability and even the desirability of situations involving these responses as a necessary part of the development and the refinement of feelings. The children's author, Catherine Storr, shows the shift of sensibility between nineteenth- and twentieth-century authors, their attitude to death, violence, and sex, arguing that symbolic representations offer a child 'what he needs to know, both more economically and at greater depth ... and what he needs to learn includes not only what threatens him from the outside but also his own responses'. John McCreesh suggests that drama and stories help in the decline of egocentrism so that children discover their feelings are also those of others and that 'this is a necessary part of all morality'. We have added an important contribution by Julia MacRae, a children's editor, made at a conference where Catherine Storr was discussing this topic. She shows how she reads the books with the children in mind and feels that resolution, the sense of an ending, is all-important. This should be compared with Alix Pirani's essay in Section three.

Children's ideas of horror and tragedy   John McCreesh

It is a fact of everyday life that children, and indeed many adults, are attracted by horror and tragedy. With this in mind, it was interesting to read Ronald Pearsall's article on horror and children's tales. He is alarmed with the incidence of savagery, brutality and cruelty which one finds in many of these books. He concludes that this tendency should be condemned. Most people concerned with children would, of course, agree with his conclusion. Others would approve of this portrayal of horror, arguing that it has a cathartic effect on the child. According to this theory, the child finds an outlet for violent feelings in a non-violent and harmless way. Whatever views are held about the possible good or evil effects, the interesting question is, 'What do children themselves think about what they read and see?' How do children of different ages interpret the horror and tragedy which they see in the world around them? The answers to these questions would help us, perhaps, to look at the content of children's reading material from a more educational point of view and help us, as teachers, to introduce children to those elements of tragedy which play an important part in our literary heritage.

From an empirical point of view, there is very little evidence to suggest, not how children interpret horror and tragedy, but whether the quality of these interpretations change as the child gets older. In an attempt to find such evidence a small piece of research was carried out a few years ago.

The problem under investigation was the ability to feel horror and tragedy in situations in which the child is not personally involved (as in reading). This seems to depend on the capacity to see in tragedy something more than the bare facts actually present in the situation. It is possible, for example, to hear or read about the horror in a serious road accident, a mining disaster, or a fire, without feeling these events as tragic in the full sense. Yet, it is possible to respond to everyday events such as these, as we become aware of what is involved for both victims and those related to the victims. We respond in certain ways because we are aware of the effects, physically, socially, and emotionally, of events which most people would describe as tragic. The question is, can everyday tragedy be understood by children because of their stage of maturity and narrowness of experience? All children have some experience of tragic situations, either within their own experience, or acquired secondhand through the various media of communication. Yet it is not known how far they are aware of all that is involved in any tragic event. If children are not aware of all that is involved in tragedy, it would tend to explain the preoccupation, in the young child, with horror, death and disaster. This preoccupation is shown in the free expression of many children through painting, free drama and many play activities. Further evidence for this comes from the delight with which some children read 'horror' comics and other magazines which specialize in portraying violent and mass death, in gory detail.

Recent work on the psychology of children's thinking has resulted in a re-evaluation of many of the assumptions about what children can or cannot understand and appreciate. Whilst these researches do not throw any direct light on what children feel about 'horror' which they read and see, they do indicate the limitations of children's thinking about his own social environment of which

J. McCreesh
'An Investigation into the Child's Concept of the Tragic' (unpublished MEd thesis, Liverpool 1968)

J. Piaget
*The Moral Judgement
of the Child*
Routledge and
Kegan Paul
1952

J. Piaget
*The Psychology of
Intelligence*
Routledge and
Kegan Paul
1950

M. E. Mitchell
*The Child's Attitude
to Death*
Barry and Rockliff
1966

tragedy is just one element. Piaget's findings indicate the extent and degree of egocentricity shown by the young child. This type of thinking could make him unaware of the effects of his own feelings on what he hears and reads. The young child tends to regard his own feelings as facts which do not require objective evaluation. It is not, characteristically, until the ages of twelve and thirteen that the child can begin to see events, both sad and joyful, from the point of view of people other than themselves.

One aspect of horror and tragedy is death and its effect on the young child. How does, in fact, the young child react to death? It seems that there is a tendency, in thinking about the horror and tragedy of, and caused by, death, for children to consider multiple deaths as more tragic than single deaths. This tendency was noted by M. E. Mitchell. She learnt that the adolescents' concept of death as a tragedy was relative. Mass death was seen as a greater tragedy than the death of an individual. 'I remember at a gathering of young people met together to look at the pictures of Hiroshima, a speaker said that one could only think of death in terms of one death. But such an idea is greeted with horror by adolescents – of course, they say, it is worse to kill a million than five hundred.'

Apart from death, most people would describe accidents and natural disasters as having tragic consequences on both victims and others involved. There is some evidence, however, that young children are puzzled and confused by accidents and disasters, as well as by death. The evidence suggests that their inability to explain these types of incidents is connected with pre-causal thinking in childhood. Again, Piaget questioned children of six and seven about death and accidents. The child, he discovered, is confused by the explanation of accidents. This, Piaget claims, is because this sort of phenomenon is inexplicable to him at the age of six or seven years. Sometimes, it seems, the child will do away with the accidental element as such, and account for it by an end. Sometimes he fails to succeed in this and tries to explain the accident causally. At a later age, however, he replaces his pre-causal explanations with a conscious realization of the accidental element in the world.

J. Piaget
*The Language and
Thought of the Child*
Routledge and
Kegan Paul
1926

The relevance of this type of research is that it indicates an inability, in the young child, to give a rational explanation for death, accidents, disaster and similar events. This may well limit the extent of a child's awareness of the consequences and implications of incidents and events which fill most people with horror. The child, it seems, would not be able to anticipate and imagine the results of many of the so-called horrible events and scenes which they see depicted in books. It is not until a child nears the age of fourteen that changes in the quality of his thinking enable him to make inferences from the facts of a story. By this age, some children are able to make more circumspect and comprehensive judgements by the invocation of imagined possibilities. In terms of 'horror' stories this probably means that the child is now more aware of the reactions of the people depicted in the story. This would make him more sensitive than the younger child to the implications of the horror and its real effects on other people. In other words, the available evidence does suggest that before adolescence the child is not intellectually equipped to appreciate the emotional reactions of other people to 'horror'. There seems to be a development in the child's capacity to discriminate the attributes of other people. It seems reasonable to suggest that this capacity would include the ability to see other people as having their own particular reactions to tragic events. Young children are very inept in cognitive interpersonal skills but there is a considerable growth in these skills in early adolescence.

E. A. Peel
'A Study of the
Differences in the
Judgements of
Adolescent Pupils'
BJEP, volume 36
1966

J. Flavell
*Developmental
Psychology of J. Piaget*
Van Nostrand
Reinhold
1963

In view of the indications revealed by previous studies, it was decided to investigate, specifically, the child's concept of the tragic. The major question was whether the concept of the tragic develops in recognizable stages, or whether it is a gradual refinement of a general idea. From the evidence, it appears that some children under the age of twelve are restricted in their awareness of most of the consequences of a tragic event. They are unable, at these ages, to grasp the full social or emotional outcome of a tragic event. This suggests that 'horror' to them is something quite different from that of an adult. They are insensitive to horrific situations by the very quality of their thinking. A full mature response to a tragic event would seem to contain a sensitivity to, and an appreciation of, the physical, social and emotional results of tragic events happening to other people and in other places. As in many other aspects of cognitive development, the younger child cannot go beyond the facts of the incident and make inferences from it.

On the other hand, the older child who has reached the level of formal operations in his thinking now has the ability to anticipate the results of an action or an event. He can make inferences from what stories are read or events seen and heard. He is able to imagine the possible social and emotional consequences. The adolescent child is growing towards sensitivity to the feelings of other people. His quality of thinking enables him to put himself in the place of another person afflicted by a tragic event. This means that the older child will view 'horror' in comics and books from a different point of view than that of the younger child. The nine-year-old will tend to interpret 'horror' objectively. Its impact may be to attract, fascinate, frighten perhaps. The real implications, however, of the 'horror' are lacking. The fourteen-year-old may still be attracted and fascinated but he will be aware of the awful consequences of what he sees and reads.

M. L. Harris (editor)
Aberfan – A book of memorial verse
Stockwell, 1967

This change in the child's quality of thinking, with age, tends to be reflected in the child's creative response to horror and tragedy. A recent book devoted to the child's creative response to the Aberfan disaster in 1966 illustrates this change. Children of all ages between seven and nineteen years were asked to write their thoughts, in poetic forms, about this tragedy. In the book 'is recorded the shock and the anger, the grief and the anguish, the love and the faith of children …' Many of these poems suggest trends in thinking about the tragic which support the views expressed here. There is evidence, in the poems, of a broadening awareness of the many implications and consequences of tragedy and horror which comes about with age. The poems range from the purely descriptive of the seven-year-old to the fuller awareness of the sixteen-year-old.

> *Silent Village*
> Some people handed cups of tea,
> Some people soothed the families,
> Others dug so furiously
> In search of children's lives.
> Lights were put upon the tip
> As a danger signal,
> A spring, they said, has caused it
> Such a tiny spring it was.
> There was a great funeral,
> Men made a big, big cross
> Of flowers on the mountain side
> That could be seen for miles and miles.
> (*Girl, aged nine years*)

In this poem there is little evidence of a general insight into the implications, social and emotional, of the tragic event. No judgements or explanations are made. The poem is purely factual and descriptive. There is no attempt to see this incident from the point of view of other people involved. As a contrast many of the fifteen-year-old children seem to have developed a full recognition of all the possible results of tragedy. Many are able to anticipate the emotional and social impact of a tragic event on both onlookers and relatives.

> *I Groped for Words*
> I groped for words, but found an arrow in my heart,

I had forgotten where I was.
Looking about I see it might be anywhere,
There are remains, the ones that make me weep,
The ruined buildings, the people ...
No! Bodies with blackened flesh,
The dreaded dark disease
Called death.
Although it is over, pain is never quick
To ease, and memories remain for ever.
Sympathy is not enough.
Even from those nearest to the thoughts in your heart
It cannot fill that empty place.
(*Girl, aged fifteen years*)

Apart from the increased sophistication in style, the trend towards a more aware, introspective mood is there. The girl can now examine her own feelings and is aware that other people may have a similar reaction ... 'It cannot fill that empty place'. Unlike the nine-year-old, this child would now react to horror in a much more sensitive way.

It is interesting to note the maturity and confidence of an eighteen-year-old girl in expressing the effect of tragedy on personal relationships. The importance of friendship as a factor in tragic situations is rarely noted by younger children. The writer of the following poem shows a full realization of the implications of tragedy on friendship.

A Friendship Ended
Tommy and I were mates, you see,
Until his death
Set our friendship free.
It's funny now he's gone away,
No one else here wants to play.
Nobody quite like Tommy and me.
Funny, how his death affected me.
Now I wander on the hills alone,
Returning early to my home.
There is no point when you are bored,
I've tried to understand the Lord.

Nobody quite like Tommy and me,
Funny, how his death affected me.
(*Girl, aged eighteen years*)

All the evidence presented so far is not an argument in favour of no selection of the content of children's stories. Rather, it merely suggests part of the reason why some children are attracted and fascinated by the details of horror and tragedy. Because the child's concept is restricted, or lacking in maturity, this would make him insensitive to the implications of suffering and misfortune in others. He is not fully aware of the consequences of the horrific things he sees and reads. The evidence does suggest, however, that there is a need for the education of feeling; for the education of the emotional reason through the medium of tragedy. It is not enough to condemn this inclination in children though one could condemn it in the writers of children's books. A much more positive approach would seem to be in educating the child's feelings away from such crude presentations of horror and tragic events, by making him aware that these are tragic in a real sense.

To educate the child in tragedy is in many ways to educate the imagination. The young child's imagination towards some aspects of tragedy appears to be limited to the concrete details of the story. Yet the reading of literature demands an imaginative response – the construction of images on the basis of a verbal description. The reading that anticipates all that is involved which transfers the reader into the action of the story so that he feels involved, needs an active, imaginative response. The evidence of the present study suggests that in the child such a response is limited by his conception of what tragedy involves. The problem is how to deepen and extend a child's imaginative awareness. Without presentation which takes account of the child's own thought forms, it is difficult to see how this can be achieved.

One way of doing this, perhaps, is through means of drama. It is a widely accepted view that drama enables the child to absorb and communicate experience. It gives the child the opportunity to play out life. Through drama the child can be encouraged to play out a variety of emotional experiences, and undergo many imaginative experiences. Sealey gives an interesting example which supports this view. A class of junior children were acting out the trial of Christ. There was no script and children interpreted this tragic incident as they wished. As a result of this experience, it was claimed that there was no doubt that these children felt deeply about the incident. In a similar way, it is possible that by acting out simple tragic themes, children may be able to experience emotions and feelings, not only

L. G. W. Sealey
and V. Gibbon,
*Communication and
Learning in the
Primary School*
Blackwell, 1962

by communicating intimate feelings known to them, but by revealing new feelings previously unfelt. The accepted way of approaching this, is to begin with unscripted plays. When a child is confined to a script, he tends to be concerned with the memorization and reproduction of the words, rather than with his own interpretation of the emotional reactions, and feelings, of the character he is portraying. The plot alone, at this stage, would determine the action. The advantage of this presentation seems to lie in the possible increase in awareness of emotional reactions that such an approach might bring. The young child through portraying emotional response, may help others, and himself, to become aware of feelings previously not experienced. Once a child begins to be aware of his own feelings, his own reactions to the tragic and the horrific, then there is more likelihood of his becoming aware of these feelings in others.

It could be argued, of course, that to lay too great an emphasis on this sort of education of feeling towards the tragic aspects of life is to encourage morbidity. On the other hand, if the teaching of this aspect of appreciation takes its limited and proper place in a general scheme of teaching, it would seem to have much to contribute to a child's awareness of the world and events which surround him. In everyday tragedy, these events can be both social and personal, both concepts in which the young child is restricted in his vision. Through social tragedy, the child can come to terms with hardly understood events. Through personal tragedy, the child is introduced to the factual world of suffering, defeat and heroism. The aim is not to destroy the optimism of childhood, but to introduce the child, skilfully and carefully, to the life around him. The argument presented here is that the child, like Lear and Gloucester, can experience an enlargement of vision through an awareness of suffering in the world.

Presuming that tragedy is presented in ways in which the child of a given age can understand, it is possible that the teaching may have certain implications for the moral education of the child. At first sight this may seem an unreasonable thesis. Yet from either a religious or humanist point of view, it is generally agreed that certain feelings and attitudes are necessary in moral awareness and behaviour. Moral virtues, about which there would be some agreement, are those concerned with man's relationship with other men. This would include sensitivity to the feelings of others, sympathy with and appreciation of the life, suffering and anguish of people we do not know. In other words, an awareness that other people think and feel, suffer and enjoy in much the same way as ourselves, seems to be a necessary part of all morality. This demands an enlargement of vision which the young child does not possess, nor perhaps some children will ever attain. This is, in a sense, the basis of all morality, the sensitive ability to share the experiences of those inflicted with misfortune. It is suggested that the ability to share such experiences can be taught, deliberately and carefully through the use of tragedy, both literary and everyday.

Whilst agreeing with Ronald Pearsall that children's stories containing thoughtless cruelty and sadism should be condemned as strongly as possible, the evidence does suggest that realism in such tales could be used to educate the child in sensitivity and feeling. In fact, the evidence does suggest that, because the quality of the young child's thinking would prevent him interpreting tragedy in a sensitive way, there is a need to help him move into the next stage, or phase, of thinking.

From *Catholic Education Today* Sept./Oct. 1970

Things that go bump in the night　　Catherine Storr

It seems curious that in a society like ours, obsessed by the omniscience of scientists and pathetically reliant on the information provided by statistical surveys, we have reached no conclusions about what scenes or ideas in books or on film might damage our children. Every now and then the subject is revived with new force, when some fresh piece of evidence turns up that suggests that violence or sex in one of these mediums has triggered off a peculiarly horrifying act of the same sort. But we don't really know the answers. The most comprehensive piece of research yet to be published was headed by Hilde Himmelweit and concerned the effects on children of watching television. But the report was published in 1958, and television programmes, films and books have changed a good deal since then.

Hilde Himmelweit
Television and the
Child
OUP, 1958

In considering the effect of television on the child, the Himmelweit Commission found that a more important factor than the degree of violence, cruelty or horror shown was the context in which it appeared. Where the background of events was fairly remote from the child's experience, either in space or time, he was not disturbed even by quite horrific actions or circumstances; but this wasn't so if the setting were more like his own life (disturbance here was measured by subsequent anxiety and fear). He could tolerate cowboys and Indians, or Cavaliers and Roundheads killing each other, better than a minor accident in a programme about children in a modern European town.

It is a question of identification. Though the child may identify with the Goodies in any programme, he apparently doesn't on this account feel threatened by the Baddies unless they are operating in a world closely related to the one with which he is familiar. As for violence on the screen provoking violent behaviour in real life, the Himmelweit Commission came to the conclusion that 'these programmes will not make normal children delinquent, though they may have an effect on latent delinquents' – a finding confirmed by a piece of research prepared for the Home Office last year.

So there is not much help from the psychologists and, as every parent and teacher knows, there are no rules among children themselves. Why is it that a child who can read the most bloodthirsty of the Grimm fairy stories without flinching, is reduced to a pulp of tears by *Black Beauty* and terrified by an illustration of a water nymph? Why can one child read ghost stories with impunity, while another can't even have the volume in the same room, yet both agree in finding Blind Pew from *Treasure Island* the most terrifying character in fiction? Why is the under-the-bed monster for this child a wolf, for that a snake, and for the third a 'spider the size of a small kitten'? The answer is that we don't know. We don't know what will frighten, what will depress (more serious in my view) or what will pervert. Apart from the broadest general guidelines, we can only guess; even for one particular child whom we know well, we can never be sure.

I suppose our anxiety about this problem is at least partly due to the psycho-analytical approach to everything, literature and children included, which has grown in this century. Certainly our predecessors were not nearly as fearful of upsetting young readers. We may think of ours as a permissive society, but what the Victorians fed to their children – thinly disguised as entertainment in many cases – smacks of a much greater permissiveness than we enjoy. Death was then, of course, a common occurrence in a child's life, but I'm not sure that this wholly accounts for the regularity with which it turns up in their books, nor for the loving detail which surrounds the deathbed scene. And it wasn't only death; extreme poverty, brutality, idiocy, alcoholism and injustice also play their part.

The settings were contemporary and the victims children. The effect is deliberately sought. Mr Fairchild, in *The Fairchild Family* by M. B. Sherwood, takes his infant progeny, who quarrelled about a doll before breakfast, to see the local gibbet, where hangs the body of a man condemned for killing his brother, as a warning of what happens to sibling rivals. Mrs Randolph, in *Melbourne House* by Elizabeth Wetherill, whips her little daughter till the blood comes, to punish her for not saying grace before meat. The twelve-year-old heroine of *A Basket of Flowers* remains imprisoned under sentence of death for some time before her innocence is proved – it wasn't she who stole the brooch, it was a magpie.

Four-year-old Sophie, in *Les Malheurs de Sophie*, who disobeyed her mama's instructions not to lag behind on a country walk, is simply left behind to be attacked by the wolves in consequence; no one sees to it that she doesn't suffer the direct results of being naughty. It seems as if the rules in force in those days about terror and the young may have been not unlike ours today on obscenity. The nineteenth-century child might be scared out of his wits, as long as he was also uplifted morally, and nowadays we may be corrupted if we are thereby titillated into culture.

It is interesting that the Victorians didn't carry their realistic attitude to children into every possible field. The one subject which was absolutely barred was sex. Birth features prominently, but there are no preliminaries; babies arrive unannounced and the parents seem as much taken by surprise as anyone. But this was a piece of backsliding which belonged to the mid-nineteenth century. The earlier writers had a much more robust approach. Marryat's Midshipman Easy was suckled by what would now be called an unmarried mother, and there's a charming scene in one of his books when a European host, stationed in the tropics, offers a lady of the district some breast of chicken and is reproved for his indelicacy; he should have said 'bosom of chicken'. Ballantyne, writing a little later, beautifully exemplifies my point. When describing the customs of the savages who inhabit Coral Island and the neighbouring shores, he merely mentions the local practice of polygamy, and then goes on to discuss the morality of the custom of all the chief's wives killing themselves on his death. But he gives a detailed and horrible description of the occasion when a victorious army launch their canoes over the living bodies of their vanquished opponents. Sex was taboo, but torture was O.K.

It is easy to ridicule the fashions of other days, less easy to accept those of our own. It is also difficult to assess *now* exactly what impact a fashionable attitude might have had *then*. Perhaps to the literate Victorian child, secure in his upper- or middle-class home, the horrors of cruelty and poverty seemed far removed from his probable experience. But it is different for children today. The class barriers are not so absolute, literacy is more widely spread and, at the same time, because of radio and television, less essential to the purposes of entertainment and learning. Before they can read, our children have the opportunity to learn about the topics which engross the adult world, and to absorb the prevalent attitudes towards those topics. Are they disturbed by them? If not, we must ask whether perhaps they ought to be? So our problem of censorship becomes extended: we have to consider not only what will frighten children and make them anxious, but also whether we are going to allow this to happen. And, if we are, in what terms we shall speak to them of terror and fear.

I believe that children should be allowed to feel fear. And I believe that they must also be allowed to meet terror and pity and evil. I was delighted to learn last summer from Kaye Webb that her friend Walter de la Mare had told her he believed that children were impoverished if they were protected from everything that might frighten them. He said that the child who hadn't known fear could never be a poet. I would add to that the worldwide folk story of *The Boy Who Didn't Know Fear*. This boy is a sort of guileless simpleton, of the kind often met with in folklore, who is brave because he doesn't foresee dangers. He can spend a night in the belfry with hobgoblins without a tremor because until he is actually attacked (when he defends himself) he recognizes no threat. In fact, he is without imagination, that fatal human quality which makes cowards of us all. In one more sophisticated version of this tale the boy wins himself a royal bride through his senseless bravery, but the marriage doesn't prosper because he can still feel no fear. It is the princess's maid who cures the young husband's inadequacy, by pouring cold water over him as he wakes up so that at last, as the story puts it, he learns to shiver.

Wagner used this idea of the hero without fear – and without knowledge – in Siegfried, who discovers man's true nature when he meets his first woman, disrobing Brünnhilde of her shield on the top of her fiery rock with the immortal words '*Das ist kein Mann!*' The myth seems to me true, though not in its obvious meaning for most animals know the meaning of physical fear; but it expresses in the language of poetry the human need for an understanding of more than meets the eye, for the power to speculate and to fantasize. The child must be allowed to daydream; and if he can dream of what he wants and of the pleasurable things that may come, he will inevitably have his nightmares too.

Once one has answered this basic question, of whether or not children are to be made aware of evil, the second problem arises of how it is to be presented. This is really a technical problem which has to be faced by every writer for children over the age of infancy. Very small children do not require, in fact find it difficult to follow, a plot. It is enough for them to hear the relation of everyday events such as happen to themselves. I've always suspected that the adult liking for factual books about a period within one's own memory springs from the feeling that one has assisted at something that has been considered worthy to be called history. Perhaps the infant who follows the tale of the child who visits his aunt in the country and finds for himself a large brown egg experiences the same pleasure. But by the time they have reached the *Little Black Sambo* age, there has to be a story; where there is a story, there must be conflict and where there is conflict, there must be Good and Evil, in however watered down a version. The Good presents no difficulties; it is, of course, oneself. But how does one feature the Evil?

You can do it in the Ian Fleming style. You can have a tale of smugglers, or dope-pedlars, or spies or a more ordinary brand of crooks, who are totally evil, totally wrong, totally unbelievable. But in a fast-moving, rattling yarn they will pass muster. In this category I would put the Buchan stories, Fleming, of course, and a good many other cops and robbers, Goodies and Baddies types. Everything is seen in the greatest possible contrast, so stark a black and white that nothing is the colour of reality. If it is done well enough you cannot put it down. But it leaves no permanent mark. This is both its weakness and its measure of security. However horrific the horror, it is unbelievable, two-dimensional. It never gets under the skin. In general this sort of book doesn't terrify; its innocuousness is in inverse proportion to its realism.

Or you can de-humanize the enemy and pit your hero against Fate in the shape of either the forces of nature, or the evils of society. Here there need be no loss of reality; man is indeed often faced by natural disasters such as fire, flood, disease and death, and social dangers like war, poverty, ignorance, prejudice and stupidity. I suppose the most outstanding example of this kind of writing is *Robinson Crusoe*. One of the marvellous things about Defoe's manner of telling the story is the contrast he draws between the almost unique situation of the hero and his essential ordinariness.

Several writers for children today use this method of casting Fate as the villain: Hester Burton has written of a great flood, Veronique Day of a landslide, Rutgers van der Loeff of an avalanche. And I think one could include here stories of animals where the animals aren't humanized: not *The Wind in the Willows* or *The Jungle Books*, but *My Friend Flicka* and *The Yearling*, because here the enemies are the natural ones of predators, illness and death.

The evils of society are kept impersonal with more difficulty; it can be tempting to identify the horrors of war with the bestiality of the people you are fighting, or to attribute the misery of poverty to the heartlessness of the rich. But neither Ian Serraillier, in *The Silver Sword*, nor Paul Berna in *They Didn't Come Back*, has vilified people; in both these books about the aftermath of the last war, it is made clear that it is the international situation that separates families, raises suspicion between friends and neighbours, and sends the innocent to be slaughtered. In a totally different context John Rowe Townsend – particularly in *Gumble's Yard*, and in his last book, *The Intruder* – shows that poverty and stupidity are as threatening and as dangerous as personal malice. No child is going to have nightmares about the characters in these books, but any child might learn from them something of the nature of the impersonal evils he may encounter.

Unreality and impersonality; a third approach is humour. If you laugh at your villain you can still use his actions as a necessary impetus to the plot, but to a certain extent you reduce his horror. Erich Kästner does this beautifully in *Emil and the Detectives*, James Barrie was less successful with the Old Etonian, Captain Hook. Another writer who ridicules villainy, though the tone of most of his books is not comic but deeply serious and moving, is Leon Garfield. He involves his readers in a situation where, identified with the hero, they see the forces of evil moving to engulf them and then, suddenly, by a delicate twist of phrase, he shows not the wickedness of the villain but his weakness and, above all, his vanity. As Thackeray pointed out, once you understand a man's vanity, he is in your power; for this reason the Garfield villains evoke almost as much sympathy as terror.

They are also distanced by time, and this is the fourth way in which evil can be depicted without the danger of overwhelming the child participant. If you are writing of a period of history very remote from the present, there is enough space between what happened then and what could happen now to prevent your readers from feeling too much threat to themselves both immediately and personally. So a first-class writer like Rosemary Sutcliff, author of many well-known historical novels, can treat desperate situations with complete realism. She never minimizes danger, but in her stories the passage of time serves the same function as the proscenium arch or the spotlight in the theatre; it enables the audience to believe in what is happening on stage while retaining the consciousness of immunity from danger.

Finally there is fantasy; the means of expression which I find most sympathetic, and the easiest to use. Not for adults; fantasy for adults can so quickly degenerate into whimsy or become portentously heavy, perhaps because adults like a clear indication of whether this is meant to be truth or not; they don't tolerate uncertainty well, they like their portions definitely labelled. But children don't make this distinction between fact and imagination. They can move without trouble from one to the other, recognizing the value of both.

It is a dichotomy that most of us never lose altogether, though we often deny it. It is seen frequently in patients with terminal illnesses, who demand to be told whether they are dying. To some of these questioners it is right to speak openly, giving one's own guess of their short expectation of life, but there are others who feel obliged to ask to whom it would be cruel and unnecessary to return a truthful answer. I have known people, one with medical degrees, who continued to believe, as Jung said one should, in the face of symptoms which they couldn't help but recognize, that they had a thousand years more to live. Hjalmar Ekdal, in Ibsen's *Wild Duck*, is one of those blind do-gooders who insists on telling everyone the truth; he won't admit the necessity most of us have to believe in what makes life possible, what will keep us sane, in defiance of the evidence. Of course, it might be better, or more admirable, if we were to face the cold facts of our lives with courage and without hope.

If this is a digression it is an important one, because it is this ability to accept two different sorts of truth at the same time, so much more evident in children than in adults, which provides the answer – for me – to the problem of how to tell children of horror and fear. Much of the telling should be in the language of poetry, the language of symbols, because in this language we can talk to the child of what he needs to know both more economically and at greater depth than in any other. And what he needs to learn includes not only what threatens him from outside, but also his own responses. While we hold his attention with the story, we are communicating at the same time with all sorts of half-conscious feelings that force him to recognize his own involvement.

Perhaps fantasy is the wrong word for this sort of writing; for no single supernatural event need be incorporated in it, but it has magic, the magic of imagination. In *A Dog So Small* nothing happens that can't be explained in factual terms, but besides telling the story of a boy who passionately wants to own a dog, Philippa Pearce is writing of the gap between promise and its fulfilment, of the necessity of fantasy, and of the adjustment to cold sober reality which every dreamer must make. But if she had written down these lessons in flat statements, who would read them? They would be as easily shrugged off as Dracula or Goldfinger, they would be seen to have validity, but no personal relevance.

If we are going to tell children about evil we owe it to them to give the subject its proper importance, just as we should if we were writing about beauty or goodness or truth. We shall succeed in doing this only if we address the child's inner ear, if we can evoke in him, as he reads, that shock of recognition which means the discovery of a fresh aspect of oneself. Because this is one of the things we must say about evil; that it is not always over there, a characteristic of other people but not of ourselves. Evil is within as well as without, and by under-standing our own feelings we have the power over evil in others that understanding gives.

There is one last point. If we talk to children about the great subjects in this way, in folk stories and myths and in any form of art which exercises the imagination, we are giving them something else besides the fruit of consciousness, the knowledge of good and evil. We are demonstrating also a way of handling this knowledge which makes it tolerable to live with. We are showing that it can be used as one of the elements of creative art to make a pattern in which both the good and the bad are essential. This is the true magic.

From *The Sunday Times Magazine*, 7 March 1971

This is part of the discussion that followed the presentation of Catherine Storr's paper:

'Fear and evil in children's books', *Children's Literature in Education*, March 1970, page 39

Julia MacRae Do you think there is a danger of the writer nowadays employing the sensational techniques of fear for fear's sake? I am thinking in particular of Ivan Southall's new novel *Finn's Folly* which I have just read and found it very worrying because although there were many issues raised, talking about death in particular and death in violent circumstances, the dice was so loaded, the book was so full of what seemed to me to be Grand Guignol effects as well, that the total effect was purely terrifying and for the first time for many, many years when I finished the book I was afraid to turn the light out in my bedroom. It had this effect on me and I did seriously wonder about a child reading this book.

Catherine Storr I very much doubt that Ivan Southall would do this deliberately. But when he started piling on the agony, when we got to the cyanide overturning and rushing down the hillside, I stopped believing. I thought all the bits where the car crashed and the lorry driver was trapped in his cab with his adolescent daughter, were good and disturbing, but when we found that the lorry had been carrying cyanide and had poisoned the whole hillside, there I thought it was Grand Guignol as you say. What is the danger, Julia?

Julia MacRae The danger seemed to me to be that the issues were raised and so much fuel was thrown in that what you were left with was an unresolved fear, that a tension is built up and you are just frightened, but there is nothing to balance this.

Catherine Storr I am not sure you haven't said something terribly important. Isn't it the unresolved bit that we ought to think about? I mean we all agree we have got to frighten children, but there must be some sort of resolution – not necessarily an overcoming of the enemy.

Julia MacRae I am not advocating that the ends all be tied up, that all solutions be given pat, but in a book where fear is employed to the extent that it is in this book, I feel that there should be some balance to redress the possible confusion and alarming of the child.

Catherine Storr Yes, I think you are right. I think perhaps Julia MacRae has given the answer to this. Oughtn't we to be able to resolve the fears that we raise in some way or other? She says, not tidily; but we ought to have some way of coping with it ourselves which we can put over. I agree, I don't think that book did. I found it depressing, not frightening, but depressing.

Realism and the testing of reality (1)

One of the recurrent arguments of those who choose books for children is that children find their way into a book if they can 'recognize themselves in it'. By this is usually meant that a certain kind of realism (e.g. non-middle-classness or bulldozers and new towns, not cottages, forests, and fairies) would represent the state of most children. In this essay, Betty Bacon, who is co-ordinator of children's services, Solano County (California) Library, criticizes the inclusion in books for the young of social problems which, however 'realistic', cannot be fully treated by the authors or understood by the reader and which convey 'deep pessimism and a sense of helplessness' without resolution. The point is extended to show that realism means truth to feeling.

From now to 1984   Betty Bacon

In 1968 the now infamous episode of the People's Park took place in Berkeley, California. It started quietly enough with a few hippies, 'street people', local young people, and a sprinkling of sympathetic adults planting trees and setting up home-made playground equipment on some unused land belonging to the University of California in the center of town. Before it was over, the city was in an uproar – rock throwing, shooting, a death, occupation by the National Guard, tear gas, helicopters clattering overhead, mass arrests, brutal treatment of prisoners at the county prison farm, and violent feelings unleashed throughout the community. Finally, a peaceable and flower-decked parade of thousands of sympathizers from all over the San Francisco Bay area calmed things down somewhat, but the cause was lost and the scars remain. As for the park, the University of California had the land surrounded with a sturdy wire fence, behind which now lie a parking lot where nobody parks and manicured playing fields where nobody plays.

Coincidentally, two children's books appeared at about the same time, both dealing with efforts by the young to gain a community park.

Tucker's Countryside by George Selden is a gentle book in which a small group of children picket ineffectually to hold back the bulldozers which are gouging out open land for building development in a Connecticut town. Nobody really pays much attention to the children. Fortunately, some ingenious and friendly animals come up with a ploy that saves the day. Too bad there was none in Berkeley!

This is the world the way it *ought* to be. The values it presents are those to which we give lip service. The book is humorous, wistful, and friendly. But what does it tell children about society the way it really is? What does it lead them to expect? Magic solutions?

The second book, *Hell's Edge* by John Rowe Townsend, is on the surface more realistic. At any rate, there are no magic animals. Two teenagers in an industrial town in England try to pry land for a park from the local aristocratic landowners, whose family motto is 'What I have, I hold.' Like the University of California, the owner hangs tough, and all appears lost until the local political boss, representative of the town's business interests, steps into the picture and carries the day. Unfortunately, Berkeley's downtown merchants did not share his civic point of view.

Townsend has an exquisite sense of class distinctions and class interests. There is violence in this book, but it has all taken place safely offstage a hundred years before at the time of the enclosure of the common lands. The *deus ex machina* is human and convincing within the terms of the story, but the result is the same as Selden's.

'I want a book about survival'

Violence in the streets, massacre at My Lai, rage in the ghetto, desperate retreat in the suburbs, uprisings on the campus, runaways and wanderers and the drug culture, while the clock ticks inexorably toward 1984. Surely, there is an overtone of all this in the voices of children who come into the library and ask, 'I want a book about survival.' Under the present circumstances isn't this a reasonable request?

Of course, what they mean are books like *Two on an Island* by Bianca Bradbury, *Hills End* by Ivan Southall, *Castaway Christmas* by Margaret J. Baker, *The Village that Slept* by Monique de Ladebat, or most of all perhaps, *My Side of the Mountain* by Jean George. In all of these, children, isolated from adults, confront the natural world alone and survive by their own efforts. Aside from the intrinsic excitement and suspense of these stories and their Robinson Crusoe charm, this is reassuring. Possibly, too, the forces of nature, impersonal as they are, hold less threat than social forces that have created a time of war, racism, violence, and depersonalization.

The authors of children's books live in this same hostile world, and they too are subject to feelings of disillusion and despair. Like the children's writers of any era, they project their own adult values and their own vision of life. Perhaps the anti-hero of the anti-novel has not yet invaded children's books to the extent that he has wormed his way into adult fiction, for we cannot quite give up all hope for the future, however disturbed we may be about the present. But the trend is there.

During the past few years, in the name of 'realism', there has been a stream of books with drunken mothers and no-good fathers. The children are left defenceless and alone in a world which they do not understand and with which they cannot deal unaided. This is the great adult 'cop-out'. To be sure, there *are* drunken mothers and no-good fathers, but the books wallow in guilt and lightly toss to the children the responsibility for cleaning up the mess, without tools. This is no more honest realism than the too-too wholesome books of a bygone era, in which adults were all-knowing and close to perfection, and children learned to be good. In the neo-realism, neither the young nor their parents are competent or worthy of respect. They are imbued with a deep pessimism and sense of helplessness in the face of a society hostile to human values. To whom can they turn?

Children and adolescents need models. And who are the models in a closed society and in an era of violent change? This is no idle question if the end result of the next decade is to be no 1984 but an atmosphere in which a child can grow up to be a full human being.

Full humanity requires dealing with the great issues of love and death and freedom and responsibility. This is never easy, and it is less so in a social order that sweeps them under the rug, whether it is in the name of realism, or sweetness and light, or law and order. *The Cay* by Theodore Taylor is a survival story of a different kind. Here, it is the love and sacrifice of a mature and responsible adult that gives the child the competence and courage to go on living. A boy and an old man are cast ashore on a remote Caribbean island after their ship is torpedoed during World War II. Their situation sets them apart from other people, but the book is not so much an exploration of man against nature as of man with man. The cooperation of two human beings – adult and child – make the survival of the child possible. This offers hope in the face of social catastrophe and a world in upheaval.*

In *The Little Fishes* by Erik Haugaard, another novel of World War II, the narrator promises in the preface that he will give 'an answer to that query, "What was it like?" which most veterans leave unanswered.' And so he tells the story of three beggar children of Naples who head north in 1943 straight into the battle of Cassino. They, too, survive – partly out of their own ingenuity, partly with the freely given help of some adults and despite the greed of others. And afterwards? At the end, the narrator remarks ruefully, 'I like to think ... that someone finally took the children in ... Yet a kind wish is like a summer cloud, it brings no rain to the parched earth.'

This is an honest, serious book for serious times. It treats both its characters and its audience with dignity. But as the author says, 'Even when life is a misery, a man must laugh.' And so must children, and they need books of laughter, fantasy, and those that are written and read for no other reason than that they are entertaining.

There are both laughter and fantasy, and the tough wisdom of the folk, in *Black Folk Tales* by Julius Lester. Controversy rages around the book. Is it proper for children to read a book with so much violence and openly expressed anger, not to mention sex? Essentially it is a book for anyone who can understand what it is talking about. Parts are within a child's scope; other parts require a more mature vision. Rooted firmly in tradition, it seems to belong very much to today. It calls things by their right names, from racism to the war in Vietnam. The black rage comes as a kind of cultural shock to the white liberal who would like to think that everybody loves him. The laughter is wry and salutary, and the sense of personal

---

* At this point in my original article of 1970, I wrote a paragraph about *The Cay* by Theodore Taylor. I discussed it solely as an example of a story in which a child is enabled to survive through the responsibility and sacrifice of a mature adult. I did not even mention that the child was white, the adult black. The ink was hardly dry on the paper when all of my black friends and colleagues, without exception, and other librarians and reviewers whom I respect began to point up the racist aspects of the book. I had concentrated so exclusively on my own special point of view that I had ignored the matrix in which the story was embedded. On rereading the book now, I still find some of the value I originally felt in it, but I also acknowledge that the critics were right, and I could not see the woods for the single tree on which I was concentrating.

Writing now in 1974, I can point to a different kind of survival story in which an adult's love and responsibility give a child at least a chance to make it, namely, *A Hero Ain't Nothin' but a Sandwich* by Alice Childress. Here the question is survival not on a desert island but in the urban ghetto. A young heroin addict cannot even begin to face his problem until the love and admiration he feels for his stepfather are returned in full measure – and even then the issue is in doubt. In 1974, I can also write about a young white girl, heroine of *Celebrate the Morning* by Ella Thorp Ellis, who tries to cope with the problems of poverty and a mother who is mentally ill. In the end, she too gets her chance to survive in the jungle of daily living through the lovingly given help of an adult neighbour. There is no adult 'cop-out' in either of these books.

dignity is unshakable.

In the last paragraph of the last story the author speaks directly to his audience:

'You ain't free as long as you let somebody else tell you who you are. We got black people today walking around in slavery 'cause they let white folks tell 'em who they are. But you be like Dave. Just keep on stepping, children, when you know you're right. Don't matter what they yell after you. Just keep on stepping.'

Homely wisdom also finds its way into a book that provides a special value for a drastic time of change and the consequent emotional and physical suffering and this is *The Borrowers* by Mary Norton. Here are small beings in a world too big for them, a world they cannot control – like today's children. But how tough and resilient they are! When disaster sweeps down upon them, no magic comes to their rescue. They rise from one defeat after another not with inhuman courage but with common sense and dogged perseverance. Without heroics, they simply cope.

These are sustaining qualities in an era of uncertainty. Perhaps this accounts for the young man who came into the library one evening. In black leather jacket and motorcycle boots he swaggered over to the shelves and picked up *The Borrowers Aloft*, defiantly pulled a chair into the middle of the floor, and sat there tensely with one eye on me and the other on the book. 'He's trying to bug me,' I said to myself and offered to help him find something more suitable.

To my surprise, he muttered, 'I read the others when I was a kid. I didn't know there was another.' We declared a truce and he read for a while. Then he called in a loud whisper, 'Hey, librarian, check this book out for me. I'm embarrassed.'

Presently, he got to his feet, marched stiffly to the circulation desk, and checked out the book himself.

I estimate that the young man will be in his early thirties in 1984. Just keep on stepping, children, when you know you're right. Just keep on stepping.

From *Wilson Library Bulletin*, October 1970

Children Selecting Books in a Library   Randall Jarrell

With beasts and gods, above, the wall is bright.
The child's head, bent to the book-coloured shelves,
Is slow and sidelong and food-gathering,
Moving in blind grace ... Yet from the mural, Care,
The grey-eyed one, fishing the morning mist,
Seizes the baby hero by the hair

And whispers, in the tongue of gods and children,
Words of a doom as ecumenical as dawn
But blanched, like dawn, with dew. The children's cries
Are to men the cries of crickets, dense with warmth
– But dip a finger into Fafnir, taste it,
And all their words are plain as chance and pain.

Their tales are full of sorcerers and ogres
Because their lives are: the capricious infinite
That, like parents, no one has yet escaped
Except by luck or magic; and since strength
And wit are useless, be kind or stupid, wait
Some power's gratitude, the tide of things.

Read meanwhile ... hunt among the shelves, as dogs do, grasses,
And find one cure for Everychild's diseases
Beginning: *Once upon a time there was*
A wolf that fed, a mouse that warned, a bear that rode
A boy. Us men, alas! wolves, mice, bears bore.
And yet wolves, mice, bears, children, gods and men

In slow perambulation up and down the shelves
Of the universe are seeking ... who knows except themselves?
What some escape to, some escape: if we find Swann's
Way better than our own, and trudge on at the back
Of the north wind to – to – somewhere east
Of the sun, west of the moon, it is because we live

By trading another's sorrow for our own; another's
Impossibilities, still unbelieved in, for our own ...
'I am myself still'? For a little while, forget:
The world's selves cure that short disease, myself,
And we see bending to us, dewy-eyed, the great
CHANGE, dear to all things not to themselves endeared.

Realism and the testing of reality (2)

This idiosyncratic piece, heavy with North American assumptions and cultural problems, raises issues that face the choosers of books for children. We include it because the problems are familiar and it may be helpful to look at them when one has less familiarity with the books. The author is a Program Director in Toronto schools.

Innocence is a cop-out   Joan Bodger Mercer

A. S. Neill of Summerhill writes of his belief that a child who pokes into drawers and purses, opens cupboards, peers into boxes, and takes toys or watches apart is a child who is looking for answers to life's sexual mysteries. 'Do you want to know where babies come from? I'll tell you!' he says is the swiftest cure for snoopiness. Perhaps the reason that generations of little girls have identified with flat-chested Nancy Drew is that instinctively they know she is looking for something more exciting than *The Secret of the Old Clock*. In vain we point to vulgar style and shallow character development as reason to shun that perennial challenger to our professional infallibility. But what do we offer in Nancy's place? Perhaps it is not better style or characterization that children need and search for, but recognition of an ultimate mystery.

In all my travels in this past year, the book that non-professionals have asked me about most often has been *The Godfather*. I began to get the feeling that in 1970–71 an uncommon number of thirteen-year-olds were reading not Segal, but the tender love story of Sonny Corleone, his oversized sex organ, and his similarly abnormal mistress.

The parents who volunteered the information about their kids' reading habits were quite ordinary people, really, not far removed from the minor characters in Mario Puzo's ethnic *Forsyte Saga*. One was a Detroit housewife who said her daughter had read the book and discussed it with her, but she had abjured her not 'to let father know'. Of the men, one was 'in dogfood', the other 'in dispensers'.

Each of them opened up when he learned I was 'in children's lit.'. I got the feeling they were a little anxious but a lot more proud about their sons' choice of reading. None of the three discussed any other part of the novel so perhaps their children didn't either. After all, there is a sort of folk tale grandeur to it, fabulous yet explicit, that lends itself to speculation. Unlike most books for thirteen-year-olds, it leaves no doubt about the nature of the sexual act nor that sex is essential to a loving relationship between man and woman. But what strikes me most forcibly is that the adults who confided in me represent the very kind of parent upon whom we project our professional paranoia. However, the moral of *The Godfather* (if there is one) is that Father knows best. This lends support to my belief that it is not sex that makes the would-be censor, but challenge to authority.

Once, when I was involved in a library censorship case, I found myself answering to a group of my fellow workers – everyone from professionals to the maintenance man. Questions were hurled at me and I tried to answer them intelligently. I felt terribly stupid because I didn't seem able to grasp the politically oriented questions being pressed upon me by a middle-aged clerk. Her color was high, her eyes glazed bright blue. She looked *enamelled*. Then I remembered: the only other time I had ever seen her look like that was when she was discussing her hot flushes!

Right then I realized that we were not discussing Communist influences in the SDS. We were discussing sex! Yet later, when the arguments turned explicitly to sex and pornography, I noticed that the conversation flipped again. Suddenly we were discussing Communism, or what passed as a definition of Communism. For a moment the fog lifted and I glimpsed the battlefield whole. *Anything new is taboo. 'Communism' is anything new. Therefore, Communism is anything that is taboo. Sex is taboo. Therefore, sex is Communistic and Communism is sexual.*

Sex, sexualism, and sexism in children's literature have been around for a long time, covert but powerful. Sex *is* power. One has to grasp only the rudiments of anthropology to perceive that whole religions and priesthoods have been attempts to explain and control the energy of propagation, the mysterious life force. 'What do the simple folk do?' asks Guinevere, having just tasted the joys of love. Innocent, yet callous, she assumes any experience so delicious must surely be reserved for the ruling classes. What do the children do? Freud has tipped us off to the fact that they are sexual little beggars but we have used our own innocence and theirs as a cop-out. We have refused to see what we did not want to see. Philippe Aries, in his fascinating study, *Centuries of Childhood*, points out that the concept of childhood is a recent invention that came into being at the onset of the Industrial Revolution. Perhaps we should face up to the fact that it was conceived as much for the profit of adults as for the children. Teachers and librarians make a living by keeping children in their place.

How long is it since you read *Black Beauty*? The swinging intellectual's stance is to despise the book's mincing prissiness, yet to tolerate shelf room for it because mothers and grandmothers come looking for it to hand on to another generation. Even more damnable, it has become a fixed 'classic' on school lists. Despite these formidable handicaps, little girls still read the book eagerly and buy cheap fuzzy-papered editions of it even while the book loses ground in sophisticated book selection circles.

Black Beauty is a funny book, hilarious if you read long passages of its Victorian prose aloud. Who wants it? Who needs it? But why did I remember – not the book, but the *feeling* of the book – so vividly? So Anna Sewell was revisited and Ginger resurrected. No wonder I was sexually aroused as I read my favourite chapter! Poor broken Ginger was put out to pasture because she had been ridden all night by the squire's son! I don't consider myself particularly precocious, but somehow I had known without knowing I knew what the book was about. Tell me, gentle reader, am I the only one?

I suppose that my confession now furnishes evidence that children's books stir prurient interests. But how to predict which book will stir which child when? We can no more do that than predict the right book for the right child, professional arrogance to the contrary. Even supposing we withhold books, how are we to prevent our patrons from receiving stimuli elsewhere? Ah, the Devil whispers, that is hardly our concern. All we have to worry about is that no child point to the Children's Room and make claim he/she found excitement there.

Last summer (1970), having several hours to spend in a large city library before going out to the airport, I asked the Young Adult librarian if I could browse through some of the new books, among them, *Girls and Sex* (Pomeroy). The book had been rejected, she explained, because it encourages girls 'to sneak behind their parents' backs'. An hour later I left the library by the front door, picking my way down the broad shallow steps and across the famous square that fronted the building. Then I began to laugh.

The reason I was stepping so carefully, blushing prettily, and murmuring, 'Oh, excuse me!' so many times was that the whole scene was carpeted by young couples sitting, standing, lying in close embrace. Any fourteen-year-old who came to the library that day would have had to run the same gauntlet that I did. He or she might do worse than to have a copy of Pomeroy in hand. Later, I interpreted

Pomeroy's remarks to mean that if any young girl were determined to have intercourse she should face up to her decision, find some place where she and her lover would not be interrupted accidentally-on-purpose. In other words, don't involve the parents or use the action as a weapon against them. This seems like old-fashioned prudery as compared to the action on the library steps!

There are many ways to hide books that have been written and published for children or young adults. One way, of course, is not to buy the book in the first place. Book budgets are tight; book selection is highly professional (read static); we must limit ourselves to the flawless. Take no chances on the Harlan Quist publications, for instance. *Book No. 1* (Ionesco) is unpleasant and upsetting. We do not eschew books because they are controversial but because of poor literary quality, weird illustrations or – favourite cop-out – disrespect to parents.

Books that are not specifically sexual are sometimes treated as though they were because of challenge to parental authority. However, as I have pointed out elsewhere, I feel that the struggle to *be* sexually, politically, individually is all intertwined. In one city I visited, Steptoe's *Up-town* was too well reviewed to be excluded from purchase but ingenious ways have been found to hide it from the kids. The modest little picture book, originally meant for five- to ten-year-olds, is relegated to the adult section because 'the father drinks beer and the grammar is substandard'. I am happy to report that in a branch library in that same city (in a neighbourhood where the fathers drink beer and the grammar is substandard), the librarians just never seem to get around to hiding the book by reclassifying it. Meanwhile, in the opposite corner of the country, the Pacific Northwest, *Lisa, Bright and Dark* (Neufeld) is hidden away in the adult psychology section. The reason is not that young people cannot understand a psychotic break (after all, the same kids can buy *You Never Promised Me a Rose Garden* in paperback) but because the book makes adults look stupid, ignorant, and neglectful.

Little old ladies still trot into the library and ask for Young Adult titles, 'a nice love story without too much sex in it', but they are in for a shock these days. Eleven-year-olds are better able to dig sex, drugs, out-of-wedlock pregnancies, and bumbling parents than are their escapist elders. Young adults read adult books. If they are not allowed to use the adult section of the library or if the Young Adult section is too timid in its selection they turn to paperbacks. But younger and younger children are reading the books that authors and publishers assumed were for young adults. Hinton's *The Outsiders*, considered a little racy for young teenagers in the early 1960s, is the hottest title for nine-year-olds in Vancouver, Wash.

In the good old days the best children's books got rid of the parents early. They either died, were already dead, were sent on a trip or were conveniently lost. From *Children of the New Forest* to *From the Mixed Up Files of Mrs Basil E. Frankweiler* children have found vicarious delight in the Robinson Crusoe dilemma of making it on their own. Whenever parents came on the scene they were so wise and strong and good that we longed to get rid of them again. One of the most frightening characters in children's literature, to my way of thinking, is the omnipotent mother in *The Runaway Bunny* (M. W. Brown). Sometimes I find myself comparing her to the Victorian briskness of Beatrix Potter's estimable Mrs Rabbit. If Peter had been born in the 1950s his mother would never have left him. There would have been no Mr MacGregor, no camomile tea. In short, no adventure.

In May, 1970, I was in Anaheim, California, attending an International Reading Association convention. It happened to be the week that Cambodia was invaded, when students were being killed at Kent and Jackson State. There was almost no mention of these things made in the speeches and workshops although the several thousand of us attending there were directly involved with the welfare and education of the young. When, at intervals, we came out of the Plato's Cave of the convention hall it was into the surreality of Disney's land. The plastic Matterhorn glittered in the smog. We did it all for the children.

I am convinced that, as usual, the conservatives and the reactionaries see the situation clearly. If we step down from our height or the children are allowed to be more free, the tension of the whole structure will be threatened. If we persist in opening up the children's section to 'adult' feelings and ideas, if we let children read where and what they want to there is no predicting what may happen. To pretend otherwise is a cop-out.

From *Wilson Library Bulletin*, October, 1971

What is a 'good' book?

Do we really know what a good book is for any child, and are the criteria of 'literary merit' applied to adult novels adequate for our purposes ? Here Elaine Moss makes clear that a story which would win no critical acclaim nowadays had the utmost significance for at least one child. This is how a child 'finds himself in a book'. At the stage when the reader's self-concern is uppermost, this kind of experience is of special value. The critic's appraisal may be at odds with the reader's needs.

The 'Peppermint' lesson   Elaine Moss

Don't go looking round the bookshops for *Peppermint*. Though this was probably the most important book in my younger daughter's early life, to your child it would probably mean very little: just another story and not a particularly good one at that.

Why, then, did mine clamour for it so often ? Why, when it was falling to pieces, did I have to glue it together ? Why was it never scribbled on, thrown out of bed, lent to a friend or given away with the jumble ? I had no idea – for years and years.

Then one day, when Alison was about eleven, out of the blue came the revelation. How could I have been so blind – but yet, was it really so obvious ? Before I give the game away I must describe *Peppermint* in some detail. If only you could see it – but you can't.

Peppermint is by an author whose name is Dorothy Grider. Dorothy Grider is also the illustrator. From the copyright matter I deduce that Miss Grider is an American and my guess is that she sold the story and pictures for an outright small sum (no royalty) to the Whitman Publishing Company, Racine, Wisconsin, who subsequently did a deal with Raphael Tuck and Sons, London, enabling them to put *Peppermint* on the market in the UK for about two bob a copy. It is a cheap book in every sense of the word, yet to one child it was, and still is in a way, pure gold.

Heaven knows how *Peppermint* got into our house – a visiting aunt must have given it to one of the children instead of a packet of jelly babies, I should think. For then, as now, I was knee-deep in review copies of new picture-books and storybooks from the good publishing houses – the only books I bought were the great classic picture-books (early *Babars*, *Clever Bill*, *Little Tim*) 'without which', as blurbs are so fond of saying, 'no nursery bookshelf is complete'.

So of one thing I am certain. With the yardsticks I was already making for myself as standards by which to judge the steadily increasing flow of high-quality picture-books for children in general (only the parent can tell whether a particular book 'takes' with his own child), I would never have forked out a penny, let alone a florin, for a book like *Peppermint*.

Peppermint has a shiny red cover from the front of which a white kitten face, sad-eyed, pink-eared and bewhiskered, looks soulfully (the adverb is important, as you'll see later) out. The word 'peppermint' is trick-printed in red and white twisty-candy-sticks above the pussy. On the back cover the series stamp (*Tell-a-Tale*) is surrounded by a cavorting pig, rabbit, lamb, goose, pony and squirrel – all loosely linked by a painted blue 'framing' ribbon. The spine, now merely desiccated sellotape, was probably once a thin strip of red paper.

The story of *Peppermint* is simply told in undistinguished (and un-Anglicized) flat American prose: Peppermint, the frail little white kitten, is the fourth of a litter of kittens born in a candy store. Is she sick? No, she's just thin and pale and nobody buys poor Peppermint – though Lollipop, Chocolate Drop and Caramel, her sisters, are all gleefully acquired by young customers. One day a little girl cries in the candy store because there is to be a Cat Show at school and she has no kitten – and no money to buy one. The candy store owner gives her Peppermint. Peppermint is taken home lovingly; she is bathed, 'blued', brushed and combed; she wins first prize in the Cat Show and she lives happily with the little girl for ever after.

Like the words, the pictures are totally without distinction. Comic-style kids and cats, blobby colours, accentuated sashes and splashes. Totally expendable, one would have thought: a watered-down, vulgarized *Ugly Duckling*. Where, oh where did *Peppermint's* special appeal to this one child lie hidden?

I'm ashamed to say that its appeal was not hidden at all. It was as clear as daylight – but I was looking in the wrong direction. Alison is an adopted child; her hair is pale straw, her eyes are blue; she was taken home, like Peppermint, to be loved and cared for and treasured. It was a matter of identification not just for the duration of the story but at a deep, warm comforting and enduring level.

So we still have *Peppermint*. Its place on the family bookshelf is assured and no longer questioned, not only because it is precious to Alison – in a way that the technically efficient and typographically superior *Mr Fairweather and his Family* (written by Margaret Kornitzer for the express purpose of explaining adoption to pre-school children) has never been but because it taught me an invaluable lesson. The artistically worthless book – hack-written and poorly illustrated – may, if its emotional content is sound, hold a message of supreme significance for a particular child. If it does, it will be more important to that child's development than all the Kate Greenaway Medal-winning books put together.

For a book by itself is nothing – a film shown in an empty cinema: one can only assess its value by the light it brings to a child's eye.

From *Books* volume 2, National Book League, Winter 1970

What the authors tell us

Introduction

The author of books for children is called on more frequently than most other
people to defend his or her choice of occupation, be it in lectures to librarians,
at conferences with teachers, in *Puffin Post*, in letters to enquiring children or to
students making research raids for special studies. The implicit question is always
the same: 'Why do you write for *children*?' and the simplest form of the answer is:
'I write the kind of stories I like to write and children seem to like them too.'
The matter could rest there, but into these apologiae creeps a note of defensiveness,
as if there were a charge to be answered, the charge of doing something easier,
more self-indulgent, than writing a book for adults. Also, these explanations,
when put alongside our concern with the reader, may yield more than the simple
plea for recognition that should have been appeased by C. S. Lewis's remark that
'the sorting out of books into age groups, so dear to publishers, has only a very
sketchy relation with the habits of any real readers'.

C. S. Lewis
'On Three Ways of
Writing for
Children'
reprinted in
Only Connect
OUP Toronto, 1967

    The most extended study of modern writers for the young is that of
J. Rowe Townsend, himself an author of repute. In his book *A Sense of Story*
he judges, rightly it seems to us, the growth in the popularity of children's books
against the decline of the adult novel.

J. R. Townsend
A Sense of Story
Longman, 1971

> 'At present (the novel) gives the impression of shrinking into a corner;
> narrow, cold, self-preoccupied. But children's literature has wild blood in it,
> its ancestry lies partly in the long ages of storytelling which preceded the
> novel. Myth, legend, fairy tale are alive in their own right, endlessly
> reprinted, endlessly fertile in their influence. Modern children's fiction is
> permeated by a *sense of story*.'

By including in his book quotations from what the writers say and by his own
description of their plots, settings, and characters in the, by now, traditional
analysis, J. Rowe Townsend comes near to providing the insights which the
enquirers feel must be there. The very sensitiveness of this critic's descriptive
analysis shows that he leaves untouched the notion of writing as *process*, the way
the author goes about his thinking, the effect of his sense of *audience* on the kind
of story he writes. (What difference *does* it make if these books are read by those

whose past is short, whose picture of the world includes contradictory notions of cause and consequence, whose moral concepts are egocentric?) It cannot simply be the same to write for an audience that includes children and one that does not.

Consequently, we have collected in Section two a number of extended statements by authors who have looked at themselves as storytellers. We ask if the way they see their readers influences the way they set about writing and the kind of stories they create. We wonder if the answer to the question 'Why write?' is really the same for them as for other authors whose audience is avowedly adult. We think that the differences may be significant in the light of what we have said about the reader and will later suggest about the critic. We have assumed the existence and availability of other pieces to which we occasionally refer but have not reprinted.

In *Only Connect*
for example

While there is some consensus, there is by no means unanimity in the way the authors see their profession. Joan Aiken insists that 'writing for children should not be a full-time job', and possibly C. S. Lewis would agree, but Alan Garner endured 'four years of dole queues' to write as he wanted to. The most significant differences lie in the mode, the narrative strategies, especially the choice of the 'point of view', the nearness to or distance from the reader chosen by the author. We can examine this in what they say of themselves. For example, Enid Blyton and Beatrix Potter testify to the existence of 'the literary perspective in the

See page 182

mnemonic mode'. Others, like Philippa Pearce speak of a book 'growing', and relate their activity to the kind of making that the young can understand. None see themselves as simple scribes of actuality, but all convey an intensity of purpose and a sustaining strength of feeling which makes it quite clear to even the most casual reader that the children's author expends great talent and skill with seriousness and verve.

A lifetime of storytelling: the author takes stock of writing books for children since 1933

No one has taken the role of the author of books for children more seriously than Geoffrey Trease. The present generation of writers owes him much. For forty years he has championed and justified the claim that writers of children's books are not producing 'juveniles' because their talent is too short-winded for adult literature. This essay sets out the core of that argument, but implies rather than states its author's effect on the historical novel, which he transformed. In 1949 he wrote 'Tales out of School' in which he made a plea for children's books to be taken seriously by adults. Lately he has moved into the field of biography, influenced perhaps by the popularity of this mode in adult storytelling, where he has shown that the lives of intriguing characters, Byron and D. H. Lawrence, can acquire a new significance for the young if the author's bond with the readers is clear and strong.

Old writers and young readers   Geoffrey Trease

'Forty years on' is a good moment for personal stocktaking. It was in 1933 that, burning my boats (not for the first time), I forsook the dubious security of a teaching post and turned my twenty-fourth birthday into a triple anniversary by getting married and becoming a full-time free-lance writer. That so much of the writing was fated to be for children was something I never foresaw and would have dismissed as almost too improbable to be worth considering.

I was not interested in children. I had just been teaching for a year, admittedly, but those two statements imply no inconsistency. In the depressed nineteen-thirties what embryo writer did not earn his bread, and deepen his depression, by serving for a spell in some kind of private, often comic, boarding school? Day Lewis, Auden – most of them did it. It was part of the apprenticeship.

Nor did children's literature present itself, even to the most desperate struggler, as a promising field in which to win fame and fortune. Of fame there

was none for the living. Children's books were in the doldrums. With a handful
of exceptions such as A. A. Milne, no writer enjoyed any public esteem. 'You
can't beat Henty and Ballantyne,' was the cry. Everyone looked backwards.
There was such a dearth of criticism that if, once in a while, a new children's author
of originality appeared, his advent was scarcely noticed. *Swallows and Amazons*
came out in 1930 and *Mary Poppins* in 1934, but it was years before the names of
Arthur Ransome and P. L. Travers meant anything to me.

If there was no fame, there was not much fortune. Children's books were
commonly published under the old system long abandoned for other types of
books. The author sold his copyright for a single payment of perhaps fifty pounds.
There was nothing to be done then but begin another, and then another. He was
on a treadmill. It was small wonder that so much of children's literature was
hackwork.

Two motives, none the less, impelled me to enter this unpromising field.
One was that great spur to inspiration, financial need. Even fifty pounds was a
fortune when an article earned only a couple of guineas. The second motive was
political.

It was not only the spell of schoolmastering that I shared with Day Lewis,
Auden and so many others, it was the Left-wing idealism of that generation, which
in my own case had drawn me to a short-lived membership not of the Communist
but of the Independent Labour Party. Now, living far from London and its
political excitements, I found another outlet for my feelings. I was already aware,
from my not-so-distant boyhood, that boys' fiction was, as George Orwell was to
declare seven years later, 'sodden in the worst illusions of 1910', and I would
certainly have agreed with him when he continued, 'The fact is only unimportant
if one believes that what is read in childhood leaves no impression behind.'
With this in mind, I wrote to a publisher with a conspicuously Left-wing list and
inquired if he would be interested in adventure-stories with a Socialist slant.

What about Robin Hood, I asked? It was an obvious suggestion, especially
from a native of Nottingham like myself. Children should realize, I argued, that
Sherwood would have been a grim place in January, and that there had been
unromantic compulsions to adopt the outlaw life. Some of the merriment should
be taken out of Merrie England. The story would gain, not lose. You could stand
Henty on his head without taking the kick out of him. Indeed, the inverted
position was often a stimulus to vigorous activity.

Such was the genesis of *Bows Against the Barons*, published early in 1934.
Though a first book of fiction, by an unknown beginner, it was accepted somewhat

unusually on a synopsis and three chapters. Before I knew where I was, the label of 'children's author' was riveted upon me. Yet there was a practical incentive for continuing along the path upon which I had stumbled. My publishers' Marxist principles forbade the exploitation even of authors and there was an unquestioned acceptance of the royalty system, at least in the context of the book trade. So, although sales were small and it was years before the royalties reached the sum I should have received for an outright sale of my story, I was led on by the hope of jam tomorrow.

How did one write for children? To entertain them was essential. At that date I knew there was a prejudice against historical fiction, which was associated with compulsory holiday reading, long-winded descriptive passages, and archaic diction, especially in the dialogue. There were too many varlets crying 'quotha!' Too many writers slipped into a stilted, didactic style which set up an unnecessary barrier between them and their readers. A conscientious author of those days, Gertrude Hollis, in *Spurs and Bride*, would produce a sentence like this:

> ' "Yonder sight is enough to make a man eschew lance and sword for ever, and take to hot-cockles and cherry pit," exclaimed the Earl of Pembroke, adding an oath which the sacred character of the building did not in the least restrain.'

An obliging footnote informed the young reader that 'hot-cockles and cherry pit' were 'popular games'.

The avid young book-lover might accept this kind of thing on the terms stated by one child, Gillian Hansard, who expressed herself thus honestly: 'Though the details of Scott's novels are not always correct they give one a very good idea of the period, and though they are rather painful to read they always give benefit.' For most children, however, this was too suggestive of a visit to the dentist. There was a widespread resistance to historical fiction, and somehow it had to be broken down.

One thing was clear. Ye olde jargon must go. In my own schooldays I had discovered Naomi Mitchison's splendid early novels, *The Conquered* and *Cloud Cuckoo Land*. I had realized what living dialogue could do. I had felt the truth of Ernest Barker's approving comment on her method, 'These ancient figures must break into modern speech if they are to touch us.' I did not know that, as I set my Sherwood outlaws talking like ordinary human beings, Robert Graves was simultaneously doing the same with his Romans in *I Claudius*, which also came out in 1934. Yet for all the influence of that famous novel and its sequel, ye olde jargon lingered for a long time. One could still find characters crying 'I joy me'

and even 'Wot you what?' while a writer of such future distinction as Carola
Oman might be caught lapsing into an unguarded *mélange* of archaic and contemporary: 'I am not in a great hurry, if you truly desire aught, but I think I
ought to be turning home now.'

Apart from a resolution to keep away from Wardour Street, I had no
confident formula for winning over a juvenile public. I would simply write for
them, I told myself, as I would write fiction for adults, but leaving out the sex.
The passage of forty years has modified both the general principle and the exception.

Granted, it is fatal to write down. 'When you write for children,' said
Anatole France, 'do not adopt a style for the occasion. Think your best and write
your best.' That is a splendid thought, something to cling to in hesitant moments,
but for the practising craftsman it is not a sufficient guide.

Granted, too, that the 1973 ten-year-old is more sophisticated than his
counterpart forty years ago, and in some respects genuinely more mature, which
is by no means the same thing. Childhood, to many people's regret, has been
telescoped into a much shorter period by varied factors ranging from earlier
puberty to the pressures of television and advertising.

Grant that in any generation children may be more intelligent than their
parents, more literate, better informed (especially about new scientific and technical
developments), and more fully endowed with that quality of 'apprehension' which
Walter de la Mare distinguished from 'comprehension'.

Grant all this, yet the writer is left with one obvious and inescapable
difference between child and adult readers: the former have not lived so long, and
in the nature of things they cannot have built up the same mental and emotional
capital of background knowledge and first-hand experience. They were not alive
fifteen years ago. To them, 'all our yesterdays' are already history that has to be
learnt.

Thus, in writing an introductory biography of D. H. Lawrence for those
school children who now quite early encounter some of his work in class, I
recently had to remind myself continually that the Nottingham of his youth,
and of my childhood, was almost as remote to them as Periclean Athens. The
clanking, swaying electric trams, the open market stalls with their scents and
colours, the pleasure steamers at Trent Bridge, the steam trains puffing into the
city from all those vanished local stations – the whole background of *Sons and
Lovers* and *The White Peacock*, which it is unnecessary to establish for the adult
reader, has to be touched in, discreetly, for the adolescent. 'Discreetly', because he
must be neither bored nor affronted by too overt explanations. But if the author is

to communicate effectively he cannot risk making too many assumptions. Can he rely, for instance, on all his young readers – especially in the United States – knowing that when Lawrence went to school Queen Victoria was still on the throne, a fact not irrelevant to his story? Can they place George V – or the Kaiser? The author who writes without some such awareness of his readers' age-group is asking for trouble.

This is not to say that every 'i' must be dotted. A book, Alan Garner has said, 'must be written for all levels of experience'. There must be, as he rightly insists, a text that works 'at simple plot level', to make the reader turn the page. 'Anything else that comes through in the book is pure bonus. An onion can be peeled down through its layers, but it is always, at every layer, an onion, whole in itself. I try to write onions.'

The onion metaphor is admirable. In forty years the frontiers of children's literature have been pushed back far beyond any horizon I could see in 1933. The comic old taboos have gone. I can recall the time when 'books for boys' and 'books for girls' were as carefully segregated as lavatories, when 'healthy reading' involved unlimited carnage but not the least hint of tenderness between the sexes, and when a Nonconformist editor rapped my knuckles for permitting two adults and four adolescents to consume a single bottle of Sauterne with their Christmas dinner. 'Is it right,' he demanded, 'to introduce children to the cocktail habit?' That was in 1952.

Now almost nothing is barred in a children's book, and it may reasonably be asked whether the pendulum has not swung too far, for the very reason already stated, that the child reader has *not* lived very long and is inevitably handicapped by a lack of first-hand experience which only time can supply. When I read in a *New Statesman* review, of a 1971 story for older children, that 'the crisis scene is first intercourse, the boy making a mess of it, and thinking himself impotent', I shudder to think of the effect upon some boys reading the book. Another recent book dealt with 'a series of promiscuous affairs … backstreet abortion … adolescent homosexuality'. The tale of a mother's suicide, told from the standpoint of her eleven-year-old son, was recommended in a specialist journal concerned with children's books as 'most suitable perhaps for the nine- to eleven-year-olds'.

I prefer the onion. The individual child peels off just as many layers as his stage of maturity impels him to.

Even in their externals, the life of D. H. Lawrence and the life of Byron (which I wrote for young readers previously) offer good stories, rich in incident, character and colourful background. Even the outer layers of the onion have

savour and some nutriment. Yet, it would be impossible to write the biographies
in question and evade such central topics as Augusta Leigh and 'Lady Chatterley'.
Their significance goes into the inner layers of the onion. A child mature enough
to have grasped the meaning of, say, homosexuality or incest does not need to
find the actual words, much less their definitions, when he reaches Byron's time
at Cambridge or his association with his sister. He will read fluently between the
lines – as he will, similarly, when he reads of Lawrence's tortured love affairs with
Jessie Chambers and Louie Burrows, or *The Rainbow*, or the police raid on
Lawrence's phallic paintings. The less mature reader will have no information
thrust upon him that he is not ready to absorb. Biography for children is an
excellent medium for learning about life, in some ways perhaps even better than
fiction, but its author must not be expected to include a manual of sex education
at the same time. As most sex educationists themselves view with disfavour the
premature answering of questions the child has not asked, the 'literary onion'
seems the right form in which an imaginative writer should present his work to
the young.

It is also the most personally satisfactory. One need feel no restrictions. The
book can be as good and as deep as the author's mind. As has often been remarked,
no first-class children's book has ever failed to hold countless adult admirers.
Given the storytelling craft to get the outer skins right – exciting, mysterious,
fantastic, or what you will – the author is free to put his own heart and soul
into the rest.

It would be misleading to convey the impression that sex was the only, or
principal, subject on which we can now write for children with a freedom unknown
when I began. As long ago as 1946 a New Zealand librarian, Dorothy Neal White,
could say, in her study *About Books for Children*: 'Children's literature has changed
inwardly. It has broadened its range and increased its depth … slowly maturing,
as modern knowledge – political science, sociology, anthropology, economics –
all impinged upon it.' Today, after a generation of further change, amounting to
nothing less than a revolution in this field, no theme that attracts the sufficiently
gifted writer can be ruled out summarily as unacceptable. To recall Anatole France
again, 'Think your best and write your best' is a safe principle.

When I chose to begin with a Robin Hood story I was deliberately taking a
hackneyed theme not from commercial caution but for the fun of turning it
upside down. Later I did the same thing with the Cavaliers, and with the aristocrats
in the French Revolution. But there is another pleasure, no smaller, in choosing
a subject unknown to most children and opening a window to show them a world

completely fresh – Moorish Spain, Norway in the time of the Hanseatic League, Urbino under the good Duke Federigo, even the old Birmingham Bull Ring in 1839, with Chartists and redcoats locked in battle.

Various factors determine the selection. Some historical events seem of such transcendental importance that, if they are being ignored by other children's writers or (one feels) wrongly presented, it appears almost a duty to relate them. Such, for me, was the Bolshevik Revolution, which I treated in a story called *The White Nights of St Petersburg*, though in a rather different manner from the one I would have adopted thirty years earlier. The desire to make political propaganda faded long ago. It is right that a children's author should have something to say in his books, and desirable (in my view) that he should speak on the side of freedom and justice. Partisan preaching is another matter. One of the differences between writing for adults and writing for children is the special responsibility which the latter involves. The adult reader is assumed to be fit to look after himself, able in theory at least to challenge the author's controversial views and verify his statements from other sources. The writer for adults is entitled, if he pleases, to argue a case like a barrister. The writer for children, however, has the same moral responsibility as a teacher. Even though his young readers demand heroes and villains he must still try – in presenting historical issues – to give the devil his due.

So, nowadays, the great political struggles of the past are only some of the themes that inspire me, and even they tend to be combined with some other, quite different, kind of inspiration. I fall under the spell of a character, like Garibaldi, and write *Follow My Black Plume* and *A Thousand for Sicily*. Or a period and setting, Mantua and Urbino in the *quattrocento*, and the result is *Horsemen on the Hills*. Even the Bolshevik story, when at last I got to writing it, drew much of its life from the loveliness of the setting in which those messy events took place – it was the first-hand memory of white nights beside the Neva in 1935 that provided the necessary spark of poetic inspiration to keep the typewriter clicking in 1966. And in writing *Trumpets in the West*, while I wanted to tell young people about the Glorious Revolution I was no less eager to tell them about the period when the English were a truly musical nation. I can still remember my delight, as a plot-maker, when I discovered a handy coincidence of dates – William of Orange's arrival in London occurred within a month or two of the first English opera, Purcell's *Dido and Aeneas*. Since the latter was presented at a girls' school in Chelsea, nothing could have slotted more neatly into a children's novel.

Often the second theme, which can contribute so much of the depth and vitality of a story, springs not from the period but from today. I can quote two very obvious examples from my own experience. The 'historian's motive' for writing *Mist Over Athelney* was the desire to tell children that our Anglo-Saxon forefathers had not been as 'rude' as old-fashioned teaching used to depict them and that pre-Conquest England enjoyed in many respects a civilization finer than what immediately succeeded it. Alfred, the book-loving fighter, was the obvious hero, Alfred, the wearer of that splendid jewel we can still see in the Ashmolean. The eventful months before and after Athelney offered the obvious frame for the plot. But the second theme, the driving force to write the story, came from the television newsreel, showing night after night the queues of prospective emigrants outside Australia House and similar offices. It was 1957. We were going through one of our wearisomely recurrent economic crises. The popular cry was 'England is finished!' It was parroted by those interviewed in front of the camera, one heard it everywhere. I heard it myself alarmingly, from young people all too near and dear. I knew that the same cry had been heard in Wessex in 878. Guthrum seemed master of the last Christian corner of England. Alfred was 'missing, presumed dead'. In Dorset and Hampshire the dispirited English were loading their portable possessions into ships and getting out, across the Channel, while the going was good. They had been mistaken. The twentieth-century English could be mistaken too. *Deor's Lament* provided an apt text: 'That passed. This also may.'

My other example is the highly topical theme of racial and religious toleration. I had long wanted to use an Andalusian setting and to depict for children the period when Arab culture had transformed southern Spain into a garden, later spoilt by the neglect of its Christian conquerors. The then tolerant attitude of the Arabs to the Jews, in striking contrast to the persecution practised by the Catholics, added a further dimension. Requiring a link with England, to make the theme less remote to my young public, I dated the story in 1289 and 1290, when Edward I expelled the Jews from his realm. Convenient coincidence once more took a hand: during those months the King and Queen Eleanor – whose final illness was also most convenient, because I wanted to work in Jewish medicine and Arab pharmacy – spent much of their time in Nottingham Castle. Thus, for the opening chapters, I could return to the familiar ground of Sherwood Forest and medieval Nottingham where my very first book had been set.

That was not so labour-saving as it sounds. The medieval town which Robin Hood entered in *Bows Against the Barons* was little more than a painted backdrop. The Nottingham depicted thirty-two years later in *The Red Towers of Granada* was a patient reconstruction, as faithful as I could make it. I knew where the tiny ghetto stood, the Carmelite convent, the river wharf where the Franciscans unloaded their barges, Lister Gate where the dyers lived, Bridlesmith Gate, Fletcher Gate, every cobbled lane and the trade that was plied there.

Historical accuracy was never more important in the children's story than it is now. Any flaw will be detected, and gleefully, by some one. I spent great pains on my Anglo-Saxon story. It passed publishers' readers and reviewers unchallenged. Then came a letter from a small boy in Aberdeen. I had described the flight of my young characters from Guthrum's winter quarters in Gloucester and, with an Ordnance Survey map of Roman Britain beside me, I had traced every yard of their journey along the snow-covered Fosse Way, *but* – in a moment of aberration – I had allowed them to sup on rabbit, stewed over a camp-fire; and, as the young Aberdonian severely reminded me, rabbits had reached England only with the Normans.

Research must be thorough, but it must also be thoroughly absorbed by the author. It must be integrated in character and action, it must not show obviously in explanatory passages which the reader will instinctively skip. Research is one of the joys of writing for children, but it also has its perils, for too much is as bad as too little. The writer must beware of falling in love with charming period details that tickle his own adult taste. He must resist the temptation to 'work them in' when they do not further the action and will only slow it down.

Sometimes the research required for some adult volume provides both the idea and the ready-made background material, so that there is very little additional 'homework' to be done. The Garibaldi stories were born of my general history of Italy, *The Italian Story*, and after writing *The Condottieri* for adults it was truly child's play to transmute the same material into the fiction of *Horsemen on the Hills*. In the process of research for a history of my native city I found fresh ideas crowding into my mind for stories, set in various centuries, that would bring the workaday life of an English provincial town alive for young readers. It was, indeed, the work needed for *Nottingham, A Biography* – research in greater depth than I had been previously accustomed to – that opened my eyes to fresh possibilities and set me wondering, a shade guiltily, whether I had not neglected the history of my own country and been too often attracted by exotic settings elsewhere. Children, however, need both to discover the treasure under their feet and to gaze on far horizons, so their authors may fairly do the same.

In any case, the writer must begin by pleasing himself and choose his theme accordingly. The communication of his own interests and enthusiasms is his function. Today he is fortunate in that, unless those interests and enthusiasms are very odd indeed, he has unprecedented freedom to communicate them to the young.

Freedom of subject-matter is matched with freedom of style. There are still people, no doubt, who imagine a children's writer as one cruelly limited in vocabulary. Such people cannot have opened any recently published children's books. They might have found, had they done so, an exuberance of language too seldom present today in the matter-of-fact pages of the adult novel with its drab, tape-recorded dialogue. As one critic has said of Leon Garfield, 'He treats the English language with a mastery that sometimes verges on outrage ... Leon Garfield can do anything with words and his touch is very sure.' It is true that, shortly after the Second World War, some publishers were frightened by certain educationists into acceptance of the theory of 'vocabulary limitation' or 'word control', which had begun like so many theories in the United States but was already losing ground there. It did not make much headway in Britain. Academic surveys of children's comics and playground speech soon confirmed what teachers and parents had always known, that children had a surprisingly, sometimes alarmingly, extensive vocabulary at their disposal. The storyteller need not ration himself, but that is not to say that, in addressing the young, he would not be well-advised to bear in mind some special considerations. But I have always felt that these were a stimulus to better writing rather than a handicap.

As a schoolboy on the Classics side, I was taught to admire the Greek and Roman preference for concrete rather than abstract expression. Children share this preference. One writes no worse for studying their taste. The dead metaphors that litter our casual language are a double evil when they appear in prose for children, for, while the adult reader can step over the corpses without noticing them, there are always some children meeting a particular dead metaphor for the first time and they will not recognize it as such. The previous sentence is a good example of how not to write for children.

Elliptical expressions and obscure (however witty) allusions will most often be blemishes in prose intended for understanding by the young, and for the same reason. They are intelligent enough and the subtler television plays have quickened their recognition of 'flash-backs' and other imaginative tricks, but, just as they have not lived long enough to acquire much historical background, so even the brightest cannot yet have acquired the linguistic equipment to catch every nuance of meaning that an older person can be relied upon to pick up. But English is none the worse for being simple, direct and unambiguous. Nor is there any need to rule out, in their proper place, those colourful, evocative, incantatory passages which supply the element of the 'rich and strange', as vital to enjoyment as complete and literal comprehension. Garfield, afore-mentioned, and a host of other talented writers are the proof of that.

Writing for children involves two other special considerations, which in turn carry with them their particular challenges and rewards. A good children's story must stand being read aloud and it must bear repetition. How many adult novelists need worry about, or hope for, either test? Yet what an encouragement they are to get one's prose just right.

A story may be read aloud by any one from a radio professional to a stumbling school-child in class. It should generally be possible to achieve a style that will create no difficulties for the child yet at the same time offer scope for the actor to display his skill. In revising his manuscript the author becomes alert to detect those awkwardnesses, embarrassments sometimes, which the silent and solitary reader would scarcely notice.

An absurd little example will illustrate this. Writing of Garibaldi's defence of Rome in 1849, I wanted to emphasize Mazzini's personal humility, which I felt would help to endear him to children. Bolton King's biography described how, when installed in the magnificence of the Quirinal Palace, the revolutionary leader 'hunted for a room small enough to feel at home in'. In my original draft I was careless enough to translate this into dialogue and make his young admirer exclaim, 'He is the most important man here and he is using the smallest room in the palace as his office!' Ancient memories of the classroom saved me. As I re-read those words I heard, in imagination, the roar of laughter that would have gone up from any group of children to whom they were read aloud. Similarly, though I could not avoid naming the palace once, there was such a risk of the accent being placed on the wrong syllable that I was not having any more 'Quirinals' than necessary.

The second incentive to careful writing has only to be stated: whereas few adults read the same novel twice, it is common for a child to read a favourite story half a dozen times, often with a lapse of years between, which gives extra force to the onion-layer analogy. Whole phrases and sentences are remembered at that impressionable age. As many a subsequent autobiography has revealed, they remain part of the reader's mental furniture for life. They ought to be good.

Perhaps we think too much about the classroom aspects of children's literature. The writer cannot afford to forget them, because the school library and the special school edition provide so much of his livelihood. Forty years ago, most teachers believed that the only good author was, like an Injun, a dead one. All that is marvellously changed. The living author is read and invited to lecture to courses.

He is made the subject of flattering 'projects' and receives, with mixed feelings, batches of children's letters demanding answers to questions which with proper guidance could have been found in the reference library.

There is a danger, however, that the role of the children's author should be regarded as educational, not artistic. Clearly, there is an overlap. So there is with Shakespeare, but Shakespeare is more than an educational tool. So, in his humbler fashion, is the children's author. He may write better than many a novelist – or he may *be* a novelist, in which case he does not stop being a literary artist when he turns to address a younger audience. Yet our histories of English Literature commonly ignore children's books as if they did not exist. In Legouis and Cazamian, for example, there is space to mention the obscure Elizabethan Thomas Hughes but no word of the man who gave us *Tom Brown's Schooldays*.

The past forty years have seen a miraculous flowering of children's books and a welcome improvement in the status of their writers, but there is still a tendency to patronize them as second-class citizens in the commonwealth of letters. They deserve better. There is nothing easy about writing for the young. Boswell admitted that long ago, when he made one of his many unfulfilled resolutions, in this case to write some day 'a little story-book' like the ones he had enjoyed as a boy.

'It will not be an easy task for me,' he noted, 'it will require much nature and simplicity and a great acquaintance with the humours and traditions of the English common people. I shall be happy to succeed, for he who pleases children will be remembered with pleasure by men.'

From *Essays and Studies*, John Murray for the English Association, 1973

The author continuing the literary tradition in children's books

The reasons for his entering the world of children's stories is admirably set down by C. S. Lewis elsewhere. He never claimed to be an 'expert' in children's literature, saying 'my knowledge is about exhausted by MacDonald, Tolkien, E. Nesbit, and Kenneth Grahame.' But we know that his interpretation of 'romance' (see page 79) was a special one, and he was unsparing in his praise of MacDonald. This letter was originally embedded in an article by James E. Higgins. Lewis was always punctilious in answering his correspondents and Mr Higgins had asked him to comment on a description of MacDonald's work in which Lewis says, 'What he does best is fantasy – fantasy that hovers between the allegorical and the mythopoeic.' The very brevity and directness of these answers belie the length of the tradition behind them and the generality of experience they are founded on.

A letter to James E. Higgins   C. S. Lewis

Magdalene College, Cambridge
2 December 1962

Dear Mr Higgins:

1. Surely I never questioned the 'legitimacy' of mythopoeia – only the propriety of classifying the art which it belonged to as 'literature'.

2. The Narnian books are not as much allegory as supposal. 'Suppose there were a Narnian world and it, like ours, needed redemption. What kind of incarnation and Passion might Christ be supposed to undergo *there*?'

3. Only after Aslan came into the story – on His own: I never called Him – did I remember the scriptural 'Lion of Judah'.

4. No. I never met Chesterton. I suppose the same affinity which made me like him made us both like MacDonald.

5. I turned to fairy tales because that seemed the form which certain ideas and images in my mind seemed to demand; as a man might turn to fugues because the musical phrases in his head seemed to be 'good fugue subjects'.

6. When I wrote *The Lion* I had no notion of writing the others.

7. Writing 'juveniles' certainly modified my habits of composition. Thus it (a) imposed a strict limit on vocabulary (b) excluded erotic love (c) cut down reflective and analytical passages (d) led me to produce chapters of nearly equal length, for convenience in reading aloud. All these restrictions did me great good – like writing in a strict metre.

    Yes. I get wonderful letters from children in the USA and elsewhere.

Yours sincerely,

C. S. Lewis.

Quoted by James E. Higgins in the article from which this letter is extracted, *Horn Book Magazine*, October 1966, (page 533)

The author as historical novelist: one of the élite

This article is a special case in the general argument made by Geoffrey Trease about the place of the historical novel in the development of books for children in the last twenty years. Authors who choose this form are amongst the most distinguished practitioners. The attractions of this kind of writing are summarized here by Mrs Burton, a Carnegie medallist, whose books are acclaimed for their recreation of the 'felt life' of the period in which they are set. Not least amongst her satisfactions is the possibility that young characters in earlier centuries than this can be more easily exposed to danger. Historical novels are always adventure stories. But at the same time situations and experiences contemporary with the reader are distanced and given 'the sense of an ending', or at best a resolution, by being presented in a historical setting. The plot is in the past; the theme is here and now. Amongst Mrs Burton's most acclaimed books are 'Castors Away' (1962); 'Time of Trial' (1963); 'No Beat of Drum' (1966); 'In Spite of all Terror' (1969); 'Thomas' (1970); 'Kate Rider' (1974).

The writing of historical novels   Hester Burton

Historical novels – like most mixed marriages – are frowned upon by the Establishment. Historians look upon them with contempt, feeling sure that their authors must have tampered with, or at least distorted, historical fact. The straight novelist regards them as unfortunate aberrations – at best, as a misuse of their writers' talents. A novelist's duty, he thinks, is to portray life as he *knows* it – namely, in the contemporary scene. Anything else must be false, for how can a writer living in the twentieth century really put himself into the mind, say, of a Roman centurion or a fifteenth-century wool merchant or one of Lord Nelson's powder monkeys? He may well learn every detail concerning the centurion's armour and the wool merchant's trade and the powder monkey's duties on board a man-of-war, but how can the most fertile imagination living today re-create the secret fears and unrecorded hopes of people living in times past?

The purpose of this article is to explain how one historical novelist – myself – answers these very serious questions.

Sooner or later, the writer of historical fiction has to make quite clear to himself where history ends and where fiction may legitimately begin. If his books are to appear on the shelves of a school library, I think it is his duty to indicate in an introduction where this dividing line comes.

I have been writing historical novels for nine years, and during this time I have formulated certain other rules for myself.

First, I must acquaint myself as thoroughly as I possibly can with the historical period and the events I am describing. Ideally, I should be so knowledge-able that I have no need to turn to a book of reference once I have actually started writing the book. I should be able to see clearly in my mind's eye the houses in which my characters live, the clothes they wear, and the carts and carriages and ships in which they travel. I should know what food they eat, what songs they sing when they feel happy, and what are the sights and smells they are likely to meet when they walk down the street. I must understand their religion, their political hopes, their trades, and – what is most important – the relationships between different members of a family common to their particular generation. Moreover, I must carry this knowledge as lightly as the contemporary novelist carries his knowledge of the contemporary scene.

My second rule is never to use a famous historical person as the pivot of my story and never to put into his mouth words or sentiments for which there is no documentary evidence. The reason for this rule is my conviction that it is legitimate for a writer such as myself to try to re-create an historical situation or event, such as the Fire of London, the Battle of Trafalgar, or the Agrarian Revolt of 1829, and then to place fictional characters in this situation and describe how they behave. It is *not* legitimate to reverse the order; namely, to take an actual historical personage and plunge him into fictional adventures.

My last rule is really more of a warning than a rule. When I come to describe the historical situation which I have chosen, I try to view it through the limited vision of a single character or group of characters. I am not all-wise or all-knowing as the historian is; but neither, it is well to remember, were the people actually taking part in the historical event I am describing. They had no access to state papers; they could merely use their eyes. Not only is it a wise caution for the writer of historical novels to limit his range of vision but it is also much better art. I first realized this when I read Stendhal's *The Charterhouse of Parma*. In an early chapter, a young man riding through the Flanders countryside strays by accident into the middle of the Battle of Waterloo. His ensuing feelings of surprise and horror at the muddled and brutal engagements going on all about him made me realize for the first time the utter bewilderment of war. It is a fictional treatment of a great battle which seems utterly right. Thackeray does the same thing in *Vanity Fair*; he views Waterloo through the eyes of the womenfolk waiting anxiously for news in Brussels. Tolstoy, too, in *War and Peace* limits his view of Borodino and so achieves the most vivid effects. In my very humble way, I applied this rule to my account of the Battle of Trafalgar in *Castors Away!* I described it through the eyes of a boy of twelve running almost non-stop from the lower deck down through the orlop deck to the powder magazine and back again, bringing powder for the gunners. The battle comes to him as a series of salvos, cries, shouts, jolts, and the grinding of wood as the ships run each other down and are grappled together.

It is much more difficult to try to answer the strictures of the contemporary novelist upon historical novels. Why, he asks, with an exciting, familiar world going on all about us, do writers, such as myself, plunge themselves into a past which they cannot hope to know as well as they know the middle of the twentieth century?

Each writer has to answer for himself. I am conscious of two reasons why I have chosen to write historical novels. The first is extremely simple and mundane. The second is more complex. The simple reason is this: As a novelist, I am primarily interested in one kind of story; it is the story of young people thrown into some terrible predicament or danger and scrambling out of it, unaided. The first book I wrote, *The Great Gale*, was not an historical novel. The predicament was the sudden flooding of the children's village in Norfolk on the night of January 31, 1953. The incidents in the story were based on what really happened all along the east coast on that night. *The Great Gale* is, in fact, what one American reviewer has delightfully called 'documentary fiction'. When I came to search for another real-life predicament set in modern times upon which I could base a second story, I could not find one. The reasons are obvious: in England, we do not suffer from the natural hazards of earthquake, tornado, or bush fire; and against all other dangers we surround our children with loving parents, school-teachers, and policemen. For a novelist, such as myself, life is far too safe for the young in the twentieth century. Therefore, I looked back in time to the beginning of the nineteenth century, when it was not at all safe to be young, when boys like Nelson himself were sent to sea at the age of eleven and might very well take part – as my Tom Henchman took part – in a battle as bloody as Trafalgar. The truth is that English history – all history for that matter – is full of robust, exciting plots for novelists who, like myself, wish to subject their characters to the test of danger.

The more complex reason why my imagination finds refuge in history was not at first apparent to me. Now, with every passing year, I am coming to realize more and more clearly how little I understand this present age. I do not understand its poetry or its art or its music. I do not understand why the young take drugs or become hippies. I am bewildered by the multiplicity and contradictions of the facts, figures, fashions, and opinions which are presented to me daily in the newspapers. I am lost in the fog. If I look back at a past age, however, the fog clears; the facts and figures fall into place. Not only have the accidents of time selected the evidence but historians have interpreted that evidence for us and taught us to see the past in perspective.

What is complex about the situation is that though the past is better sign-posted than the present, I, the traveller, carry with me the anxieties and preoccupations of the twentieth century. I am quite conscious that I choose an event or theme in history because it echoes something I have experienced in my own life. For example, when I described the autumn of Trafalgar in *Castors Away!*, I consciously relived the summer of 1940. Both seasons were a time of great national danger, stress, and joy; in both we were threatened by invasion and were fighting for our lives. In the courage of Nelson, I felt again the inspiration of Winston Churchill, a personal experience of feeling which I have tried to recapture in my book *In Spite of All Terror*. In a quieter way, the themes of *Time of Trial* and *Thomas* echo a contemporary experience, namely the growing concern of many of us at the encroachment of the State upon the rights of the individual; while the theme of *No Beat of Drum* is perhaps the most insistently modern of all, since it is concerned with the bitter misery of the poor in a world of the rich. Whether it is right to use history in order to explore one's own problems, I do not know; but it certainly adds a deep and adult pleasure to storytelling.

In further reply to the contemporary novelist's criticisms, I would add that having chosen a historical event in which one can hear one's own heart beat, it is not so impossible to imagine oneself living a hundred and sixty years ago – or more; for so much in England is still the same. Large parts of the Suffolk coast are the same, and the line of the South Downs, and the Cotswold villages, and a field of standing wheat undulating in the wind, and the weather. By concentrating on the sameness, one can gradually slip into what is different. The most important sameness, of course, is human nature. Men and women and children have always known happiness, felt terror, been angry, felt irritable, known despair. The emotions are the same; it is what evokes them that changes down the ages. Remembering our own ever-present terror of the nuclear bomb, it is not so impossible to imagine a seventeenth-century Puritan's terror of hell-fire. The courage of the three astronauts circling the moon is matched by the courage of Drake sailing round the world – and our response to both is the same.

Every novelist finds joy and an extension to his life in the characters which he creates in his stories, but the writer of historical fiction has yet another pleasure, which is his alone. It is the pleasure of discovery. The results of the research necessary before the writing of any historical novel open up for the author a new and absorbing world. I can only compare this experience with that of looking through a microscope at a number of formless blobs on one's slide and then twiddling the knobs until, suddenly, the blobs come into focus and an intricate network of cells and nerves and structures is clearly revealed.

When I came to write *Time of Trial*, it was necessary for me to find out as much as possible about life in London in the year 1801. The little that I already knew was vague and formless. In search of information, I went to the Bodleian Library in Oxford and read as much contemporary material as I could discover in the catalogue. This, among many other books, included *A Guide to Visitors to London Newly Come Up from the Country*. In this guidebook, I learned which coffeehouses were patronized by what profession or political party, where the best tea gardens were, in which church I could hear the best sermon, and how I ought to behave when I visited that most popular attraction for sightseers – Newgate Prison – in order to stare at the prisoners. I discovered, too, various street maps, a ground plan of the prison known as Poultry Compter (to which I sent my unfortunate bookseller-hero, Mr Pargeter), and a book of etchings of the most noteworthy buildings in the metropolis. I looked also at contemporary cartoons and had the good fortune to light upon a little sixpenny book published especially for children. This consisted of coloured plates illustrating the many street vendors in the city, with their particular street cry printed below; for example, a boy carrying a flat basket of fish on his head with the caption 'Mackerel. Fresh Mackerel,' and a dustman with his cart crying 'Dust O! Bring out your dust!' From oddly assorted material such as this, a strange, exciting, rather savage city gradually came into focus. I could lie in bed and listen – as Margaret Pargeter lay and listened in the first chapter of the book – to the countless church bells, the harsh grinding of iron wheels over the cobbles, the street cries, and the mutter of angry, half-starved men and women living in the terrible attics and cellars of the dark courts. The London of 1801 had mysteriously burst into life for me.

If writing historical novels has its own special pleasures, it also has its own special difficulties – especially if one knows that one's books are going to be read primarily by children. Children are not less intelligent than grown-ups. The problem is that they *know* less. In particular, they know less history. The first difficulty, then, is to give the historical setting of one's story and to impart the necessary historical facts without appearing to teach or to preach and – what is more important – without slowing up the pace of the narrative. Both the child and the writer want to hurry on to the action of the story. Yet, if the historical background is not firmly painted in, both child and author come to grief. The characters in the story move in a kind of featureless limbo, and both reader and writer lose interest in them. For this reason, I find the writing of the first chapter of every novel extremely difficult. There is so much to do all at the same moment: there are the characters to describe, the geographical setting to depict, the plot to be introduced, and, on top of all, the problem of history. I know from children themselves that I have not entirely mastered this difficulty, for I sometimes receive letters which begin: 'I liked your story except for the beginning which I found boaring (sic).'

Another difficulty lies in children's susceptibilities: their capacity to be frightened or appalled. Yet, if one is drawn to write historical novels, what is one to do? History is not pretty. The Nazi concentration camps aside, I think people were far more cruel to each other in times past than they are today. The law was certainly more cruel. So was poverty. So was the treatment of children. How then is the writer to deal honestly with history and show sympathetic understanding toward his reader? One certainly does not want to cosset children in their reading. In my own case, the kind of story I like writing precludes such softness and emotional cosiness. Yet, the difficulty remains: The brutality of times past may shock the over-sensitive.

If one can only overcome these difficulties, both the writing and the reading of historical novels bring great rewards. The writer acquires much factual information from his researches which, if he is skilful, he can pass on pleasurably to his readers. Yet this, happily, is not his chief aim. The prime object of writing an historical novel is an exercise of the *heart* rather than the head. It is an exploration of the imagination, a discovery of other people living at other times and faced with other problems than our own. In other words, it is an extension of the author's human sympathies.

Writing my historical novels has made me far more understanding of human nature. I feel that it is not I who brought compassion to the writing but the actual writing that gave it to me. And if I have in any measure passed on this experience of sympathy to my readers, then I am indeed rewarded as a writer.

From *Horn Book Magazine*, June 1969

The author as the ally of the reader

The plea that this article contains is a powerful one: no one should write for children except 'with the whole heart'. Most of the points made by Joan Aiken reinforce the claims of other authors but in some she stands on her own: in her resistance to scarcely concealed didacticism, for example. But, most clearly, there emerges her sense of audience – the child reading or the adult reading to the child – her awareness of the reader's bond with the author. Most of Joan Aiken's books for children have Dickensian plots, a weird realism which makes a threatening world full of wolves, towering adults, and natural hazards. They exploit the conventions to the limits of credibility but carry along at great speed all the incidents that have 'the crazy logic of magic'. John Rowe Townsend says she is 'one of the liveliest and most exuberant of today's writers for children, an original', but concludes that she is 'a lightweight because her books lack moral or psychological complexities'. In this essay we feel the strength of her concern and some of her originality. The points she makes are serious ones.

Purely for love   Joan Aiken

To begin this rambling series of disjointed meditations, questions without any answers, and impracticable suggestions, I am going to give a couple of quotations whose relevance can probably be guessed. Here is the first:

' "Do you know where the wicked go after death?"

"They go to hell," was my ready and orthodox answer.

"And should you like to fall into that pit and be burning there for ever?"

"No, Sir."

"What must you do to avoid it?"

I deliberated a moment; my answer, when it did come, was objectionable.

"I must keep in good health and not die."

"How can you keep in good health? Children younger than you die daily. ...

Here is a book entitled *The Child's Guide*; read it with prayer, especially that part containing an account of the awfully sudden death of Martha G –, a naughty child addicted to falsehood and deceit."…

"I am not deceitful: if I were, I should say I loved *you*; but I declare I do not love you: I dislike you the worst of anybody in the world, and this book about the liar, you may give to your girl Georgiana, for it is she who tells lies …" '

That, of course, is from *Jane Eyre*. And the other, quite different, is shorter:

'Me and my brother were then the victims of his feury since which we have suffered very much which leads us to the arrowing belief that we have received some injury in our insides, especially as no marks of violence are visible externally. I am screaming out loud all the time I write and so is my brother which takes off my attention and I hope will excuse mistakes …'

(*Nicholas Nickleby*)

I will leave those for the moment and go on.

I keep my gramophone records in old wooden coalboxes. Quite by chance a long time ago I discovered that old wooden coalboxes are exactly the right size and shape for keeping gramophone records in. Don't worry – there is a connection here: for someone who has been writing children's stories on and off for the last thirty years, the sudden rise to importance of children's literature has affected me rather in the same way that it would if I were to wake one day and find that university courses and seminars were being held on the necessity of keeping one's discs in old wooden coalboxes, and journals printed called *Wooden Coalbox News*, and even that an industry had sprung up for making imitation plastic wooden coalboxes. I do not wish to sound snide or ungrateful. In a way it's wonderful suddenly to find one's occupation so respectable, at least in certain circles. For it isn't yet with the general public. In most circles the confession that one writes children's books always produces the same response, and a very daunting response it is. I'll give an example.

A couple of months ago I went to a party with two friends. It was a very mixed party of all incomes, classes, and professions, young and old; some guests were in TV, some in films or advertising, some wrote. The only common factor was that they were all very intelligent because the host was very intelligent. The friends with whom I went, started off by introducing me as their friend Joan who wrote children's books. But they soon stopped that. Because at the phrase *children's books* an expression of blank horror would close down on every face, people would be unable to think of a single conversational topic, they obviously expected me to start reciting poetry about fairies in a high piping voice, they just could not wait to get away from that part of the room to somewhere safer and more interesting. My friends observed this phenomenon so they changed their tactics – they started introducing me as somebody who wrote thrillers. Instantly all was well, faces lit up. People love thriller-writers because everybody reads a thriller at one time or another, so they felt able to talk to me and I had a good time and came away from the party with a curious feeling of the relativity of identity. And wondering, too, who is a real adult – if anybody is, all the time, that is to say.

Obviously children's writing – writing for children – is regarded by society as a fairly childish occupation. But then it occurred to me that most people's occupations are pursued at a number of different levels – at varying mental ages. A man runs his business affairs with a 50-year-old intelligence, conducts his marriage on a pattern formed at age 20, has hobbies suitable to a 10-year-old, and a reading age that stuck at Leslie Charteris: is he an adult or not? And if he is not, how would you classify his reading-matter? There is a lot of what I would classify as non-adult reading: thrillers, funny books, regency romances, horror stories, westerns. Of course some of these, because of outstanding qualities, may fall into the adult sphere, but lots do not. And yet it is considered perfectly all right for a forty-five-year-old company director to read, say, Ian Fleming, whereas he would be thought odd if he read, say, Alan Garner, a much better writer. And there is the same ambivalence in the social attitude to the writers. If you say that you write books for children because you enjoy doing so, people instantly assume that you are retarded. Whereas, sad but true, if you say, 'Of course I'd *rather* write adult fiction but writing for children is more paying,' (not so, incidentally) people accept that as a perfectly logical, virtuous viewpoint. But to write children's books for pleasure – that, nine times out of ten, is considered almost as embarrassing as making one's money from the manufacture of contraceptives or nappy liners. And yet writing thrillers is acceptable. It's odd – because the really interesting point here is the strong similarity that in fact exists between thrillers and children's fiction: the moral outlook is the same, the pattern of mystery, danger, capture, escape, revenge, triumph of good over evil, is very similar indeed.

So society regards people who write for children as odd. And one can't help stopping from time to time and saying to oneself, 'Maybe society is right about this. Why do people write for children? Is it a good thing that they should? Up to the nineteenth century children managed all right without having books specially written for them. Up to the nineteenth century children were not regarded as a different species, but were clothed, fed, and treated in most ways as if they were adults of a smaller size. Are they, in fact, better off for being treated as a separate minority? And, turning to the people who write for children, ought they to indulge themselves in this way? And what started them doing so, in the middle of the nineteenth century? Was it the need of the children or the need of the writers to write in that particular way? And, if people are to be allowed to write for children, what ought they to write?'

Why do people write for children? I am afraid there are quite a number who do it because it seems like easy money – especially in the present boom of children's literature. Their idea is that in children's fiction you can get away with a minimum of factual background, a skimpy story and a poverty-stricken vocabulary. But let's set all those on one side. If they found an easier racket, they would switch to it. Let's consider the ones who *like* to write for children – let's consider why, in spite of it being an embarrassing, ill-paid, guilt-producing, and socially unaccept-able thing to do, quite a number of people in fact *do* it, instead of – or as well as – writing adult novels, or plays, or TV scripts, or biographies. What sort of people are they?

Fairly soon we shall know the answers to some of these questions in detail, because Berkeley Department of Motivational Studies, University of California, is conducting a massive research project into the motivations of children's writers. They sent out a great questionnaire, which took a solid six hours to fill in going at top speed, and presently they will have the results all tabulated by computers. Though of course these results are bound to be an average only of the writers they selected – and who did the selecting, one wonders? Anyway, I'm going to guess ahead and predict that presently they will be able to say that most children's writers come from broken families, may have been ill when young, or handi-capped, or misfits, or at least unsociably inclined. And when they do come up with this result, I'm not sure where it will get us; we have left behind the era when boys were castrated so they would always be sure of a part in opera; you would hardly break up your home in the hope that your child might become a second Lewis Carroll. (It really is too bad that Berkeley started too late to send their questionnaire to *him*.)

However let's – rather sketchily – survey a few peaks sticking up out of the general landscape of children's literature. We can agree that Dickens (I include Dickens because, though not a children's writer, he has so many of the essential qualities of one: mystery, slapstick, simple emotion, intricate plots, marvellous language – and anyway, children enjoy him, and you could say he wrote for a mental age of 15) Dickens had a very unhappy childhood. So did Kipling and

Masefield. Beatrix Potter had tyrannical, dominating parents, so did Charlotte Yonge. Ruskin and Lewis Carroll never entirely grew up. Hans Andersen's father died when he was small and his mother drank. Blake suffered from visions and was so gifted, *that* in itself must have made his childhood troubled. De la Mare was delicate, so was Robert Louis Stevenson who, moreover, had to endure a hellfire upbringing which caused him to have frightful nightmares and guilt fantasies. The theme certainly seems clear enough: writers who had unhappy childhoods tend to address themselves to children, not necessarily all the time, not necessarily their whole output, but, obviously, as a sort of compensation, to replace part of the childhood they lost. They are writing for the unfulfilled part of themselves. It would be invidious to talk about living writers in this context, but I can think of a couple among the top rank who were ill when young or suffered from broken homes. Here's an interesting thing, though – and in my list of classics it obtains too – this seems to apply to male writers more than to females. Plenty of well-known women children's writers had stable happy childhoods and normal lives. Maybe women just take naturally to producing children's tales, it's an occupational occupation. They don't get such a complete break from childhood as men do, because they are more likely to be continually in contact with children between youth and middle age.

So we can guess that when Berkeley produce their profile of the children's writer, there will be a troubled childhood in the background. And here's where I'm going to put another question aimed at starting argument: is it a good thing that these disturbed, unhappy characters should be doing this particular job? Are the people who write for children the ones who *ought* to be writing?

There are quite a few professions – for instance, politics, the police, the prison service, maybe the civil service – which, one suspects, attract to them the very last people who ought to be in them. The very desire to be a prison warder or a prime minister should disbar one from eligibility. I dare say by the next century anybody expressing a wish to go into politics will be psychoanalysed and put through all kinds of vocational tests, as they ought before matrimony or being allowed to drive a car on the public roads. I know this is a shocking suggestion, verging on fascism, but we are moving into a more and more controlled way of living. Our environment has to be controlled. We are subject to restraints in many areas already: fluoridation, smokeless zones, no-parking areas, contraception, industrial regulations, the decision whether or not to die of nicotine cancer. Control is not enjoyable, it is just necessary because there are such a lot of us. Many industries already have their own personnel selection tests; before taking an advertising job in which I wrote copy for Campbells' soup tin labels I had to undergo a whole series of ability tests and finally a psychologist spent two hours trying to make me lose my temper. If one needs such stringent tests in order to write advertising copy, whose end-purposes may reasonably be regarded as frivolous – if not downright nefarious – how much more necessary might it not be thought to subject to some kind of psychological screening those people who are directing their energies into such a frighteningly influential area as children's books, material that can affect the outlook of whole generations to an incalculable degree? I know this is an outrageous suggestion: who would give the tests, what would they consist of, who would assess the results? The whole idea bristles with impossibilities. It certainly runs flat counter to the growing permissiveness in the adult field as to what can be written and published. I'm not suggesting it quite seriously. But it's worth talking around. After all, you need a licence to keep a dog, you need all kinds of official authority before you can adopt or foster a child or start a school or even run a playgroup – yet any paranoid can write a children's book. The only indirect control is the need to find a publisher and that's not too difficult.

I'm now going to stick my neck out a bit farther. I've heard that the average child in the course of childhood is estimated to have time to read six hundred books. Judging from myself and friends and children, it is probably less, because children read books over and over – which is a good thing: better read *Tom Sawyer* four times than four second-rate stories. So, six hundred or less. The book industry is unlike nearly all other industries in one marked particular: its products never perish. So those six hundred books have already been written. Without a shadow of doubt, any children's librarian could produce a list of six hundred titles, including all the classics and plenty of good modern books, enough to last any child right through. So where is the need to write any more? Particularly since writing for children is such a suspect, self-indulgent, narcissistic activity?

I'll leave that question in the air too and think a bit more about writers. Of course a troubled childhood in the background isn't the only contributory factor, or the world would be stuffed with children's writers. Plenty of people who suffer from childhood handicaps go on to become politicians or psycho-analysts or bank robbers. To be a writer you have to have the potential – to be a children's writer you have to have imagination, iconoclasm, a deep instinctive morality, a large vocabulary, a sense of humour, a powerful sense of pity and justice. … Besides that, I for one feel strongly that the ideal writer for children should do something else most of the time. Writing for children should not be

a full-time job. Let me repeat that because it is probably the most important thing
I have to say here: writing for children should not be a full-time job. And that's
another thing Dickens, Masefield, de la Mare, Lewis Carroll, Ruskin, Kipling,
Hans Andersen and William Blake had in common – children's writing was a
sideline with them. (If indeed they were really writing for children at any time?)
They had plenty of other professional interests. Which meant, first, that their
writing was enriched by their other activities, knowledge, background – that
it had plenty of depth; second, that they wrote, when they did write for children,
purely for love. And that is the way children's writing should be done; it should
not be done for any other reason.

Think of those six hundred books again – what a tiny total that is. It is
frightful to think that a single one of them should have been written primarily to
earn an advance of £250 on a five per cent royalty rising to twelve and a half per
cent – or to propagate some such idea as that it is a very enjoyable thing to be a
student nurse. And I might as well add that I do not think any kind of fringe
activity connected with children's literature should be a full-time occupation –
editing, reviewing, publishing, anything – everyone connected with these professions ought to leave the children's field from time to time so as to get a different
perspective. After all, children live in the world with the rest of us, they aren't a
separate race. I'm a bit uneasy about this cult of treating children as creatures
utterly divorced from adult life. In the BBC 2 television series, *Family of Man*,
which compared the social habits of different races, what struck me forcibly about
the New Guinea tribesmen, the Himalayans, the Kalahari bushmen, the Chinese,
is how very serene and well-adjusted their children seemed to be – because they had
their established place in the adult world. And yet I'm ready to bet not a single
one of them had a children's book. There's no need to point a moral here and
anyway we can't reverse the course of civilization. So I will go on to mention a
danger that every children's writer is likely to encounter.

Most writers – most people – have at some point the idea for a good children's
book. And maybe something fetches it out: an unresolved trauma from childhood
to dispose of, or just the circumstance of having children and telling them stories
which seem worth writing down – anyway, this person, due to some environmental factor, writes a good book, maybe two or three and then – although the
formative circumstances no longer exist – is too caught up in the business to quit.
Financial pressure, pressure of success, pressure of habit – it is easy to succumb.
I can think of several people who wrote one or two good children's books and
then their interests developed elsewhere in a natural progression and they

stopped. I can think of several more who wrote one or two good children's books and should have stopped there but didn't. And I need hardly say, as my previous remarks will have made my opinion clear, but I will go on and say it again because I feel so strongly about it – writing anything for children unless one has a strong genuine impulse not only to write at all but to write that one particular thing – writing anything without such an impulse is every bit as wicked as selling plastic machine-gun toys, candies containing addictive drugs, or watered-down penicillin.

Another reason why children's writers should have some other, predominant occupation, is simply because children have a greater respect for them if they do. Children, bless their good sound sense, are naturally suspicious of adults who devote themselves to nothing but children. For one thing, such adults are too boringly familiar – there aren't any mysteries about them. Don't you remember how at school the teachers who disappeared to their own pursuits after school were respected and how the ones who were always at hand doing things with the children as if they had nothing else to do, no better way of occupying themselves were despised? Elizabeth Jenkins, in her book *Young Enthusiasts*, says, 'It is of course admirable to want to teach children, but the question all too seldom asked is: What have you got to teach them?' Parents, after all, are not occupied exclusively with their children – or heaven help them both. Surveys of distraught young mothers in housing estates who never have a chance to get away show what a very unnatural state of affairs this is, and how undesirable.

When I was a child, one of my greatest pleasures was listening to my elder brother play the piano. He was a lot older and he played pretty well. But the point was that he was playing for his benefit, not for mine. Part of my pleasure was the feeling that it was a free gift, that my brother and I were independent of one another. Another part was the understanding that some of the music was beyond my scope, which intensified my enjoyment of the easier bits. If my brother had said, 'I'll play for you now, choose what you'd like?' I would have been not only embarrassed and nonplussed, but also horribly constricted by such a gesture, it would have completely changed the whole experience. I think the essence of the very best children's literature is this understanding that it is a free gift – no, not a gift, a treasure trove – tossed out casually from the richness of a much larger store. Of course there are exceptions to this generalization – I can think of several fine children's writers now at work who do nothing else *at present* – but my feeling is that they have the capacity to, and probably will do something else in due course.

I listened to a fascinating broadcast by Arthur Koestler recently, first delivered at the 1969 Cheltenham Festival. Its subject was literature and the law of diminishing returns, and Mr Koestler first of all was discussing whether or not there is progress in art comparable with progress in science, where discoveries and the growth of knowledge can be continually recorded and tabulated. He came to the conclusion that there *is* progress in art but of a different kind – it proceeds by leaps and bounds instead of in a measurable upward graph, and it skips from one form to another; each art-form proceeds through four stages, a stage of revolution, a stage of expansion, a stage of saturation, when the audience has had enough of it, and the only way their attention can be held is by exaggeration or involution – and then a final collapse, as something else comes to the fore.

I suppose, judged in those terms, one could say that writing for children is just leaving its revolutionary stage, having been going for less than a hundred years, and is still expanding; just now, because it is expanding, it attracts people who fifty years ago would have been writing novels. I wonder what will have happened in, say, another twenty years? Maybe involution will have set in, there will be a kind of Kafka vogue in children's literature. I wouldn't be surprised. I believe one can see traces of it already.

I was thinking about this question of progress, after Koestler's talk – thinking that you cannot have progress without loss: you acquire nylon, you lose the spinning-wheel. You acquire colour photography, you lose Breughel. You acquire logic, you lose fairy tales. Our brains now have to contain such a frightening amount of *stuff*, just in order to carry on normal life: electronics, the decimal system, knowledge of what is happening all over the world, psychology, ecology, how to deal with parking meters and supermarkets and yellow tube tickets – when you think of all this information that has to be rammed in and stored at the front of our minds compared with, say, the necessary equipment for comfortable and rational living at the beginning of the nineteenth century, you can see why some people worry about what in the meantime may be trickling away at the back and being irretrievably lost. Sherlock Holmes, if you remember, had an idea that the brain's capacity was strictly limited. When Dr Watson, rather scandalized, discovered that Holmes knew nothing about the solar system, and started telling him, Holmes brushed his proffered instruction aside, saying 'I managed very well before, without this information, and what you have told me I shall now do my best to forget.' I'm sure, whether or not this idea of the mind's limited capacity is correct, many people entertain it; consciously or unconsciously it forms part of their fear of progress: the feeling that if you acquire enough basic data about space flight to be able to understand what is going on in the lunar module, you will probably forget your wife's birthday or the theme of the first movement of the third Brandenburg concerto. I sometimes cheer myself up by remembering that in Peru they didn't learn about the wheel until bicycles were invented. I'm sure most children's writers are natural opponents of progress, unable to adapt to the world entirely, fighting a rearguard action, like people salvaging treasures in a bombardment; for growing up, of course, involves the severest loss of all, the one that is hardest to accept. Children's writers are natural conservatives in the sense that they want to *conserve*.

The notion of any restraints or controls at all over writers is a horrifying one, I'm glad to think. And yet on the other side of the Iron Curtain such controls are in force. And in the field of children's literature, both in this country and America, I have come across educators who made fairly plain their feeling that some children's writers are a bunch of tiresome anarchists who could perfectly well be a bit more helpful if they chose, in the way of incorporating educational material and acceptable ethics into their writing. As if they were a kind of hot-drink vending machine and you had only to press the right knob to produce an appropriately flavoured bit of nourishment. I do not agree with this point of view. I do not think it is possible to exercise any control over what a creative artist produces, without the risk of wrecking the product. The only possible control is to shoot the artist. This view may seem inconsistent with what I have said before about who should be allowed to write for children. So it is. I don't pretend to have consistent views.

I would not dream of making suggestions to other writers as to what they should write. But I do have strong views as to the kind of intentions one should *not* have when setting out to write anything for children. Childhood is so desperately short, and becoming shorter all the time: they are reading adult novels at 14, which leaves only about nine years in which to get through those six hundred books – nearly two books a week, that means. Furthermore, children have so little reading-time, compared with adults, and that is growing less – there's school, there's bedtime, all the extra-curricular activities they have now. I am not decrying adventure playgrounds, and drama groups, and play classes, and organized camp holidays, I think they are splendid – even television has its points – but all this means a loss of reading-time, and *that* means that when they do read, it is really a wicked shame if they waste any time at all reading what I am going to group under the heading of Filboid Studge. *Filboid Studge*, if you recall, was the title of a short story by Saki about a breakfast food which was so dull and tasteless that it sold extremely well because everybody believed that it *must* be good for them. (Really it is a pity we don't have an excretory system for mental waste matter as well as for physical. Children, at an age when their minds are as soft and impressionable as a newly tarred road, pick up such a mass of un-nourishing stuff and what happens to it? It soaks down into the subconscious and does no good there, or it lies around taking up room that could be used to better purpose.)

It is lucky that at least children have a strong natural resistance to phoney morality. They can see through the adult with some moral axe to grind almost before he opens his mouth – the smaller the child, the sharper the instinct. I suppose it's the same kind of ESP that one finds in animals – the telepathy that transmits to one's cat exactly which page of the Sunday paper one wishes to read so that he can go and sit on it. Small children have this to a marked degree. You have only to say, 'Eat your nice spinach' for a negative reaction to be triggered off. You don't even have to add 'because it's good for you'. They pick that up out of the atmosphere. They sense at once when we want them to do something because it suits *us*. It's sad to think how much at our mercy children are: ninety per cent of their time we are organizing them and guiding them and making them do things for utilitarian reasons – and then, the remaining ten per cent, likely as not, we are concocting pretexts for getting rid of them. I can remember the exact tone of my mother's voice as she invented some errand that would get me out from under the grown-ups' feet for half an hour. And I now remember too with frightful guilt how pleased I was when my children learned to read. Apart from my real happiness at the thought of the pleasure that lay ahead of them, I looked forward to hours of peace and quiet.

On account of this tough natural resistance, I'm not bothered about hypo-critical moral messages. That's where the Jane Eyre quotation comes in. It is a beautiful example of the calm and ruthless logic with which children bypass any bit of moral teaching they are not going to concern themselves with.

'What must you do to avoid going to hell?'

'I must keep in good health and not die.'

It's an example of lateral thinking, anticipating Edward de Bono by 120 years.

Unfortunately, as children grow older, this faculty becomes blunted because of education. So much of education consists of having inexplicable things done at one for obscure reasons, that it's no wonder the victims presently almost cease to resist. I can see that some education is necessary, just as the wheel is necessary. We have to learn to get into gear with the rest of the world. But it is remarkable how little education one *can* get along on. (This, incidentally, was a fact that emerged from a conference on the role of children's literature in education at

Exeter last year – a large proportion of the writers there had had little formal
education. And I don't think you could say of that group that they had taken to
writing for children because they were unequipped to do anything else.)

It is a dangerous thing to decry education. But I feel there's something wrong
with our whole attitude to it. The trouble is, we have taken away the role of
children in the adult world. Instead of being with their parents, learning how:
helping on the farm, blowing the forge fire, making flint arrowheads with the
grown-ups, as would be natural, they are all shoved off together into a corner. And
what happens then? We have to find them something to do to keep them out of
mischief. I think too much – far, far too much – of education is still fundamentally
just this: something cooked up to keep children out of their parents' hair till they
are grown. I don't see how you can learn to have a spontaneous, creative,
intelligent, sensitive reaction to the world when for your first six or twelve or
eighteen years there is such a lot of this element of hypocrisy in how you are
treated. And the worst of it is that this element is not only present in education,
but in reading-matter too.

There's a whole range of it – from *The Awfully Sudden Death of Martha G –*,
through *A Hundred And One Things To Do on a Wet Saturday and Not Plague
Daddy*, and *Sue Jones Has a Super Time as Student Nurse*, to the novels, some of
them quite good, intended to show teenagers how to adjust to the colour problem
and keep calm through parents' divorce and the death of poor Fido. I even saw
in a publisher's catalogue a series of situation books for *under-sixes*. I suppose
they serve some purpose. But just the same I count them as Filboid Studge. And
how insulting they are! Adults are not expected to buy books called *Mrs Sue
Jones – Alcoholic's Wife*, or *A Hundred And One Ways to Lose Your Job and Keep
Calm*. Maybe some adults would be better adjusted if they did. It's true people will
swallow things wrapped in this form of fictional jam. They will swallow it because
they have been conditioned to it all their lives, because from the first primer their
reading has become more and more impure – I'm not using impure in the sense of
obscene, but in the sense of being written with a concealed purpose. In that same
publisher's catalogue, advertising a series of basic vocabulary classics aimed at
backward readers, the blurb said that in secondary schools a surprising number
of children read nothing for pleasure except comics. Can you wonder, if the poor
things have had nothing but situation books handed out to them? If you are
bombarded with Filboid Studge, either you go on strike, or you become dulled,
you cease to recognize propaganda when you hear it. I'm sure if children's
reading were kept unadulterated, they would be quicker and clearer-minded

as adults, more confident in making judgements for themselves.

I can see an objection coming up here – some of the greatest and best-known children's books have a moral message. C. S. Lewis and George MacDonald: the Christian religion. Kipling: how to maintain the British Empire. Arthur Ransome: how to get along without parents just the same as if they were there. They had a moral message mostly because they were rooted in the nineteenth century when moral messages came naturally; everybody wore them like bustles. As we get farther and farther away from the nineteenth century the moral message has become more cautious and oblique, though it is still often there. Don't mistake me – I'm not opposed to a moral if it is truly felt – you can't have life without opinions, you can't have behaviour without character. I just don't like tongue-in-cheek stuff. Konrad Lorenz said somewhere that our intuitive judge-ments of people are partly based on their linguistic habits which is an interesting idea and I'm sure it is true. I certainly find it true in myself and not only on an intuitive level: from someone who uses sloppy secondhand phrases I would expect sloppy inconsiderate behaviour, whereas a person who uses vigorous, thoughtful, individual language will apply the same care to his behaviour – and this applies with double force to the written word. What I mean is that the author of a really well-written book needn't worry about inserting some synthetic moral message – it will *be* there, embodied in the whole structure of the book.

Let's get back to the Dickens quotation a moment: 'I am screaming out loud all the time I write and so is my brother which takes off my attention rather and I hope will excuse mistakes.'

The reason why I love that so much is because it was plain that it was written with extreme pleasure. You can feel his smile as the idea came to him and he wrote it down. You can feel this smile in plenty of children's masterpieces – in *Jemima Puddleduck*, and in James Reeves's poem *Cows*, and in Jane Austen's youthful history of the kings and queens of England – to pick a few random examples. And there's a serious counterpart of the smile – a kind of intensity – you feel the author's awareness that he is putting down *exactly* what he intended – in for instance, *The King of the Golden River*, and *A Cricket in Times Square*, and *Huckleberry Finn*, to pick some more at random. Really good writing for children should come out with the force of Niagara, it ought to be concentrated; it needs to have everything that is in adult writing squeezed into a smaller compass. I mean that both literally and metaphorically: in a form adapted to children's capacities, and at shorter length, because of this shortage of reading-time. But the emotional range ought to be the same, if not greater; children's emotions are just as powerful as those of adults, and more compressed, since children have less means of expressing themselves, and less capacity for self-analysis. The Victorians really had a point with all those deathbed scenes.

Recently I had a home-made picture-book sent me from a primary school in Cornwall: it was about Miss Slighcarp, the villainess in one of my books. Each of the children had drawn a picture of her and written on the back why they hated her. And then under that their teacher had evidently suggested that each should write down his own personal fear: 'In the kitchen, where the boiler is, the ventilator rattles and frightens me. I hate Mrs Rance next door. Every time the ball goes in her garden she keeps it and I am frightened of her. I am frightened of the teacher and my mum and dad when they are angry.' At first it was rather a worrying thought that my book had triggered off all this hate and fear, but then I thought, at least they are expressing their fears, and plainly they had an interesting time comparing their bogies and nightmares, maybe it was really a good thing for them.

This is another thing a children's story ought to do, I suppose, put things in perspective; if you think about it, a story is the first step towards abstract thought. It is placing yourself on one side and looking at events from a distance; in psychological terms, mixing primary mental process – dream-imagery, wish-fulfilling fantasy – with secondary process – verbalization, adaptation to reality, logic. A story is like a *roux* in cookery: by the chemical process of rubbing fat into dry flour you can persuade it to mix with a liquid. So by means of a story you can combine dream with reality and make something nourishing. I think this mixing dream with reality, far from confusing children, helps them to define the areas of both.

I said something in my talk at Exeter last year which I would like to repeat here: it is about the texture of children's books. Children read in a totally different way from adults. It's a newer activity for them. To begin with they have to be wooed and kept involved. And then, when they are involved, reading isn't just a relaxation for them, something to be done after work. It's a real activity. (Children, after all, don't differentiate between work and non-work.) You see a child reading, he is standing on one leg, or squatting, or lying on his stomach, holding his breath, absolutely generating force. Children's reading-matter is going to be subjected to all sorts of strains and tensions, it needs to be able to stand up to this at every point. Children read the same book over and over, or just make for the bits they like best, or read the book backwards; there's a psychological explanation for all this re-reading, apparently it fulfils a need for security, a need to make sure the story is still there. (Or you could just call it love, of course.) And children may read very slowly or very fast, they gulp down books or chew them, they believe passionately in the characters and identify with them, they really participate. In order to stand up to all this wear and tear a book need almost be tested in a wind-tunnel before being launched. Furthermore, if it is going to be read and re-read, by the same child, over a span of perhaps ten years – my children certainly did this – it needs to have something new to offer at each re-reading. It is impossible to predict what a child's mind will seize on at any stage. Their minds are like houses in a staggered process of building – some rooms complete with furniture, others just bare bricks and girders. A lot of children will miss humour in a story at first reading while they concentrate on the plot. Richness of language, symbolism, character – all these emerge at later readings. Conversely anything poor or meretricious or cheap may be missed while attention is held by the excitement of the story, but sticks out like a sore thumb on a later reading. Reading aloud, of course, is the ultimate test – an absolutely basic one for a children's book – and I must add here that any adult who isn't willing to read aloud to a child for an hour a day I personally think doesn't deserve to *have* a child. I know this is probably an impossible ideal – both parents may be working, and there are so many counter-attractions and distractions – but just the same there is *nothing* like reading aloud for enjoyment and for building up a happy relationship between the participants.

Another factor which I think is of tremendous importance in this enrichment of texture is a sense of mystery and things left unexplained – references that are not followed up, incidents and behaviour that have to be puzzled over, language that is going to stretch the reader's mind and vocabulary. (Words, in themselves, are such a pleasure to children – and even the most deprived childhood can be well supplied with *them*.) Talking about mystery, I recently came across a fascinating analysis of Wilkie Collins's *Moonstone* in psychological terms by Dr Charles Rycroft. (*Imagination and Reality*, Hogarth Press, 1968.) He begins his essay by saying that people who have a compulsion to read detective novels do so as a kind of fantasy defence against incomprehensible infantile memories connected with their parents – they, as it were, keep on solving the problem over and over to their own satisfaction and pinning the guilt firmly on to somebody else. It's a very ingenious theory, I'm not sure that I agree with it altogether, I can think of plenty of reasons for reading thrillers – but I daresay that is one of the reasons why we all love a mystery.

As I said before, there's a very close connection between writing thrillers and writing for children – I know two or three people who, like myself, do both. And since, presumably, a wish to keep solving the unresolved problems of childhood over and over characterizes the writer of detective fiction, as well as the reader, this ties in neatly with our image of the children's writer as someone with a troubled past.

As for children themselves – it is not surprising they are fascinated by mysteries. An immense proportion of the world they live in, after all, must be mysterious to them, since they are expected to take most adult behaviour on trust, without explanations – not only adult behaviour but anything else that adults themselves can't explain or haven't time to account for. And there's no doubt that children do love mysteries; they are poets, too; they have a natural affinity for the crazy logic of magic. And they like open endings that they can keep in mind and ponder.

Since children's reading needs richness and mystery, and a sense of intense pleasure, and dedication, and powerful emotion, and an intricate story, and fine language, and humour – it is plain that only one lot of people are competent to write for children. They, of course, are poets – or at least people with the mental make-up of poets: writers who can condense experience and make it meaningful by the use of symbols.

Not surprisingly, the best children's writers *are* poets – I wonder if Berkeley will find that out?

I've said that I don't think children ought to be filled with Filboid Studge. And that the best children's writers should be mostly otherwise occupied, and should be poets. And I've ruminated a bit about what should be written or not be written. But – except insofar as what I've said may have been a conscious summing-up of unconscious processes – I can't claim to practise what I preach. There's a relevant fairy tale, which crops up in many folklores, so it must be a pretty basic message, the one about the helpful pixies. I expect you remember it. Mysterious little helpers do the farmwife's work for her every night – spin the flax, collect the eggs, make the butter, and so forth; but when she watches and discovers who is helping her and, to reward them, makes all of them tiny suits of clothes, they put on the clothes, they are pleased, to be sure, and dance all about, but that's the end of them; they disappear and never return. That tale is a powerful warning against too much tinkering about with one's subterranean creative processes. I can't claim to write according to any of the lofty ideals I've put forward. But I said nobody should write for children unless it is with the whole heart. And I can claim to do that.

From *Books*, volume 2, National Book League, Winter 1970

The author confides in her audience: how a story grows

One of the most successful radio broadcast series in the schools service of the BBC has been 'Listening and Writing'. This article was originally a talk Philippa Pearce gave to children to tell them how an author goes about writing a book – in this case 'A Dog So Small', which many of the listeners would know. The audience, then, for this piece is composed of children (between eleven and fifteen) in school, learning how to write stories. Philippa Pearce gives both the story of how 'her' story emerged, and, indirectly, offers advice about the relevance of memory, individual experience, imagination, and first stage planning. In J. Rowe Townsend's book 'A Sense of Story' he quotes her as saying, 'I used to think – and to say in print – that authors of children's books usually wrote out of childhood experience, that I myself certainly did. Now I'm not sure. Almost, I'm sure not. That is, I think I write out of present experience, but present experience includes – sometimes painfully – the past.' These introspections and those in the talk are the more valuable from an author whose reputation is very high although her output is small. 'Tom's Midnight Garden' has been described as 'the best English children's book since the war'. A recent collection, 'What the Neighbours Did' shows new strengths.

Writing a Book   Philippa Pearce

A book that is worth writing, that you really care about, is only partly *made*. You may be able to make all the parts hold neatly and strongly together, as a carpenter does a good job on a box; but from the very beginning – perhaps even before you think of writing a story at all – the story must *grow*. An idea grows in your mind as a tree grows from a seed. The idea of the story is a seed, and it grows with the slowness of natural growth.

The idea of a story springs from your experience, from what you have seen and heard and done and felt and thought, going back for weeks, months, perhaps

years, perhaps even to the day you were born. So you would often find great
difficulty in saying exactly where an idea sprang from; it is much easier to mark its
growth – its gaining in strength and in size and its branchings out. That is what
I am going to do for one of my stories now. I shall tell you mostly about growth
and the encouragement of growth – the cultivation, as a gardener would say; and
there will also be something about making, as a carpenter makes. Making and
growth can go on together as long as the first is never allowed to interfere with
the second.

You have these ideas for stories too. You have them, although perhaps you
do not recognize them for what they are. Remember that these ideas may not look
like stories at all to begin with: you need to be on the watch for them, to recognize
them. Certainly my idea did not look like a story; it looked like a person, a boy who
longed to have a dog. It began with the longing itself, and at first that was all I
knew of the boy. I never did know, and never bothered to wonder, what exactly
he looked like: the colour of his hair or eyes, his height, or his exact age. I did not
care about the boy's appearance because I started knowing him from the inside –
his desires, his thoughts, his feelings – so there was no need to look at him from
the outside, as you do a stranger passing in the street. I knew that at the very
centre of that boy – at the heart of him – was his longing for a dog. That was my
idea for the story, and from that the boy grew, and the story grew round him
because what he wanted and what he was caused the story.

The idea grew in my mind in this way. The boy's longing was intense, so
intense that at last it created what it could not have: the boy imagined a dog for
himself. He became absorbed in a waking dream of a dog more wonderful than
any flesh and blood dog could ever be. The dream could not last for ever; later the
boy was alone again, without even an imaginary dog but with the old longing.
Yet that was not the end of the story, I was sure, although I did not yet know
what the end would be.

As soon as the boy existed in my mind as a presence, as somebody there, I
began trying out different scenes and scenery behind him. Some fitted, some did
not. This was like carpenter's work – fitting the right pieces together so that they
would hold. I tried the boy out, for instance, in various kinds of family and house
and district. Only one suited him: a large family living in a poky house in a back
street of London. I shall explain why this fitted. In the family the boy had two
younger brothers, who did everything together, and two elder sisters, who did
everything together; and my boy, in the middle, was always on his own and lonely.
That was why he longed for a dog as a companion. But he could not have one

because the house was too small and had no garden and there was too much dangerous traffic in his part of London. You will notice that in the finished story it seems as if the boy began to long for a dog *because* he belonged to that family and as if he could not have a dog *because* he lived in that house and that district. But in fact, in my imagining of the story, the exact opposite happened: that family, house, and district were the result of the boy's hopeless longing. They were the only ones that fitted it.

I tried out different scenes for the boy, some of them only glimpses, others complete scenes, as in a film. One of the scenes that came to me earliest of all was set on Hampstead Heath in London late one summer evening. I know the Heath well, and that is when I like it best. Perhaps that was why I put my boy there then. When everyone else had gone home, he was still wandering on the Heath; he was the only thing you could see moving in that failing light. There was absolute stillness, too, until he called to somebody or something. I liked the dramatic way his voice cracked the silence. Then there was an answering sound from over the Heath – a dog barking – and out of the dusky distance a dog rushed toward him, a living dog for him alone. The boy and his dog met, overjoyed, and then they went over the Heath together, their shapes melting into the dusk again. And that, I suddenly realized, was the end of my story.

Thus, long before I had the beginning of my story, I had the end. (It can be encouraging to have the end of your story early in your thinking. The end becomes a landmark, a destination to be aimed at.) All the same, this end that I had found asked more questions than it answered. It answered one big question: Did the boy ever get the real dog he longed for? Yes. But it asked others: Where did this dog come from? How did the Heath come into the story? How could the boy have a dog now and not earlier? These were difficult questions, and they gave me great trouble later. Already I looked ahead toward them with anxiety: they appeared as big gaps in the story. Not only were there gaps, there was no beginning to the story either. A story without a beginning does not look like much of a story.

This is just the time when you can easily begin to feel stuck. You may want either to give up altogether in despair or to *make* the story work out – to force it as you might force a lock. But forcing it would be just as fatal to the story as giving up – at least, to the life of the story. The life of my story was in the boy, in his longing. Everything had either to grow naturally from the boy's longing, or be made to fit it, as the family, house, and district had been made to fit. So the boy himself must never be forced to do anything. If I had begun doing that, the boy would have become a dummy boy that I moved about in a dead story.

No, the important thing at this stage is to wait – to think about your story only when you want to; and even then not to think hard, not to reason, but to let your mind rove freely, almost lazily. In any time when you have not positively to be thinking of something else, your mind can be wandering about in your story, exploring its possibilities. A good time for this is in bed at night. Falling asleep or nearly falling asleep frees your mind to try out possibilities that might otherwise seem too weird, but one of them may fit or lead to another that fits. Next morning, remembering, you may find that you have half dreamed the answers to questions.

I have said that you cannot force your story along, or you will almost certainly kill it or kill that part of it. But you can feed its growth. There will be things that you suddenly remember from long ago or things that you have always known or things that you notice freshly – incidents and details from your own experience, which you can try out in the story to nourish its growth. So the alert, observant part of your mind that notices what goes on round about you can be useful to your story, as well as the part that is meditative, half dreaming.

It was this noticing part of my mind that eventually helped me to find the missing beginning to my story. You will remember that so far I had only the end, on Hampstead Heath, and rather a misty middle, which was the boy imagining a dog for himself. I had nothing earlier than that middle, and so I had to work backward from that. Three things I had seen or heard took me backward to a beginning.

First of all, up from my memory came something I had noticed in a naval museum several years before. A section of the museum was devoted to Lord Nelson, and, in addition to a great many relics of sea battles, there was a pretty bronze brooch or medallion of a dog. The label said that it had belonged to Nelson's daughter when she was hardly more than a baby. Her father had promised to give her whatever she chose as a present, and she had asked for a dog. But her father thought – or perhaps he was persuaded – that a dog was too rough a pet for such a young child. So, to keep his promise and yet not keep it, he gave her the representation of a dog in bronze. As I read that in the museum I thought how bitterly disappointed, perhaps furiously angry, the little girl must have been. And now I thought of this again and wondered what had happened next. Did she go on longing for a dog, as my boy did?

The story of the brooch seemed to fit with my story of a boy and his longing. But the fit could not be exact: for one thing, a brooch could never be a present for a boy.

Then came a second thing (it had been there all the time), a little, old-fashioned picture of a dog, embroidered in wool, hanging on my wall at home. I had seen it every day for years, but now suddenly I saw it in my story. My picture might do instead of a brooch.

And lastly, even while all this was whirling round in my mind, I happened to have a conversation with a friend about seeing with your eyes shut. You can often remember the look of a thing more exactly if you close your eyes. And if you have been staring at something very intently and then shut your eyes, you seem to see it particularly vividly.

And as that conversation continued, I seemed to hear a click in my mind like the sound of a key turning in a lock, opening something. I saw the way through that my story could now go, naturally, without any forcing. I could now find a way back from the middle of my story, which I knew, to the missing beginning. In the middle of the story, the boy was imagining a dog. Suppose he saw his imaginary dog only when he had his eyes shut. Yes; and suppose this vision came in the first place from staring at a picture of a dog like my woolwork picture. He owned the picture; but – wait a minute – he did not want to own a picture of a dog; he wanted to own a real dog. Yes, but that could be the whole point, as it had been with Nelson's little daughter. The boy wanted a real dog, and he was given the representation of a dog instead. That would be a bitter disappointment, if he had actually been promised a dog as a present, say, on his birthday.

And then, you see, I found I had travelled backward from the middle of the story to what could be a good beginning: the boy's birthday and his expecting a dog.

Now, suddenly finding myself at the beginning of the story, I wanted to start writing at once. I knew there were gaps in the story ahead, particularly, you may remember, toward the end. There was some mistiness elsewhere as well, but both the gaps and the mistiness were a good way ahead in the story. So I did not let them worry me. I do not believe in putting off writing when you really want to, even if you have not got everything planned. After all, you can pause for days if you like between stretches of writing – between chapters, perhaps – and think ahead again. And if things do go wrong, you can go back afterward and put them right. Rewriting may be a nuisance, but it is less dangerous than putting off writing when you feel ready. The danger then is that you may forget what was at the tip of your pen; you may lose the excitement that would lead you to write in the best possible way.

So I started to write the first chapter. The story fell into chapters as I went along, and it was only occasionally that I was in doubt as to where exactly to make a chapter end. In the finished story there were nearly twenty chapters, but long before the end I had begun to see that the story was also going into a natural pattern of three big sections. These were made by the three different dogs the boy had, one after the other: the woolwork picture of a dog, the imaginary dog, the living dog that came over Hampstead Heath.

The end of the first section about the woolwork dog actually overlapped a little with the beginning of the next about the imaginary dog that the boy saw with his eyes shut; and this overlap came in the middle of a chapter. I remember the particular excitement with me when I wrote that chapter because I felt myself at a turning-point in the story. And a phrase of the conversation at that turning-point gave me a title for the story when it was finished: *A Dog So Small* – a dog so small that you could only see it with your eyes shut.

From *Horn Book Magazine*, June 1967

The author as exemplifying the actual transformed by the imagination and memory

·garet Lane
*Tale of
'rix Potter
·ne, 1946

Beatrix Potter wrote this account of herself in 1929 for an American audience. She had been asked to speak about the 'roots' her work had sprung from. In her biography, Margaret Lane makes it clear that the life of the author of 'Peter Rabbit' was far from being as straightforward as this account suggests. So that in common with all other writers of stories, Beatrix Potter makes one up about herself to hold the experience she used in her books. See how the needs of the invalid child, the audience for Peter Rabbit, focused the writing. Note the author's persistence in the face of publishers' reluctance: a conviction of worth which transcended rejection. Then compare this account with Maurice Sendak's, and see how the double facet of author–artist works. In both cases the remembrance of things read and seen in childhood is central. The enclosed world of Beatrix Potter is now open to every critical wind that blows, but the process of writing for children has a remarkable continuity.

'Roots' of the Peter Rabbit Tales   Beatrix Potter

The question of 'roots' interests me! I am a believer in 'breed'; I hold that a strongly marked personality can influence descendants for generations. In the same way that we farmers know that certain sires – bulls – stallions – rams – have been 'prepotent' in forming breeds of shorthorns, thoroughbreds, and the numerous varieties of sheep. I am descended from generations of Lancashire yeomen and weavers; obstinate, hard-headed, *matter-of-fact* folk. (There you find the downright matter-of-factness which imports an air of reality.) As far back as I can go, they were Puritans, Nonjurors, Nonconformists, Dissenters. Your *Mayflower* ancestors sailed to America; mine at the same date were sticking it out at home; probably rather enjoying persecution. The most remarkable old 'character' amongst my ancestors – old Abraham Crompton, who sprang from mid-Lancashire, bought land for pleasure in the Lake District, and his descendants seem to have drifted back at intervals ever since – though none of us own any of the land that belonged to old Abraham.

However – it was not the Lake District at all that inspired me to write children's books. I hope this shocking statement will not distress you kind Americans, who see Peter Rabbits under every Westmorland bush. I am inclined to put it down to three things – mainly – (1) the aforesaid matter-of-fact ancestry; (2) the accidental circumstance of having spent a good deal of my childhood in the Highlands of Scotland, with a Highland nurse girl, and a firm belief in witches, fairies and the creed of the terrible John Calvin (the creed rubbed off, but the fairies remained); (3) a peculiarly precocious and tenacious memory. I have been laughed at for what I say I can remember; but it is admitted that I can remember quite plainly from one and two years old; not only facts, like learning to walk, but places and sentiments – the way things impressed a very young child.

Does not that go a long way towards explaining the little books? I learned to read on the Waverley novels; I had had a horrid large-print primer and a stodgy fat book – I think it was called a *History of the Robin Family*, by Mrs Trimmer. I know I hated it – then I was let loose on *Rob Roy*, and spelled through a few pages painfully; then I tried *Ivanhoe* – and the *Talisman* – then I tried *Rob Roy* again; all at once I began to READ (missing the long words, of course), and those great books keep their freshness and charm still. I had very few books – Miss Edgeworth and Scott's novels I read over and over.

I only cared for two toys; a dilapidated black wooden doll called Topsy, and a very grimy, hard-stuffed, once-white, flannelette pig (which gradually parted with a tail made of tape). The pig did not belong to me. Grandmamma kept it in the bottom drawer of her secretaire. The drawer had to be solemnly unlocked, and I nursed the precious animal, I being seated on a crossbar under-neath the library table; the tablecloth had a yellowy green fringe, and Grand-mamma also had very hard gingersnap biscuits in a canister. I remember one of my teeth (milk-teeth) came out in consequence (on purpose?) while I was under the table. Children were much better brought up in those days. Thank goodness, my education was neglected; I was never sent to school. Of course, what I wore was absurdly uncomfortable; white piqué starched frocks just like Tenniel's *Alice in Wonderland,* and cotton stockings striped round and round like a zebra's legs. In those early days I composed (or endeavoured to compose) hymns imitated from Isaac Watts, and sentimental ballad descriptions of Scottish scenery, which might have been pretty, only I never could make them scan. Then for a long time I gave up trying to write, because I could not do it. About 1893 I was interested in a little invalid child, the eldest child of a friend; he had a long illness. I used to write letters with pen and ink scribbles, and one of the letters was Peter Rabbit.

Noel has got them yet; he grew up and became a hard-working clergyman in a London poor parish. After a time there began to be a vogue for small books, and I thought *Peter* might do as well as some that were being published. But I did not find any publisher who agreed with me. The manuscript – nearly word for word the same, but with only outline illustrations – was returned with or without thanks by at least six firms. Then I drew my savings out of the post office savings bank, and got an edition of 450 copies printed. I think the engraving and printing cost me about £11. It caused a good deal of amusement amongst my relations and friends. I made about £12 or £14 by selling copies to obliging aunts. I showed this privately printed black-and-white book to Messrs F. Warne and Company, and the following year, 1901, they brought out the first coloured edition. The coloured drawings for this were done in a garden near Keswick, Cumberland, and several others were painted in the same part of the Lake District. Squirrel Nutkin sailed on Derwentwater; Mrs Tiggywinkle lived in the Vale of Newlands near Keswick. Later books, such as *Jemima Puddleduck*, *Ginger and Pickles*, the *Pie and the Patty Pan*, etc., were done at Sawrey, in this southern end of the Lake District. The books relating to Tom Kitten and Samuel Whiskers describe the interior of my old farmhouse, where children are comically impressed by seeing the real chimney and cupboards.

I think I write carefully because I enjoy my writing, and enjoy taking pains over it. I have always disliked writing to order; I write to please myself. I made enough by books and a small legacy from an aunt to buy a home at the Lakes which has gradually grown into a very large sheep farm; and I married very happily at forty-seven. What are the words in the *Tempest*? 'Spring came to you at the farthest, in the latter end of harvest.' I have always found my own pleasure in nature and books.

The reason I am glad I did not go to school; it would have rubbed off some of the originality (if I had not died of shyness or been killed with overpressure). I fancy I could have been taught anything if I had been caught young; but it was in the days when parents kept governesses, and only boys went to school in most families.

My usual way of writing is to scribble, and cut out, and write it again and again. The shorter and plainer the better. And read the Bible (*unrevised* version and Old Testament) if I feel my style wants chastening. There are many dialect words of the Bible and Shakespeare – and also the forcible direct language – still

in use in the rural parts of Lancashire.
Sawrey, near Ambleside, 1929

From *Horn Book Magazine,* 5, (2), 1929

The author meeting the challenge of the form

From her experience of writing for both children and adults, Jill Paton Walsh draws a clear distinction between them as audience. The craft of composing for children is something she has studied deeply; her novels are not variations on a theme of childhood, but all different kinds of writing. At the heart of her thinking about books for children she puts the education of the reader's emotions, no less in her novel about the fall of Constantinople, 'The Emperor's Winding Sheet', than in her modern romance, 'Goldengrove'. Here she suggests there is an art form called a children's book but when it appeals to adults it is because 'the mainstream novel has turned its back on the story in a way that children's writers cannot'. Adults then have to see that the 'multivalency' of a good children's book calls on all the writer's craft, and what looks like simple skill is, in fact, significant expertise.

The rainbow surface   Jill Paton Walsh

Is there such a thing as a children's book? Is the children's book an art-form, distinct from other fiction, having its own particular excellence? Or is it just the novel made easy, in which everything is the same as in an adult book, only less so? If the second possibility were the truth it would surely be the case that all (rather than some, as Kevin Crossley-Holland recently suggested) children's authors would know themselves for adult authors *manqué*. If children's books are them- selves an art-form, albeit a minor art, then a writer may perfectly well have a talent more apt to them than to mainstream fiction, just as he may have a talent more apt to short stories than to novels.

From the writer's standpoint, there certainly is such a thing as a children's book, because a number of more or less conscious adjustments have to be made in writing them. The children's book presents a technically most difficult, technically most interesting problem – that of making a fully serious adult statement,

as a good novel of any kind does, and making it utterly simple and transparent.
It seems to me to be a dereliction of some kind, almost a betrayal of the young
reader, to get out of the difficulty by putting down the adult's burden of knowledge
and experience, and speaking childishly; but the need for comprehensibility imposes
an emotional obliqueness, an indirectness of approach, which like elision and
partial statement in poetry is often itself a source of aesthetic power. I imagine
the perfectly achieved children's book something like a soap-bubble; all you can
see is a surface – a lovely rainbow thing to attract the youngest onlooker – but
the whole is shaped and sustained by the pressure of adult emotion, present but
invisible, like the air within the bubble. Many themes can be treated indirectly
in this way which crudely and directly broached would not be 'suitable' for
children; perhaps one may hope their emotions may be educated by the shape of
the rainbow surface, in preparation for more conscious understanding of hard
things. I am thinking here of a book like *The Owl Service*.

The simplicity-significance problem is, however, a profoundly complex one,
to which there is more than one solution. In another kind of book the adult
statement runs alongside, rather than within, the book; a sort of exterior analogue.
Here I have in mind *The Mouse and his Child*, a book which no adult could read
without seeing in it a fable of our times, our century familiar with rubble heaps,
with destruction, with displaced persons. But the child with his merciful short
memory reads an unhaunted tale, a tale for its own sake, complete and satisfying
for itself. Indeed in this case, he may even be *protected* to some degree by the
make-believe quality inherent in humanized toys, small mammals, etc., as characters,
from the realization of the truth that people too have been battered, discarded,
exploited and hounded like that. Read in innocence, the book is a lesson in the
long and necessarily painful education of the heart.

Another type of solution is the use of fantasy or surrealism (dreams, magic,
time shifts, *et al.*) to make Freudian journeys to the heart of the interior. This is
not the kind of book I write, yet from my writer's viewpoint it seems clear that this
approach offers a whole range of interesting and fruitful solutions to the
significance-simplicity problem, at the cost of extreme difficulties in execution.
Penelope Farmer once pointed out to me that even the simplest magical occurrence,
if met in real life, would in fact terrify to the point of unhinging minds; she is
right, and this generates a continuous credibility problem about such stories,
demanding a high degree of literary skill to make them seem real. For no child
will tremble for the danger threatening a Hobbit, if he does not believe in Hobbits.
Likewise in stories which use dream there is an ever-present technical difficulty;

dreams 'float', and it is difficult to use them in an advancing narrative structure. Nevertheless, some of the most beautiful and powerful children's books are of this kind, when the writer measures up to the task – Catherine Storr's *Marianne Dreams*, for example, or William Mayne's recent *A Game of Dark*.

In this book the 'plot', with danger, the need for courage, the narrative tension, has been transposed to the surreal level, so that the reality of Donald's life appears as interruptions in the dream, rather than the dream interrupting reality. Adult understanding of this book demands comprehension of the relation of life and dream; but the transposing device ensures that the least aware reader following the 'story' will have his attention nailed at the level of nightmare. This book is as terrifying as self-knowledge, which is saying a lot. I do not doubt, however, that terror is good for children. I am in favour of exercising all the muscles of the heart. It is a device with story that brings off this *tour de force*. The story is indispensable to children's books – the necessary continuous thread to bring young readers through any kind of labyrinth. The children's book is an essentially narrative form, being in this respect much less versatile than the mainstream novel, which can do other things as well, or instead.

Let us look now at the current relationship between adult fiction and children's books. I think there is no doubt it is a very curious one. I am not the first person to be dazzled by the galaxy of formidable talents that adorn contemporary children's literature. In any other age most of them would have been let out of the nursery, and allowed to entertain the adults. Their talents would have been appropriate to the novel, when obliquity and indirectness was compulsory in the treatment of a vast swathe of adult experience. That restraint has now completely gone; it may well be that some contemporary writers are voluntarily seeking stimulating discipline in choosing to write for children. But we all work in a context; and the present context is one in which *any* book with a strong plot and no extreme erotic scenes, and *any* book dealing in magic or fantasy seems to many people to be a book for children.

The *Odyssey* has for 3,000-odd years attracted the serious attention of the most brilliant and educated minds, yet if it were written today there is no doubt it would be published for children. One can almost imagine the reviews: 'Mr Homer has a lively vein of invention and a fresh eye for detail that will entrance the nine-to ten-year-old ...' and then a disapproving eyebrow raised at the slaughter of the suitors. In this context it is not surprising that there is an upsurge of interest in children's books; much of it is not pedagogic, or parental at all, but is the simple pleasure of a reader enjoying himself. Really it seems to me that the defining quality of children's literature is to be sought not in children, nor in children's writers, but in the peculiarities of the adult market.

The mainstream novel in our century has turned its back on the story – and the space, and hopefulness, that good stories need: the epic balance, that to 'they wept long and bitterly for their comrades' always adds, 'and then prepared a meal and slept till morning' has come to be felt by the adult sensibility as unreal, deluding, wishful thinking. But the appetite for story remains. It has lived in humble forms before, when the grander literature disowned it. It has lived in ballad and broadsheet, and unwritten folk tale. For a while in the nineteenth century the novel in all its splendour served it, and now it runs in byways again, in spy-thrillers, and science fiction, and children's books.

Children's writers will probably always meet with a good deal of con-descension; some of it from people whose inability to see the multivalency of a good children's book hardly inspires confidence in their ability to read the kind of difficult modern novel that the children's writer does not write; we should blow our soap bubbles unconcerned; we are working in a literary tradition that goes back not to *Ulysses* but to Odysseus.

From *The Times Literary Supplement*, 3 December 1971

The author extending the form and the vision: showing not telling

The claim that a novel for children is a symbolic representation of their universe is nowhere made more powerfully than here, in the mildly sardonic tone of a man who has given everything to his art and asks only to be taken seriously. Alan Garner's books make demands on his readers as great as many an adult masterpiece, although they can always be read at the level of 'what happens next'. He tells in this piece how he comes to 'write onions'. 'It is my job to show, not tell.' Thus the rhetoric of his fiction is a challenge. This essay is also related to another theme of this collection: that 'fantasy is an intensification of reality'. The books which rouse most discussion are 'The Owl Service' (1967) and 'Red Shift' (1973).

A bit more practice   Alan Garner

'When you've had a bit more practice, will you try to write a real book?' This frequent question is asked in the context of my having written four novels 'for children', and by now there is a stock answer ready that seals off the conversation harmlessly, without bloodshed.

I don't write for children, but entirely for myself. Yet I do write for children, and have done so from the very beginning. This paradox may be explained by two levels at which the brain works. Hindsight gives scope for rationalization, but at the time, the conscious motive for an action is usually crude and opportunist.

For this reason any romantic picture of The Artist must be discarded straight away. I became an author through no burning ambition, but through a process of elimination which lasted from the age of sixteen to twenty-one, rejecting everything until I had isolated the only occupation to offer what seemed necessary: complete physical and mental freedom from the tyranny of job, place, boss and time. The fact that ever since that decision I have worked a twenty-four-hour day, seven-day week, fifty-two-week year is a nice irony.

No publisher is interested in an unknown with nothing to show, nor is it common to find the sympathetic publisher and editor for a manuscript at the first attempt. I was lucky. Two years to write the book; one year to find the publisher; one year to publish. Four years of dole queues and National Assistance. Some sharp lessons in the problems of human communication were learnt in this period, and one interview with the committee of the National Assistance Board was so hilarious (in retrospect) that it provided material later for a play. But 'success' changes public attitude, and what was once called skiving is now called integrity.

Yet why children? The crude, conscious reason was that, at the age of twenty-one, I could not imagine that I had anything worth saying to people twice my age – but if I wrote to the full extent of ability and experience there might be something to be salvaged by people half my age.

The result, *The Weirdstone of Brisingamen*, is a fairly bad book, but there had to be a start somewhere, and consolation rests in the even worse first drafts of the opening chapters, which I pin up when things seem to be going too well. At that stage I was indeed writing for children and the result was the usual condescending pap. Luckily I saw this in the first month, and thereafter wrote for myself.

Only recently have I come to realize that, when writing for myself, I still am writing for children – or, rather, for adolescents.

By adolescence I mean an arbitrary age of from, say, ten to eighteen. This group of people is the most important of all, and, selfishly, it makes the best audience. Few adults read with a comparable involvement.

Now, within this group, the age of the individual does not necessarily relate to the maturity. Therefore, in order to connect, the book must be written for all levels of experience. This means that any given piece of text must work at simple plot level, so that the reader feels compelled to turn the page, if only to find out what happens next; and it must also work for me, and for every stage between. My concern for the reader is not to bore him. Anything else that comes through in the book is pure bonus. An onion can be peeled down through its layers, but it is always, at every layer, an onion, whole in itself. I try to write onions.

The disciplines of poetry are called for to achieve such multi-level validity. Simplicity, pace, compression are needed, so that the reader who has not experienced what I am getting at will not be held up, since the same text is also fulfilling the demands of the plot. And my requirements are satisfied, because this discipline has made me reduce what I have to say to its purest form, communicating primarily with the emotions. Didactic writing is unworked writing. It is my job to show, not tell.

I make the first draft of a book in longhand, revised to the point of illegibility, and the result is typed, some revision taking place on the typewriter. This first typescript is corrected, and when it is as good as it can be made, a clean, second typescript is prepared, corrected and sent to the publisher, who sends back a long editorial comment. Any second thoughts engendered by this are put into the typescript, and I consider the book finished. Proof corrections are almost entirely of compositor's errors.

The internal activities of a story's growth, however, are almost impossible to describe. Each book is the first – or ought to be. By this I mean that any facility gained through experience should be outweighed by one's own critical development. The author should become harder and harder to please. And not only is every book the first by this definition, but no two books ever arrive through the same door. Yet, as a rough generalization, there does seem to be a flexible pattern common to them all.

It is this. An isolated idea presents itself. It can come from anywhere. Something that happens; something seen; something said. It can be an attitude, a colour, a sound in a particular context. I react to it, usually forget it; but it is filed away by the subconscious.

Later, and there is no saying how long that is, another idea happens involuntarily, and a spark flies. The two ideas stand out clearly, and I know that they will be a book. This moment is always involuntary and instantaneous, a moment of very clear vision.

The spark must be fed, and I begin to define the areas of research needed to arrive at the shape of what the story is going to say. It is a pure hallucination, but there is always the feeling that the book exists already, and the task is not so much invention as clarification: I must give colour to the invisible object so that other people can see it.

The period of research varies in length. It has never been less than a year, and the most was three years.

The spark struck by the primary ideas is all that originality is or can be, and the discovery of the point where hitherto unconnected themes may meet is the great excitement of writing. For instance, in the third book, *Elidor*, I had to read extensively textbooks on physics, Celtic symbolism, unicorns, medieval watermarks, megalithic archaeology; study the writings of Jung; brush up my Plato; visit Avebury, Silbury, and Coventry Cathedral; spend a lot of time with demolition gangs on slum clearance sites; and listen to the whole of Britten's *War Requiem* nearly every day. A major block in the writing was resolved by seeing Robert Stephens's performance as Atahualpa in *The Royal Hunt of the Sun* at Chichester.

Such an absurd list may give an idea of the variety of subjects to be considered, but perhaps a more easily presented example would be the fourth book, *The Owl Service*. It took four years of unbroken work to complete, after the spark, but the research was less diffused than in other books.

Like all the books so far, *The Owl Service* contains elements of fantasy, drawing on non-Classical mythological themes. This is because the elements of myth work deeply and are powerful tools. Myth is not entertainment, but rather the crystallization of experience, and far from being escapist literature, fantasy is an intensification of reality.

When I first read the Welsh myth of Lleu Llaw Gyffes and the wife who was made for him out of flowers, who destroyed him and was herself turned into an owl, it struck me as being such a modern story of the damage people do to each other, not through evil in themselves, but through the unhappy combination of circumstance that throws otherwise harmless personalities together. So far (and for about three years), no more than that.

Then I happened to see a dinner service that was decorated with an abstract floral pattern. The owner had toyed with the pattern, and had found that by tracing it, and by moving the components around so that they fitted into one another, the model of an owl could be made.

The spark flew.

Welsh political and economic history; Welsh law; these were the main areas of research. Nothing may show in the book, but I feel compelled to know everything before I can move. This is a weakness, not a strength.

I learnt Welsh in order not to use it. Through the language it is possible to reach the mind of a people, but just as important seemed the avoidance of the superficial in characterization – the 'Come you here, bach' school of writing. Presented with such a sentence, we know that the speaker is Welsh. We may guess that the author knows Welsh, especially if he inserts from time to time a gratuitous, and untranslated, line of the language. We can admire the author's erudition: but we do not experience what it is to be Welsh. This is reality laid on with a trowel, and it remains external and false.

By learning the language I hoped to discover how a character would feel and think, and hence react, in situations. The importance is not to know that someone is Welsh ('Diolch yn fawr, I'm sure', said Williams the Post), but to experience the relevance of the fact. The success or failure of *The Owl Service* here is impossible for me to judge, but I am warmed to learn that the publishers have been approached to negotiate the Welsh translation rights of the book.

On a more general level – the ideas have struck a spark, and the spark has been fed. There is nothing else to be done but to write. At this stage panic sets in, because the ground has been covered, and there just is no story.

Coming to terms with this phase has been difficult. The analogy of a computer may be apt. The mind is programmed by the long period of reading and note-taking, and it must then be left alone for the subconscious to scan, select and analyse the material. This has taken anything from a month to a year, and while it is going on I find myself unable to function at any but the lowest levels. The days are spent asleep, or reading pulp novels, and the evenings are devoted to the worst of television. Then a sudden, unpredictable, brilliantly original idea erupts, which makes me race around for a while, prophesying a great future – and then I remember where the idea came from. It is an idea woven from strands of that book, and that film, and that conversation, and that book, and those notes, and that book, and that book. ...

There follows a string of such unexpected flashes of worked-out ideas which have to undergo another process of shaping and selection, but this part is relatively straightforward, and it is possible to get on with the excitement of telling the story. The worked-out ideas form stepping-stones over which the book must move with simple logic. The details are never planned, but grow from day to day, which helps to overcome the deadly manual labour as well as to give the whole an organic development.

This has been, of course, merely a statement of intent, since all books fall short of the vision, and the original question is truer than the questioner ever knows. There is always the hope that, with a bit more practice, a real book will emerge. If it is good enough, it will probably be for children.

From *The Times Literary Supplement*, 6 June 1968

The author as creator of a social relation

Implicit in our concern about the stories we offer children is a belief, as yet imprecisely formulated, that these stories contribute to cognitive development and affective growth. It is demonstrably true that children form an attachment to certain authors to whom they look for 'virtual experience', whatever the verdict of adults about the worth of the stories or the literary status of the authors.

In this essay Professor Harding examines the quasi-social bond which exists between the author and his reader and the nature of the reader's pleasure that 'some other human being found it satisfying to contemplate such and such and such possibilities of experience and evaluate them in such and such a way'. Although the essay deals with the subject matter of literary criticism it shows how the dimensions of virtual experience can be examined from the earliest stories onward. It offers a model for an examination of how the adult writer controls the response of the young reader and thus makes more clear these areas of imprecision about what reading does for children.

The bond with the author   D. W. Harding

Any but the most naïve kind of reading puts us into implicit relation with an author. A novelist (or a playwright) may be directing our attention mainly to the action and experience of his characters, and part of our job is to enter imaginatively into them. But he is at the same time conveying his own evaluation of what is done and felt, presenting it (to mention simpler possibilities) as heroic, pathetic, contemptible, charming, funny ... and implicitly inviting us to share his attitude. Our task as readers is not complete unless we tacitly evaluate his evaluation, endorsing it fully, rejecting it, but more probably feeling some less clear-cut attitude based on discriminations achieved or groped after. Even the older discussions of Shakespeare's plays in terms of characters used to bring up the

question of his attitude to Falstaff, Malvolio, Shylock, for instance, and whether
modern readers could fully share it. Again, if we flinch a little from the histrionic
elements in the self-portrait in 'Adonais' we separate ourselves to that extent from
Shelley.

The more widely we read the more this relation with the author will be
influenced by comparisons with other authors; at the back of our mind, very
faintly perhaps, is the knowledge that there were different ways in which the
material could have been handled. Our awareness of a literature as distinct from
a collection of separate writers consists partly in this. Look, for instance, at
Crabbe's sharply realized picture of Widow Goe in *The Parish Register* and his
account of her death after a life of busy superintendence:

> No parish-business in the place could stir
> Without direction or assent from her ...
> The lazy vagrants in her presence shook,
> And pregnant damsels fear'd her stern rebuke;

then suddenly, in the midst of her successful farming, she feels her end upon her:

> When pleased she look'd on all the smiling land,
> And view'd the hinds, who wrought at her command;
> (Poultry in groups still follow'd where she went;)
> Then dread o'ercame her, – that her days were spent.
>   'Bless me! I die, and not a warning giv'n –
> 'With *much* to do on Earth, and ALL for Heav'n! –
> 'No reparation for my soul's affairs,
> 'No leave petition'd for the barn's repairs;
> 'Accounts perplex'd, my interest yet unpaid,
> 'My mind unsettled, and my will unmade; –
> 'A lawyer haste, and in your way, a priest;
> 'And let me die in one good work at least.'
> She spake, and, trembling, dropp'd upon her knees,
> Heaven in her eye and in her hand her keys;
> And still the more she found her life decay,
> With greater force she grasp'd those signs of sway:
> Then fell and died! – In haste her sons drew near,
> And dropp'd, in haste, the tributary tear,

Then from th'adhering clasp the keys unbound,
And consolation for their sorrows found.

Our enjoyment may be complete: we may be thoroughly attuned to Crabbe's robust simplifications, with him all the way. Or we may wonder if he has loaded the dice against her a little, perhaps in her sons' reactions, and whether the mode of satire justifies the abrupt, externalized awareness of her approaching death, whether the episode is touched too much by the element of convention and the ready-made in Crabbe's whole outlook. And then if it occurs to us that the Widow Goe has something in common with Mrs Norris we are bound to see that with the technique of the novel in the hands of Jane Austen a much subtler and more particularized picture is given, with the result that the reader's acceptance of Jane Austen's attitude will survive much closer attention and much further reflection than his acceptance of Crabbe's. Even without Jane Austen's known admiration for Crabbe it would be apparent that they had affinities of outlook, especially in their broader moral and social judgements, and a reader who finds both of them congenial takes them as allies, but still finds himself sharing Jane Austen's viewpoint more closely than Crabbe's, from which he stands a little to one side. This kind of relation with authors is, needless to say, only one element in literary experience; it is largely unspoken and un-thought-about, but it still forms an integral part of the experience.

Because of the importance of sharing or demurring to the author's attitudes and the values they imply we may be tempted to feel that we must establish what he 'intended'. But this would lead us astray. It may be quite impossible ever to know what his intention was.

Even if he happens still to be alive (and most authors aren't) he could perhaps tell us nothing, and if he did tell us something it might be irrelevant. For one thing we might have to reply that what he says he intended didn't come across, a fatal and final objection. More important is the fact that much of the author's intention exists in no form separable from what he achieves; it is only in the course of writing that his intention defines itself in full detail. And moreover he may not himself always perceive what he has said – there is no reason why he should. He may not, for instance, be able to expound the full implications of a symbol he has used, but they may still be vitally important to the total effect of the poem (or the play or the novel). It seems unlikely that Shakespeare ever worked out for himself all that modern critics have found in his plays, but probably many of these insights into what he actually did – whether or not he could have said in other terms what he had done – are perfectly valid.

Not what the author intended, and not what he was aware analytically of having created, but the work as he consented to leave it is the thing that concerns the reader. He is not likely to have been completely content with it. He may have reluctantly consented to consider it finished because a deadline had arrived or, like Valéry after years of work on 'Cimetière Marin', because an editor friend insisted on taking it away and publishing it. All we need know is that he was satisfied enough to let it go and acknowledge it. The full background, of experience and personality, that made him set to work is something he need never have thought out, and he might be equally unanalytic about the reasons for his satisfaction with the finished work. He could even be positively wrong if he tried to explain it – critical analysis may be no part of his creative strength.

So the reader (or 'critic') is faced with work that strikes him as more satisfying or less satisfying for such and such reasons (which may be very complex) and he draws other people's attention to them and invites them to agree with him about what he sees in the work and what he likes and dislikes in it. If he and they disagree the matter can never be settled by asking the author if he intended this, or whether he noticed that or the other in the finished work. What he intended and what he noticed are less important than what he did.

At this point we could easily make a different mistake. We could take the line that here, in this poem, we have a complex object, often an ambiguous object, which interests and stirs us in some way and which may interest and stir someone else in a totally different way, and the wide difference between one reader and another is of no account; there is no reason why they should see the same thing in the poem. This would amount to treating the poem as projection material, the equivalent of a Rorschach blot or a TAT picture, with no right or wrong set of perceptions and interpretations. It might be argued that this would be a satisfactory position: the writer's job would be to provide material which combined high ambiguity with high suggestiveness, which would stimulate responses of maximum intensity and minimum predictability. There would be no expectation of any consensus of interpretation among readers. The responsibility of the writer would be extremely limited; in fact natural objects, like flames, smoke, clouds, odd-shaped rocks or lichen stains on an old wall would serve equally well, especially if the spectator had taken a suitable narcotic or stimulant drug. This is the extreme towards which those playwrights tend who leave the ending of a play completely ambiguous; the spectator makes up his own mind, and what he thinks the play means is just as good as what the author or some other spectator may think. (This is of course an entirely different thing from a work – for instance Cozzens' *By Love Possessed* – which ends with a defined uncertainty arising from the situation the book has examined.)

The tendency towards leaving the reader's response very imperfectly controlled has been strengthened by several related lines of activity in literary criticism. One of these is the recognition, based on the suggestions of depth psychology, that a writer may be expressing more, perhaps in his symbolism or in the juxtaposition of his events, than a simple reading would suggest and *perhaps* more than he himself has noticed. And a living author, bothered by the enquiries of earnest interpreters and symbol hunters, may take the self-protective line of replying in effect, as Eliot evidently did, 'Well, if this is what you see in my work it's doubtless there – who am I to deny it?' A second factor making in the same direction is the immense effort of criticism to show the unsuspected depth and subtlety of great works that earlier generations have enjoyed in a simpler way; much Shakespeare criticism of the last forty years means that our response is different, and probably rightly different, from our forebears' response to the plays. And thirdly there has been determined and imaginative exegesis of writing – Blake's is the obvious example – that previous readers have dismissed as hopelessly obscure.

At first sight it seems paradoxical that these three lines of work, all of them aiming at elucidation, should have contributed to the acceptance of unintelligibility or great uncertainty, about a work's meaning. It comes about partly because some critics have pressed their interpretations to such lengths with such conviction and without any discrimination between the possible and the probable that timid readers dare deny nothing and, faced with unintelligibility, doubt their own powers to comprehend rather than questioning the author's comprehensibility. Moreover a critic who has invested immense pains in puzzling out an obscure piece of symbolic writing is much more likely to rejoice in his success than to lament the author's needless obscurity. These related critical lines of work have beyond all doubt justified themselves. Objections only arise when the trend they help to set in motion reaches the point of questioning the necessity for the author to exercise any control over the reader's response or for the reader to submit to any control, and therefore by implication questioning whether any consensus of understanding among readers is to be looked for. The final outcome of this trend would be to eliminate the author. It would be quite easy, instead of a play, to have a large number of scenes, sounds, bits of dialogue and human actions electronically randomized and presented on TV in unpredictable and indefinitely varying order, as in a kaleidoscope, and the impact of the sequences on different people would be certain to produce occasional striking emotional effects.

If this would lack something that we expect from literature we must ask what is missing. And what is missing is a relation between spectator and author. Implicitly we think of a work as being offered to us by someone, as having had significance for another person and not being an impersonal accident like the flickering of flames. Part of our own satisfaction is the sense that some other human-being found it satisfying to contemplate such and such and such possibilities of experience and evaluate them in such and such a way, that when we share his satisfaction some mutual sanctioning of values is occurring, and that we have this quasi-social relation with him even if he is dead or totally inaccessible. Abridgments of books and expurgated editions are unsatisfactory to the more practised reader because he knows that something has been interposed – some selective procedure – between him and the author. Although dramatized versions of novels may be accepted as a sort of entertainment in themselves, even the fairly unsophisticated spectator feels some uneasiness if he hears or suspects that the dramatization does violence to the original.

The existence of this relation between reader and author is confirmed by the quandary readers experience when an author revises his work in a way which they think spoils it. It was a reader who pleaded with Wordsworth to restore, after an ill-judged revision,

The light that never was, on sea or land ...;

otherwise, if we had wanted to keep the line in mind we should have had to do so with the uneasy feeling that Wordsworth himself had discarded it. In some cases readers have held so firmly to what first gained currency that they have ignored the writer's revision. Few if any of Fitzgerald's extensive changes in the Quatrains have gained either attention or acceptance. Most people still think of the first as being

Awake! for Morning in the Bowl of Night
Has flung the Stone that puts the Stars to Flight:
And Lo! the Hunter of the East has caught
The Sultán's Turret in a Noose of Light

whereas Fitzgerald's final version runs:

Wake! For the Sun, who scatter'd into flight
The Stars before him from the Field of Night,
Drives Night along with them from Heav'n, and strikes
The Sultán's Turret with a Shaft of Light.

Most readers who prefer the first version will feel a shade of regret that Fitzgerald changed it. Why should they? They still have the first version. But they are preferring something he discarded and they have to argue against the natural wish to go with the author; they have perhaps to distinguish the younger from the older Fitzgerald, the one who preferred dramatic suddenness of action from the one who preferred more accurate description of the gradual dawn. They feel the need to justify, one way or another, something that disturbs their usual sense of being with the author while they read.

In a similar way earlier readers of Blake had to reconcile themselves, when Sampson's edition appeared in 1905, to alterations in what they had supposed Blake to have written. In 'To find the western path', for instance, 'Sweet mercy leads me on' had previously been read as 'Sweet morning leads me on' and the change brought a shift of emphasis. Committing himself at all points to Blake's final version, Sampson added 'Instances will be noted where … these changes are the reverse of improvements …' Editors in such a situation, at least modern editors, don't cheerfully print what they prefer; they feel an obligation to respect the author's judgement. They do so, I think we must say, because a poem is not just a happening but somebody's offering; and this is the basis of the quasi-social relation the reader has with the author.

The fact of this relation raises the question whether biographical knowledge about the author is relevant to our reading of his work. Essentially, perhaps, it is not; but the problem is puzzling. The essential thing is that some fellow-being wrote this poem or this play; and that defines him sufficiently for the crucial purpose of our joining with him in the values he affirms, whether we join whole-heartedly or with reservations. And yet – if the author is identified and anything is known about him we do inevitably want to fit this poem and his other poems and the biographical facts into some sort of pattern, if only the pattern made by puzzling contrasts. It is for this reason that the simpler admirers of a writer, Dickens, for instance, or Ruskin, have been disturbed by discreditable biographical facts brought to light after a decent period of *nil nisi bonum*. (Even in Ruskin's lifetime the rumours of scandal led Mrs Gaskell to write 'I cannot bear to think of the dreadful hypocrisy if the man who wrote those books is a bad man,' *Letters,*

editor Chapple and Pollard, page 288.) But whatever our literary sophistication
the problem is a real one; facts of the author's life, once known must come to
mind as we read. Henry King's 'Exequy' is no less moving an expression of
grief and intended constancy when we are told that he remarried six years later,
but the fact adds a touch of wryness to the total state of mind in which our reading
of the poem is embedded. However, there is nothing here peculiar to literature;
in ordinary social life we don't doubt the genuineness of our friend's grief because
he recovers from it, but we do afterwards bear in mind, in the midst of sympathy,
that grief passes. Our quasi-social relation to a writer whose life we know about
is bound to include some of these complexities. We can hardly be unaffected,
one way or another, by learning that Proust's account of Albertine was based
mainly on his love affairs with Albert Nahmias, his secretary, and Alfred Agostinelli,
his chauffeur (George D. Painter, *Marcel Proust: a Biography*, London, 1965).

At the other extreme from the poem our reading of which is complicated by
what we know of the author lies the anonymous, often traditional poem. Here,
it might be said, there is no one with whom we can have a relation. But this would
be to overlook our capacity for social response – expressed in interest, concern,
sympathy – to people living long ago of whom we know nothing but their
situation and the fact that they *were* people. There was that coachman, for instance,
when the plague was spreading, who drove Pepys more and more slowly along
Holborn, and 'at last stood still, and come down hardly able to stand, and told
me he was suddenly struck very sicke, and almost blind, he could not see; so I
'light and went into another coach, with a sad heart for the poor man and trouble
for myself, lest he should have been struck with the plague ...' (17 June 1665).
We need know nothing about this coachman in order even now to feel some
concern about his fate. In the same way, with traditional poetry, which may never
have had a single author, we still feel that there were people who registered their
deep interest in the battles, the love affairs, the heroism, and the treacheries, and
we join, with or without reservations, in the concerns and the emotions their
ballads offer us.

If we believe that a work of literature creates a potential link between the
reader and the author we must believe that the author's control of the reader's
response counts for something. Exact control of every detail of the response is
out of the question, and types of writing differ in the extent to which they
circumscribe the experiences the reader can have while still remaining keyed to
the work. At least it would seem so if we compare, say, Pope with Shelley. But
some degree of control and direction by the author is essential. This amounts to

saying that unless we treat reading as a purely individual creative or projective activity there is such a thing as misreading. To say at what point misreading begins is always a critical problem – one that I. A. Richards has examined in an essay on 'Variant Readings and Misreadings' (in *So Much Nearer*, New York, 1968). He takes it that the distinction between the two is 'a chief operating assumption in most education' – 'the recognition, on the one hand, of the inevitability and desirability of diverse understandings and, on the other, their sharp contrast with the mistake, the inadmissible interpretation'. There is a question how far we go with him in this initial assumption that variant readings are not only inevitable but desirable too. The eighteenth century would presumably have been doubtful about any such idea; critics then would have been more inclined to think that what is correctly written can and should be correctly read. But we can at any rate agree that some variant readings are inevitable, knowing that the full effect of any writing, at least any emotive writing, must depend in part on the unique structure of personality and experience to which it is assimilated by each reader.

The vital practical question is how we justify our decision that a given interpretation is a misreading. Although Richards addresses himself to this problem he is not explicit. I think our judgement must be made on the ground of two sorts of coherence or consistency: first, the compatibility of the interpretation of any part of the poem (a line or phrase or word) with the rest of the poem; and, second, the compatibility of the interpretation of a word or phrase with its use in other contexts of the language at the period of writing. To focus the problem more sharply we can consider whether we have a variant reading or a misreading in Helen Gardner's interpretation of the last line of Eliot's 'The Hollow Men':

Not with a bang but a whimper

She sees the whimper as the birth cry of the newborn, heralding the life of religious commitment that Eliot entered on two years after the publication of the poem. In rejecting that interpretation I would argue that it fails to harmonize with two contexts, that of ordinary language usage and that of the poem. 'Whimper', a quiet, subdued, frightened kind of cry, is not appropriate to the much more sudden, wail of the birth cry, which is better conveyed by Blake's line on the new-born infant, 'Helpless, naked, piping loud'. Secondly, and more important, the hint of a new birth is difficult to reconcile with the desolate tenor of the poem as a whole; and even this last section which makes fragmentary use of Christian prayer sets the note of arid futility with its opening lines ('*Here we go round the prickly pear ...*'). The last lines deal explicitly with an ending. Self disgust and the failure of personal relation –

> At the hour when we are
> Trembling with tenderness
> Lips that would kiss
> Form prayers to broken stone

– these bring him to a terminus, an abandonment of living effort, which is signalled not by an explosion – he hasn't the accumulated energy which that would demand – but by the whimper of the miserable child at the end of his emotional tether. With hindsight, after Eliot's next poems, it is easy to say that 'The Hollow Men' expressed the nadir of despair at one's own efforts, from which some people do turn to religion, and that the new development was implicit in the poem, but hindsight would have been equally confident in a different reading if Eliot's next step had been suicide or psychosis instead of conversion.

It is useful to examine a disputable interpretation like this, instead of the gross kind of blunder Richards shows his Harvard students making, because it illustrates the great difficulty of deciding at what point a variant reading becomes a misreading. Eliot, living, could not have settled the question even if he had been willing; although he might not have intended the hint of a birth cry he would, once the suggestion had been made, have been in the position of other readers, having to ask himself 'Is this a valid reading in view of the meaning of "whimper" and the general tenor of the poem?' It would be tempting to say that this is a case simply of variant readings, each admissible. But that would be unsatisfactory. The poem becomes a sharply different thing according as you take Helen Gardner's reading or the other, as I think more natural, one. And this is not a valuable ambiguity in which both readings have their justification and give a complex state of balance or deliberate uncertainty and suspense. The clash is too sharp and comes too near making the poem into a piece of projective material, each reader's version being peculiar to himself and not an experience shared with others.

No objective demonstration of a misreading is possible, except perhaps where a critic has misunderstood the plain sense of a word or misread the author's sentence structure. Otherwise only discussion of the probabilities and mutual attempts at persuasion are open to us. But these are vital. There really are probable and less probable senses and implications of the poet's words or the playwright's sequences of scene and action. Admittedly we may not identify them and sort them out at first reading: the conviction that a poem is rewarding, or promises to be rewarding after closer acquaintance, may be strongly held long before we can support it with any discursive statement of its sense. It is this fact that may tempt us, as it did A. E. Housman in discussing some of Blake's lyrics, to say that the whole thing is just incantation, the magical property of words whose sense it would be useless to seek. Yet there seems no doubt that in the poems Housman had in mind the emotional effect is obtained through the meaning of words, phrases, statements – even though they may not be connected into one continuous logical whole – through evocations of imagery, reminders of experience and events, suggestions of imaginary events, echoes of other writing and so on. And all these things do convey fragmentary meanings that, taken together, define an area within which the sense of the poem lies, even though that sense may be difficult to formulate and different interpreters may put the emphasis differently. Unless we attempt to formulate it, broadly at least, we have no way of knowing whether we and other readers are valuing the poem for anything like the same reasons.

With rather more appearance of reason than A. E. Housman, Eliot has gone some distance in the same direction when he speaks of St J. Perse's *Anabasis* requiring that the reader should 'allow the images to fall into his memory successively without questioning the reasonableness of each at the moment; so that, at the end, a total effect is produced'. He goes on to say 'Such selection of a sequence of images and ideas has nothing chaotic about it. There is a logic of the imagination as well as a logic of concepts.' If we expand this cryptic statement it would seem to imply that some indication could be offered of the broad area of interest and outlook covered by the poem (and in fact Eliot does offer this much) and also of the main transitions from one group of images to another and what these transitions or modulations convey. Eliot says that the obscurity of *Anabasis* comes from the suppression of links in the chain of connecting matter. If nevertheless the sequence of images has some recognizable logic it should be possible to reconstruct at least in outline the main development of the writer's thought. That may well be possible with *Anabasis*, as it is with the Blake poems to which Housman referred. Trying to say – of course only very broadly – what we think the poet has done, what he is talking about, is the only way of discovering whether we and other readers are sharing the poem. Otherwise we are limited to exclaiming Oh and Ah and reporting shivers down the spine.

There is a knife-edge balance between too little commitment to a definite reading of a poem's sense and too extensive an exegesis. It may be very difficult to judge where to draw the line and stop following up more and more remote associations and recondite allusions. Winifred Nowottny's analysis of Eliot's *Four Quartets* ('The Common Privileges of Poetry', *Proc. Brit. Acad.*, Volume LII, 1966) left me dazed with its intricacies of erudite interpretation and despondently convinced that I ought never to have attempted to read the poems. I could only gradually recover the belief that I had gained great satisfaction from them even with my innocent reading, and I began (perhaps as a process of defensive rationalization) to suspect that a law of diminishing returns might be at work and that the added value of the furthest extensions of analysis was slight even if their validity could be accepted. The fact is that when you follow out all the possible associations of imagery, sound, meaning and allusion, everything does connect with everything else, and the decision – essential if we are not to emulate the over-inclusive thinking of some schizophrenics – to stop at this or that point, to decide that further allusions are too improbable or too little cogent to be worth pursuing, must always be arbitrary, a matter of personal assessment, not logic.

Up to this point it may have seemed that all the responsibility for making sense of an author was assumed to fall on the reader. Of course the author shares the responsibility, and when impenetrable obscurity or irreconcilable diversities of interpretation are met with the author has failed in part of his task, in his control of the reader's response. Among the great writers Blake seems most open to criticism on this count. One after another the modern critics have come along with their interpretations not only of the prophetic books but of the lyrics, and each of them offers an illuminating and plausible reading, but each different. It is heresy at the moment to suggest that the difficulty stems from any defect in Blake's writing, but when such diverse readings can be offered by competent critics the suspicion must arise that the work is inadequately defined and may have elements of confusion as well as complexity. A more or less adequate contemporary audience (such as Blake lacked) is a partial safeguard against such a danger by providing readers whose failure to understand can be taken seriously by the author. This is not to suggest that a great writer must be fully appreciated by his contemporaries – it is unlikely that he will be – but a very great disparity between his best potential and their best ability to read brings waste.

Although a literature may be said to exist even when it consists of works that are not read or are only partly understood, a living literature is much more than a collection of books: it has characteristics of a social institution, with an active social or quasi-social process going on between readers and author and between one reader and others. One feature of this process is a gradual extension in the relevance of a work of literature. When a great work has been vigorously alive for many generations it may seem to undergo an accretion of meaning, to have implications and applications for later readers that it could not have had for the author's contemporaries. I have suggested (*Experience Into Words*, 1963, Chapter 9) that this process can go too far; when, for instance, Madariaga sees Don Quixote as tilting not just at his windmills but at the whole vast mechanism of modern industry as we now know it, he comes too near the medieval readers who saw a passage of Virgil as an unconscious prophecy of the birth of Christ. Going to these lengths dissociates the reader's response from anything that could have contributed to the author's satisfaction in the work. On the other hand when a modern reader of *Troilus and Cressida* assimilates to it his knowledge of grander wars than Shakespeare's he is right in feeling that Shakespeare knew it all already – the bogus glory, the dubious motives, the waste and futility. Lasting works are always being given current relevance by their later readers; the question is whether the new reading is derived from the author's own paradigm or is a contemporary creation foisted upon him. If the latter, the individual author has been reduced to the mere initiator of a social process, and what we enjoy is not something he too enjoyed but a late stage of that social process. The work has become rather like a folk product, a nursery rhyme, a fairy tale or a ballad.

But if so it is a folk product with an essential difference, for it is now exposed to continuous revision along the lines of prevailing interests and attitudes. It may seem that this is no bad thing. It might be claimed as a gain, something like audience participation in the theatre, and in line with the view I have argued of literature as a process of social interaction. It becomes necessary to look more closely at the nature of this social interaction. There would be real danger if it were taken to mean that our society at any given moment of time were rightly engaged in remodelling literature in its own likeness. To some extent, admittedly, this process of remodelling goes on willy nilly without our intending it, a process of reinterpreting the literature of the past, rediscovering some, neglecting very much, disparaging this, overvaluing that, sometimes providing new insight, often bringing just a change of fashion. The sinister possibilities of the process in the totalitarian regimes are too familiar. But even when no political directive is restricting our range of exploration and disturbing our perception the ordinary pressures towards conformity and fashion are at work to bring us into line.

Opposed to this process is the fact that no tyrannies of uniformity have yet obliterated the uniqueness of individual people which springs from a great diversity of circumstance interacting with a great diversity of genetic constitution.

Though most of us conform in the main to contemporary values, we are nearly all deviant or at least harbour questionings in some directions, and this is part of our contribution to any society that is not static or dominated by a small minority. But we are not likely to retain any significant questioning of majority values in complete isolation. Solomon Asch's studies of conforming, in which an unsuspecting individual could be brought to deny the evidence of his senses when five or six people conspired to disagree with him, showed that individual resistance to this kind of group pressure was enormously increased if the dupe was given just one other member of the group who agreed with him in reporting things as they really were. A literature provides us with the almost indispensable ally, with the sense of there having been someone who felt as we do.

Although it is sometimes said that a literature enshrines a culture's values, the fact is that it includes a vastly wider range of values than any one period of society can compass, among them sentiments and ideals that have been positively rejected. It provides a record of explorations in interest and feeling, of compassions, brutalities of attitude, subtleties and crudities of personal relations, varieties of humour, conceptions of holiness, of tragedy, of generosity – possibilities of feeling inexhaustible by any one person or contemporary group. Almost any experience we may have and almost any reaction to it, however far from what is currently acceptable, will find an echo somewhere in literature and be understood and sanctioned by some writer. Shakespeare alone will echo most moods, from Thersites' to Prospero's. And if our attitudes to love are in question we have a choice ranging at least from Malory to Wycherley. Is this to view literature as a depository in which every deviant and misfit can find something to his taste? He probably can. And no doubt literature could be used to lend sanction to our most transient impulse and disorganized mood swing.

But against this two things have to be considered. One is that, to the experienced reader at least, no single author stands alone; there is Wycherley but there is Malory too; there is *Wuthering Heights* but there is also *Mansfield Park*; not only Keats but Pope. A literature does not sanction any particular outlook or scale of values; it is committed only to the belief that human experiences and our ways of evaluating them must be brought to light and looked at, probed and discussed. The reader must make his own value decisions, but he makes them in the light of a much richer consideration of human possibilities than one lifetime's experience in his contemporary group could have given him. The second check on treating literature simply as an indulgence of our own moods, a reinforcement of our own prejudices, a narcissistic reflection of our self, is that the greater works, at least, are organized systems of checks and balances as well as driving power. To find our experiences reflected in them and to see our impulses and possibilities of feeling explored, is totally different from projecting our own outlook and attitudes on to ambiguous material that we can interpret or select from as we wish. In literature we can seldom follow the whim of the person we already happen to be: we find our experiences set in somebody else's context and examined within the framework of his values. He is not controllable by us. In the end we must judge him, but not until we have followed his working out of a pattern of perceptions, interests, views of human probability, choices of action, glimpses of consequences. Responding adequately to a great work means becoming something different from your previous self. And this process of entering into another person's pattern of growth is an essential difference between real literary experience and free imaginative response to a barely intelligible or completely ambiguous piece of writing, however suggestive and stimulating to our own latent creativeness that may be.

From *The Use of English*, volume 22, number 4, 1971

The author as the maker of the personal myth

Lucy Boston writes most passionately about 'place'. In her books about Green Knowe the house is the chief character; it is also where she is living and writing so that it is the symbolic representation of all her thoughts and imaginings. It is possible to see her books as presenting a kind of personal myth on which this essay is a commentary. Implicit in what she says here, and borne out in her autobiography, 'Memory in a House', is the feeling that children make the best audience because their simplicity is a profound and untainted wisdom that most adults, preoccupied with material things of no beauty, have turned their backs on. In her writing Mrs Boston sees herself as offering a way back to this wisdom for a reader of any age who can share her singular viewpoint. The characters are absorbed into their surroundings and emerge the wiser. For a critic's view of this kind of writing see page 325.

A message from Green Knowe   Lucy Boston

Green Knowe, the house which is the underlying symbol in all my books, is where I live. It came into my hands when I was suffering from what seemed total disillusion. From the moment I saw it, the meaning of such a find began to grow and to take more and more into itself.

I get lyrical about it. I think of it as a miracle, and nobody ever felt that they owned a miracle, so I must be acquitted of boasting. It is so old and so easily contemporary that to succeed in reconciling these two ideas is to go up in the air. One is bewitched from that moment.

I am not a historian. You would laugh if you knew the feebleness and anxiety of my research into such periods of history as I put in the books. It is not the affixing of serial numbers to years, months, and days that fascinates me; it is the total loss of that fragmentation of time.

The outside of the house – it is in essence a one-roomed hall – is like a much-loved face. You do not ask yourself, 'What was it like when it was alive?'

It is there, answering all questions. Inside, partly because of the silence within the massive stone walls, partly because of the complexity of incurving shapes, you get a unique impression of time as a coexistent whole. I cannot tell you with what sense you know it. It is simply given.

In the first few days after I came to live there, a small boy digging for treasure by the moat brought me a tooth that he thought must belong to a sabre-toothed tiger. Like me, he was prepared for anything. We took it to be identified and were told it was a beaver's incisor. I put it carefully away in a little box, where it has since disintegrated.

Beavers in Britain are contemporary with bison and bears. What a leap the imagination has taken, and what a great lungful of time one has breathed in with the gasp! And still, every bad winter, the Great Ouse fills up the hollows of ancient waterways, and the whole setting of Green Knowe becomes marshland as before. Wild duck, wild geese, swans, and herons retake it as their own. The herons, so like the pterodactyls in their angular shape, are mercilessly harried by birds of more modern flight. Watching them, you are watching the Ice Age break up. The elms round the moat continually lean, tilt, and topple into the water, damming the flow. You could think beavers were still at work.

About the same time the midland marshes were inhabited by Peterborough Man, Stone Age fisherfolk, who lived in wattle huts, spearing and netting fish, and sometimes, with luck and organization, even killing a wild boar. I touched on them in a vein of reckless fantasy in *The River at Green Knowe*.

The moat is undoubtedly a natural watercourse, exploited for defence. When the Romans built the Via Devana, only a mile away – which was used for the movement of troops for centuries after – any steadholder would have thought of protecting himself. It only needed sense.

By Saxon times Green Knowe was already important. In 1008 the owner, Boggo, got into trouble with Hardecanute and the Church and forfeited his lands. I take him to be the father of all the Boggises. Hence Boggis the gardener. Boggo's descendants were reinstated as tenants under the Normans and were therefore collaborators and the enemies of Hereward the Wake, who crossed the Great Ouse at the ferry just downstream on his flight from the Norman court at Cambridge. When Tolly looks out of his attic window in winter, he sees what Hereward knew intimately.

One of Boggo's descendants built the present house, and a daughter married into the Norman family, De Grey, their landlords. The De Greys were very prominent Crusaders, and the Knight's Hale, as Tolly called it, is still a place for

Crusaders to return to. They would find it surprising, but still very recognizably home. It was so used in the last war when a friend and I ran it as a music club for the bomber crews of Wyton Aerodrome, who, having – as they used to say – no future, seemed to find great comfort in belonging to so enduring a past. I like to remember that the old house played a small but lively part in the last great crisis.

Of course, when I am writing, I lie freely. It is allowed in the rules of the game. I put back at will what has ceased to exist or sweep away what has recently come. I even bring in what is somewhere else. St Christopher, for instance, is actually in Cheshire, where my son was a child, and so properly comes in. When I wrote *The Children of Green Knowe*, I never imagined there would be a series to follow, and St Christopher has been an embarrassment to me since then. No subsequently story has really needed him, and yet he has been put there and can't be dismissed. Orlando the dog has also been unrequired lately, and dear Boggis sent away on altogether too many holidays. Neither could have coexisted with Hanno. Also, I must confess that Toseland Thicket is imaginary. So is the family group of black-eyed Oldknows over the fireplace – often asked for by visiting children. The eighteenth-century mansion and the fire in 1799 were real, and so is a picture embroidered in human hair.

I do keep to fact wherever I can and put in all the objects about the house. One small girl repaid me by saying, 'When you see so many things that are true, you know the rest of the book must be, don't you?' But I find most children at eight less naïve, perfectly able to understand that imagination only needs a springboard. I never cease to be surprised at their quickness in taking up a hint.

Readers of *The Children of Green Knowe* might suppose Green Knowe was my family home. This is not so. It came to me by accident because at that moment, with the war imminent, nobody else wanted it. My passionate desire that it should have a future made me provide it in the books with such a firm lineage. I do not know who will have it after me. I work to bring lovers to it, so that it may not go by default. I work desperately hard against organized local resistance to keep intact the stillness, the wholeness, the surprise of this living heritage.

To all children, and particularly to small children, a love of the past is natural. It is the soil at their roots. They have but recently emerged from the stuff of it. It gives them comfort, security, and a pattern.

Of course, rising adults of fifteen and upwards are bursting out at all the seams and want to throw away everything that has been handed down to them. That is as it should be. But the young of today are suffering less from growing pains than from a racial wound. A generation that invented and used the atom bomb deserves the contempt of its heirs even while they invent more and worse. If, looking at the world they were born into, they see the evolution of man and all the sufferings of individuals from the Ice Age until now as ending in the lunacy of hydrogen bombs all round, what value is there for them in past, present, or future? For time has all its values indivisible.

These young people have passed beyond children's libraries, but I believe their ideas and feelings seep down through the age groups more than grown-ups remember. To every child the brother and sister two removes older is an oracle who lets in truth from outside, beyond the careful screening of the parents, if modern parents screen at all.

I think the present pessimism explains why all my child heroes, and one animal hero too (always considered by me as within the hierarchy), are dispossessed and looking for what they have lost.

May I quote from the least liked of my books, *The River at Green Knowe*, which is also the one where this idea is least explicit. I must remind you that the three children have seen the Stone Age marsh dwellers dancing in honour of the moon in front of a wattle-built godhouse, similar in outline to Green Knowe and occupying the same place in space. Green Knowe itself has, for the duration of the nightmare, ceased to exist.

'... the moon had now met the shoal of cloud and passed behind it, so that from one moment to the next everything became dim and shadowy. A cold shudder of wind blew on the back of their necks and ears, and rustled the balancing surface of blade and leaf along the river's edge and across the wide meadows. They were standing at midnight, alone, under a sky that was there before either earth or moon had been and would be there long after. In this agonizing second of revelation that ALL passes, the bark of a disturbed heron caused them to clutch each other and jerked loose their tongues.

' "Where can we go?" asked Ida. "Where is there for us to go to now? [And from Oskar] We are *really* displaced now."

'Yet they turned instinctively toward the house ... because where else? Above its obscure silhouette the cloud was outlined with silver on its upper edge, where suddenly a dazzling diamond-white segment appeared and the moon came out. She dropped the cloud from about her, and round and brilliant as a singing note she hung in the centre of the sky.

'Under her lovely light Green Knowe was revealed again, gentle, heavy, and dreaming, with its carefully spaced bushes and trees standing in their known positions enriched with moonlight on their heads and shadows like the folds of Cinderella's ball dress behind them.

'The children gasped with joy and relief, and slowly taking in, holding, and keeping what they saw, they moved toward home.'

The young of the race continue to be born with their hope intact. They are popping into time at the rate of I don't know how many a minute. If I could be their fairy godmother, I would bring two gifts – veneration and delight, because you can't have one without the other.

Now, although an author obviously has nothing to give except what engages him, there must be no propaganda nor the faintest hint of patronage. This applies to children every bit as much as to adults. I deplore the tendency to come down to a supposedly childish level in subject and in language; to make it easy, to provide predigested food – to eliminate, in fact, the widening of the horizon. That will never form reading habits of value.

All art is an invitation to share the creator's world: a door thrown open or a mesh to ensnare. I prefer in this context the word *mesh*, because in a mesh every strand is equally important; lose one and there is a big hole in no time. In a work of art every word or pencil stroke or note has a reference to every other! They interrelate, foreshadow, recall, enlarge, and play all over each other to produce a specific feeling – *not* a moral. A word arbitrarily changed – presuming the writing to be organic – could change a book. It is difficult to calculate how much, since the whole process is so largely from the subconscious. When I am asked to alter the text of a book, I get panicky because I don't know if it will be merely a local botch, like a knot in knitting, or a fault running all through.

I sense that people are unprepared to consider children's books as works of art, and, of course, one can get away with almost anything, because children are such artists themselves and transform what is given them. On the other hand, they react to style with their whole being. I want to stress this. Style has an irresistible authority.

I learned to read when I was six and clearly remember going to school at seven and having my first reading lesson there. The august passage that was set for us, familiar as it is to you all, is startlingly modern. To a seven-year-old Algerian it might be, I suppose, her own daily experience. To me, in my Victorian innocence, it was supremely mysterious and at the same time *recognizable* (I believe in racial memory). This magnificent and beautiful message came to me straight from the real thing – the outside, non-nursery truth; and I received it with as much appreciation of the language as I can bring to it now. It marked me for life. How can we tell, when the seven-year-olds turn their clear-eyed faces to us, what is going on inside?

'Remember now thy Creator in the days of thy youth, while the evil days come not, nor the years draw nigh, when thou shalt say, I have no pleasure in them. While the sun, or the light, or the moon, or the stars, be not darkened, nor the clouds return after the rain. In the day when the keepers of the house shall tremble, and the strong men shall bow themselves, and the grinders cease because they are few, and those that look out of the windows be darkened. ... Also when they shall be afraid of that which is high, and fears shall be in the way, and the almond tree shall flourish, and the grasshopper shall be a burden, and desire shall fail, because man goeth to his long home and the mourners go about the streets. Or ever the silver cord be loosed, or the golden bowl be broken, or the pitcher be broken at the fountain, or the wheel broken at the cistern. Then shall the dust return to the earth as it was, and the spirit shall return unto God who gave it.'

Ecclesiastes 12: 1-3, 5-7

Children's problems are bigger than the ones psychologists assign to their different stages of development. Theirs are the problems inherent in being human.

From *Horn Book Magazine*, June 1963

Most popular author: writing as private screen printing from the eidetic image

Wherever stories for children are discussed, the works of Enid Blyton are mentioned. The vast output, the energetic marketing, and the appeal to a great number of children of a wide age-range rouse adults to extremes of polemical fury about the deleterious effect of 'unreal' characters and situations, or to passionate defence of a childhood sub-culture which children recognize as their own. No one is above the battle.

In the course of writing his book 'Imagination and Thinking', Peter McKellar carried on a long correspondence with Enid Blyton about her methods of work. He is interested in the relationship of the kind of thinking that occurs in dreams and similar states to the thinking that is adjusted to everyday reality. This is the passage which contains Enid Blyton's answers to the questions he sent her to ask about how she works. It shows that she is recalling in a special way 'all the things I have ever seen or heard'. This throws light on her writing as process rather than product.

Enid Blyton   Peter McKellar

Miss Enid Blyton's stories for children cover several different age ranges and in all she has written several hundred books. The cinematographic imagery processes responsible are of considerable interest. They are described, not as typical of literary creativeness, but as representing one interesting form in which it *can* occur. Miss Blyton reports: 'I shut my eyes for a few minutes, with my portable typewriter on my knee; I make my mind a blank and wait – and then, as clearly as I would see real children, my characters stand before me in my mind's eye ... The story is enacted almost as if I had a private cinema screen there.'

The strongly autonomous character of the imagery is apparent from Miss Blyton's further description of her psychological processes: 'I don't know what anyone is going to say or do. I don't know what is going to happen. I am in the happy position of being able to write a story and read it for the first time, at one and the same moment.' The authoress uses the term 'under-mind' to denote the source of her autonomous imagery, and interprets the phenomenon of her literary creativeness as a perfectly natural, though somewhat unusual, psychological process. The activities of the 'under-mind' are at times amusing. 'Sometimes,' she writes, 'a character makes a joke, a really funny one that makes me laugh as I type it on my paper, and I think: "Well, I couldn't have thought of that myself in a hundred years!" And then I think: "Well, who *did* think of it?".'

An interesting feature of this autonomous imagery is its resistance to interference. Sometimes Miss Blyton has been troubled when, as she says, 'Something crops up in the story which I am sure is wrong, or somehow out of place. Not a bit of it! It rights itself, falls into place – and now I dare not alter a thing I think is wrong.' Another interesting feature is that the 'under-mind' is receptive to directives from the 'editorial' functions of consciousness as to the appropriate length of the stories. No matter what length Miss Blyton is writing to, the story completes itself, and she reports, 'ends, almost to the word, the right length'.

Miss Blyton writes that this interesting imagery began in childhood, in what she called 'night stories'. She mentions her surprise when she learned that other children were not subject to similar 'night stories'. In response to questions she clearly distinguished what we might call the 'cinematographic eidetic imagery' responsible for her literary work from both dreams and hypnagogic imagery. While her imaginative characters may find their way into her dreams, the imagery itself is of a different kind, and she distinguishes it also from a number of descriptions of hypnagogic experiences sent to her by the writer. She adds: 'The simile of a "private cinema screen" is the best I can think of. But it's a three-dimensional screen, complete with sound, smell, and taste. This is why I can describe things so realistically in my stories "as if I had been there". I have been there – but only in my imagination.' Miss Blyton is not subject to other kinds of atypical imagery such as number-forms or colour associations.

One might expect that a person subject to such impressive autonomous imagery would interpret the occurrence in some a-scientific way. It is therefore the more interesting to find that this type of explanation is rejected by the authoress herself, who is sympathetic to our associationist theory that the content of her imagery is composed of rearrangements of past experiences. She reports recognizing 'many things thrown up from my under-mind, transmuted and changed – a castle seen long ago, a dog, a small child, words long forgotten – in a new setting'. Elsewhere she writes: 'There are, for instance, many islands in my stories, many old castles, many caves – all things that have attracted me in my travels. These things come up time and again in my stories, changed, sometimes almost unrecognizable – and then I see a detail that makes me say: "Yes, that's one of the Cheddar Caves surely!" ' Such occasions of recognition are interesting and suggestive for the theory that we can apparently recollect, and thus seem to 'imagine', many past percepts which we are *not* in this way able to recognize. In the same letter Miss Blyton expressed her more general view of her imaginative process: 'I think my imagination contains all the things I have ever seen or heard, things my conscious mind has long forgotten.' This view is consistent with our own thesis as to the perceptual origins of both the content and form of imaginative thought products.

It is significant that Miss Blyton experiences this strongly autonomous visual imagery only when she is writing imaginative stories. It did not occur, for instance, when she was writing her autobiography. This, she reports, 'was written in exactly the same way as most writers write – by thinking and planning ...' In a later letter Miss Blyton expanded this remark: 'If I have to write an article – something serious, abstract, or considered – then I am as slow as anyone else doing the same thing. I think hard – deliberate – write a sentence or two – erase one – rewrite – think again, and so on.'

Aware of this difference between her considered and imaginative writing, Miss Blyton sat down to write her first play without anticipating any difficulty. This is what happened:

'To my dismay and bewilderment, I could not get going at all. I began, read what I had written, knew it to be all wrong, and tore it up. This went on for two and a half days ... Then I suddenly knew what was wrong. I was using the same procedure for a play as for a book – and this was utterly wrong. (After this realization) in half a second my mind cleared, and I saw a big stage, in all its details. I saw Toyland there as represented by scenery. I saw exits and entrances through which the characters could come. And of course they came.'

It took a little time for Miss Blyton's 'private cinema screen' to become adjusted to the new medium; but when it did, auditory imagery was prominent, especially in songs (about twenty-five lyrics). Of one of these she writes: 'It was not a song I would have thought of myself, if I had *tried* to write it, and seemed to burst out spontaneously from the characters then on the stage (about twenty-five or so) so that I saw them dancing to it, and heard them singing it.'

The work of Miss Blyton is an interesting instance (of a somewhat atypical kind) of a process wherein the 'author' (as opposed to the 'editor') functions of creativity operated in a strongly visual way. As has been already suggested, this process of visual imagining, like other forms of thinking (however creative and original) owes its content to prior perceptions, often dating from long ago.

From *Imagination and Thinking: a psychological analysis,* Cohen & West, 1957

The author as fabulist: the nature of 'overt significance'

Any discussion of distinctions between adults' and children's books will always include William Golding's 'The Lord of the Flies'. Regularly set as a school text, it presents all the problems of ambiguity, of mature literary allusion, and of the complicated rhetoric of fiction, discourse, and growth to which Moffett refers in our first quotation (page 8). Yet it can still be read as a tale of 'What happens next?'

When he was lecturing in the USA in 1962, Golding saw a chance to reply to some of the standard questions students constantly asked him and at the same time to elaborate his idea of the novel as a fable and the writer as a fabulist offering 'overt significance' to his readers. This essay is the result. He makes a strong, austere claim for the contribution that imaginative fiction makes to the history of ideas. It is also related to the theme in section one of this collection about the author and the reader in the role of spectator (q.v. Harding and Britton). In this case the fabulist is concerned that his judgements be recognized as 'overt'. This gives a new slant to the old argument about didacticism in tales for children.

Fable   William Golding

'Nuncle,' says the Fool in Lear, 'thou hast pared thy wit o' both sides and left nothing i' the middle. Look – here comes one of the parings.' The paring in question is Goneril and she gives him a dirty look. No one has ever been quite sure what happened to the Fool later on. He disappears halfway through the play in mysterious circumstances, but we need not be surprised. He asked time and again for summary measures to be taken against him. Oh, the uncomfortable counsel he gave! 'Thou did'st little good when thou mad'st thy daughters thy mothers.' He tries to comfort Lear; to turn his mind from his sorrows; but ever and again the bitter truth will out. Notice that he never says 'It was a piece of folly to put yourself in the power of your bloody-minded daughters.' Always the truth is metaphorical. So he disappears; and though Shakespeare nowhere says so, it is plain enough to me that Lear's daughters got him in the end. For the Fool was a fabulist, and fabulists are never popular. They are those people who haunt the fringes of history and appear in miscellanies of anecdotes as slaves or jesters, rash courtiers, or just plain wise men. They tell the dictator, the absolute monarch what he ought to know but does not want to hear. Generally they are hanged, or beheaded, or even bow-stringed, unless they have the wit to get out of that hole with another pretty jest. It is a thankless task, to be a fabulist.

Why this is so is clear enough. The fabulist is a moralist. He cannot make a story without a human lesson tucked away in it. Arranging his signs as he does, he reaches, not profundity on many levels, but what you would expect from signs, that is overt significance. By the nature of his craft then, the fabulist is didactic, desires to inculcate a moral lesson. People do not much like moral lessons. The pill has to be sugared, has to be witty or entertaining, or engaging in some way or another. Also, the moralist has to be out of his victim's reach, when the full impact of the lesson strikes him. For the moralist has made an unforgivable assumption; namely that he knows better than his reader; nor does a good intention save him. If the pill is not sufficiently sugared it will not be swallowed. If the moral is terrible enough he will be regarded as inhuman; and if the edge of his parable cuts deeply enough, he will be crucified.

Any of Aesop's fables will do as examples to begin with. The fox who loses his tail in a trap and then tries to persuade all the other foxes to cut theirs off, because a fox looks better that way, is a situation that may be paralleled in human experience easily enough. But, you cannot make a scale model. This is why *Animal Farm*, George Orwell's splendid fable, having to choose between falsifying the human situation and falsifying the nature of animals, chooses to do the latter. Often, we forget they are animals. They are people, and Orwell's brilliant mechanics have placed them in a situation where he can underline every moral point he cares to make. We read his funny, poignant book and consent to the lesson as much out of our own experience as out of his. There are fables from other centuries, *Gulliver's Travels*, *Pilgrim's Progress*, perhaps *Robinson Crusoe*. Children love them, since by a God-given urgency for pleasure, they duck the morals and enjoy the story. But children do not like *Animal Farm*. Why should the poor animals suffer so? Why should even animal life be without point or hope? Perhaps in the twentieth century, the sort of fables we must construct, are not for children on any level.

With all its drawbacks and difficulties, it was this method of presenting the

truth as I saw it in fable form which I adopted for the first of my novels which
ever got published. The overall intention may be stated simply enough. Before
the Second World War, I believed in the perfectibility of social man; that a correct
structure of society would produce goodwill; and that therefore you could remove
all social ills by a reorganization of society. It is possible that today I believe something of the same again; but after the war I did not because I was unable to. I had
discovered what one man could do to another. I am not talking of one man
killing another with a gun, or dropping a bomb on him or blowing him up or
torpedoing him. I am thinking of the vileness beyond all words that went on,
year after year, in the totalitarian states. It is bad enough to say that so many Jews
were exterminated in this way and that, so many people liquidated – lovely,
elegant word – but there were things done during that period from which I still
have to avert my mind lest I should be physically sick. They were not done by the
headhunters of New Guinea, or by some primitive tribe in the Amazon. They were
done, skilfully, coldly, by educated men, doctors, lawyers, by men with a tradition
of civilization behind them, to beings of their own kind. I do not want to elaborate
this. I would like to pass on; but I must say that anyone who moved through those
years without understanding that man produces evil as a bee produces honey,
must have been blind or wrong in the head. Let me take a parallel from a social
situation. We are commonly dressed, and commonly behave as if we had no
genitalia. Taboos and prohibitions have grown up round that very necessary part
of the human anatomy. But in sickness, the whole structure of man must be
exhibited to the doctor. When the occasion is important enough, we admit to
what we have. It seems to me that in nineteenth-century and early twentieth-
century society of the West, similar taboos grew up round the nature of man.
He was supposed not to have in him the sad fact of his own cruelty and lust.
When these capacities emerged into action they were thought aberrant. Social
systems, political systems were composed, detached from the real nature of man.
They were what one might call political symphonies. They would perfect most
men, and at the least, reduce aberrance.

Why, then, have they never worked? How did the idealist concepts of
primitive socialism turn at last into Stalinism? How could the political and
philosophical idealism of Germany produce as its ultimate fruit, the rule of Adolf
Hitler? My own conviction grew, that what had happened was that men were
putting the cart before the horse. They were looking at the system rather than the
people. It seemed to me that man's capacity for greed, his innate cruelty and selfish-
ness was being hidden behind a kind of pair of political pants. I believed then,

that man was sick – not exceptional man, but average man. I believed that the condition of man was to be a morally diseased creation and that the best job I could do at the time was to trace the connection between his diseased nature and the international mess he gets himself into.

To many of you, this will seem trite, obvious and familiar in theological terms. Man is a fallen being. He is gripped by original sin. His nature is sinful and his state perilous. I accept the theology and admit the triteness; but what is trite is true; and a truism can become more than a truism when it is a belief passionately held. I looked round me for some convenient form in which this thesis might be worked out, and found it in the play of children. I was well situated for this, since at this time I was teaching them. Moreover, I am a son, brother, and father. I have lived for many years with small boys, and understand and know them with awful precision. I decided to take the literary convention of boys on an island, only make them real boys instead of paper cutouts with no life in them; and try to show how the shape of the society they evolved would be conditioned by their diseased, their fallen nature.

It is worth looking for a moment at the great original of boys on an island. This is *The Coral Island*, published a century ago, at the height of Victorian smugness, ignorance, and prosperity. I can do no better than quote to you Professor Carl Niemeyer's sketch of this book.

'Ballantyne shipwrecks his three boys – Jack, eighteen; Ralph, the narrator, aged fifteen; and Peterkin Gay, a comic sort of boy, aged thirteen – somewhere in the South Seas on an uninhabited coral island. Jack is a natural leader, but both Ralph and Peterkin have abilities valuable for survival. Jack has the most common sense and foresight, but Peterkin turns out to be a skilful killer of pigs and Ralph, when later in the book he is separated from his friends and alone on a schooner, coolly navigates back to Coral Island by dead reckoning, a feat sufficiently impressive, if not quite equal to Captain Bligh's. The boys' life on the island is idyllic; and they are themselves without malice or wickedness, tho' there are a few curious episodes in which Ballantyne seems to hint at something he himself understands as little as do his characters. ... Ballantyne's book raises the problem of evil – which comes to the boys not from within themselves but from the outside world. Tropical nature to be sure, is kind, but the men of this non-Christian world are bad. For example the island is visited by savage cannibals, one canoeful pursuing another, who fight a cruel and bloody battle, observed by the horrified boys and then go away. A little later, the island is again visited, this time by pirates (i.e. white men who have renounced or scorned their Christian heritage) who succeed in capturing Ralph. In due time the pirates are deservedly destroyed, and in the final episode of the book the natives undergo an unmotivated conversion to Christianity, which effects a total change in their nature just in time to rescue the boys from their clutches.

'Thus Ballantyne's view of man is seen to be optimistic, like his view of English boys' pluck and resourcefulness, which subdues tropical islands as triumphantly as England imposes empire and religion on lawless breeds of men.'

Ballantyne's island was a nineteenth-century island inhabited by English boys; mine was to be a twentieth-century island inhabited by English boys. I can say here in America what I should not like to say at home, which is that I condemn and detest my country's faults precisely because I am so proud of her many virtues. One of our faults is to believe that evil is somewhere else and inherent in another nation. My book was to say: you think that now the war is over and an evil thing destroyed, you are safe because you are naturally kind and decent. But I know why the thing rose in Germany. I know it could happen in any country. It could happen here.

So the boys try to construct a civilization on the island; but it breaks down in blood and terror because the boys are suffering from the terrible disease of being human.

The protagonist is Ralph, the average, rather more than average, man of goodwill and commonsense; the man who makes mistakes because he simply does not understand at first the nature of the disease from which they all suffer. The boys find an earthly paradise, a world, in fact like our world, of boundless wealth, beauty, and resource. The boys were below the age of overt sex, for I did not want to complicate the issue with that relative triviality. They did not have to fight for survival, for I did not want a Marxist exegesis. If disaster came, it was not to come through the exploitation of one class by another. It was to rise, simply and solely out of the nature of the brute. The overall picture was to be the tragic lesson that the English have had to learn over a period of one hundred years; that one lot of people is inherently like any other lot of people; and that the only enemy of man is inside him. So the picture I had in my mind of the change to be brought about was exemplified by two pictures of the little boy Ralph. The first is when he discovers he is on a real desert island and delights in the discovery.

'He jumped down from the terrace. The sand was thick over his black shoes and the heat hit him. He became conscious of the weight of clothes, kicked his shoes off fiercely and ripped off each stocking with its elastic garter in a single movement. Then he leapt back on the terrace, pulled off his shirt, and stood there among the skull-like coconuts with green shadows from the palms and the forest sliding over his skin. He undid the snake-clasp of his belt, lugged off his shorts and pants, and stood there naked, looking at the dazzling beach and the water.

'He was old enough, twelve years and a few months, to have lost the prominent tummy of childhood; and not yet old enough for adolescence to have made him awkward. You could see now that he might make a boxer, as far as width and heaviness of shoulders went, but there was a mildness about his mouth and eyes that proclaimed no devil. He patted the palm trunk softly; and forced at last to believe in the reality of the island, laughed delightedly again, and stood on his head. He turned neatly on to his feet, jumped down to the beach, knelt, and swept a double armful of sand into a pile against his chest. Then he sat back and looked at the water with bright, excited eyes.'

This is innocence and hope; but the picture changes and the book is so designed that our last view of Ralph is very different. By the end, he has come to understand the fallen nature of man, and that what stands between him and happiness comes from inside him; a trite lesson as I have said; but one which I believed needed urgently to be driven home.

Yet if one takes the whole of the human condition as background of a fable it becomes hopelessly complex, though I worked the book out in detail.

Let us take, for example, the word 'history'. It seems to me that the word has two common meanings, each of them of aweful importance. First there is what might be called academic, or if you like campus history. To my mind this is not only of importance, but of supreme importance. It is that objective yet devoted stare with which humanity observes its own past; and in that stare, that attempt to see how things have become what they are, where they went wrong, and where right, that our only hope lies of having some control over our own future. The exploration of the physical world is an art, with all the attendant aesthetic pleasures; but the knowledge we get from it is not immediately applicable to the problems that we have on hand. But history is a kind of self-knowledge, and it may be with care that self-knowledge will be sufficient to give us the right clue to our behaviour in the future. I say a clue; for we stand today in the same general condition as we have always stood, under sentence of death.

But there is another kind of force which we call history; and how uncontrollable that force is, even in the most detached of men, was amusingly demonstrated to me only the other day. I was being driven over the last battle-ground of the war between the States, a historical episode which I am able to observe with some objectivity. My driver was a Southerner and scholar. His

exposition to me of the situation was a model of historical balance. He explained
to me how the South had embarked on a war which they could not hope to win,
in support of a pattern of society which could not hope to survive. He was,
perhaps a little harder on the South than a Northerner would have been; but
judicially so. As the day wore on, his voice began to return to its origins. Emotion
crept in – not very far, because of course he was a scholar, and scholars are
detached and unemotional are they not ? – At a discreet forty miles an hour we
followed the wavering fortunes of battle down into Virginia. Here, he told me,
Lee had performed that last incredible tactical feat in the defence of Richmond;
here, Grant had sidestepped – but what was this ? His voice had lost all pretence
of scholarship. Insensibly the speed of the car had increased. When we came to
the Appomatox, this educated, and indeed rather cynical man grunted – 'Aw,
shucks!' and drove past the place where Lee surrendered to Grant at seventy-five
miles an hour.

This is a different force from campus history. It is history felt in the blood
and bones. Sometimes it is dignified by a pretty name, but I am not sure in my
own mind, that it is ever anything but pernicious. However this is a political and
historical question which we need not settle here and now. My point is that
however pathetic or amusing we find these lesser manifestations of prejudice,
when they go beyond a certain point no one in the world can doubt that they are
wholly evil. Jew and Arab in the name of religion, Jew and Nordic in the name of
race, Negro and white in the name of God knows what.

And it is not only these larger more spectacular examples of frozen history
which do the damage. I am a European and an optimist. But I do not believe
that history is only a nominal thing. There have been many years when as I
contemplate our national frontiers, I have fallen into something like despair.
Frontiers in Europe may be likened to wrinkles in an aged face, and all that will
remove them is the death of the body. Now I know you will point out to me that
Europe is already moving towards some confederation; and I would agree and
add that that confederation has the full support of every man of goodwill and
commonsense. But the wrinkles are so deep. And I cannot think of a confederation
in history, where the members voluntarily bowed to supranational authority
without at least one of the members fighting a war to contest it. In Europe there
is and has been, a terrible fund of national ill will, handed down from generation
to generation. There are habits of feeling which have acquired the force of
instinct. These habits of feeling may be encouraged in school or college, but they
are rarely taught there. They are an unconscious legacy wished on children by their

parents. A woman, like one old French lady I knew, who had gone through the
business of being conquered three times, in 1870, 1914, and 1940, had acquired an
attitude to the Germans which was a hate so deep that she shook when she thought
of them. Indeed, as I make these words, I am aware in myself of resentments,
indignations, and perhaps fears which have nothing to do with today, with the
England and Germany of today, in a word, with reality, but are there, nevertheless.
I got them from off-campus history; and unless I make a conscious effort I shall
hand them on. These impulses, prejudices, even perhaps these *just* hates which are
nevertheless backward-looking are what parents luxuriating in a cheap emotion
can wish on their children without being properly conscious of it and so perpetuate
division through the generations. A less painful example of this is the way in
which, where one Englishman and one American are gathered together, that
sad old story of the eighteenth century will raise its head, so that the American
whose ancestors have perhaps been in the States since 1911 will be arrogating to
himself all the splendours of that struggle, while the Englishman who may have
spent his life in the pursuit and furtherance of liberal principles may find himself
forced into the ridiculous position of defending his fellow Englishman George III.
My own technique on these occasions, is to start talking about the vicious
occupation of my country by the Romans and the splendid resistance to them by
our own heroes, Queen Boadicea and King Arthur. Some of these examples are
silly, meant to be silly, and are understood as silly by the contestants. They are
less severe than the partisanship roused by games of one sort or another;
nevertheless they are symptomatic. We ought not to underestimate the power or
the destructiveness of these emotions. The one country to leave the British
Commonwealth of Nations in recent centuries, is the Union of South Africa,
forced out by a universal, if sometimes smug condemnation of her policy towards
her own black population. But a quarter of a century ago England and Australia
were shaken to the very roots of their common interests by a game of cricket.
Those of you who find this incredible, either do not understand the tenuousness
of the bond that holds Australia and England together, or else do not understand
the fierce passions that can be roused by cricket. But the point is that many
Englishmen and Australians did in fact begin to think of each other as objectionable, irrational, ill-disposed, vindictive. For a moment each nation, or at least the
sillier members of each – and there are always enough silly people in any country
to form a sizable mass-movement – each nation stood squarely behind their
culture's heroes, the one a very fast and accurate bowler, the other a batsman who
objected to being struck repeatedly on the head. If the random agglomeration

of nations which is the Commonwealth seems to you to have any power for good, you may consider it lucky that England and Australia are twelve thousand miles apart. Had they been separated, not by half a world, but by a relatively small ocean, Australia might have taken her bat and gone off fiercely to play cricket by herself. It was George Orwell who commented on the destructive force of international contests. Anyone who has watched a television programme of a game between two European nations must agree with him. There's savagery for you. There's bloodlust. There's ugly nationalism raising its gorgon head.

What I am trying to do is to add together those elements, some horrible, some merely funny, but all significant, which I suppose to be the forces of off-campus history. They are a failure of human sympathy, ignorance of facts, the objectivizing of our own inadequacies so as to make a scapegoat. At moments of optimism I have felt that education and perhaps a miracle or two would be sufficient to remove their more dangerous elements. When I feel pessimistic, then they seem to constitute a trap into which humanity has got itself with a dreary inevitability much as the dinosaur trapped itself in its own useless armour. For if humanity has a future on this planet of a hundred million years, it is unthinkable that it should spend those aeons in a ferment of national self-satisfaction and chauvinistic idiocies. I was feeling pessimistic when I tried to include a sign for this thing in a fable.

The point about off-campus history is that it is always dead. It is a cloak of national prestige which the uneducated pull round their shoulders to keep off the wind of personal self-knowledge. It is a dead thing handed on, but dead though it is, it will not lie down. It is a monstrous creature descending to us from our ancestors, producing nothing but disunity, chaos. War and disorder prolong in it the ghastly and ironic semblance of life. All the marching and counter-marching, the flags, the heroism and cruelty are galvanic twitches induced in its slaves and subjects by that hideous, parody thing. When I constructed a sign for it, therefore, it had to be something that was dead but had a kind of life. It had to be presented to my island of children by the world of grown-ups. There was only one way in which I could do this. First I must take the children at a moment when mature council and authority might have saved them as on so many occasions we might have saved our own children, might have been saved ourselves. Since a novelist ought not preach overtly in a fable, the situation had to be highlighted by the children having some dim knowledge that wisdom, that commonsense even, is to be found in the world of grown-ups. They must yearn for it, now they have begun to find the inadequacy of their own powers. I took a moment therefore, when they had tried to hold a council meeting to discuss ways and means but had found that other questions came up – questions which they would sooner have ignored. Finally the meeting breaks down. The children who are retrogressing more rapidly have gone off into the war dance with which they fortify their own sense of power and togetherness. It is dark. The few remainder, puzzled, anxious, surrounded by half-perceived threats and mysteries; faced with a problem which once looked so simple of solution, the maintenance of a fire on the mountain, but which proved to be too much for them – these few, men of goodwill, are searching for some hope, some power for good, some commonsense.

'If only they could get a message to us,' cried Ralph desperately. 'If only they could send us something grown-up – a sign or something.'

What the grown-ups send them is indeed a sign, a sign to fit into the fable; but in the fable sense, that arbitrary sign stands for off-campus history, the thing which threatens every child everywhere, the history of blood and intolerance, of ignorance and prejudice, the thing which is dead but won't lie down.

'There was no light left save that of the stars. The three bigger boys went together to the next shelter. They lay restlessly and noisily among the dry leaves, watching the patch of stars that was the opening towards the lagoon. Sometimes a little 'un cried out from the other shelters and once a big 'un spoke in the dark. Then they too fell asleep.

'A sliver of moon rose over the horizon, hardly large enough to make a path of light even when it sat right down on the water; but there were other lights in the sky, that moved fast, winked or went out, though not even a faint popping came down from the battle fought at ten miles height. But a sign came down from the world of grown-ups, though at that time there was no child awake to read it. There was a sudden bright explosion and a corkscrew trail across the sky; then darkness again and stars. There was a speck above the island, a figure dropping swiftly beneath a parachute, a figure that hung with dangling limbs. The changing winds of various altitudes took the figure where they would. Then, three miles up the wind steadied and bore it in a descending curve round the sky and swept it in a great slant across the reef and the lagoon towards the mountain. The figure fell and crumpled among the blue flowers of the mountainside, but now there was a gentle breeze at this height too and the parachute flopped and banged and pulled. So the figure, with feet that dragged behind it, slid up the mountain. Yard by yard, puff by puff, the breeze hauled the figure through the blue flowers, over the boulders and red stones, till it lay huddled among the shattered rocks of the mountain top. Here the breeze was fitful and allowed the strings of the parachute to tangle and festoon; and the figure sat, its helmeted head between its knees, held by a complication of lines. When the breeze blew, the lines would strain taut and some accident of this pull lifted the head and chest upright so that the figure seemed to peer across the brow of the mountain. Then, each time the wind dropped, the lines would slacken and the figure bow forward again, sinking its head between its knees. So as the stars moved across the sky, the figure sat on the mountain top and bowed and sank and bowed again.'

I have no time to prolong this quotation, nor is it necessary, since I am glad to say the book itself remains in print. But it is perhaps worth noticing that this figure which is dead but won't lie down, falls on the very place where the children are making their one constructive attempt to get themselves helped. It dominates the mountain top and so prevents them keeping a fire alight there as a signal. To take an actual historical example, the fire is perhaps like the long defunct but once much hoped-over League of Nations. That great effort at international sanity fell before the pressures of nationalism which were founded in ignorance, jealousy, greed – before the pressures of off-campus history which was dead but would not lie down.

Having got thus far, I must admit to a number of qualifications, not in the theory itself but in the result. Fable, as a method, depends on two things neither of which can be relied on. First the writer has to have a coherent picture of the subject; but if he takes the whole human condition as his subject, his picture is likely to get a little dim at the edges. Next a fable can only be taken as far as the parable, the parallel is exact; and these literary parallels between the fable and the underlying life do not extend to infinity. It is not just that a small-scale model cannot be exact in every detail. It is because every sort of life, once referred to, brings up associations of its own within its own limits which may have no significant relationships with the matter under consideration. Thus, the fable is most successful *qua* fable, when it works within strict limits. George Orwell's *Animal Farm* confines itself to consideration and satire of a given political situation. In other words, the fable must be under strict control. Yet it is at this very point, that the imagination can get out of hand.

I had better explain that I am not referring now to normal exercises of imagination, which we are told is the selection and rearrangement of pictures already latent in the mind. There is another possible experience, which some may think admirable and others pathological. I remember, many years ago, trying to bore a hole with a drilling machine through armour plate. Armour plate is constructed to resist just such an operation – a point which had escaped me for the time being. In my extreme ignorance, I put the drill in the chuck, held by half an inch of its extreme end. I seized the handle and brought the revolving drill down on the armour. It wobbled for a second; then there was a sharp explosion, the drill departed in every direction, breaking two windows and taking a piece of my uniform with it. Wiser now, I held the next drill deep in the chuck so that only the point protruded, held it mercilessly in those steel jaws and brought it down on the armour with the power behind it of many hundred horses. This operation was successful. I made a small red-hot hole in the armour, though of course I ruined the drill. If this small anecdote seems fatuous, I assure you that it is the best image I know for one sort of imaginative process. There is the same merciless concentration, the same will, the same apparently impenetrable target, the same pressure applied steadily to one small point. It is not a normal mode of life; or we should find ourselves posting letters in letterboxes which were not there. But it happens sometimes and it works. The point of the fable under imaginative consideration does not become more real than the real world, it shoves the real world on one side. The author becomes a spectator, appalled or delighted, but a spectator. At this moment, how can he be sure that he is keeping a relationship between the fable and the moralized world, when he is only conscious of one of them? I believe he cannot be sure. This experience, excellent for the novel which does not claim to be a parable must surely lead to a distortion of the fable. Yet is it not the experience which we expect and hope the novelist to have?

It might be appropriate now to give an example of a situation in which something like this happened. For reasons it is not necessary to specify, I included a Christ-figure in my fable. This is the little boy Simon, solitary, stammering, a lover of mankind, a visionary, who reaches commonsense attitudes not by reason but by intuition. Of all the boys, he is the only one who feels the need to be alone and goes every now and then into the bushes. Since this book is one that is highly and diversely explicable, you would not believe the various interpretations that have been given of Simon's going into the bushes. But go he does, and prays, as the child Jean Vianney would go, and some other saints – though not many. He is really turning a part of the jungle into a church, not a physical one, perhaps, but a spiritual one. Here there is a scene, when civilization has already begun to break down under the combined pressures of boy-nature and the thing still ducking and bowing on the mountain top, when the hunters bring before him, without knowing he is there, their false god, the pig's head on a stick. It was at this point of imaginative concentration that I found that the pig's head knew Simon was there. In fact the pig's head delivered something very like a sermon to the boy; the pig's head spoke. I know because I heard it.

'You are a silly little boy,' said the Lord of the Flies, 'just an ignorant, silly little boy.'

Simon moved his swollen tongue but said nothing.

'Don't you agree?' said the Lord of the Flies. 'Aren't you just a silly little boy?' Simon answered him in the same silent voice.

'Well then,' said the Lord of the Flies, 'you'd better run off and play with the others. They think you're batty. You don't want Ralph to think you're batty do you? You like Ralph a lot don't you? And Piggy and Jack?'

Simon's head was tilted slightly up. His eyes could not break away and the Lord of the Flies hung in space before him.

'What are you doing out here all alone? Aren't you afraid of me?'

Simon shook.

'There isn't anyone to help you. Only me. And I'm the Beast.'

Simon's head laboured, brought forth audible words.

'Pig's head on a stick.'

'Fancy thinking the Beast was something you could hunt and kill!' said the head. For a moment or two the forest and all the other dimly appreciated places echoed with the parody of laughter. 'You knew didn't you? I'm part of you? Close, close, close! I'm the reason why it's no go? Why things are what they are?'

The laughter shivered again.

'Come now,' said the Lord of the Flies. 'Get back to the others and we'll forget the whole thing.'

Simon's head wobbled. His eyes were half-closed as though he were imitating the obscene thing on the stick. He knew that one of his times was coming on. The Lord of the Flies was expanding like a balloon.

'This is ridiculous. You know perfectly well you'll only meet me down there – so don't try to escape!'

Simon's body was arched and stiff. The Lord of the Flies spoke in the voice of a schoolmaster.

'This has gone quite far enough. My poor, misguided child, do you think you know better than I do?'

There was a pause.

'I'm warning you. I'm going to get waxy. D'you see? You're not wanted. Understand? We are going to have fun on this island. Understand? We are going to have fun on this island! So don't try it on, my poor misguided boy, or else –'

Simon found he was looking into a vast mouth. There was blackness within, a blackness that spread.

'– Or else,' said the Lord of the Flies, 'we shall do you. See? Jack and Roger and Maurice and Robert and Bill and Piggy and Ralph? Do you. See?'

Simon was inside the mouth. He fell down and lost consciousness.

That then is an example of how a fable when it is extended to novel length can bid fair to get out of hand. Fortunately the Lord of the Flies' theology and mine were sufficiently alike to conceal the fact that I was writing at his dictation. I don't think the fable ever got right out of hand; but there are many places I am sure, where the fable splits at the seams and I would like to think that if this is so, the splits do not rise from ineptitude or deficiency but from a plenitude of imagination. Faults of excess seem to me more forgivable than faults of coldness, at least in the exercise of craftsmanship.

And then I remind myself that after all, the last lecture on sign, symbol, fable, and myth, and this one more particularly on fable, are exercises not in crafts-manship but in analysis. I suspect that art, like experience is a continuum and if we try to take elements out of that continuum, they cease to be what they were, because they are no longer together. Take these words, then, as efforts to indicate trends and possibilities rather than discrete things. May it not be that at the very moments when I felt the fable to come to its own life before me, it may in fact have become something more valuable, so that where I thought it was failing, it was really succeeding? I leave that consideration to the many learned and devoted persons, who in speech and the printed word, have explained to me what the story means. For I have shifted somewhat from the position I held when I wrote the book. I no longer believe that the author has a sort of *patria potestas* over his brainchildren. Once they are printed they have reached their majority and the author has no more authority over them, knows no more about them, perhaps knows less about them than the critic who comes fresh to them, and sees them not as the author hoped they would be, but as what they are.

At least the fable has caught attention, and gone out into the world. The effect on me has been diverse and not wholly satisfactory. On the good side it has brought me here, 7000 miles from home, jet-propelled though somewhat jaundiced. It has subjected me to a steady stream of letters. I get letters from schoolmasters who want permission to turn the book into a play so that their classes can act it. I get letters from schoolmasters telling me that they *have* turned the book into a play so that their classes can act it. Now and again I get letters from mothers of boys whose schoolmasters have turned the book into a play so that their classes can act it. I get letters from psychiatrists, psychologists, clergymen – complimentary, I am glad to say; but sometimes tinged with a faint air of indignation that I should seem to know something about human nature without being officially qualified.

And at the last – students. How am I to put this gently and politely? In the first place, I am moved and fulfilled by the fact that anyone of your generation should think a book I have written is significant for you. But this is the standard form of the letters I get from most English speaking parts of the world:

Dear Mr Golding, I and my friend so and so have read your book *Lord of the Flies* and we think so forth and so forth. However there are some things in it which we are not able to understand. We shall be glad therefore if you will kindly answer the following forty-one questions. A prompt reply would oblige as exams start next week.

Well there it is. I cannot do your homework for you; and it is in some ways a melancholy thought that I have become a school textbook before I am properly dead and buried. To go on being a schoolmaster so that I should have time to write novels was a tactic I employed in the struggle of life. But life, clever life, has got back at me. My first novel ensured that I should be treated for the rest of my days as a schoolmaster only given a longer tether – one that has stretched 7000 miles.

From *The Hot Gates*, Faber, 1963

The artist as author: the strength of the double vision

Based on the transcript of a discussion which was held at the Library of Congress in Washington in 1970, where Virginia Haviland is head of the Children's Book Section, this article presents the thoughts of one of the most acclaimed artists at present working in the field of children's books. He tells of the books he read (and bit into) as a child, of the influence of Disney and of fairy stories, and the impact of earlier artists. Sendak touches on many things about reading and fantasy in childhood which, because of their sensuous nature, are recalled in visual terms that give his argument a concrete quality, a directness, which he finds in the ' "primal" images of the fairy story'. The recurrence of a metaphor about eating is significant. He did not know the classic children's books as a child. He 'doesn't believe in people who consciously write for children ... The great ones have always first written books.' His comments on the work of other illustrators are valuable for the explicitness of their insights: he does not want books to be 'showcases for artists'. As storybooks for the youngest children are usually picture-books, Sendak's commentary is the most significant statement we have found on this topic. 'Where the Wild Things Are' (1963), 'Higglety Pigglety Pop!' (1967) and 'In the Night Kitchen' (1970) have the artistic 'rightness' of children's classics.

Questions to an artist who is also an author   Maurice Sendak

Miss Haviland As a starter, let's ask: What did a book mean to you as a child? And what kinds of books did you have?

Mr Sendak I think I'll start with the kinds of books, because back in the thirties I didn't have any 'official' children's books (I refer to the classics). The only thing I can remember is cheap paperbacks, comic books. That's principally where I started. My sister bought me my first book, *The Prince and the Pauper*. A ritual began with that book which I recall very clearly. The first thing was to set it up on the table and stare at it for a long time. Not because I was impressed with Mark Twain; it was just such a beautiful object. Then came the smelling of it. I think the smelling of books began with *The Prince and the Pauper*, because it was printed on particularly fine paper, unlike the Disney books I had gotten previous to that, which were printed on very poor paper and smelled poor. *The Prince and the Paper – Pauper –* smelled good and it also had a shiny cover, a laminated cover. I flipped over that. And it was very solid. I mean, it was bound very tightly. I remember trying to bite into it, which I don't imagine is what my sister intended when she bought the book for me. But the last thing I did with the book was to read it. It was all right. But I think it started then, a passion for books and bookmaking. I wanted to be an illustrator very early in my life; to be involved in books in some way – to make books. And the making of books, and the touching of books – there's so much more to a book than just the reading; there is a sensuousness. I've seen children touch books, fondle books, smell books, and it's all the reason in the world why books should be beautifully produced.

Miss Haviland Our questions to you, which are questions I think you have often answered for university and other groups, come as questions to you as an author and questions to you as an artist. Let's begin with the group of questions that have to do with you as an author. What part do you think fantasy should play in a child's life?

Mr Sendak Well, fantasy is so all-pervasive in a child's life: I believe there's no part of our lives, our adult as well as child life, when we're not fantasizing, but we prefer to relegate fantasy to children, as though it were some tomfoolery only fit for the immature minds of the young. Children do live in fantasy *and* reality; they move back and forth very easily in a way that we no longer remember how to do. And in writing for children you just must assume they have this incredible flexibility, this cool sense of the logic of illogic, and that they can move with you very easily from one sphere to another without any problems. Fantasy is the core of all writing for children, as I think it is for the writing of any book, for any creative act, perhaps for the act of living. Certainly it is crucial to my work. There are many kinds of fantasy and levels of fantasy and subtleties of fantasy – but that would be another question. There is probably no such thing as creativity without fantasy. My books don't come about by 'ideas' or by thinking of a particular subject and exclaiming 'Gee, that's a terrific idea, I'll put it down!' They never quite come to me that way; they well up. In the way a dream comes to us at night, feelings come to me, and then I must rush to put them down. But these fantasies have to be given physical form, so you build a house around them, and the house is what you call a story, and the painting of the house is the bookmaking. But essentially it's a dream, or it's a fantasy.

Miss Haviland Are you, yourself, remembering daydreams? And a belief in fantasy that came out of your own childhood?

Mr Sendak I can't recall my childhood any more than most of us can. There are sequences and scenes I remember much as we all do. But I do seem to have the knack of recalling the emotional quality of childhood, so that in *Wild Things* – I can remember the feeling, when I was a child (I don't remember who the people were, but there were people who had come to our house, relatives perhaps) and I remember they looked extremely ugly to me. I remember this quite clearly, and that when people came and, with endearments, they leaned over and said 'Oh, I could eat you up!' I was very nervous because I really believed they probably could if they had a mind to. They had great big teeth, immense nostrils, and very sweaty foreheads. I often remember that vision and how it frightened me. There was one particular relative (I have some relatives in the audience, so I won't mention who it was) who did this to me, and it was really quite terrifying. Well, he is forever immortalized in *Wild Things*. *Wild Things* really is the anxiety and pleasure and immense problem of being a small child. And what do children do with themselves? They fantasize, they control fantasies or they don't control fantasies. It's not the recollection of my own particular childhood that I put down in books, but the feeling – like that particular feeling of fear of adults, who are totally unaware that what they say to children is sometimes taken quite literally. And that when they pinch your cheek out of affection, it hurts; and that, when they suggest they could 'hug you to death', you back away – any number of such things.

Miss Haviland It would be interesting to find out whether you can account for the fact that college students seem to enjoy *Where the Wild Things Are* and *Higglety Pigglety Pop!* as much as children do. The question is: whom do you see as your audience?

Mr Sendak Well, I suppose primarily children, but not really. Because I don't write for children specifically. I certainly am not conscious of sitting down and writing a book for children. I think it would be fatal if one did. So I write *books*, and I hope that they are books anybody can read. I mean, there was a time in history when books like *Alice in Wonderland* and the fairy tales of George MacDonald were read by everybody. They were not segregated for children. So I'd like to think I have a large audience, and if college students like my books, that's fine. I think young people tend to be freer about reading children's books. They don't think it's an odd thing to do particularly, if it's a good piece of fantasy, or even if it's just a good piece of fun. They aren't as hung up as perhaps we were about reading 'children's' books. I know a lot of students think that I was 'turned on' when I wrote some of my books. That is not just a guess, because I've had lots of enquiries about what I smoked during certain chapters of certain books. And that may be partly the interest that they have in such things. Writing fantasies is really being quite sufficiently high (without anything more than an Empirin).

Miss Haviland Some other college students have asked how you, as a writer in this post-Freudian era, can resolve the problem of not consciously manipulating the unconscious.

Mr Sendak [After a pause] Well, that's a problem. The Victorians were very fortunate. *Alice in Wonderland* is full of images and symbols, which are extremely beautiful and sometimes frightening. We know that Carroll had no Freud, and the book came pouring out of his unconscious, as happened with George MacDonald in *Princess and the Goblin*. These authors touched on some very primal images in quite a fascinating way. It is more difficult for us to do because we do know so much, we've read so much. I hope I don't consciously manipulate my material. I do not analyse my work; if something strikes me and I get excited, then I want it to be a book. If it begins to die as I work, then of course it's not a book. But I think I do get away occasionally with walking that fine unconscious line. The things I've written in which there are conscious unconscious things, are very – you can't put your finger on it, certainly children can put their fingers on it, they are *the* most critical audience in the world, they smell a rat instantly. You cannot fool them, you really cannot fool them. They're tough to work for. And if they sense – and they know adults do these books – if they sense for one minute that I was faking this, I would know it. Now, *Wild Things* walked a very fine line in this particular sense. It was accepted by children largely, and that's the only proof I have that I've done it.

Miss Haviland Another college student has asked about the recurring symbol of something eating something, ingesting something, and then giving it out again. For instance in *Pierre* the lion eats Pierre and then gives him out; and in *As I Went Over the Water* a sea monster ingests a boat, then gives it out; in *Higglety Pigglety Pop!* Jenny eats a mop and then gives it out; and in *The Night Kitchen* Mickey is engulfed in dough and then springs out. Would you comment on this?

Mr Sendak I don't know if it's safe to, but I began by telling you how much I liked to bite into my first books, and that is perhaps a clue to this subject. And, so far as I'm aware, I'm not an overeating person, but perhaps it is a hang-up from childhood. A pleasant one, I think. The business of eating is such an immensely important part of life for a child. Grimms' *Fairy Tales* is full of things being eaten and then disgorged. It's an image that constantly appeals to me; I love it. In *As I Went Over the Water*, the scene where the monster eats the boat and then regurgitates it is hilarious! I have the mind of a child, I think that's very funny. I will sit home and laugh myself sick over what I've done. Whether it appeals or makes sense to anyone else, I honestly don't know. It just seems right and occasionally children laugh too, so we laugh together.

Miss Haviland Some readers have been intrigued by the relationships between your characters Kenny, Martin, Max, and Mickey. Would you say in what way these children may be the same child, or in what ways they are not?

Mr Sendak They are the same child, of course. Three of them have the initial 'M'. I don't think that's an accident, although I thought of that only while I was working on the last book. The first boy was Kenny, and he was named after a specific person. But a thread of meaning connects all the children. I can do a very rough analysis, I suppose. Kenny is a frustrated and introverted child. And Martin is fussy and sulking and not very brave. Max is tremendously brave but in a rage. And Mickey is extremely brave and very happy. I can follow that – I don't know if you can – but in the characters there is a kind of progress from holding back to coming forth which I'd like to think is me, not so much as a child or pretending that I'm a child but as a creative artist who also gets freer and freer with each book and opens up more and more.

Miss Haviland Many persons right now are asking what inspired you to produce this new book, *In the Night Kitchen*?

Mr Sendak Well, that is a difficult question. It comes out of a lot of things, and they are very hard to describe, because they are not so clear to me. There are a few clues. When I was a child there was an advertisement which I remember very clearly. It was for the Sunshine Bakers. And the advertisement read 'We Bake While You Sleep!' It seemed to me the most sadistic thing in the world, because all I wanted to do was stay up and watch. And it seemed so absurdly cruel and arbitrary for them to do it while I slept. And also for them to think I would think that was terrific stuff on their part, you know, and would eat their product on top of that. It bothered me a good deal, and I remember I used to save the coupons showing the three fat little Sunshine bakers going off to this magic place, wherever it was, at night to have their fun, while I had to go to bed. This book was a sort of vendetta book to get back at them and to say that I am now old enough to stay up at night and know what is happening in the Night Kitchen! The other clue is a rather odd fantasy of mine when I was a child. I lived in Brooklyn and to travel to Manhattan was a big deal, even though it was so close. I couldn't go by myself, and I counted a good deal on my elder sister. She took us – my brother and myself – to Radio City Music Hall, or the Roxy, or some such place. Now, the point of going to New York was that you *ate* in New York. Now we get back to eating again. Somehow to me New York represented eating. And eating in a very fashionable, elegant, superlatively mysterious place like Longchamps. You got dressed up, and you went uptown, and it was night when you got there, and there were lots of windows blinking, and you went straight to a place to eat. It was one of the most exciting things of my childhood, to do this. Cross the bridge, and see the city approaching, and get there, and have your dinner, and then go to a movie, and come home. So, again, *In the Night Kitchen* is a kind of homage to New York City, the city I loved so much and still love. It had a special quality for me as a child. It also is homage to the things that really affected me aesthetically. I did not get to museums, I did not see art books. I was really quite rough in the sense of what was going on artistically. *Fantasia* was perhaps the most aesthetic experience of my childhood, and that's a very dubious experience. But mainly there were the comic books and there was Walt Disney, and, more than anything else, there were the movies and radio, especially the movies. The early films, such as the Gold Digger movies and *King Kong* and other monster films, were the stuff that my books are composed of now. I am surprised, and this is really unconscious – I was looking at *Where the Wild Things Are* not too long ago with a friend, who had found something which amused her a good deal. She is a film collector, and she opened the book to one page where one of the wild things is leaning out of the cave. And then she held alongside it a still from *King Kong*, and it was, literally, a copy. But I had not seen the still, of course; I could not have remembered the sequence. Obviously, it had impressed itself on my brain, and there it was: I mean, exactly the proportions of cave to cliff, and proportions of monster coming out of cave. It was really quite extraordinary, the effect the films did have on me.

It was only much later, when I was a practising illustrator and writer, that I got to know the classic children's books and read them. I did not know them as a child; I did not know pictures or paintings or writing when I was growing up. Brooklyn was a more or less civilized place, let me assure you, but this particular thing didn't get to me until quite late. And I think it's reflected in my work. I am what is commonly referred to as a late bloomer. I am happy for that.

Miss Haviland That brings us to the question of whom you believe to be some of the great writers for children? You have made some allusions already, but would you enlarge on that?

Mr Sendak George MacDonald I think of as probably the greatest of the Victorian writers for children. It's the combination of planes, levels, that he worked on. George MacDonald can tell a conventional fairy tale; it has all the form that a fairy tale must have. At the same time, he manages to inundate the story with a kind of dream-magic, or unconscious power. *The Princess and the Goblin:* Irene's travels through the cave with the goblins are so strange, they can only come out of the deepest dream stuff. The fact that he can weave both of these things together is exactly what I love so much in his work, and what I try to emulate. And he is a model; he is someone I try to copy in many ways. There are other writers, like Charles Dickens, who has precisely this quality of the urgency of childhood. The peculiar charm of being in a room in a Dickens novel, where the furniture is alive, the fire is alive, where saucepans are alive, where chairs move, where every inanimate object has a personality. This is that particularly vivid quality that children have, of endowing everything with life. And Dickens sees and hears as children do. He has a marvellous ear for what's going on socially and politically, and on one level he's telling you a straightforward story. But underneath there is the intensity of the little boy staring out at everything and looking, and examining, and watching, and feeling intensely, and suffering immensely, which is what I think makes Dickens a superb writer. The same is true of George MacDonald. Another favourite writer is Henry James. I first became enthusiastic over Henry

James when I read some of the earlier novels about young children. His incredible power of putting himself in the position of young children, viewing the adult world; and his uncanny sense of how difficult and painful it is to be a child. And even harder to be an adolescent. Now, these are people who write from their child sources, their dream sources. They don't forget them. William Blake is my favourite – and, of course, *The Songs of Innocence* and *The Songs of Experience* tell you all about this: what it is to be a child – not childish, but a child inside your adult self – and how much better a person you are for being such. So that my favourite writers are never writers who have written books specifically for children. I don't believe in that kind of writing. I don't believe in people who consciously write for children. The great ones have always just written books. And there are many more, but I can't think of them now.

Miss Haviland Now let's take a group of questions set to you as an artist. In a photo bulletin issued by our State Department, a comment is made that critics credit – and I'm quoting now – 'a hidden little boy, Maurice, between four and eight, with the dreamlike quality of the pictures created by Sendak the man.' And further in this piece, the journalist quoted you as saying that your new book, *In the Night Kitchen*, is your idea of what books looked like to you as a four-year-old. Would you elaborate on this quotation?

Mr Sendak Well, I think I did that already. I mean, the city as I felt it as a child. It also was an attempt to capture the look of the books that meant so much to me in the thirties and the early forties – they were not glamorous, 'artistic' books; they were very cheap, full-colour books that, up to a short time ago, I thought were contemptible. But for some odd reason, my old love for them has returned. My taste in English graphics and German fairy tales came much later, and it really is, I think, on my part at least an honest attempt to get back to those things that did mean an awful lot to me as a child. They weren't fancy, they were good, and *In the Night Kitchen* was an attempt to make a beautiful book that at the same time still suggested those early inexpensive books that were read by most children I knew.

Miss Haviland One librarian recalls hearing you speak in the 1950s, a time between the publishing of your illustrations for *A Hole Is To Dig* and of those for *Little Bear*, when you said that your roots go back to Caldecott. And this past April, when you accepted the Hans Christian Andersen International Medal, you named another string of artists whom you credit with stimulating you. I remember you mentioned William Blake, whom you've already spoken of here, George Cruikshank and Boutet de Monvel, Wilhelm Busch, Heinrich Hoffmann.

Mr Sendak That's right.

Miss Haviland Could you talk about the specific elements that you think you find there that are particularly relevant to the children's book illustrator?

Mr Sendak I hated school and my own particular way was to learn by myself. Many of the artists who influenced me were illustrators I accidentally came upon. I knew the Grimms' *Fairy Tales* illustrated by George Cruikshank, and I just went after everything I could put my hands on that was illustrated by Cruikshank and copied his style. Quite as simply as that. I wanted to crosshatch the way he did. Then I found Wilhelm Busch and I was off again. But happily Wilhelm Busch also crosshatched, so the Cruikshank crosshatching wasn't entirely wasted. And so an artist grows. I leaned very heavily on these people. I developed taste from these illustrators. Boutet de Monvel, the French illustrator, who is still not terribly well known (which is a great surprise to me), illustrated in the twenties, or earlier perhaps – had the most glorious sense of design and refinement of style. His pictures are so beautifully felt and they are supremely elegant as only French illustration can be. They are very clear, very transparent, extremely fine. At the same time, they can be very tragic. There are things in his drawings, which perhaps now would even seem too strong for children – although at one point, they did not. There is a perfect example of his method in one of his illustrations for the *Fables* of La Fontaine – 'The Wolf and the Lamb'. They are a series of drawings, very much like a comic strip. It's like a ballet. The little lamb moves toward the stream and begins to drink, and the ferocious wolf appears and says: 'What are you doing here? This is my water!' Of course, he's rationalizing the whole thing, he's going to eat the lamb up anyway, but he's putting on this big act about it being his water. Now, the lamb knows that there's no chance for escape, and while the wolf is bristling – and in each drawing his chest gets puffier and his fangs get fangier, and his eyes are blazing, and he looks horrendous – now, in proportion to him, growing larger on the page, the lamb dwindles. It has immediately accepted its fate, it can't outrun the wolf, it doesn't even listen to the words of the wolf, this is all beside the point: it is going to die, and it prepares itself for death. And while the wolf goes through this inane harangue, the lamb folds itself in preparation for its death. It leans down, it puts its head to one side, it curls up very gently, and its final gesture is to lay its head down on the ground. And at that moment the wolf pounces and destroys the lamb. It is one of the most beautiful sequences I've ever seen and one of the most honest in a children's book. There's no pretence of the lamb escaping, or of there being a happy ending – this is the way it is, it does happen this way sometimes, that's what de Monvel is saying. And this is what I believe children appreciate. People rage against the Grimms' fairy tales, forgetting that originally the brothers Grimm had – I'm going off the track a little bit – assembled the tales not for children but for historical and philological reasons. They were afraid their past was being lost in all the upheavals of that period, and the tales were put out as a scholarly edition of peasant tales not to be forgotten as part of the heritage of their homeland. Well, lo and behold, children began to read them. And the second edition was called *The Household Tales* because children were devouring the books – not literally – I'm going to be so conscious of that from here on. The whole point I'm making, although I have forgotten the point frankly, is that those illustrators and writers that attracted me were the ones who did not seem at all to be hung up by the fact that their audiences were small people. They were telling the truth, just the way it was. This could be done if it were aesthetically beautiful, if it were well written – simply, if it were a work of art, then it was fine. Now *Der Struwwelpeter* was one of the books that I loved very much – graphically, it *is* one of the most beautiful books in the world. One might complain about the cutting off of fingers, and the choking to death, and being burned alive, and might well have a case there – but, aesthetically, for an artist growing up it was a good book to look at and a lot of my early books were affected strongly by the German illustrators. When I came to picture books, it was Randolph Caldecott who really did put me where I wanted to be. Caldecott is an illustrator, he is a songwriter, he is a choreographer, he is a stage manager, he is a decorator, he is a theatre person; he's superb, simply. And he can take four lines of verse that have very little meaning in themselves and stretch them into a book that has tremendous meaning – not overloaded, no sentimentality in it. Everybody meets with a bad ending in *Froggie Went A-Courting*. Froggie gets eaten at the end by a duck, which is very sad, and the story usually ends on that note. But in Caldecott's version, he introduces, oddly enough, a human family. They observe the tragedy much as a Greek chorus might – one can almost hear their comments. In the last picture, we see Froggie's hat going downstream, all that remains of him. And standing on the bank are mother, father, and child – and it's startling for a moment until you realize what he's done: the little girl is clutching the mother's long Victorian skirt. And it's as though she's just been told the story, she's very upset, obviously. There are no words; I'm just inventing what I think this means – Froggie is dead, it alarms her, and for support she's hanging on to her mother's skirt. Her mother has a very quiet, resigned expression on her face. She's very gently pointing with her parasol toward the stream as the hat moves away, and the father is looking very sad. They're both expressing to the child, 'Yes, it is very sad, but this does happen – that is the way the story ended, it can't be helped. But you have us. Hold on, everything is all right.' And this is impressive in a simple rhyming book for children; it's extremely beautiful. It's full of fun, it's full of beautiful drawings, and it's full of truth. And I think Caldecott did it best, much better than anyone else who ever lived.

Miss Haviland One critic, at the last Biennale of Illustration at Bratislava, said: 'There is no fundamental difference between illustrations for children and those for adults.' Would you comment on that?

Mr Sendak I don't agree at all, of course. I intensely do not believe in illustrations for adults. For pre-school children who cannot read, pictures are extremely valuable. But even children who do read move in a very different world. As for adults, I personally find it offensive to read, I will *not* read, a novel that is illustrated. I always use this example, and many people here who know me have heard me carry on about this particular one, the case of *Anna Karenina*: the audacity of any illustrator who would draw Anna after Tolstoy has described her in the best way possible! Now, everyone who's read the book knows exactly what she looks like, or what he wants her to look like. Tolstoy is superb. And then to get an artist so asinine as to think he's going to draw Anna! Or Melville: it's incredible. People illustrate *Moby Dick*. It's an insane thing to do, in my estimation. There is every difference in the world between illustrations for adults and illustrations for children. I don't know why there *are* illustrations for adults. They make no sense to me at all.

Miss Haviland Out of that same Biennale of Illustration, where you represented the United States as our juror, there was considerable disagreement, I recall disagreement in theory, on the importance of kinds of art as illustrations. You were there, could you bring this into the picture?

Mr Sendak Well, I'm not sure I know exactly what you mean, but as I recall there was a European point of view as to what illustrations accomplish in a children's book, as opposed to what we believe is the function of illustration. I didn't know such a difference of opinion existed until we were in Czechoslovakia. And it was quite extraordinary. Partly, perhaps, because there is a dearth of original writing, they tend more often to reillustrate their classic and fairy tales, and the illustrations take on a dominance and importance which I, as an illustrator, do not approve of. The books often become showcases for artists. I mean, you turn pages and there are extremely beautiful illustrations, but so far as I can see they could be taken out of one book and put into another. Whereas here, we are very much involved in making the illustrations work in a very specific way inside a book. Now, a picture is there, not because there should be a picture there; there is a purpose for a picture – we are embellishing, or we are enlarging, or we are involving ourselves in some very deep way with the writer of the book, so that the book (when it is finally illustrated) means more than it did when it was just written. Which is not to say we are making the words more important; we are perhaps opening up the words in a way that children at first did not see was possible. In the United States we work to bring pictures and words together to achieve a wholeness in the book, which I was very surprised to find is not at all important in many European countries. It's not a matter of right or wrong, it's just that it is so different! There it was so much a matter of graphics, of beauty of picture; here graphic acrobatics are less important.

Miss Haviland One critic has asked why you changed from the 'fine engraved style' of *Higglety Pigglety Pop!* back to what this person calls the 'fat style' of your earlier work?

Mr Sendak Umm, 'fat style'. Well, I think the only way to answer that is to discuss the business of style. Style, to me, is purely a means to an end, and the more styles you have, the better. One should be able to junk a style very quickly. I think one of the worst things that can happen in some of the training schools for young men and women who are going to be illustrators is the tremendous focusing on 'style', on preparation for coming out into the world and meeting the great, horned monsters, book editors. And how to take them on. And style seems to be one of the things. It's a great mistake. To get trapped in a style is to lose all flexibility. And I have worked very hard not to get trapped in that way. Now, I think my work looks like me, generally speaking; over a series of books, you can tell I've done them (much as I may regret many of them). I worked up a very elaborate pen and ink style in *Higglety*, which is very finely crosshatched. But I can abandon that for a magic marker, as I did in *Night Kitchen*, and just go back to very simple, outlined, broad drawings with flat, or flatter, colours. Each book obviously demands an individual stylistic approach. If you have one style, then you're going to do the same book over and over, which is, of course, pretty dull. Lots of styles permit you to walk in and out of all kinds of books. It is a great bore worrying about style. So, my point is to have a fine style, a fat style, a fairly slim style, and an extremely stout style.

Miss Haviland This question comes to you as both an artist and an author. Do you think of your books first in words or in pictures?

Mr Sendak In words. In fact, I don't think of the pictures at all. It's a very strange, schizophrenic sort of thing; I've thought of that very often. Sometimes after I've written something I find that there are things in my story that I don't draw well. And if it were any other person's book, I'd consider not doing it. But I've written it and I'm stuck with it, which is proof to me that I have not (at least consciously) been seduced by the tale's graphic potential. I don't think in terms of pictures at all; I find it's much more interesting and difficult to write, and illustration now becomes secondary in my life. So far as I'm aware, I think strictly in terms of words. And then when it's finished, it is almost a surprise as to 'How'm I going to draw *that*?' or 'Why did I do that?' I'm stuck with an airplane, or I'm stuck with a building. If I'm stuck with an automobile, I'm ready to blow my brains out.

Miss Haviland Some artists feel that creating a work is a very separate experience and vastly more satisfying than what happens when the work goes out into the world. How do you evaluate the private experience as compared with the public experience?

Mr Sendak Well, there really is no comparison. The private experience is extraordinary, because it's all yours, nobody knows about it, nobody's going to find out about it, and you have it all to yourself for as long as it takes you to finish the book. *In the Night Kitchen* took two years of concentrated work. *The Wild Things* took about the same length of time, maybe a little less. During that time you are completely absorbed in this dream, this fantasy, whatever it is. The pleasure you get is extraordinary. You live in a very strange world, really quite divorced from this dull, real world. When I'm working on a book, I see very few people, do very few things but think about my book, dream about my book, love it, hate it, pull hairs out of my head; and the only time I speak to people is when I want to complain about it. And then it's over, and then it's finished, and the great shock comes when it is printed! And that's much like giving birth, and always a difficult birth. A book being printed is a major topic in itself; it is a very difficult thing to see through. What was once very dreamlike and transparent and what you thought was a magic moment has now become a real thing in a printing press, and it's going through a big machine, and it looks lousy, and it has to be done all over again. And so gradually your particular transparent little dream is becoming more real, and more terrible every moment. And then finally it is a book. And you become extremely depressed, because you realize that what was so superb and different is really just another book! How strange. It looks like all the other things you've done. And then it goes out into the world, and your child, who was so private and who was living with you for two years, now is everybody's child. Some people knock him on the head, some kick him in the rump, and others like him very much. It's a totally different experience. It takes me a long time to shift gears. I am now in the process. It's only a few weeks since the book came out, and I don't know quite yet how to adjust to the fact that people are looking at it, and criticizing it.

Miss Haviland Looking at the publishing world, we can see a very big question: Do you think that children's book publishing is significantly different today than it was when you began in the early fifties ? And, if you do, in what respect do you see this ?

Mr Sendak Well, yes, of course, it is very different than when I began in the early fifties. For one thing, the world seemed quieter then, and there was more opportunity to do experimental kinds of books. More important, there was time for young people to grow quietly. If you're an artist, you really need the time to grow quietly and not feel competitive or pushed. It was that way in the early fifties. One could develop gradually. Now, of course, it is much more competitive, and we do many more books but, alas, not many more great books. Something is lost. There is a rush, we are flooded with books, books come pouring out of the publishing meat grinder. And, the quality has dropped severely. We may be able to print a book better, but intrinsically the book, perhaps, is not better than it was. We have a backlist of books, superb books, by Margaret Wise Brown, by Ruth Krauss, by lots of people. I'd much rather we just took a year off, a moratorium:

no more books. For a year, maybe two – just stop publishing. And get those old books back, let the children see them! Books don't go out of fashion with children; they only go out of fashion with adults. So that kids are deprived of works of art which are no longer around simply because new ones keep coming out. Every Christmas we are inundated with new books, and it's the inundation which I really find quite depressing.

Miss Haviland Would you generalize in any way on what has been happening in other countries as you have travelled abroad and looked at picture books?

Mr Sendak Since I've generalized all this time, I could go a little further. There was a great moment in the middle fifties when, suddenly, the foreign books came to America. Books from Switzerland, the Hans Fischer books and the Carigiet books. We'd never seen them; it was a revolution in American bookmaking. We suddenly began to look very European. It was the best thing that could have happened to us, we *looked* terrific! But, of course, Europeans were then doing the most superb books. England invented the children's book as we know it. And now, in the sixties and seventies, certainly America is leading the world in the manufacture of children's books. It's disappointing, I find, going to Europe (with the exception of England and Switzerland) and finding so few contemporary children's books. I don't know if you found this to be true, but I did. In France there is *Babar* and the great old ones, but there are very few new ones. There *are* new ones, of course, but none that we get to see and none that seemingly even French people or Italians get to see – it seems they have dropped back considerably. I could be wrong. In my travels I've discussed this matter with illustrators and editors – and this is certainly the impression I've gotten.

Miss Haviland Is there any point that you would like to make, aside from the questions that have been brought up to you before and which you've answered again tonight?

Mr Sendak I love my work very much, it means everything to me. I would like to see a time when children's books were not segregated from adult books, a time when people didn't think of children's books as a minor art-form, a little Peter-panville, a cutesy-darling place where you could Have Fun, Laugh Your Head Off. I know so many adult writers whom I would happily chop into pieces, who say, 'Well, I think I'll take a moment and sit down and knock off a kiddy book! It looks like so much fun, it's obviously easy –.' And, of course, they write a lousy book. You hope they will and they do! It would be so much better if everyone felt that children's books are for everybody, that we simply write books, that we are a community of writers and artists, that we are all seriously involved in the business of writing. And if everyone felt that writing for children is a serious business, perhaps even more serious than a lot of other forms of writing, and if, when such books are reviewed and discussed, they were discussed on this serious level, and that we would be taken seriously as artists. I would like to do away with the division into age categories of children over here and adults over there, which is confusing to me and I think probably confusing to children. It's very confusing to many people who don't even know how to buy a children's book. I think if I have any particular hope it is this: that we all should simply be artists and just write books and stop pretending that there is such a thing as being able to sit down and write a book for a child: it is quite impossible. One simply writes books.

From *Quarterly Journal of the Library of Congress*, October 1971

The author's response to the teacher's demand: when 'readers' are books not people

Although this is a journalistic 'spoof' article, the instance it offers is crucial. Most children are taught to read from books in which the subject and vocabulary are controlled so that the essential nature of reading – the bond with the author especially – is exchanged for a process of word recognition. The producers of the new series described here have rightly judged the importance of asking an imaginative writer for children like Catherine Storr to help them. They failed to see that, while the author can accept the limitations of the form, as poets do, the rest must be left to her. The only possible movement in these fetters is a 'danse macabre'. But behind this lies the basic question: from what kind of books should children be taught to read: 'real' ones or 'made up' ones?

How to earn a dollar every four words   Catherine Storr

A transatlantic corporation who shall be nameless has just sent me a fascinating document describing a project they are nursing and in which they invite me to co-operate. It is to provide 'language experience in reading' for children aged between five and ten.

They are asking writers – with whose work they are kind enough to say they are familiar, and which meets the required 'standards of excellence' – to submit manuscripts on certain topics, set out as Units 1 to 8 for each of the different age groups. They want 'a variety of fiction and nonfiction of different kinds, grade levels, and topics.' They suggest also poems and plays. There are helpful suggestions on content and style. 'Conceptual level, syntax, and vocabulary should be less complicated for a Grade 1 story than for a Grade 3 story. When you use difficult words or talk about concepts that might not be familiar to children, try to define them in context. Avoid artificial enthusiasm, characterized by excessive use of such adjectives as wonderful and exciting. If something truly is wonderful and exciting, it shouldn't be necessary to point it out.'

There follows a page on the setting out of the manuscript, and then the rate per thousand words. It is very high. It is an inducement to us all to have a go. It works out, by my reckoning, at something like a dollar on average for every four words.

So far so good; now let's see the units (topics). The age groups are divided into three: Grade I for ages 5–8, Grade II for ages 6–9, Grade III for 7–10. Eight units to each grade. But now comes the really astonishing thing. At the head of each set of topics is the 'acceptable length' of each piece to be submitted. For Grade I, 75–250 words. And in case anyone is not immediately familiar with totting up words at a glance, let me add that this paragraph contains about 100 words.

The next step seemed to be to survey the units. Some of the suggestions are:
The child – his or her physical, factual self.
Animals live here too ... familiar animals in the child's environment. These animals can have fins, fur, or feathers ... You might even want to include insects.
Inventions that exist just for fun, such as balloons, see-saws, milkshakes, fireworks, swings, ice-cream, cotton candy ...
Real and imaginary monsters ... horrifying beings of prehistory, fiction and their own private imaginings. Frankenstein, Count Dracula, the Abominable Snowman, dinosaurs, and brontosaurs are all possibilities.

No lack of scope. My agent, whom I next consulted, told me to write and ask for samples of the sort of thing they were thinking of; but I pointed out that a letter would inevitably take up more than seventy-five words; why should I write that many words for nothing, when I could send in a playlet of not more than 250 which might rake me in the promised dollar per four words?

For instance, taking to heart the very first piece of advice on style: 'Don't write down for children,' how about this?

Waiting for God knows who

It is night. Two immaculately dressed gentlemen are waiting on a railway platform.

1st man It will be awkward for you if the train's late.

2nd man You can say that again. Last week I'd only just found myself a seat when midnight struck, and my charming companions were not best pleased with my transformation. They would, indeed, have called the guard, but that I was able, by swift action, to put their fears – and themselves – at rest.

1st man It is certainly more agreeable to be able to conduct one's affairs without undue haste. I prefer to make a full, mature relationship with my vict – my mistresses before proceeding to the ecstatic and final embrace.

2nd man It must be a great advantage never to have to abandon the human form completely. I have to be so careful about time. You can't think how frustrating it is, when you're doing very nicely as a man, to find that you've changed into a wolf. The appetites of the two species are not exactly identical.

1st man Interesting. I seldom find myself seriously inconvenienced. The passionate kisses of a human lover, merge almost imperceptibly with the vampire's thirst. It's simply a question of touching the right vein.

2nd man Ah! The train at last. Goodnight, Count.

1st man Bon soir. And, in the words of a great English poet – Good Hunting!

Not bad, for dramatic impact in just over 200 words for dialogue, plus – but I don't know if they have got to count or not – about thirty more for title, stage directions, and indication as to who is speaking. But a little farther on in the advice on style, I see that I'm warned not to write 'cute' stuff which only adults will understand. Perhaps the old Beacon Reader style would be rather nearer the mark.

Familiar animals in our environment

Janet Mother see John.

John I have a bee.

Janet Let me see the bee. It is a big bee.

John The bee can fly. See his wings.

Janet John, see the cow. The cow is in the pen.

John The cow cannot fly.

Mother Janet, see the fly.

Janet A fly is in the pen.

John A bat is in the pen.

Mother (the know-all) Dracula is in the pen. (Define difficult concepts in context.)

Janet What is Dracula?

Mother Drac-ula is not a cow. Drac-ula is not a fly. Drac-ula is not a bee.

John (a logician, will probably read P.P.P. at Oxford in time) Drac-ula is a bat.

Janet Mother, see Dracula. See Drac-ula drink. He drinks from the cow.

Mother (one of these progressive young mums who believe in telling their children the facts of life early on): Soon Drac-ula will drink from us. He will drink blood.

Janet Come, Drac-ula come. Mother, see Drac-ula come.

This style is definitely more economical. Around 110 words of dialogue, but fifty-seven for title, speakers' names, and directions.

Perhaps poetry is really what I should be trying.

See, Mother, see
The bee has wings!
Be careful, child.
It also stings.

Mother, see funny Frankenstein,
He is a pretty toy.
Be careful, child, his maker, taught
Him only to destroy.

See, Mother, see this monstrous spoor
On Himalayan snows.
My child, th' abominable Snowman cometh,
The beast that no man knows.

Seventy-five words exactly. Need I write more?

From *The Guardian*, 1974

Approaches to criticism

Introduction

Criticism as I. A. Richards understood it – 'the endeavour to discriminate between experiences and evaluate them' – has been applied to children's literature over a long period and for a wide variety of purposes. Mrs Trimmer, the first to undertake it seriously, saw her role as the guardian of children's social as well as religious morals; she could denounce *Little Goody Two Shoes* on the grounds that 'In these times, when such pains are taken to prejudice the poor against the higher orders, and to set them against the parish officers, we could wish to have a veil thrown over the faults of "oppressive squires and hard-hearted overseers" ' (1802). Later, children's books began to be treated on a similar basis to adults': 'The finest thing we have had since Martin Chuzzlewit', said Henry Kingsley of *Through the Looking-Glass* (1871). And finally a more scholarly view was provided for us by Harvey Darton's great survey *Children's Books in England* (1932), which he regarded as 'a minor chapter in the history of social life'.

Mrs Trimmer
The Guardian of Education
volume 1, 1802
quoted in Haviland
Children and Literature
1973

Each of these approaches to criticism is to be found flourishing today. The guardians of public morality range from David Holbrook to members of the Working Group for the Eradication of Colour Prejudice who call for the banning of *Little Black Sambo*: 'Many schools are still using books which reflect attitudes more suitable to a colonial generation.' Meanwhile, fastidious literary critics continue to encourage, flatter, needle, or put the knife into children's authors so that Ivan Southall was driven to complain: 'Beyond the writer, between him and the child, has grown a barbed-wire entanglement through which his book, beating with his own blood, must thrust its way.' And, of course, general surveys of the literature abound, though none so learned as Harvey Darton's.

Ivan Southall
A Critique of Children's Book Reviewing
1969; reprinted in Haviland, *Children and Literature*, 1973

To the serious man of letters, much of this will appear a faintly ridiculous activity – adults earnestly writing for each other about books that weren't intended for them in the first place. Nothing they produce gets through to the children themselves. No critic, however sensitive, tolerant, and well informed about childhood, is likely to make a statement about *Beano*, or, for that matter, *Tom's Midnight Garden*, that will help a child to understand or enjoy it any better. So why bother?

There are a number of possible answers. The first is purely practical. Every day, authors, publishers' editors, booksellers, librarians, teachers, and parents are called upon to make complex evaluative decisions on behalf of children about what sort of stories to provide for them and why. They can, of course, enlist children's help in making these decisions, but their comments are likely to be even more capricious than the adults' and formulated in terms of liking and disliking which, though ultimately crucial, are not helpful. Adults are forced to seek advice from each other, however responsive they may be to the views of children.

Out of this need has grown a body of informed opinion that exchanges views in the specialist journals, the review pages of newspapers and the *Times Literary Supplement* and at the annual conference in Exeter. They are led by a group of professional connoisseurs of children's literature who have an interesting time awarding prizes to the authors they enjoy most. They appear to have reached a consensus on who the good authors are and a fairly stable corpus of big names (Mayne, Pearce, Sutcliff, Garfield) is promoted by them for our attention.

Alongside these, but generally assuming a less fastidious and more 'consumer-oriented' approach, are those who combine an interest in literature with specialist knowledge of psychology, education, or academic criticism. The contributors to Section Three mostly fall into this category since it is they who are most likely to take the study into new directions. Conspicuously absent from the discussion have been the people one would expect to be most concerned – practising English teachers; as victims and agents of a system that promotes literature as an object of textual study rather than as a source of private satisfaction to the reader, their contribution to the thought represented in this volume has been negligible, (see Blishen, page 376). Things might be changing now. Aidan Chambers has helped a lot (q.v. Bibliography). It was possibly in reaction to the slowness of English teachers in treating children's literature in a humane fashion that so many thoughtful parents were drawn into Anne Wood's Federation of Children's Book Groups.

We might now separate the critics into two main categories. There are those who undertake what John Rowe Townsend calls 'stern critical appraisal' according to high literary standards on behalf of the discerning adult. The novelists who can withstand this sort of treatment are the ones who use children's literature to communicate their own significant thoughts and experience because, as C. S. Lewis said, 'a children's story is the best art form for something you have to say'. And there are those who look at children's literature on behalf of the child, trying to understand his needs and advising parents and teachers accordingly.

Conspicuous among the latter has been Elaine Moss, who manages to reach her public where it matters – on Woman's Hour and in the *Sunday Mirror* as well as at the National Book League exhibitions.

The papers assembled in this section exemplify some of the current criticism. But they also indicate ways of moving forward in a direction that is less possible in 'adult' literature – towards a notion of what a *story* consists of. Schlegelmilch in the opening piece introduces some of the issues and Margaret Meek in her contribution takes us considerably further with a study of the rhetoric – 'the way in which a writer makes a world and invites a reader to share it with him'. This concern with storymaking as a *process* has been helped by the fact that children's authors are generally much more willing to discuss their own aims and methods than their 'adult' equivalents. And when we see these studies alongside that of Labov (q.v. Bibliography) we realize finally that though the audience of children's literature is juvenile, its *matter* is highly complex, potent, and a proper study for scholars.

R. Peacock
Criticism and Personal Taste
Clarendon Press
1972

The direction in which we have unfortunately not been able to pursue our enquiries is that of Ronald Peacock (1972) – 'criticism as the justification for personal taste' – which raises all the questions about the origins and nature of personal taste. It is a fascinating and unexplored area.

The wide variety of approaches that have been discussed are all useful and mutually compatible. As John Rowe Townsend says in his important critical study *A Sense of Story* (1971), 'Different kinds of assessment are valid for different purposes. The important thing is that everyone should understand what is being done.'

The critic as analyst of technique

Dr Schlegelmilch describes the work of Hugh Lofting in terms of its narrative form – in particular the author's shift from the conventions of fairy tale, which can have no sequels, to those of the memoir which can be perpetuated into successive volumes. In the course of his examination, he makes useful general comments on the conventions and limitations of first- and third-person narrative (cf. Booth 1961). He focuses clearly on many of the problems raised in the first section of this collection: Story as revisualized experience, 'the tension between reminiscence and reminiscing', the storyteller who 'authenticates the reliability of his story by temporal fixation' and the shift from naïve to elaborate descriptive commentary. Detailed non-evaluative analyses of this kind are needed if we are to understand more fully the task of the storyteller. This article first appeared in an international journal addressed to those professionally interested in children's literature.

From fairy tale to children's novel   Wolfgang Schlegelmilch

Hugh Lofting's Dolittle books originated in a genuine narrative situation, with the child listening. They share this creative starting point with several other famous children's books, with Lewis Caroll's *Alice's Adventures in Wonderland*, Rudyard Kipling's *Just So Stories*, A. A. Milne's *Winnie-the-Pooh* – just to mention a few English titles.

In 1916–17, Lofting wrote letters from the front in France to his children Elizabeth and Colin; later he read them bedtime stories. Their hero was, in Lofting's own words,

'An eccentric country physician with a bent for natural history and a great love of pets, who finally decides to give up his human practice for the more difficult, more sincere and, for him, more attractive therapy of the animal kingdom. He is challenged by the difficulty of the work – for obviously it requires a much cleverer brain to become a good animal doctor (who must first acquire all animal languages and physiologies) than it does to take care of the mere human hypochondriac.'

Quoted from
Edward Blishen
Hugh Lofting
Bodley Head
1968 (page 13)

It was only natural that Lofting, who was already active in the press, revised the material for publication, and so, in 1920, the first Dolittle book, *The Story of Doctor Dolittle*, appeared in America where the English author had made his home. In 1922 followed *The Voyages of Doctor Dolittle*, which was awarded the Newbery Medal.

In spite of the wealth of adventures in these and later volumes (altogether twelve have been published), Dolittle's character remains unchanged. He is a blessed child of fortune, for whom, in spite of his helplessness in practical things, even the most dangerous situations take a turn for the better in mysterious ways. He is good-natured and penniless as a result of his boundless generosity; patient and unselfish; a Franciscan figure living in harmony with nature. In the same way that he untiringly aids sick animals, loyal animal helpers support him in the dangers and adventures he encounters in his travels. Lofting's text and drawings quickly and unforgettably imprint Dolittle's pudgy little figure with its friendly round face and thick bulbous nose and the indispensible (and equally indestructible) physician's tall hat in the reader's mind.

All the Dolittle
books have been
published in the
Puffin series of
Penguin Books
between 1967 and
1970

It is worth mentioning that Lofting first found the final style for the series in his second Dolittle book, although *The Story of Doctor Dolittle* was an immediate success with the critics and the public. For example, Oskar Loerke wrote an introduction to the German edition (1926) in which he praised the book as 'one of the clearest, cleverest and most ingenious children's books that exist'. The change in narrative style from *The Story of Doctor Dolittle* to *The Voyages of Doctor Dolittle* can be sketched as follows.

Blishen (l.c., p. 23)
refers to the change
in 'tone' and
'manner', from the
joke to the serious
memoir

The Story begins:

'Once upon a time, many years ago – when our grandfathers were little
    children – there was a doctor; and his name was Dolittle – John Dolittle, MD.'

Hugh Lofting
*The Story of Doctor
Dolittle*
Penguin Books
1967, (page 13)
All quotations are
taken from this
edition. The page
numbers directly
follow the quotation

A fairy tale is being related here. It is the voice of the fairy-tale narrator which begins with the old opening formula 'once upon a time'. The story is removed to that indefinite Anytime in which all fairy tales take place. Therefore the time span between the story and its telling also remains very indefinite; 'Long ago, when Doctor Dolittle was alive' (page 76) must be sufficient. An indefinite time relationship also exists between the single episodes. Something just happens 'once', 'one day', 'another time' or simply, 'soon', 'very soon', 'then'. Duration is rarely indicated and if so then only in stock phrases like 'Now for six whole weeks they went on sailing' (page 40) or 'Three days they had to wait' (page 136). Such formal abstract use of determination of time is reminiscent of the folk fairy tale, in which characters have no temporal experience.

Still other fairy-tale characteristics are evident in the first Dolittle book, especially the fact that individual things are not described, but merely named. The author succeeds in avoiding lengthy descriptive passages.

This genuine epic technique of mere naming allows everything which is named to appear to us as a conclusively earmarked entity. Every approach to more detailed description awakens the feeling that only a fraction of what could be told has really been said; every detail lures us further into infinity, shows us the confusing depth of the thing. Mere naming, on the other hand, allows the things to become automatically rigid in simple little pictures.

Cf. Max Lüthi
*Once upon a Time:
on the Nature of
Fairy Tales*
Frederick Ungar
1970

A good example of this narrative technique is the short passage about the storm and shipwreck during Dolittle's trip to Africa in *The Story of Doctor Dolittle*.

'Then a great storm came up, with thunder and lightning. The wind howled, the rain came down in torrents, and the waves got so high they splashed right over the boat.

'Presently there was a big BANG! The ship stopped and rolled over on its side.

' "What's happened?" asked the Doctor, coming up from downstairs.

' "I'm not sure," said the parrot; "but I think we're shipwrecked. Tell the duck to get out and see."

'So Dab-Dab dived right down under the waves. And when she came up she said they had struck a rock; there was a big hole in the bottom of the ship, the water was coming in, and they were sinking fast.

' "We must have run into Africa," said the Doctor.' (page 42)

Nothing is described in detail, only that which is important for the development of the plot is mentioned. 'The meagre designation outlines and isolates the things into solid contours.' In a few co-ordinated sentences the roughly sketched picture of the storm becomes clear; the shipwreck is established in a few words, the location of the catastrophe is imparted through a meagre dialogue and short report. This style has something unambiguous about it; nothing irrelevant is introduced; there are no incidental remarks; everything is straightforward and clear. In this way the style is able to approach the abstractness of a formula. The last chapter announces Dolittle's homecoming.

'March winds had come and gone; April's showers were over; May's buds had opened into flower; and the June sun was shining on the pleasant fields,

when John Dolittle at last got back to his own country.' (page 149)
The narrative does not aim at specific characterization, but rather at naming that
which is typical. March is windy, April brings showers, May is the month of
flowers and in June the sun shines on friendly meadows. The essential is captured.
A bit later the 'abstract' fairy-tale style becomes even more clear.

'And one fine day, when the hollyhocks were in full bloom, he came back to
Puddleby a rich man, to live in the little house with the big garden.' (page 151)
The formal time period connected with the image-evoking picture of the blooming
flowers, the standardizing adjective to the substantives of human existence – all
this comes together into a sharply outlined, exhaustive statement. Simple things
and simple actions are set down naturally and without question. The advantage
is clear, but so is the price of this form of narrative: transparent luminosity,
playful lightness, sharply outlined unambiguousness are purchased at the price
of reality-saturated fullness and realistic individuality of the world portrayed.

The Voyages of Doctor Dolittle opens with a 'Prologue'. A first-person
narrator introduces himself – old Tommy Stubbins, who was Dolittle's apprentice
and assistant as a little boy. Thus he was able to observe the doctor-explorer at
close quarters and unintentionally became a partner in Dolittle's adventures.
Stubbins, now an old man, writes down his memories of the great doctor. This is
somewhat different from the first book (the author of which Stubbins, to the
reader's surprise, acknowledges to be) which referred to events which were known
to the narrator purely through hearsay. 'But I now come to set down that part
of the great man's life which I myself saw and took part in.' A witness appears
and his report calls for authenticity. Whenever the narrator's memory begins to
fail him, it is revived with the aid of the extraordinary power of recollection of
the parrot Polynesia from Dolittle's household. 'If there is anything I am not
quite sure of, she is always able to put me right, to tell me exactly how it took
place, who was there and everything about it.' (page 7)

Thus, instead of a fairy tale, a book of memoirs, a biography by someone who
was there. Instead of the voice of a story teller, the record of a precise biographer.
But that life which he describes lies far back. Between the time of the experiences
and the telling of them many years have elapsed. Thus, in the new story the
tension between reminiscence and reminiscing, between the man who experienced
and the man who relates is established. A story told from recollection allows for a
composed style, occasional reversion or anticipation and, above all, the formation
of judgement.

Finally, the narrator fulfils the important function of mediator between the

Hugh Lofting
*The Voyages of
Doctor Dolittle*
Penguin Books
1967, (page 7)
All quotations are
taken from this
edition

Cf. Franz K. Stanzel
*Typische Formen
des Romans*
(Typical novel
forms)
Vandenhoeck and
Ruprecht,
Göttingen, 1965
(page 31 ff.)

reader and the hero of the book. The reader easily identifies with bright little Tommy and sees the great doctor through his eyes; he experiences Dolittle's friendship with Tommy and the animals, takes part in the mysterious scientific projects with the same delighted astonishment and curiosity as the doctor's young assistant.

A correct and accurate storyteller also authenticates the reliability of his story by temporal fixation. *The Voyages of Doctor Dolittle* is certainly not just a barren chronicle; however, the more precise temporal fixation stands out again and again. Right at the beginning of the first chapter Tommy introduces himself as a nine-and-a-half-year-old boy, and a bit later we learn that Dolittle's visit to Tommy's parents is still remembered today by an inscription over the front door. 'John Dolittle, the famous naturalist, played the flute in this house in the year 1839.' (page 38 f.) The claim to historical authenticity could not be made more definitely.

Also the temporal relationship of single events to one another is more strongly emphasized. Something happens 'the next morning' or 'the next day', 'two days after that' or 'early in the morning of the sixth day'. The flow of time is precisely perceived by the characters. 'We will have been on this island seven months tomorrow' (page 241) or 'By the end of next month it will be two whole years since we left England' (page 259). He who reckons time like this experiences the irretrievability of times past.

The recollector attempts to visualize once again what he has experienced. He pays particular attention to exactness and entirety. He wants to tell it as it happened, wants to put others in his place by concrete description. In *The Voyages* there is also the report of a storm which ends in shipwreck. This thematically similar chapter clearly shows the change in style when compared with the corresponding one in *The Story*. The chapter 'Bad Weather' (pages 164–7) begins with Tommy's observation of the wind. A dead calm delays the trip, then a quick wind blows up, the sky and water change colour, ragged clouds chase across the dark sky. Finally the storm breaks.

'When that storm finally struck us we leaned right over flatly on our side, as though some invisible giant had slapped the poor *Curlew* on the cheek.

'After that, things happened so thick and so fast that what with the wind that stopped your breath, the driving, blinding water, the deafening noise and the rest, I haven't a very clear idea of how our shipwreck came about.

'I remember seeing the sails, which we were now trying to roll up upon the deck, torn out of our hands by the wind and go overboard like a penny balloon – very nearly carrying Chee-Chee with them.

'And I have a dim recollection of Polynesia screeching somewhere for one of us to go downstairs and close the port-holes.

'In spite of our masts being bare of sail, we were now scudding along to the southward at a great pace. But every once in a while huge grey-black waves would arise from under the ship's side like nightmare monsters, swell and climb, then crash down upon us, pressing us into the sea; and the poor *Curlew* would come to a standstill, half under water, like a gasping, drowning pig.

'When I was clambering along towards the wheel to see the Doctor, clinging like a leech with hands and legs to the rails lest I be blown overboard, one of these tremendous seas tore loose my hold, filled my throat with water and swept me like a cork the full length of the deck. My head struck a door with an awful bang. And then I fainted.' (page 166 f.)

The narrator revisualizes his perceptions from memory, he chooses his words with care, describes every step as it happened without losing himself in details. The claim of truth shines through the narrator's limited perspective. Only that is related which he himself experienced and which his memory has preserved; only that can be clarified which one has understood himself. Thus the reality appears in concrete situations, relived in the narrator's consciousness. Such scenic descriptions draw the reader into the event, allow him to experience it as if it were happening once again. In *The Voyages*, too, Dolittle returns home in the end, accompanied by Tom Stubbins and the Negro prince Bumpo, the parrot Polynesia, the dog Jip and his other household animals. The huge sea-snail deposits all of them on the English coast after a long ocean trip.

'As we stepped down upon the marshy land we noticed that a fine, drizzling autumn rain was falling.

' "Can this be Merrie England?" asked Bumpo, peering into the fog – "doesn't look like any place in particular. Maybe the snail hasn't brought us right after all."

' "Yes," sighed Polynesia, shaking the rain off her feathers, "this is England all right. – You can tell it by the beastly climate."

' "Oh, but fellows," cried Jip, as he sniffed up the air in great gulps, "it has a smell – a good and glorious smell! – Excuse me a minute: I see a water-rat." ' (page 268 f.)

This section could be quoted even further, until the end of the book fifteen lines later. However, it is already very clear how the individual characteristics build up a concrete picture. English drizzle and English rain, the smell of the damp marshlands are evoked. Within this background individual voices speak: sarcastically affirming, cheerful and enterprising.

Lofting discovered in *The Voyages* a style for the Dolittle books which permitted sequels to follow. A sequel to a fairy tale is difficult to imagine. On the other hand, the reminiscing biographer or historian can always produce or add something new. If Lofting wanted to continue to write after the success of the first book, he had to find a new narrative form. The fictitious biographer made detailed, realistic description possible and, at the same time, gave him free berth for his fancy. The formal realism in no way excludes fantastic content. Dolittle's character and his adventures remain irrational, that is, beyond practical experience and logical thought processes. Following the example of *Gulliver's Travels*, the accurate report indeed intensifies the fantastic events. From a theoretical viewpoint, Lofting's second book took the step from the loose poetical narrative 'romance' to the realistic 'novel' form.

> 'The novel is realistic; the romance is poetic or epic: we should now call it "mythic" ... The two types, which are polar, indicate the double descent of prose narrative: the novel develops from the lineage of non-fictitious narrative forms – the letter, the journal, the memoir or biography, the chronicle or history; it develops, so to speak, out of documents; stylistically it stresses representative detail, "mimesis" in its narrow sense. The romance, on the other end, the continuator of the epic and the medieval romance, may neglect verisimilitude of detail (the reproduction of individuated speech in dialogue, for example) addressing itself to a higher reality, a deeper psychology.'

René Wellek and Austin Warren *Theory of Literature* Penguin Books 1963, (page 216)

The titles and dedications of the two Dolittle books discussed here once again support this distinction in a convincing manner. By the title, *The Story of Doctor Dolittle*, the doctor's story itself is announced. It is understood as complete. On the other hand, with a title like *The Voyages of Doctor Dolittle*, a specific chapter, a piece of Dolittle's adventurous life, is promised. The dedication of the fairy tale is for all children, large and small: 'To all children – children in years and children in heart. I dedicate this story.' The novel is dedicated to two particular children, his own: 'To Elizabeth and Colin.'

From *Bookbird*, 4, 1970

The critic as judge of quality

Elizabeth Cook compares alternative versions of 'Cinderella' from the point of view of style and conformity to what she takes to be the true meaning of the story. Her interpretation of the central theme of the folk tale (Cinderella's triumph is recognition of her true status, not promotion into something different) is plausible and enlightening, though alternative views are possible. Her evaluation of the text is based on norms established by herself and those who think like her and we should feel free to disagree with some of her judgements. Her comments on, for example, 'Oh dear you are making fun of me' (in version B) might not be generally shared, and is 'vulgar' a proper term with which to condemn the language of a folktale? Nevertheless, the procedure that she adopts (firmly rooted in the Cambridge tradition) is an extremely valuable contribution to the discussion of children's literature.

Cinderella's sisters get ready for a ball   Elizabeth Cook

A. 'Our young misses were also invited; for they cut a very grand figure among the quality. They were mightily delighted at this invitation, and wonderfully busy in chusing out such gowns, petticoats and head clothes as might best become them. This was a new trouble to Cinderilla; for it was she who ironed her sisters' linen, and plaited their ruffles. They talked all day long of nothing but how they should be dressed. "For my part (said the eldest) I will wear my red velvet suit, with French trimming."

' "And I (said the youngest) shall only have my usual petticoat; but then, to make amends for that, I will put on my gold-flowered mantua, and my diamond stomacher, which is far from being the most ordinary one in the world."

'They sent for the best tire-woman they could get, to make up their head-dresses, and adjust their double pinners, and they had their red brushes

and patches from Mademoiselle de la Poché. Cinderilla was likewise called
up to them to be consulted in all these matters, for she had excellent notions,
and advised them always for the best; nay, and offered her service to dress
their heads, which they were very willing she should do. As she was doing
this, they said to her, "Cinderilla, would you not be glad to go to the ball?"

' "Ah! (said she) you only jeer at me; it is not for such as I am to go
thither."

' "Thou art in the right of it (replied they) it would make the people laugh
to see a Cinderbreech at a ball." Anyone but Cinderilla would have dressed
their heads awry; but she was very good, and dressed them perfectly well.
They were almost two days without eating, so much they were transported
with joy. They broke above a dozen of laces in trying to be laced up close,
that they might have a fine slender shape, and they were continually at their
looking-glass. At last the happy day came; they went to court, and Cinderilla
followed them with her eyes as long as she could, and when she had lost
sight of them, she fell a crying.'

Charles Perrault
Cendrillon
translator Guy Miège
at some date between
1697 and 1719:
text exactly
reproduced in
*Histories or Tales
of Past Times*
Nonesuch Press, 1925
(limited edition) and
Fortune Press, 1928
(limited edition)
and reproduced with
a few very slight
alterations in Lang's
Blue Fairy Book

B. 'Our two young ladies received invitations, for they cut quite a figure in
the country. So there they were, both feeling very pleased and very busy
choosing the clothes and the hair-styles which would suit them best. More
work for Cinderella, for it was she who ironed her sisters' underwear and
goffered their linen cuffs. Their only talk was of what they would wear.

' "I", said the elder, "shall wear my red velvet dress and my collar of
English lace."

' "I", said the younger, "shall wear just my ordinary skirt; but, to make
up, I shall put on my gold-embroidered cape and my diamond clasp, which
is quite out of the common."

'The right hairdresser was sent for to supply double-frilled coifs, and
patches were bought from the right patch-maker. They called Cinderella
to ask her opinion, for she had excellent taste. She made useful suggestions
and even offered to do their hair for them. They accepted willingly.
'While she was doing it, they said to her:

' "Cinderella, how would you like to go to the ball?"

' "Oh dear, you are making fun of me. It wouldn't do for me."

' "You are quite right. It would be a joke. People would laugh if they saw
a Cinderbottom at the ball."

'Anyone-else would have done their hair in knots for them, but she had a sweet nature, and she finished it perfectly. For two days they were so excited that they ate almost nothing. They broke a good dozen laces trying to tighten their stays to make their waists slimmer, and they were never away from their mirrors.

'At last the great day arrived. They set off, and Cinderella watched them until they were out of sight. When she could no longer see them, she began to cry.'

Charles Perrault
Cendrillon
translator Geoffrey
Brereton, Penguin
Books, 1957

C.   'Ashputtel's two sisters were asked to come. So they called her up, and said, "Now, comb our hair, brush our shoes, and tie our sashes for us, for we are going to dance at the King's feast." Then she did as she was told, but when all was done she could not help crying, for she thought to herself she should have liked to go to the dance too; and at last she begged her mother very hard to let her go. "You, Ashputtel?" said she. "You have nothing to wear, no clothes at all, and who cannot even dance – you want to go to the ball?"'

Jacob and Wilhelm
Grimm
Aschenputtel
translator Edgar
Taylor, 1823
Puffin, 1948

D.   'They thought of nothing but dances and parties. So, when they got an invitation to the grand ball at the castle, they could not eat for two days, they were so excited.

'"You must come and do our hair," they told Cinderella. "You must make it look beautiful because the Prince himself will be there."

'"I wish – Oh, how I wish that I, too, might go to the ball," Cinderella said, as her clever fingers shaped their curls.

'"What, you!" exclaimed the Ugly Sisters, and they laughed so unkindly, that anyone else but Cinderella would have tugged at their hair. But Cinderella was Cinderella – as good as she was pretty. And so she did her very best to make the Sisters look handsome. She pressed their fine dresses, and she fetched and carried all day long, until at last they were ready to leave for the wonderful ball.

'"Now I am really all alone," Cinderella told her white cat, as she sat down by the fire. "You are the only one who loves me ..."

'But Cinderella did have someone else to love her besides her little white cat.'

My Book of Cinderella
Odhams All Colour
Book Series, 1960
(name of writer
not given)

E.   'The younger sister who was short and dumpy chose a cloak of emerald green. Cinderella thought it was quite the wrong colour, and made her less graceful than ever. It hurt her not to be able to tell her stepsister so, and to see the soft flower-like colours which she loved cast aside.

'At last the night of the ball came. Poor Cinderella! Her stepmother and sisters were so bad-tempered, and scolded and ordered her about so much that she did not know who to obey first.

' "That curl is not right. Brush it out and do it again," said the younger sister when Cinderella was trying hard to make her hair look nice. Anyone could see that both sisters were angry at having to have their hair curled with hot irons, while Cinderella stood there with lovely, naturally curly golden ringlets glinting in the candlelight.

'Cinderella tried again to make the stiff curls lie neatly, but it was no use trying to please. "You are brushing too hard, you clumsy girl," shouted the younger sister. "You'll spoil the whole effect" ...

'Cinderella imagined what the ball would be like. She thought of the glittering lights, the lovely dresses, sparkling jewels, and of the handsome Prince dancing in the minuets. In fact, Cinderella almost imagined she really was at the ball!

' "Oh, how I wish I could go with you!" she said.

' "Don't be such a foolish girl," said her stepmother. "You know quite well that you cannot come. Just look at you now! Wouldn't the Prince laugh if he were to see you!"

'Cinderella was thoughtful for a moment then screwed up her courage to say:

' "Couldn't you let me have one of the dresses you have in that big chest? There are so many that surely one would fit me. I promise you would not be ashamed of me if you let me go with you."

' "Don't say any more, child! You can't go, and that's the end of it," answered her stepmother angrily.'

Cinderella
Nelson, 1958
(name of writer not
given)

F. 'Invitations to the ball were sent to all the Princesses, Duchesses, and great ladies, and among others to Cinderella's two proud sisters.

'No one even thought of inviting poor Cinderella, but the proud sisters were very much excited. Cinderella was so kind that she didn't say a word about being disappointed, but sewed and ironed for her proud sisters, helping them to get their dresses ready. When the day of the ball came she helped them to dress, and brushed and arranged their hair for them, and they just called and shouted for anything they wanted. At last they were ready, and

Amabel Williams-
Ellis
Cinderella, in
Princesses and Trolls
Barrie, 1950

Cinderella went to the door and saw them go off in a grand coach drawn by four horses.

'Then at last poor little Cinderella began to cry.'

G. 'At last the first day of the festival arrived and the two sisters began dressing for the big ball. It took them all afternoon, and when they had finished, they were worth looking at.

'They were dressed in satin and silk. Their bustles were puffed, their bodices stuffed, their skirts were ruffled and tufted with bows; their sleeves were muffled with furbelows. They wore bells that tinkled, and glittering rings; and rubies and pearls and little birds' wings! They plastered their pimples and covered their scars with moons and stars and hearts. They powdered their hair, and piled it high with plumes and jewelled darts.

'At the last minute Cinderella was called in to curl their hair, lace up their bodices and dust off their shoes. When the poor little girl heard they were going to a party at the King's palace, her eyes sparkled and she asked her stepmother whether she might not go too.

' "You?" cried the stepmother. "You, all dusty and cindery, want to go to a party? You haven't even a dress to wear and you can't dance." '

Wanda Gàg
Cinderella, in
Tales from Grimm
Faber, 1937

The tale of Cinderella deserves its fame, but does not deserve the cheapening and distortion that so often follow fame in the nineteenth and twentieth centuries. It is a folk tale which was 'retold' at the turn of the seventeenth century so sensitively that for ever afterwards it has been remembered as an aristocratic children's story. It is not a story about Wishes Come True, although people are always saying so, even in forewords written for children; it is a story about Trial, Recognition and Judgement. In traditional stories people who wish always come to a bad end. Cinderella is her father's true heir, and is born to be a queen. Her place in the family is usurped by the Proud Sisters, and they try to prevent her from entering the contest by which the right to the kingdom is to be decided. Her situation is the same as that of the untried Theseus, or Sigurd, or Arthur, or Beaumains, or La Cote Male Tale; the glass (or fur) slipper has the same place in her story as the Sword in the Stone has in the story of Arthur's kingship. The knights have no weapons or tournament armour; she has no ball-dress. She differs only in being a woman instead of a man, and in suffering more from her foster-parent and foster-sisters, since one of the usurpers has married her real father. In stepmother stories representation of the heroine's true house and lineage is divided

The position of women as heroines in folklore might have something to do with memories of a matriarchal society, or with the transmission of the stories by successive generations of old wives and nurses between the Father and the Prince, just as in exposed-baby stories the role of usurper is divided between the upstart king and the unknowing foster-father.

As soon as one sees that Cinderella is 'really' a princess, and that her cindery rags are a disguise which is stripped away by magic, the story can never be told as the story of a little waif, without name or inheritance, who dreams of an unnatural transformation of herself and finds that magic makes it 'come true'. The imagery latent in the tale does not shadow adolescent wishfulfilment. It suggests the stripping away of the disguise that conceals the soul from the eyes of others – even the shedding of the ragged personalities that prevent it from manifesting itself as it should by nature or by grace. Cinderella must be a virtuous maiden, and she must suffer at the hands of the usurpers, but she must suffer like a princess, and not like an ignorant and repining little girl.

Perrault (A and B) makes his Cinderella a girl whom we can accept as a candidate for the throne, when she comes to the test; she will be a good queen, for she is getting through the present initiation with dignity. She is intelligent and has good taste; she performs the appointed tasks thoroughly, but without servility. She is not making a martyr of herself. She does more than is required, but Perrault's short record of it in 'even offered to do their hair for them' does not suggest self-righteousness. 'She had a sweet nature' is originally *elle estoit bonne*, which is quite simple and undemonstrative. When the usurping Sisters taunt her, she replies with 'Oh dear, you are making fun of me', which is natural, and unruffled, and also shows a certain urbanity; she knows quite well what they are up to, and is not going to be drawn. There is no pleading, and no self-pity, *and no wishing*. She follows them with her eyes as long as she can, and only then begins to cry. The nearest she gets to a wish is the 'If only I could ...', in the midst of her tears, in her later reply to her godmother's point-blank question as to why she is crying. It takes only a few seconds for her to recover her wits enough to make useful suggestions about raw material, such as rat-traps, for her godmother to use in her magic.

The Grimms' early nineteenth-century Cinderella (C and G) is not quite as self-controlled. She does plead with the Stepmother, and she does burst into tears before the Sisters have left. Nevertheless the passage is so short in the original, closely translated in C, that there is no time for Cinderella to explore her own emotions. In G Wanda Gàg sensibly leaves this part alone, expanding only the description of the Sisters' toilette. It is natural that there should be more dialogue between Cinderella and her stepmother in the Grimm variant of the story: the contrast between stepmother and real mother is more important throughout,

Of course these interpretations are heads and tails of the same penny; it is quite possible to say that we like to think we are princesses when we are 'really' scullery-maids by origin. I am concerned only to point out the likeness between *Cinderella* and legends which are not commonly seen as images of wishfulfilment. In *The Myth of the Birth of the Hero* Otto Rank gives the same wishfulfilment interpretation to all of them.

In an early version of *Cinderella*, and in the related *Donkey-Skin*, the heroine is understandably disgraced; either she herself has murdered a previous stepmother, or else her father has contracted, or tried to contract, an incestuous union with her. In these variants her exile among the cinders is an expiation or a cleansing from pollution, and the ring or shoe by which the Prince knows her is even more clearly a token of restoration to an original state from which she has fallen and later it is a magic bird and a magic tree on the real mother's grave that throw down the gold and silver clothes which are Cinderella's birthright.

D and E have been included to show how much the figure of Cinderella has been diminished in the popular storytelling of the present time. It is not just a matter of vulgar language or sentimental trimming. The heroine herself has been turned into a cry-baby, a child rather than a young woman, and a very unpleasantly sugary and self-satisfied child at that. She has to be 'as good as she was pretty'. She is given 'lovely, naturally curly golden ringlets glinting in the candlelight' (after doing the rough housework and sitting in the ashes?) and seems to feel some complacency in watching the Sisters' annoyance when their straight hair will not curl like hers. She is plentifully endowed with a capacity for daydreaming, and we are asked to consider it a virtue, as if it were a kind of artistic genius:

> 'She thought of the glittering lights, the lovely dresses, sparkling jewels,
> and of the handsome Prince dancing in the minuets. In fact, Cinderella
> almost imagined she really was at the ball!'

She tries to make the Stepmother 'feel awful' by pleading that she has plenty of dresses of her own in the chest; no wonder the Stepmother loses her temper. She is 'hurt' by the taste of the Sisters; she did not tell them, but one cannot help feeling that she made it very apparent. She catches up the white kitten when she is feeling passionately sorry for herself. 'You are the only one who loves me', she says, and the kitten must have hated it.

In Perrault Cinderella is a girl undergoing the tests that will show whether she is a queen or not; in this respect she is a heroine comparable with the heroes of legend. But A and B are quite different in temper from any of the other original sources that I have reproduced in this section. This original source is already a children's story, and one that shows a shrewd knowledge of children's tastes. Perrault knew that very young children like humour, and repetition, and conversations, and little touches of detail from the daily life of their own families. He also knew that they are frightened if they see grown-ups displaying strong personal emotion. Consequently his *Cinderella* is more light-hearted, familiar and everyday than the folk tales incorporated by poets in Greek legends, or taken down from peasant storytellers in the nineteenth century. It is not put back in time into some heroic or golden age; it is given a definite contemporary setting in the court of Louis XIV. Cinderella's family belongs, or almost belongs, to 'the quality'. The Sisters talk for days about the various garments that make up a fashionable *toilette* in 1700: a 'petticoat' (*jupe*) or underskirt, quilted and flowered, and nearly all revealed in front by the 'mantua' (*manteau*), a silk overgown cut somewhat loosely, open to the waist, with the skirt looped back into a bustle; a *barrière*, which A equates with the English 'stomacher', or embroidered cover for the front of the laced corset, seen between the edges of the 'mantua' bodice; and the 'double pinner' (*cornettes à deux rangs*), a head-dress of two upstanding stiffened lace frills, which is almost a uniform in polite society. All this must have been tremendously entertaining to the Perrault children, who no doubt overheard young women gossiping about clothes, and giggled at exclamations over broken corset laces.

A *Cinderella* as easy and amusing as this could now be produced only by stripping the folk tale down again to its bare plot, and setting it in a modern house, with modern clothes, and dishwashers, and motorcars, and sherry parties. To a writer this would mean his own house, and his wife's clothes. In addition to unavoidable national overtones there would be the unmistakable class characteristics about which we now feel so embarrassed. The resulting tale might be entertaining to children of five or six, but only to the writer's own children, and to others like them. And there is nothing much like kingship in modern society. As tradition has canonized Perrault's coach and footmen, and even his corset laces, it seems better to agree that he has fixed the action of *Cinderella* in 1700 for all successive generations, and take advantage of the fact that none of us, however we live, know what the court of Louis XIV was like, without having pictures to look at. If the storyteller exploits the period charm of the tale, it will raise the age at which it can first be told, perhaps to eight or nine or even ten. At this age children can listen to Perrault himself; nothing could be more fresh and crisp and even than his narrative. However the period detail begins to worry the storyteller when it comes to choosing a translation.

> It has been done by Osbert Sitwell, but only as a grown-up satire on the self-pitying Cinderella depicted in D and E

A is very nearly contemporary with Perrault's book, and it delights the grown-up reader by giving him the flavour of life and literature at the turn of the seventeenth century. 'Our young misses' is just the right term for the Sisters. They are not exactly ladies of the court; they are on the fringe of it, being members of the 'ever-rising rising middle class', then making new pretensions to leisure and culture. The Stepmother is a 'madam', like the London 'City Madams'. 'Mightily delighted with the invitation, and wonderfully busy in chusing out such gowns … as might become them' is written in the fashionable colloquial English that we hear in Restoration comedy, and it suits the tale. The articles of attire discussed by the Sisters present no problem to Guy Miège, because they are still being worn, and he can use the ordinary English names for them.

I do not think that much of this pleasure will be shared by children of eight. They may notice an indefinitely old-fashioned effect, but nothing more. Some of them will be put off by the un-English use of 'thou' and 'you', where Perrault's *tu* and *vous* show that the Sisters are addressing Cinderella as a servant, and that she is replying to them as her mistresses. Yet Lang, who was a good judge, thought that Miège's translation would be attractive to children; in 1889 he used it for all the Perrault stories in his *Blue Fairy Book*, although he had more recent versions to choose from. The few alterations he made were very slight; the rude nickname 'Cinderbreech' was changed into the less improper 'Cinderwench', and some of the fashion-vocabulary was modified. Oddly enough, Miège's fashion-vocabulary may now be a help rather than a hindrance to the storyteller who brings plenty of pictures with him. 'Double pinner' has no previous associations for children, and they can attach the word to their picture at once. 'Coif' may already be associated with other things, for instance with a nun's head-dress, which is as unlike the 'double pinners' as anything could be. Some of the dialogue of the Sisters may have to be cut, even though it expresses their snobbery so well; it is interesting to come across two or three new names for clothes, but six or seven would be tedious.

These two translations are probably of equal value for reading to children; one group may be happier with the old, and another with the new. B is lively, and manages to imitate Perrault's neat, brisk manner in modern English. A class of children who had not heard many old stories would probably prefer it to A.

Some teachers and storytellers feel that the less well-known variant of *Cinderella* collected by the Grimm brothers is more interesting than Perrault's story. C does not give a fair impression of it, because in this variant the Sisters are less important than the Stepmother, and none of the usurpers are given as much prominence as the magic bird and the magic tree. In preparing his Proud Sisters for the king's three-day feast – a much more heroic or mediaeval affair than Perrault's ball – Grimm may be influenced by Perrault; literary fairy tales can turn back into folk tales transmitted by word of mouth.

The Grimm brothers never try to follow Perrault's method of adapting a peasant tale by putting in details from their own children's everyday life. There is no description at all of contemporary fashion. The phrase translated in 1823 as 'tie our sashes for us' (C), which does suggest Regency ball-dresses, is *schnalle uns die schnallen*, and probably means 'buckle our shoes, do up our shoe-buckles, or shoe-straps'. The tale is timeless, and the sadness of Cinderella's ordeal is not relieved by any wit or humour. It was never a story for children under eight, and it never will be.

If one chooses this variant of the story, there will be no temptation to make it brisk in the Perrault manner; but in telling it to children one may have to go beyond the original words. Edgar Taylor's fairly literal contemporary translation (C) shows that the Grimm narrative is fluent but bleak. There is no word-painting, and no impersonation. The spoken word is not at all vivid; no one would ever say,

> 'You, Ashputtel? You have nothing to wear, no clothes at all, and who cannot even dance – you want to go to the ball?'

A little rearrangement and spontaneous development produces the audibly shrill protest of Wanda Gàg's outraged Stepmother (G):

> 'You? You, all dusty and cindery, want to go to a party? You haven't even a dress to wear and you can't dance.'

The character is created in the words. Wanda Gàg's description of the scene in which the sisters are dressing is exuberant, and lightens the tone of the story. She puts them into the clothes of about 1700, without using any of the technical terms of the period; she is probably remembering Perrault here. This mixture of sources does not matter much, since the Grimm tale has no period of its own. The mixture that is deadly to its spirit is Walt Disney's ugly patchwork in which magic worked by a godmother is stitched on to magic worked by a bird and a tree. The 'book of the film' is still available.

G is probably the best version of the Grimm story to read to eight- and nine-year-olds. Wanda Gàg's Cinderella is a practical, high-spirited person who 'does not mope or cry' and washes the cinders out of her hair herself. There is honest homeliness, as well as serious magic, in this writer's storytelling. It is a pity that she calls Cinderella a 'little girl' throughout the story, because although Cinderella may have been 'little' when she planted the magic hazel twig that grew into the magic tree, she cannot be 'little' when she rides off as the Prince's bride, even allowing for the mediaeval custom of child marriage; but this only means remembering to leave out one word.

In a preface of 1947 Wanda Gàg explains how she first came to 'retell' the Grimm stories. She made a literal translation, and found that some of them, especially those in dialect, sounded clear and lively as they were.

> 'Others, which were smooth, warm and colourful in the original, came out thin, lifeless and clumsy. It seemed evident that in the case of the latter, only a free translation could convey the true flavour of the originals.'

Not all her alterations and developments were determined by the kind of German written by the Grimm brothers. Some were made on purpose to interest modern children in stories that were first written down for an audience that included adults, because although she herself was 'avidly reading fairy tales' at fourteen, she thought in the mid-1930s that 'the fairy-tale age limit' had dropped by about two years, and therefore envisaged an audience of four- to twelve-year-olds. Her account of the language that she was compelled to use is so good that it should be quoted in full.

'It seemed advisable to simplify some sections in order that a four-to-twelve age group might be assured of getting the full value of the stories.

'By simplification I mean:

1. freeing hybrid stories of confusing passages;
2. using repetition for clarity where a mature style does not include it;
3. employing actual dialogue to sustain or revive interest in places where the narrative is too condensed for children.

'However, I do not mean writing in words of one or two syllables. True, the *careless* use of large words is confusing to children; but long, even unfamiliar words are relished and easily absorbed by them, provided they have enough colour and sound-value.'

The quality of Amabel Williams-Ellis's work for children is not well represented by F: it is flat in comparison with the free and lively writing in her collection of Grimm stories, which does not include *Cinderella*. F is given here as an example of a very short and simple *Cinderella* which is inoffensive, and could be read by a teacher who had some particular reason for telling the story to a class of five- or six-year-olds. At least it would be better to use F than to use D or E.

I do not believe that reading from D or E could be justified in any situation. The language in which these passages are written is as objectionable as their portrait of Cinderella. Yet whereas one can argue about Cinderella herself, it is almost impossible to produce reasons for saying that the language of D and E is sentimental and vulgar. Any attempt to dispute the question with someone who wants to defend D and E will look like a display of snobbery instead of an exercise in logic.

Those who dislike D and E will probably fasten upon phrases like 'as her clever fingers shaped their curls', 'to see the soft flower-like colours which she loved cast aside', 'lovely, naturally curly golden ringlets glinting in the candlelight', 'the glittering lights, the lovely dresses, sparkling jewels, and the handsome Prince dancing in the minuets'. Talking among themselves, they will probably say, 'It's like a woman's magazine'.

This is an opinion, not an argument. What can be said in reply to the defendant who claims either that women's magazines are good, or that, since they are the only publications that many children see at home, a teacher might as well make use of their language in order to make good stories seem natural to them ? Not very much, but something may be better than nothing.

The words I have just quoted from D and E are words that cheat, and if children are used to cheating language there is all the more reason for introducing them to honest writing. They cheat because, like a gushing man or woman, they gush with feeling that is not stirred by anything in particular, and is always the same; never fear, or admiration, or awe, or hunger, but a comfortable brooding satisfaction that prevents the reader from seeing what the story would otherwise put in front of his eyes. If he *saw* Cinderella the reader would feel respect for her skill or self-control, excitement by, or admiration for her beauty, and contempt or amusement when the Sisters chose the wrong clothes. '*Clever* fingers *shaped*' and 'lovely, naturally curly' and 'flower-like colours cast aside' obliterate these distinctions in a single response: 'Oh, how sweet!' A common cosiness silvers everything.

One observation drawn from experience might be allowed to qualify as an argument. Many readers who once knew and liked the stories in women's magazines have changed their minds and now like the novels of Jane Austen much better. I have yet to meet a reader who once knew and liked the novels of Jane Austen and then rejected them for the stories in women's magazines. By the same token, a reader who really knows Perrault and Wanda Gàg's Grimm is most unlikely to go back to the anonymous modern versions I have been castigating.

From *The Ordinary and the Fabulous*, CUP, 1969

The critic diagnosing the author

I. A. Richards
*Principles of Literary
Criticism*
Routledge and
Kegan Paul, 1924

M. Laski
*Mrs Ewing, Mrs
Molesworth and
Mrs Hodgson Burnett*
Barker, 1950

P. Green
*Kenneth Grahame
1859–1932*
Murray, 1959

I. A. Richards persuaded the Cambridge English School that 'whatever psychoanalysis may aver, the mental processes of the poet are not a very profitable field for investigation. They offer far too happy a hunting-ground for uncontrollable conjecture'. And Marghanita Laski in her monograph decided that Frances Hodgson Burnett's books were 'far more enjoyable if one knows as little as possible of what they reveal of her own pesonality'. Nevertheless, the lives and personalities of authors continue to intrigue us and our curiosity is fed by a steady stream of intimate biographies. Some of these throw light on the processes that produce great literature while others remain at the level of gossip. Peter Green's life of Kenneth Grahame is of the former category since it shows how the obsessions of a disappointed man can be relieved by storytelling. We might add that biographies have themselves been described by Margaret Meek (page 325) as 'simply another kind of fiction where the author borrows from life on behalf of art'.

Exile from the Golden City   Georgina Battiscombe

Kenneth Grahame was born on 8 March a hundred years ago. In 1933, a year after his death, Mr Patrick Chalmers published a biography which, according to Mr Green, 'has long been out of print and is far from being a satisfactory account'. Satisfactory or not, it has remained for twenty-seven years the only available Life of Grahame, so that Mr Green's own book is not only a fitting tribute to mark the centenary year but also a valuable and badly needed addition to the sum of literary biography.

Mr Green adopts what may be called the psychological method. He uses Kenneth Grahame's writings, and more especially *The Wind in the Willows*, as guides to their author's thought and character, presuming that in his books Grahame 'was letting his anarchic Id out for a fictional romp'. The dangers of such a method are obvious, especially when the author in question has declared, as Grahame did most emphatically, that his book holds 'no second meaning'. But authors do not always speak truth about their inner motives, and in this particular biography the use of the psychological method has been brilliantly justified by results. Most of Mr Green's psychological deductions are solidly based on facts attested by documentary evidence – the formidable collection of notes is almost too weighty for a book presumably intended for the general reader rather than for the student – and the resulting portrait of Kenneth Grahame is accurate, life-like, and extremely lively.

The Golden Age, Dream Days, and *The Wind in the Willows* are still selling in their thousands, yet although Kenneth Grahame is one of the best-known writers of childhood tales, it seems that he was not particularly interested in children as such, but only in the child who had once been Kenneth Grahame. Not a particularly happy child either, yet it is without irony that he describes childhood as 'the golden age'. For this golden age is also dream days. He is not thinking of the everyday life which he remembered only too well, a life filled with lessons and punishments and apparently unavoidable misunderstandings with the grown-ups whom he was later to satirize as 'the Olympians', a title which Mr Green describes as 'diabolically well chosen'; rather, he is referring to that life of the imagination which is the special prerogative of children and poets. Mr Green rightly indicates the inner meaning of the incident in *The Wind in the Willows* when Mole consoles Rat for his vanished dream of foreign parts by sitting him down to scribble away, pencil in hand, but he omits to call attention to the significant point that Rat is scribbling verse. Kenneth Grahame was a poet *manqué*; had he been a poet indeed he would have been a happier man, because he would have retained his right of entry into this lost world of the imagination.

Yet, poet or no poet, all his life Kenneth Grahame clung to the core of his childhood's imaginings, which was the vision of the City. At first it was the golden city of a child's daydream, where, in Traherne's phrase, 'the dust and stones of the street were as precious as gold, the gates were at first the end of the world'. Later, in adolescence, the City became identified in some mysterious but vital manner with the actual stones of Oxford. Mr Green is certainly right in supposing that his Uncle John's refusal to allow him to go up to Oxford was the most crushing blow that Kenneth Grahame ever received. Remembering the many sorrows and disappointments of his personal life, his unhappy marriage, and the tragedy of his only son, this statement may well seem a little exaggerated, but nothing was to affect his character so deeply as the destruction of his Oxford dream. As he said years later to his wife, 'You like people but I like places.' He had grown to know and to love Oxford in the years which he spent there at St Edward's School, but the schoolboy could only walk as a stranger through 'the streets where the great men go'. No one can be truly of Oxford who is not of Oxford University. As the head of his school with a sheaf of prizes to his credit Grahame had well and truly earned his right to enter that university, nor could the financial difficulty in his way be counted an absolutely overwhelming obstacle. True, the Grahame children themselves were more or less penniless, but the uncle who stood like an angel with a flaming sword forbidding him entrance into Eden was himself a comparatively wealthy man who could well afford to pay the cost of a university education. 'What passed between the two of them at the crucial interview will never be known,' says Mr Green, but it is reasonable to guess that the nephew pleaded to be sent to Oxford, promising to refund the cost when once he should be launched upon a career and earning his own living, a plea which the uncle decisively and scornfully refused. When we remember how large an income Kenneth Grahame was to earn both as Secretary to the Bank of England and as the author of three 'best-sellers' that refusal takes on a tragically ironic aspect.

Children who are brought up without, to use Grahame's own phrase, 'a proper equipment of parents' are very apt to feel themselves to be 'outsiders'. In Grahame's case this feeling was most unfortunately confirmed and intensified by his uncle's attitude over this question of Oxford.

> 'Uncle John put his high-falutin nephew into a practical job to bring him
> to his senses and to teach him his role in society as a *de facto* orphan [says
> Mr Green]. It was not that he could not afford to send Kenneth to Oxford;
> he disapproved of such a step on principle.'

But the essence of Kenneth Grahame's grievance did not lie in the fact that he had been deprived of the education which most boys of his class and upbringing took as a matter of course, 'part of the natural order of things, as inevitable as moon, sun and stars'. His justifiable bitterness had deeper roots. Oxford had come to stand in his mind as the image of his Golden City, and it was the citizenship of that City which he was now denied. The loss of Oxford meant that he must for ever remain an outsider, not merely on the conscious level but in the most profound depths of his being. It is significant that Oxford should figure over and over again in his dreams, those dreams which he himself described as 'a reaction from life'. 'I constantly at night ran down to a fairy Oxford,' he writes, 'the real thing, yet transformed.' In time the dream Oxford almost came to displace the real one in his affection so that when he revisited that still-beloved city he could only say,

'I like the fairy one better.'

This same sense of disappointment at the discrepancy between actual and ideal was to mar Kenneth Grahame's first visit to Rome, the place which came nearest to Oxford in his affection – 'the beauty of Rome was not just that particular beauty that we had caught a glimpse of through the magic casement of our own idealism'. No place was ever to prove a satisfactory embodiment of his dream, an outward and visible showing-forth of the invisible City. In *The Golden Age*, when child and artist are discussing their dream city, the artist quotes the famous saying of Marcus Aurelius, 'the poet says, "dear city of Cecrops," and wilt thou not say "dear city of God"?' It was an affirmation and an identification that Kenneth Grahame was never able to make. The Scottish Calvinism hereditary in his family he found almost wholly repugnant, while the religious attitude of his Olympian relatives had not been calculated to appeal to any child – true, 'they went to church regularly of their own accord', but 'they betrayed no greater delight in the experience than ourselves'. Neopaganism was the literary fashion of Kenneth Grahame's youth, a philosophy which Mr Green describes as 'a kind of synthetic pantheism based on nature-worship'; significantly enough, one of the first of Grahame's published essays is entitled 'The Rural Pan'. Such 'pagan' writers as Henry Harland and Oscar Wilde, John Davidson and W. E. Henley provided him with his first taste of literary society, and it comes as somewhat of a shock to discover that at least two of the stories which were later collected together as *Dream Days* made their original appearance in *The Yellow Book*. Selina and Charlotte, Edward and Harold must have found themselves in strange company alongside Cynara and the creatures of Aubrey Beardsley.

The oddest part of Kenneth Grahame's career is this period, which Mr Green so aptly describes as 'his uneasy literary flirtation with the Beardsley group'. Although he could not subscribe to their very vocal expressions of religious belief, both by taste and temperament Grahame would have been much more at home with Belloc and Chesterton and their cult of ale and the open road. Nevertheless, in their own manner the children of *The Golden Age* and *Dream Days* are very much *fin de siècle* characters. They stand midway between the dutiful Victorian children of Miss Yonge's imagining and the cheerful modern extroverts of *Swallows and Amazons*. The world is changing; no longer can they take for granted with Miss Yonge a stable state of affairs in which children are always and unquestionably subject to their elders, but neither can they conceive of the affectionate relationship based on an easy, natural 'give-and-take' between adult and child which is one of the most pleasant features of Mr Arthur Ransome's stories. True, the Amazons are possessed of a very trying pair of great-aunts, but it seems that although mothers may nowadays attain to the status of 'the best of all natives', aunts of any sort are always and irredeemably Olympian.

The essential difference between Kenneth Grahame's Olympians and Mr Ransome's natives lies in the fact that the natives recognize and respect the existence of a world of childish imaginings which the Olympians entirely ignore. And although they admit its existence the 'good natives' do not infringe its privacy: a grown-up may be invited into that world, as Kenneth Grahame's children invite the curate and the artist and the absent-minded old scholar-parson, but they must never intrude. Even if invited they should not outstay their welcome; in Mr Ransome's story Mrs Walker rows away again with the Ship's Baby, leaving the Swallows alone on Wild-Cat Island.

Writing of *The Golden Age* and *Dream Days* contemporary reviewers found fault with 'the ambiguous status of the narrator, fluctuating in viewpoint between child and adult'. Mr Green endorses their objection, but at the risk of differing from so strong a consensus of critical opinion it must be pointed out that on a second reading both books seem to be written from one unvarying viewpoint, which is that of an adult. The 'I' of the stories is surely not a child but a grown-up looking back on childhood, and most of the humour and pathos depend upon the fact that this 'I' knows very well, for instance, that the Roman Road does not lead to Rome, and that the Sleeping Princess is merely a nineteenth-century girl in love. Things are otherwise in books written for children rather than about them. To return once again to Mr Ransome and the Swallows and Amazons, Kanchenjunga *is* Kanchenjunga even if it is also Coniston Old Man, and the North Pole *is* the North Pole although it is situated at the head of Windermere. The reader is not let into the author's Olympian secret; if the characters are under an imaginative illusion he shares in that illusion with them.

This distinction, which is so easy to see and so difficult to explain, becomes perfectly clear when *The Golden Age* and *Dream Days* are compared with *The Wind in the Willows*, the only book by Kenneth Grahame which can properly be described as a children's book and not a book about children. This animal fantasy originated with the bed-time tales which Kenneth Grahame told to his small son. It has become one of the most popular of nursery classics, beloved by three generations of children, but perhaps to be properly understood and appreciated only by their elders. The book is full of overtones, audible enough to children but not comprehensible even to the most precocious. Mr Green lists the memories, conscious and subconscious, which went to the making of *The*

Wind in the Willows:

> 'Summers of casual Mediterranean wandering; the childhood pattern set by
> Berkshire meadows and the lazy Thames, the eternal solitary lure of the
> Ridgeway; paganism, Pan, and *The Yellow Book*; the odd, near-eccentric
> friends who were or had been especially close to him – Furnivall, Henley,
> Q, 'Atky'; years of political unrest, the collapse of the country squirearchy,
> urban radicalism which meant strikes and riots; the London Scottish
> Territorials; the winding creeks and quiet backwaters of Fowey; books by
> the hundred, known and re-read time and time again – the Odyssey, Grimm,
> Andersen, Aesop, William Morris, Anstey, Wilde, Matthew Arnold; his
> own life with its chequered pattern of repressions, disappointments and
> compromises; above all, the small child for whom, night after night, he
> wove the beginnings of the fabric – all these met, mingled, were transformed
> in the light alembic of that delicate mind.'

No child could possibly disentangle that fabric's subtle pattern or appreciate the
full flavour of the mixture distilled in that alembic. Still less could a child follow
'the rising curve of unconscious, implicit symbolism' which Mr Green traces
through Kenneth Grahame's early essays and his stories about children until it
becomes 'all-pervasive' in this his last book. Mr Green's chapter on *The Wind in
the Willows* is christened 'The Road to Xanadu' after Professor Livingston Lowes's
famous study of the subconscious memories out of which Coleridge fashioned the
magic of *Kubla Khan*. A critical method which is admirably suited to the dissection
of a major poem written by a drug-addict might appear to be a disproportionately
powerful instrument to apply to a children's story. Occasionally Mr Green does
indeed lose his sense of proportion and allow his psychological imagination –
should it perhaps be 'his imaginative psychology'? – to run away with him. Is
there any really valid reason to suppose that the tragedy of Oscar Wilde 'sank
deep into Grahame's impressionable mind', so deep, in fact, that twelve years
later 'the core of that terrible episode, re-emerged transmuted and scaled down
to animal fantasy in the misfortunes of Mr Toad'? One wonders which of the two,
Mr Toad or Mr Wilde, would be the more affronted by this suggestion. On the
whole, however, Mr Green brings back rich treasure from his explorations into
the unconscious, and 'The Road to Xanadu' is the most fascinating chapter of a
fascinating and perceptive book.

The last word, however, must not be for Mr Green but for his subject.
Kenneth Grahame died on July 6, 1932. By his books he had given delight to
thousands of people, grown-ups and children alike, but to himself life had brought

disillusionment and deep personal unhappiness. It is comforting to know that he is buried at Oxford; after all, he did in the end come to rest within the walls of his City.

From *The Times Literary Supplement*, 13 March 1959

The critic as spokesman for the mature reader

In his article 'A Bit More Practice' (page 196) Alan Garner explains the
problem shared by many serious writers of children's fiction: 'I don't
write for children, but entirely for myself. Yet I do write for children ...'
His books, particularly the latest, 'Red Shift' (1973) never resolve this
paradox and consequently make great demands on even the most
experienced reader. In this otherwise commendatory review of 'The Owl
Service' (1967) Philippa Pearce decides that what is wrong is not Garner's
failure to explain (novelists need not do that) but simply his unwillingness to
make plain. This is as important to her as an adult reader as it is to the child.

The article, published in 'Children's Book News', provides reassurance
to fellow-readers of Garner who share her confusion. One of the critics'
best functions is to make explicit our own misgivings about a work.
Philippa Pearce's position as a distinguished fellow-author of novels that
explore the frontiers between a child's inner and outer reality lends authority
to her statement.

The Owl Service   Philippa Pearce

Alan Garner's writing is marked by hard thinking and hard, fierce imagining.
These have been brought to bear upon a distinctive choice of subject: the meeting-
plane of two contiguous worlds. One is the world that most of us agree to
describe, however inadequately, as ordinary, everyday, or by some such term.
The other is the world of folklore and myth, dream and nightmare and vision.
The wall between these two worlds is tough, but of less than tissue-paper thinness.
Where the thinness can be worn into a transparency or where the unusual pressure
of one world bursts its way into the other, there is the beginning of a Garner story.

In *The Weirdstone of Brisingamen* and *The Moon of Gomrath*, which can be
considered as consecutive parts of the same story, the two worlds were unequally
balanced: the weight of the reader's interest was with the other world, not with

the two ordinary, convenient children who broke through into it.

Then came *Elidor*, realistic-apocalyptic, comic-sublime: the author's art held his two worlds together in exact balance, in a perfection of narrative tension. Here was a splendid achievement.

After that, what *could* he engage upon, unless with unworthy repetition or with abandonment of that special field of the imagination?

The fourth and latest book, *The Owl Service*, brings the worlds together again; but with a difference of method and effect. The story is contained within a remote Welsh valley where the power of that other world lies like some bottomless lake. Into this place are gathered the everyday people who are at the centre of the story: two boys and a girl, no blood relation, yet brought together so closely that at one time it seems as if only the spilling of blood can separate them. The young people discover an old dinner-service with an owl pattern round the edge, which becomes the girl's obsession. This is the beginning of a series of discoveries, mysterious and deeply disturbing. The discoveries allow themselves to be made, but thereafter take charge, driving the story onwards, apparently towards some tragic conclusion.

Early in the story the girl, Alison, is sitting out of doors reading in the sun; the two boys arrive to tackle her on the subject of the owl service. One, Gwyn, is stung into violent quarrelling and kicks the book out of her hand. It lands yards away from Alison on the grass:

> 'Gwyn could see himself reflected in her sunglasses, and at the corner of the lens something fluttered like a wounded bird. He turned his head. It was the book. It came for him through the air. Its pages rattled, and disintegrated, but still came for him, like a tail after the red binding. Gwyn dropped the flour bags and protected his face as the book swarmed at him.
> "No!" he shouted.'

This is only one of the nonsensical and violent happenings that in the telling (what a word is *swarm*, in this context!) defies disbelief. The incident is particularly important because here the double-dealing of the story begins to emerge. For the possessed book is the 'Mabinogion', whose Fourth Branch tells of the bewitched valley. A certain man was under a curse to have no natural wife, so a woman was conjured for him out of the flowers of the valley, oak and broom and meadow-sweet. But what is it like to be a woman made for another's purpose, instead of born to your own? This woman made of flowers betrayed her husband for a lover, and two men were killed through her; her punishment was to be changed into an owl. All this happened a long, long legendary time ago; but the valley flowers still bloom, owls still hunt, and human natures can still be suddenly filled with hate as with love.

This is partly a *roman à clef* and, properly to understand what is going on, the reader needs every aid: the publisher's explanatory blurb, the endpaper design of the owl plate, the author's acknowledgements and three quotations before the story begins – and the Fourth Branch. Even with these, the narrative power of the book may be the undoing of the susceptible reader, hurrying him on in headlong excitement towards a total of mental confusion. It isn't up to an author to *explain* everything, of course; but he should *make plain*. In *Elidor* there are plenty of inexplicables, but this happens; in *The Owl Service*, on the whole, it does not.

Yet parts of *The Owl Service* are as good as anything comparable in *Elidor*; and there are new strengths, too. In particular, there is a masterly appreciation of class idioms and snobberies, and an awareness of their deadly potentiality as weapons. Not the happiest of subjects for young readers, some may say. Others will be almost certain to add that even unhappier is the choice of illegitimacy and adultery, jealousy and revenge as recurring themes in the story.

My repeated objection, however, is not that young readers (and adults too, for that matter) may understand too much, but that they are likely to understand too little. This is a great pity in a story by Alan Garner.

From *Children's Book News*, July/August 1967

The critic drawing the line between children's and adults' fiction

Opinions about the 'strong' treatment of disaster and death in books for children have always been part of the critic's stock-in-trade. A general agreement that an author does not gratuitously or irresponsibly exploit the feelings of a young reader is regularly challenged by stories which push to the tolerated limits the emotions aroused by catastrophe and distress. Ivan Southall is an Australian author whose stories are set against a background of threatening circumstances and his characters are always at risk. In this essay Alix Pirani, who teaches in a London comprehensive school, defends Southall's treatment of fear and his exploitation of the gaps in the relationships between children and adults on the grounds that this is to show responsibility towards adolescents by refusing to shelter them from reality. It should be compared with Catherine Storr's article in Section one.

Ivan Southall   Alix Pirani

In a *Times Literary Supplement* of 1968 a reviewer, bemoaning Ivan Southall's choice, and treatment, of themes, said, 'It seems that the moment has come for [him] to decide for whom he is writing ...' More recently in *Books for Your Children*, David Holbrook delivered an impassioned attack on *Finn's Folly*, condemning, among other things, its subject matter: 'a bad accident, death ... problems of parentage'.

Ivan Southall's work has increasingly posed the question: Where is the borderline between children's and adult fiction? And it seems to me that it has of its nature demonstrated that there can be no definite borderline, any more than exists between childhood and adulthood themselves.

Perhaps this question of 'suitability' and 'teenage fiction' could be discussed further by teachers in this journal. These days a child's experience, through the mass media, is extensive, even though vicarious; this, and generally earlier maturing, may dismay older generations – but children need active help to make

sense of these experiences. Helping the child to come to terms with the violence
and pain of life is important; not indulging in, nor exploiting the pain. All children
are in some way afraid to grow up, and fiction can help them. The problem is that
there is an area from thirteen years on when maturity is developing in individuals
at very different rates, and only sensitive familiarity with any one child's degree of
awareness and shelteredness can determine whether he is ready for certain books.
Publishers should be more wary of what they prescribe on book jackets. On the
other hand, newspaper reviews are directed at the more sheltered middle classes.
Southall's realistic treatment of child–parent conflicts, for instance, appeals
immediately to working-class children, whereas their middle-class fellows may be
upset by the presentation of tensions which their families take pains to conceal.

Finn's Folly, then, is about a car-crash – death, and the dissolution of
adult–child relationships – not unfamiliar experiences to today's children.
Mr Holbrook's complaints are partly justified, in that Southall isn't always in
control in this novel, and it slips into ghoulishness, particularly in the earlier
chapters. But if in some ways it has failed, there are positive strengths in it which
are characteristic of Southall and shouldn't be missed. The relationship between
Max, whose parents have been killed in the crash, and Alison, who lies trapped in
the wreckage next to her dead father, is life-giving and testing in a crucial way.
It is portrayed with a moving realism, without sentimentality, and though their
inevitable separation is poignant, Max goes on to face his tragedy and new
responsibilities with a convincing increase of maturity and a positive hold on life.
One of his responsibilities is the mongol little brother whose limitations and
helplessness, yet vivid quality of living, are so successfully conveyed, and central
to the book's affirmations.

Finn's Folly's confrontation with death and the violence of life was a logical
step in the direction Southall's work had been taking. Behind his writing lies the
belief that all fears can be met, understood, and overcome. Each of the novels
guides the young reader through an experience which might at first seem
unthinkable, in such a way as to help him apprehend the realities of disaster, the
nature of fear, the possibility of human survival. In the behaviour of his children
and adults, Southall portrays the negative and positive emotions that have to be
handled in all of us, and explores the way our relations with one another influence
that process. The outcome isn't always success, but there are individual children
whose hold on life is proved and who come through. Thus each novel is a
declaration of faith: indeed Southall is in some ways a deeply religious writer.
There is a quality of rhythm in *Ash Road*, for instance, which seems to suggest

that the spirit of courage, the maturing and development of love and responsibility in the children and adults, actually bring about the rainstorm which finally halts the bushfire.

The simplest statement of Southall's faith, *Let The Balloon Go*, perhaps the most consistently successful of the novels, is a moving account of a twelve-year-old spastic boy's determination to climb a tree on the first day he has ever been left alone. Climb it he does, and falls too. Southall's imaginative grasp of the boy's mind and feelings, his weighing up of what the adults' attitudes mean to this child's life, the final realization of his new identity, are all admirable, and this short book is a gem of inspired writing. The boy is every child, hemmed in by the limited expectations of the adults around him, yet he is, too, every man, striving against his own physical and psychological limitations.

Mr Holbrook believes that Southall is influenced by Golding, who gives him a 'licence, whatever the conscious intention, to convey hatred of the child, and to express it to the child himself ...' Mr Holbrook cannot have read *Hill's End* and *To The Wild Sky* which seem to me between them to provide a decisive answer, humane, realistic, honest, to *Lord of The Flies*. In each novel a group of children is left alone in a deserted place to cope without adults. They go through despair, helplessness, surprising revelations of their own weakness and potential, clashes of personality – and they survive. In each case a quality of leadership, the remnant of a civilized tradition, asserts itself unexpectedly in one of the boys when the anarchy of despair is threatening. In *To The Wild Sky* there is furthermore a clear affirmation that it is the primitive qualities these polished town children find so painfully in themselves on their barren island which are going to be their strength (not, as in Golding, their downfall). This novel ends with only a slender expectation of rescue but with a sense of hope and dignity and, at the achievement of making fire, a feeling that civilization is beginning anew. Through their experience of the past day the children have begun to learn how to live together: the most poignant moment of self-awareness for them is at the burial of the dead pilot (– and they have to overcome fear and revulsion to bring themselves to bury him), a ceremony which they find they can't imbue with traditional religion but which becomes even so a moment of mutual dedication, a heightening of understanding. Is it Southall's deliberate answer to the Beast role of Golding's dead pilot?

The stories are all significantly rooted in their Australian background: the children are second or third generation immigrants, the adults behind them solid, self-made, 'successful': the archetypal settlers whose strength and pioneering qualities have elsewhere lent themselves to the mythical approach of Patrick White and the tragic drama of Ray Lawler. Their children tend to feel over-shadowed. In *Hill's End* Adrian's father, Ben Fiddler, is a Jehovah-like figure who has severely limited his sons' growth. At the remarkable end to the novel Ben arrives in the storm-wrecked township and minimizes shockingly the children's achievement of restoration. His grief at the loss of 'his' town is greater than pride in his son's efforts. It is another boy, and an old spinster, who confront and humble Ben, reinforcing what the novel has already established – that there is as much strength and imagination in the children as their parents were once able to muster – and more than their parents have now.

Southall's critical attitude to adults has disturbed some reviewers, who presumably like to be reassured by the presence in a children's book of at least one strongly featured 'good' adult on whom the children are meant to rely, even model themselves. Southall offers no such comforting situation, only an honest, humble assessment of the possibilities of growth in a world where everyone is imperfect and has to learn. This seems to me one of the unique values of his work – its sense of continuity between childhood and adulthood, affirmed at a time when the boundaries between the two are shifting, as are the patterns of authority which once held those boundaries in place.

In one of Southall's recent novels, *Chinaman's Reef is Ours*, adults and children struggle side by side to make sense of their lives – the boundaries disappear under stress. The pattern of interactions between them is explored with remarkable subtlety. The setting is crucial: they are threatened with the destruction of their outworn civilization, their decayed little mining town, by men and machines intent on building something new and more profitable. (The children quickly recognize the martial nature of what is happening.) The book is about survival, and about civilization – at the point where it touches people most nearly, in their close family and community life and social aspirations. At the same time it is an allegory of twentieth-century 'progress'. One of its interesting aspects is the fluctuating role of the Sunday School teacher who embodies the strengths and weaknesses of traditional religion in that setting. As elsewhere in Southall's writing, men and women find significantly, unpredictably different kinds of strength and awareness. His observation of the way men's actions are prompted by their women or children is particularly interesting, and in this novel he uses most successfully his familiar method: the viewing of events through the eyes of many different characters, and the faithful rendering of conversation, with all its illogicalities and trivia, to display the fabric of relationships. Yet after this complexity he went on to write, with equal success, in *Bread and Honey*, a simple, short novel focused on a single boy and the ordinary, but terrifying fears that any growing boy might have, of his own physical and emotional inadequacies and the loss of the world of childhood. And again there is the wholly convincing step forward, the transformation into something nearer maturity.

Southall's writing is indeed, at its best, powerful and assured. His novels have a conviction and a realism which grip young readers right from the start. He can convey massive threat and disaster with compelling detail, while his rendering of the subtle give and take of emotions in conversation shows a remarkable ear for language. There are weaknesses: a too obsessive examination of tense situations, leading to repetitiveness, and, occasionally, a loss of the fine poise necessary to hold children's reactions to disaster above the level of schoolboy story response. If his control sometimes falters, however, there remain the positive, rare achievements of humanity, humility, and a sensitive, constantly groping awareness of the possibilities and complexities of human relations and maturity. Above all, Southall has an unsanctimonious respect for and trust in children.

From *The Use of English*, volume 22, number 3, 1971

The critic as spokesman for popular taste

Mordecai Richler, a Canadian-Jewish novelist, identifies himself with the popular taste of his generation. His racy anecdotal style is only slightly ironical and the tone is one of nostalgia rather than of disapproval for the dominant myth image of American childhood — Superman. But the message one gets is that of Raymond Williams' 'Culture and Society' (1958): literature, particularly popular literature, does not occur in a social and ideological vacuum.

The great comic book heroes   Mordecai Richler

'Quiet! a revolution is brewing,' begins a recent advertisement for the *New Book of Knowledge*.

> 'This is Gary. Age 11. He's a new breed of student. A result of the "quiet revolution" in our schools. He's spent happy hours on his project. Away from TV. Away from horror comics. Completely absorbed. Learning! Reading about cocoons, larvae, butterflies ...'

No, no, Gary is no new breed. I recognize him. In my day he always did his homework immediately he came home from school. He never ate with his elbows on the table. Or peeked at his sister in the bath. Or shoplifted. Or sent unwanted pianos, ambulances, firemen, and bust developers to the class teacher, the unspeakable Miss Ornstein, who made us suffer creative games, like 'Information Please' or 'Increase your word power with the *Reader's Digest*'. Gary ate his spinach. He was made president of the Junior Red Cross Club and pinned *The 10 Rules of Hygiene* over his sink. He didn't sweat, he perspired. And he certainly never swiped a hard-earned dime from his father's trousers, the price of a brand-new comic book. Oh, the smell of those new comic books! The sheen, the glossy feel! *Tip-Top*, *Action*, *Detective*, and *Famous Funnies*.

Each generation its own nostalgia, its own endearing fantasy-figures. For my generation, born into the depression, beginning to encourage and count pubic hairs during World War II, there was nothing quite like the comic books. While bigger, more mature men were cunningly turning road signs to point in the wrong direction in Sussex, standing firm at Tobruk, Sending For More Japs, holding out at Stalingrad, making atomic bombs, burning Jews and gassing gypsies; while General ('Old Blood and Guts') Patton was opening the Anglo-American service club in London, saying, 'The idea of these clubs could not be better because undoubtedly it is the destiny of the English and American people to rule the world …' and Admiral William F. ('Bull') Halsey was saying off-the-record, 'I hate Japs. I'm telling you men that if I met a pregnant Japanese woman, I'd kick her in the belly'; we, the young, the hope of the world, were being corrupted by the violence in comic books. Ask Dr Fredric Wertham, who wrote in *Seduction of The Innocent* (1954).

> '… a ten-year-old girl … asked me why I thought it was harmful to read *Wonder Woman* … She saw in her home many good books and I took that as a starting-point, explaining to her what good stories and novels were. "Supposing," I told her, "you get used to eating sandwiches made with very strong seasonings, with onions and peppers and highly spiced mustard. You will lose your taste for simple bread and butter and for finer food. The same is true for reading strong comic books. If later you want to read a good novel it may describe how a young boy and girl sit together and watch the rain falling. They talk about themselves and the pages of the book describe what their innermost little thoughts are. This is what is called literature. But you will never be able to appreciate that if in comic-book fashion you expect that any minute someone will appear and pitch both of them out of the window." '

Or Kingsley Martin, who wrote that Superman was blond and saw in him the nefarious proto-type of the Aryan Nazi. Never mind that Superman, the inspired creation of two Jewish boys, Jerome Siegal and Joe Shuster, was neither blond nor Aryan. It was a good theory. We were also being warped by *Captain Marvel*, *The Human Torch*, *The Flash*, *Sheena, Queen of the Jungle*, *Hawkman*, *Plastic Man*, *Sub Mariner*, and *Batman and Robin*. Our champions; our revenge figures against what seemed a gratuitously cruel adult world.

This is not to say our street was without intellectual dissent. After all social realism was the thing, then.

'There's Tarzan in the jungle, week in and week out,' Solly said, 'and he never once has to shit. It's not true to life.'

'What about Wonder Woman?'

'Wonder Woman's a dame, you schmuck.'

Wonder Woman was also a waste of time. Uncouth. Like ketchup in chicken soup. Or lighting up cigarette butts retrieved from the gutter. Reading was for improving the mind, my Aunt Ida said, and to that end she recommended *King's Row* or anything by John Gunther. Wonder Woman, according to Dr Wertham, was a dyke as well. For boys, a frightening image. For girls, a morbid ideal. Yes, yes, but as Jules Feiffer observes in his nostalgic *The Great Comic Book Heroes*, 'Whether Wonder Woman was a lesbian's dream I do not know, but I know for a fact she was every Jewish boy's unfantasied picture of the world as it really was. You mean men weren't wicked and weak? ... You mean women didn't have to be *stronger* than men to survive in the world? Not in *my* house!'

Jules Feiffer
The Great Comic Book Heroes
Dial Press, NY
Allen Lane
1965

The Batman and Robin, the unsparing Dr Wertham wrote, were also kinky. 'Sometimes Batman ends up in bed injured and young Robin is shown sitting next to him. At home they lead an idyllic life. They are Bruce Wayne and "Dick" Grayson. Bruce Wayne is described as a "socialite" and the official relationship is that Dick is Bruce's ward. They live in sumptuous quarters, with beautiful flowers in large vases ... Batman is sometimes shown in a dressing-gown ... It is like a wish dream of two homosexuals living together.' Unfortunately I cannot personally vouch for the sexual proclivities of 'socialites', but I don't see anything necessarily homosexual in 'beautiful flowers in large vases'. This strikes me as witch-hunting. Sexual McCarthyism. Unless the aforesaid flowers were pansies, which would, I admit, just about clinch the good doctor's case. As, however, he does not specify pansies, we may reasonably assume they were another variety of flora. If so, what? Satyric rambling roses? Jewy yellow daffodils? Droopy impotent peonies? Communist-front orchids? More evidence, please.

Of more significance, perhaps, what Dr Wertham fails to grasp is that we were already happily clued in on the sex life of our comic-book heroes. As far back as 1939, publishers (less fastidious than the redoubtable Captain Maxwell) were offering, at fifty cents each, crude black and white comics which improvised pornographically on the nocturnal, even orgiastic, adventures of our champions. I speak here of *Gasoline Alley Gang Bang, Dick Tracy's Night Out, Blind Date with the Dragon Lady*, and the shocking but liberating *Captain America meets Wonder Woman*, all of which have long since become collector's items. It is worth pointing out, however, that I never came across anything juicy about Superman and Lois Lane, not even gossip, until dirty-minded intellectuals and Nazis had their say.

Item: Richard Kluger writes (*Partisan Review*, Winter 1966): 'He could, of course, ravage any woman on earth (not excluding Wonder Woman, I daresay) ... Beyond this, there is a tantalizing if somewhat clinical and highly speculative theory about why Superman never bedded down with Lois, never really let himself get hotted up over her; Superman, remember, was the Man of Steel. Consider the consequences of supercoitus and the pursuit of The Perfect Orgasm at the highest level. So Supe, a nice guy, had to sublimate ...'

Item: When Whiteman, one of the many Superman derivatives, this one published by the American Nazi Party, is asked whatever became of the original Superman, he replies: 'Old Supey succumbed to the influence of Jew pornography ... It seems Superman was putting his X-ray vision to immoral use and was picked up by the vice squad as a Peeping Tom.'

Superman of course was the original superhero. 'Just before the doomed planet Krypton exploded to fragments, a scientist placed his infant son within an experimental rocketship, launching it toward earth!' Here Superman was discovered and finally adopted by the Kents, who gave him the name Clark. When they died 'it strengthened a determination that had been growing in his mind. Clark decided he must turn his titanic strength into channels that would benefit mankind. And so was created ... SUPERMAN, champion of the oppressed, the physical marvel who had sworn to devote his existence to helping those in need.' Because Superman was invincible, he soon became something of a bore ... until Mort Weisinger, a National Periodical Publications vice-president who has edited the strip since 1941, thought up an Achilles' heel for him. When exposed to fragments from the planet Krypton, Superman is shorn of his powers and reduced to mere earthly capabilities. A smooth touch, but the fact is the real Superman controversy has always centred on his assumed identity of Clark Kent, a decidedly faint-hearted reporter. Kent adores Lois Lane, who has no time for him. Lois is nutty for Superman, who in true 'aw shucks' tradition has no time for any woman. 'The truth may be', Jules Feiffer writes, 'that Kent existed not for purposes of the story but the reader. He is Superman's opinion of the rest of us, a pointed caricature of what we, the non-criminal element, were really like. His fake identity is our real one.' Well, yes, but I'm bound to reveal there's more to it than that. Feiffer, like so many before him, has overlooked a most significant factor: the Canadian psyche.

Yes. Superman was conceived by Toronto-born Joe Shuster and originally worked not for the *Daily Planet* but for a newspaper called *The Star*, modelled on the Toronto *Star*. This makes his assumed identity of bland Clark Kent not

merely understandable, but artistically inevitable. Kent is the archetypal middle-
class Canadian WASP, superficially nice, self-effacing, but within whom there
burns a hate-ball, a would-be avenger with superhuman powers, a smasher of
bridges, a breaker of skyscrapers, a potential ravager of wonder women. And (may
those who have scoffed at Canadian culture in the past please take note) a universal
hero, Superman, first drawn by Shuster in 1938, now appears in twenty languages.
This spring, God willing, Lois Lane, who has pined for him all these years, will
be married off to a reformed mad scientist, Dr Lex Luthor. I am indebted to
another *aficionado*, Alexander Ross, a *Macleans* editor, for all this information.
Last March Ross went to visit Joe Shuster, fifty and still single ('I have never
met a girl who matched up to Lois Lane,' he has said), at Forest Hills, Long Island,
where he lives with his aged mother. Shuster, sadly, never did own the rights on
his creation. It is the property of NPP, who say that by 1948 the legendary Shuster
was no longer able to draw the strip because of failing eyesight. He was discharged
and now earns a living of sorts as a free-lance cartoonist. 'He is trying', Ross
writes, 'to paint pop art – serious comic strips – and hopes eventually to promote a
one-man show in some chic Manhattan gallery.' Such, Ross might have added,
is the inevitable fate of the artistic innovator under capitalism.

If Superman, written and drawn by a hard-faced committee with 20–20
vision these days, continues to flourish, so do the imitations; and here it is worth
noting how uncomfortably the parodies of the anarchistic left and broad Jewish
humour have come to resemble the earnestly meant propaganda of the lunatic
right.

On the left, *The Realist* has for some time now been running a comic strip
about LeRoi Jones called *Supercoon*. Little LeRoi becomes mighty Supercoon,
threat to the virtue of white women everywhere, by uttering the magic curse,
'Mother-fucker'. Jones, I'm told, was so taken with this parody that he wrote
the script for an animated cartoon called *Supercoon* which he wished to have made
and released with the film version of his play *Dutchman*. It has, however, yet to be
produced. On a more inane level, *Kosher Comics*, a one-shot parody, published in
New York, which runs strips called *The Lone Arranger* (with the masked marriage
broker and Tante), *Tishman of the Apes*, and *Dick Shamus*, also includes Supermax,
who is called upon to defeat invaders from the planet Blech. The invaders are
crazy for matzoh balls.

Meanwhile, back at American Nazi headquarters in Arlington, Va., the
Stormtrooper magazine has recently given us *Whiteman*. '*Jew Commies Tremble …
Nigger Criminals Quake In Fear … Liberals Head For The Hills … Here Comes*

WHITEMAN.' In his first adventure Whiteman, whose costume is a duplicate of Supey's, except that the emblem on his chest is a swastika rather than an *S*, 'fights an interplanetary duel with a diabolical fiend ... THE JEW FROM OUTER SPACE.' He also does battle with SUPERCOON. In real life, Whiteman is a milkman named Lew Cor (Rockwell spelt backwards, for Nazi Commander George Lincoln Rockwell) and is transformed into Whiteman by speaking the secret words, '*Lieh Geis!*'

> ' "With my super-vision [Whiteman says] I can see three niggers have been caught in the act of trying to burn down a Negro church. If they had not been caught in the act, some poor southern white man would have been blamed for it." '

He soon beats up the Negro arsonists ('Sweet dreams, Jigaboo'), but meanwhile, inside a mysterious spacecraft, MIGHTY MOTZA is creating SUPERCOON with an atomic reverse-ray gun. The emblem on Supercoon's chest, incidentally, is a half-peeled banana, and naturally he is no match for Whiteman, who quickly eliminates him.

> ' "So long Supercoon! You just couldn't make the grade with your second-class brain. With my white man intelligence, I have reduced you to a super-revolting protoplasmic slime. Ugh! Looks like a vile jellyfish." '

In the past, comic strips, or derivatives thereof, have been put to less extreme political purpose. All of us, I'm sure, remember the late Vicky's Supermac. Parallax, publishers of *Kosher Comics*, have also brought out *Great Society Comics*, with SuperLBJ and Wonderbird; and *Bobman and Teddy Comics*, featuring the Kennedy brothers. Then day by day, in the Paris edition of the *New York Herald Tribune*, *Washington Post*, and hundreds of other newspapers, Steve Canyon and Buzz Sawyer risk their lives for us in Vietnam. Canyon, a more politically conscious type than Sawyer, has recently had some sour things to say about dove-like congressmen and student peaceniks: neither fighter has yet had anything to say about Whiteman. If and when the crunch comes on the Mekong Delta, it remains an open question whether or not Buzz and Steve would accept Whiteman's support.

Canyon's political past, incidentally, is not unblemished. When he came to serve at a US Air Force base in northern Canada in 1960, the Peterborough (Ont.) *Examiner* took umbrage.

> 'We have become disturbed by the political implications of the strip. The hero and his friends were on what was obviously Canadian soil, but it seemed to be entirely under the domination of American troops who were

there as a first-line defence against the Russians.'
There was only one manly answer possible; Canadian-made strips such as *Larry Brannon*, a non-starter, who was to glamorize the face of Canada. In his first adventure Brannon visited 'Toronto, focus of the future, channel for the untold wealth of the north, communications centre of a vast, rich hinterland, metropolis of rare and precious metals.' The last time we were asked to make do with Canadian comics was during the war years when in order to protect *our* balance of payments the government stopped the import of American comic books. The Canadian comic books hastily published to fill the gap were simply awful. We wouldn't have them. Banning American comic books was a typically unimaginative measure, for whatever pittance the government made up in US currency, it lost in home-front morale. Comics, as Feiffer has written, were our junk. Our fix. And before long a street corner black market in *Detective* and *Action* comics began to flourish. Just as we had come to the support of Americans during the prohibition years, thereby founding more than one Canadian family fortune, so the Americans now saw that we didn't go without. Customs barriers erected against a free exchange of ideas never work.

I have no quarrel with Feiffer's selection from the comics for his *The Great Comic Book Heroes*, but his text, the grammar and punctuation quirky, seemed to me somewhat thin. Feiffer is most knowledgeable, a veritable Rashi, on the origins and history of the comic books. He is at his most absorbing when he writes about his own experience as a comic-book artist. He learned to draw in the schlock houses, the art schools of the business. 'We were a generation,' he writes. 'We thought of ourselves the way the men who began the movies must have.' And indeed they went to see *Citizen Kane* again and again, to study Welles' use of angle shots. Rumours spread that Welles in his turn had read and learned from the comic books. Fellini was certainly a devotee.

In the schlock houses, Feiffer writes, 'Artists sat lumped in crowded rooms, knocking it out for a page rate. Pencilling, inking, lettering in the balloons for ten dollars a page, sometimes less ...'; decadence setting in during the war. The best men, Feiffer writes, went off to fight, hacks sprouting up everywhere. 'The business stopped being thought of as a life's work and became a stepping stone. Five years in it at best, then on to better things: a daily strip, or illustrating for the *Saturday Evening Post*, or getting a job with an advertising agency ... By the end of the war the men who had been in charge of our childhood fantasies had become archetypes of the grown-ups who made us need to have fantasies in the first place.'

But it was Dr Wertham, with his *Seduction of The Innocent*, who really brought an end to an era. His book led to the formation of a busybody review board and an insufferable code that amounted to the emasculation of comic books as we had known them.

1.   Respect for parents, the moral code, and for honourable behaviour, shall be fostered.
2.   Policemen, judges, government officials, and respected institutions shall never be presented in such a way as to create disrespect for established authority.
3.   In every instance good shall triumph over evil and the criminal punished for his misdeeds.

To be fair, there were uplifting, mind-improving side-effects. Culture came to the news-stands in the shape of *True Comics*, *Bible Comics*, and the unforgettable series of *Classic Comics*, from which Feiffer quotes the death scene from Hamlet.

> Fear not, queen mother!
> It was Laertes
> And he shall die at my hands!
> … Alas! I have been poisoned
> And now I, too, go
> To join my deceased father!
> I, too – I – AGGGRRRAA!

Today men in their thirties and forties trade old comic books with other addicts and buy first issues of *Superman* and *Batman* for fifty dollars or more. If the original boyhood appeal of the comic books was all but irresistible to my generation, I have not gone into the reasons until now for they seemed to me obvious. Superman, The Flash, The Human Torch, even Captain Marvel, were our *golems*. They were invulnerable, all-conquering, where we were puny, miserable, and defeated. They were also infinitely more reliable than real-life champions. Max Schmeling could take Joe Louis. Mickey Owen might drop that third strike. The Nazi Rats could by-pass the Maginot line and the Yellow-Belly Japs could take Singapore, but neither dared mix it up with Captain America the original John Bircher, endlessly decorated by FBI head J. Arthur Grover, and sponsor of the Sentinels of Liberty, to which we could all belong (regardless of race, colour, or creed) by sending a dime to Timely Publications, 330 West 42nd St, NY, and signing a pledge (the original loyalty oath?) that read: '*I solemnly pledge to uphold the principles of the Sentinels of Liberty and assist Captain America in his war against*

Finally, many of our heroes were made of paltry stuff. The World's Mightiest Man – Powerful Champion of Justice, Captain Marvel, was mere Billy Batson, newsboy, until he uttered the magic word, '*Shazam!*' The Flash is another case in point.

'Faster than the streak of lightning in the sky ... Swifter than the speed of light itself ... Fleeter than the rapidity of thought ... is *The Flash*, reincarnation of the winged Mercury ... His speed is the dismay of scientists, the joy of the oppressed – And the open-mouthed wonder of the multitudes!'

Originally, however, he was as weak as you or me. A decidedly forlorn figure. He was Jay Garrick, 'an unknown student at a midwestern university ...' and, for my money, a Jew. The creators of *The Flash*, Gardner Fox and Harry Lampert, like Arthur Miller, wrote at a time, remember, when Jews were still thinly disguised as Gentiles on the stage, in novels, and comic books. There is no doubt, for instance, that *The Green Lantern* has its origins in Hassidic mythology. Will Eisner's *The Spirit*, so much admired by Feiffer, is given to cabalistic superstitions and speaking in parables. With *The Flash*, however, we are on the brink of a new era, a liberated era. Jay Garrick is Jewish but Reform. Semi-assimilated. In the opening frame lovely Joan (significantly blonde) won't date him, because he is only a scrub on the university football team while Bull Tyron is already a captain. 'A man of your build and brains', she says, 'could be a star ... A scrub is just an old washwoman! You won't put your mind to football ...!' Jay, naturally, is intellectually inclined. Probably he is taking freshman English with Leslie Fiedler. An eye-opener! Huck Finn and Nigger Jim, like Batman and Robin, are fags. Jay, however, spends most of the time in the lab with his professor. Then one day an experiment with hard water goes 'wrong'. Jay, overcome by fumes, lurches forward. ('It's ... it's ... too much for me ...') He lies between life and death for weeks, coming out of it endowed with superhuman powers. 'Science', the doctor explains, 'knows that hard water makes a person act much quicker than ordinarily ... By an intake of its gases, Jay can walk, talk, run, and think swifter than thought ... He will probably be able to outrace a bullet! ! He is a freak of science!' Briefly, he is now The Flash.

How puerile, how unimaginative, today's comic strips seem by comparison. Take Rex Morgan, MD for instance. In my day to be a doctor was to be surrounded by hissing test tubes and vile green gases. It was to be either a cackling villain with a secret formula that would reduce Gotham City to the size of a postage stamp or to be a noble genius, creator of behemoths who would bring hope to the oppressed multitudes. The best that can be expected of the loquacious Dr Morgan is that he will lecture us on the hidden dangers of medicare. Or save a student from LSD addiction. There's no magic in him. He's commonplace. A bore.

From *Encounter*, May 1967

The critic as protector

It is the assumption of all censors and most critics who adopt a firm moral standpoint that attitudes are modified by what we know and much of what we know comes to us through literature. D. W. Harding says that 'since his (the reader's) response includes in some degree accepting or rejecting the values and emotional attitudes which the narration implicitly offers, it will influence, perhaps greatly influence, his future appraisals of behaviour and feeling ... Most values are culturally derived'.

Mrs Trimmer knew all this and censored accordingly. And Janet Hill, a distinguished children's librarian, is seen to adopt a relatively moderate 'standpoint when she asks us to discard books which seem to encourage unacceptable attitudes to immigrants – though she offers a reprieve to Little Black Sambo'. The questions we are left with are: Who should be making these decisions if they need to be made? And, if we do suppress books that are thought to be harmful, are we denying readers the opportunity to make their own rejections?

A minority view   Janet Hill

'England could be reconstructed almost entirely from its children's books,' wrote Paul Hazard in *Books, Children, and Men*. How will future generations assess our attitudes to racial prejudice in this country in 1967 in the light of his statement? Already some readers will be irritated by my opening sentences. 'Surely we don't have to bring this issue into children's books,' they will say. But of course we do. Children live in the world, and books for them should do the same. (Similar arguments apply to the familiar vexed question of the social setting of children's books. Many people find discussion of the subject wearisome, and try to dismiss it as of no account, usually either on the theory that underprivileged children don't like to read about children in situations like their own or on the grounds that, because there are now some half dozen reasonable books on the theme, the matter is settled – which it is not.) The racial issue, however, is rarely discussed. It is not, to take one example, that librarians have decided they don't subscribe to the view that golliwogs should be discarded. They simply haven't thought it necessary to see this as an issue to which they must react one way or the other. Recently I took part in a discussion on *Late Night Line-up*, which arose from the Jackanory treatment of *Uncle Remus* and was concerned with our awareness, or lack of it, regarding racial matters. The interviewer was rather surprised when, in preparation for the programme, she had rung a reputable children's library in London to ask their views on Helen Bannerman and received a bemused reply to the effect that the issue had never really come up there and was not something they had considered.

What about *Little Black Sambo*? Written by a Scotswoman stationed in India at the end of the last century, it has been popular both here and in the United States for generations. The illustrations are stylized, the text repeats the refrain 'little black …', and according to the dictionary 'sambo' is a term of abuse. My own feeling is that this book and others in the series should be available in public libraries. Most American librarians would probably disagree with me. If the word 'sambo' is widely used as an abusive term in Great Britain, I would reconsider my decision, but so far as I know, it is not. These books are extremely popular, particularly in my experience with West Indian children in Brixton. As May Hill Arbuthnot says in *Children and Books*: 'If "black" applied to people is a cause of grief to some of our children, then the book should be omitted from school lists. But Sambo is happy and completely triumphant, the envy of all young hero worshippers – he outwits the tigers over and over.'

This book has historical value, was written in innocence, and has been continuously popular since it first appeared. All books written before our own time should be carefully re-assessed in the light of current sensibilities and a decision made as to whether their literary value outweighs their dated attitudes. I object to the recent re-issue of *Two Dutch Dolls* by Florence Upton. In the first place, the book is hardly an important piece of literature, merely a curiosity. It had been forgotten. The golliwog is treated in an offensive way, and it seems to me to be an example of insensitivity on the part of the publisher to bring out a new edition in 1966. Leading periodicals reviewed the book without mentioning the golliwog even as a questionable point.

Our attitude towards contemporary books should necessarily be more stringent, as there is now no excuse for obtuseness about racial factors in modern writing for children. One recent book I feel very strongly about is *Ginger and*

Number 10 by Prudence Andrew. It was well reviewed, but apparently no one noticed that 'Negro' is spelt 'negro' throughout, or that the principal West Indian character is grossly caricatured. He is never mentioned without his physical characteristics being pointed out and emphasized: 'Odya rose to his feet. Andy put the open book in his dark brown hands. Odya looked at it. His melon grin wavered and then disappeared. He closed his dark brown lips ... Ginger guessed that, under his chocolate skin, he was blushing with shame.'

This is no unusual excerpt: there are similar passages throughout the book. The author clearly intended to write a story with a fine moral – which, of course, is also what is wrong with it. Blatant didacticism rarely succeeds, nor should it. Ginger, the hero, champions the cause of a Negro family who have moved into the neighbourhood; his motivation is a sense of guilt, because he was the cause of a wave of anti-Negro feeling when he convinced the police that the man he saw robbing a local store was a Negro. The story has a happy ending, with the family accepted by everyone. It is ironical indeed that the author obviously thought she was furthering the cause of racial harmony – whereas, in fact, the whole tone of the book seems to me to be condescending and full of stereotyped attitudes. The result of her well-meaning efforts is unfortunate, to say the least. When I raised objections to the book at a selection committee for a booklist, I think I was regarded as rather a crank: certainly there was no active support for my viewpoint.

A splendid contrast to *Ginger and Number 10* is afforded by Edward Eager's *The Well-Wishers*, which also treats of the arrival of a Negro family in a previously all-white neighbourhood, this time in the United States. That the family are Negroes is never mentioned. The point is made with great skill and subtlety. Thus, the first encounter of one of the Martin girls with the new family:

'And when Deborah saw the family, she realized for the first time why it was that the Smugs had tried to keep them from moving in.

'Her voice rang out loud and clear. "Oh," she said, "is that all it was?"

' "Yes," I told her, "that's all it was."

' "Why, how perfectly silly!" said Deborah.'

Increasingly, Negroes will feature in children's books about contemporary life in England. So far, one of the most delightful characters to appear is Profound d. Pew, the exuberant and kindly West Indian bus conductor in William Mayne's *The Rolling Season*. In *The Latchkey Children* by Eric Allen, Duke Ellington Binns, a West Indian, belongs to the group of boys who scheme together to prevent the removal of a favourite tree from their playground. In Nina Bawden's *On the Run*, Ben helps two friends to escape from their respective homes – one a fatherless young Cockney girl, the other the son of an East African politician in exile, whom he first encountered in a neighbour's garden. These last two books are both quite lightweight, the Negro characters are casually and naturally introduced – and this is just as it should be.

In *The Chimneys of Green Knowe* Lucy Boston creates a memorable character, Jacob, the West Indian boy Captain Oldknow rescues from slavery in Barbados, and brings home to become a faithful lifelong companion to Susan, his blind daughter. The reactions of an eighteenth-century family to a Negro in their midst are predictable and extremely well handled. Jacob quietly and gravely establishes himself as a person to be reckoned with.

There are a good number of historical stories which deal with various aspects of Negro history. One excellent example is *Looking for Orlando* by Frances Williams Browin, an American writer. In it Sam Chase, a convinced young Southerner, finds his beliefs challenged when he encounters a runaway Negro slave while visiting his Quaker grandparents in Philadelphia. A recent, highly interesting book is *Marassa and Midnight*, undoubtedly one of the outstanding British children's books published in 1966. The moving story of twin brothers living in eighteenth-century Haiti during a period of turmoil and upheaval on the island, has immediacy and warmth and is, above all, exciting and popular with children. The book jacket depicts two crude Negro caricatures intended, presumably, to represent the sensitive and individual brothers who are heroes of the story. How could a publisher do an author such a disservice? The jacket gives a totally misleading and unfavourable impression of the book. The fact that no one realized this depiction could be offensive is one more indication of the lack of sensitivity I have mentioned previously.

American editors and librarians have long been aware of a blindspot in some English children's books. They find it extremely puzzling and difficult to understand. In fact, they go through most of our books with a fine-toothed comb. The situation in their country is different from ours, and they have lived with it far longer. We have much to learn from their experience. Many years ago they began to think about the treatment of Negroes in children's books. There is no better short guide to the subject than *Books about Negro Life for Children*, an annotated booklist, published by the New York Public Library (revised edition, 1963), compiled by Augusta Baker, Co-ordinator of Children's Services there. The brief, reasoned introduction notes points to look for in assessing books, and the annotations are very helpful.

Certainly we need more books featuring Negroes; also more factual books

about the countries from which most of them have come to England – a point
one can only make in passing in a short article. The dangers in declaring the need
are obvious. John Rowe Townsend, writing in the April 1967 issue of the *Horn
Book Magazine*, decried the spirit of didacticism in modern children's books. I
sympathize with him entirely when he reports his negative response to the
publisher who wanted him to write a novel condemning racial discrimination.
Every author must write about the truth as he sees it, even when he is writing
purely for entertainment. His own attitudes will be implicit in what he writes.
Above all, books must be true to life to be valid and artistically acceptable. (I
have heard recently that the phrase 'integrated book' has become common
currency amongst some American publishers. I know of an American author who
wrote a simple story about two families. Her editor asked that one of the families
be made Negro, because it would make a good 'integrated book'. No legitimate
case can be made for this spurious, facile approach.)

I am well aware that many people will think it wrong to single out books
about Negroes and scrutinize them with a magnifying glass. I cannot agree. My
brief comments on a few books and the reactions to them will, I hope, be sufficient
indication that the children's book world in this country mirrors in miniature
those intangible conditions described in the recent PEP report on race relations
in Britain. Blatant racialism is expressed rarely (probably supremely in Enid
Blyton's *Little Black Doll*, which was attacked so forcefully in a *Guardian* article by
Lena Jeger in 1966). Indifference and unawareness exist. So does total acceptance,
as demonstrated by the superb picture book by Ezra Jack Keats, *Whistle for Willie*,
in which the small boy who teaches himself to whistle just happens to be a Negro.

I am convinced that we shall have to become much more colour conscious
about children's books in this country before we can become truly colour blind.

From *Children's Book News*, May 1967

The critic chooses the best

**In the opinion of many critics Philippa Pearce has written some of the best
children's books since 1950. Based on a slender output, her reputation stands
up to the test of time and fashion, so that 'What the Neighbours Did' (1973),
although written at different times as a series of short stories, is as much a
book of the seventies as 'The Minnow on the Say' (1955) is of the fifties.
Brian Jackson examines some of the reasons for the success of these stories,
drawing particular attention to the balance of experience of the outside
world and the essential inwardness of the dominant feelings of childhood.
He links his analysis to a point which other critics make – that the weakness
of the adult novel has encouraged those who work in narrative to write for
children. Since this article appeared Philippa Pearce has written 'The Elm
Street Gang' (1970), 'The Squirrel Wife' (1972) and 'What
the Neighbours Did' (1973).**

Philippa Pearce   Brian Jackson

Ours is the golden age of children's literature. It took a thousand years to hammer
out the folk and fairy tales. It took two full centuries to give us a small shelf of
classics which, like *Gulliver's Travels*, were hungrily drawn into children's culture.
Or which, like *Alice*, prettily married an adult's disintegrating vision to a child's
kaleidoscopic sense of life's logics and meanings. Or which, like *Treasure Island* or
Kidnapped, extended the adult novel downwards until it caught and mirrored back
the adolescent's dawning perception of the ambiguities, the disappearing black
and white of life. The quarrel between Davie and Alan, or Jim Hawkins' conflicting
sense of Long John Silver's malice and radiance are the entry to the adult novel
and to adult life.

By and large, the children's classics of the eighteenth and nineteenth centuries
tell us something of the unsatisfied needs of the child who reads books – what pains
he would go to, to quarry out his fiction. Or they show us adults on strange

subterranean travels posing their problems via children. Or they represent the
threshold of the novel proper.

I suppose the Edwardians – J. M. Barrie, A. A. Milne, Kenneth Grahame –
are the outstanding example of adults pretending to write for children, when they
are really writing for other adults. Of course they do this with an intermittent
brilliance that redeems the sometimes cloying sweetness of their art. And of course
there are writers – like E. Nesbit – who would require a quite different account.

Nevertheless, it does not seem surprising that the classics of the past (and
too often they still constitute *the* children's classics) have lost so much relative
ground with children over the last thirty years. I suppose that what has happened
is first of all the creation of a universal child public. The overwhelming majority
of children can, for the first time, read for pleasure. And the overwhelming
majority are different from the readers (or the read-to) of the past in that they are
the children of the common man and not of the middle-class nursery. Secondly,
it is certainly true that we are by far the most child-centred society that any
civilization has created. Perhaps it was the eighteenth century which really
discovered childhood, and the nineteenth which conspired to treasure it as a
special state. But it is this century which has revealed its breadth and richness.
To Swift, children were miniature adults—as they are in eighteenth century
paintings. To Carroll, or later Barrie, they were ourselves during a fragile, transient
stage of innocence. But what can *we* say except that children are children? We
expect them to live, and not die; to be slowly and carefully educated, not tossed
into child labour. We expect them to have their special tastes in food, dress,
amusement. They are for the first time a market to some, an audience to others.
And we see them of course through eyes imperceptibly altered by Freud.

Perhaps this goes some way to explaining why it was possible for ours to
be the golden age of children's literature – and why the old classics begin to
settle into a different perspective. The great writers of our time – like Meindert
De Jong, Rosemary Sutcliff, René Guillot – have a sense of the child's inward
life, of the normalities of growing up, and an ease and naturalness in their address
to children, which is quite fresh.

Unfortunately, it is probably true that most adults interested in books have
little awareness of what is transient or abiding in the crammed shelves of the
children's libraries (consider the fact that there *are* children's libraries). And
naturally they are guided by the books that impressed their own childhood, before
the great creative explosion took place. In this note I'd like to give some account
of Philippa Pearce. Not because she is one of the greatest. Or not yet. But because

her achievement, wonderful enough in itself, is representative of how (without forsaking the adult note) a truly gifted writer can now write directly for the child, and for the ordinary child, in a way seldom achieved before.

Philippa Pearce published her first novel *Minnow on the Say* in 1955. In plain lucid prose, wholly accessible to a child between eight and twelve, she tells the story of two boys, their canoe and their hunt for an Elizabethan treasure hidden and lost 'over the water'. The tale has the hypnotic craftsmanship of a first-class detective story. And as the story winds its fascinating course, the book engages the reader even more deeply in the lovely recreation of a boy's life in a small East Anglian village. In doing so, it brings back many childhoods – how tall the walls are, how beckoning the holes in fences, how the fingers reach to caress the dents and bulges in old stonework or to savour the speed and weight and coolness of dripping water or running streams. It spills over with a child's geography, places that only a child would know – like the fallen tree bridge over the river, from where they observe the punters below; or views that a child might specially sense, like the roof-well on Adam's house:

> 'The door opened on to something quite different: a kind of minute court-yard, floored with lead and with the slopes of the slate-roofing for its four walls. It was a well in the middle of the roof, of the kind that is quite often found in old houses. From below roof-level, one would never have suspected its existence. It made a charming secret retreat, airy and sunny; it was a perfect hiding-place.
>
> 'Together they peered over the ridge, looking outwards and downwards – far – far. Codlings' was an exceptionally high-built house – probably the highest building in Great Barley, not counting the church. It gave a view over roof-tops and tree-tops, and far out over the countryside. The boys could see the River Say winding away towards the bridge at Little Barley; they could see the railway line, and the place where it crossed the little iron bridge over the old channel of the Say – they watched a train pass over, on its way to London; they watched its smoke drift with the wind over the water-meadows – drift and dissolve.
>
> ' "I say!" said David, awed. "You're lucky to have a roof like this, Adam!" '

It is, if you like, a very conservative book. Children are expected to be polite to adults, to make things – scraping and varnishing their canoe – not to destroy. There are all the tiny ceremonies of inviting friends to tea, or calling on strangers. Pocket money is earned and carefully counted, and very neatly you pick up the nuances of children and adults observing the codes:

'David was not yet in despair. "Mr. Ellum pays me my newspaper money at the end of this month; perhaps he'd pay me for as much delivery as I've done so far."

'Mr. Ellum, when the difficulty had been twice explained to him, agreed to the arrangement David suggested. The money from Mr. Ellum, together with what very little Adam and David already had, was given to Mr. Moss on one of his trips to Castleford. He visited the boat-yards in his dinner-hour and brought back to David the container quite filled.

' "I say," said Adam, when he saw it, "that's more than I expected for the money."

' "Is it?" said David, puzzled. "My father just said, 'Here's your varnish.' It's the right kind, I know."

' "Anyway," said Adam, "we've so much, we ought to be able to put the second coat on outside, and one inside as well." '

Of course, the boys – being boys – are sometimes rude and destructive, thoughtlessly or at moments of stress. There is the moment when Adam, obsessed by the treasure, suspects treasure under the lovely pinky-yellow rose bush that stands by itself in the garden:

'Adam handed the garden-fork to David. "Hold that," he said. He passed quickly indoors; he was back again in a minute.

' "She's busy in the kitchen," he said. "It's all clear." He took the fork from David, and, with speed and force, drove the prongs in at the foot of the rose-tree.

' "Here!" cried David, bewildered and horrified. "Adam!"

' "I told you," Adam gasped, as he dug away. "It's a single rose – the only single rose in the garden."

'David watched in a state of dazed apprehension: he seemed to be in a waking nightmare. It was almost a relief when the inevitable spectator appeared: Squeak Wilson came, trundling a wheelbarrow and whistling. He stopped both, when he saw Adam and what he was doing. For once, Squeak was too appalled to be frightened for himself.

' "That's the Empress of Chiny you're at there!" he shrilled. Adam worked on, paying no attention.

' "That's your grandpa's Empress of Chiny rose! He'd be that úpset!"

'Adam turned his head. "Go away and be quiet!"

'Squeak left his wheelbarrow, and went away, but he could not have

obeyed the rest of Adam's order. In a few minutes, Miss Codling appeared
at the garden-door, with Squeak peering out from behind her.

'"Adam!" she shouted – no, she screamed it, rather.

'Adam had only a little more digging to do, and he did not stop now.
David could see the sweat rolling off his cheeks like tears; his muscles flowed
and knotted and flowed again; the fork thrust and heaved and whirled up and
away, like a gleaming, deadly instrument of war.

'Miss Codling screamed again, and set off across the lawn towards Adam.
She reached him at the exact moment that the fork completed its work: it
had made a deep, raw hole, empty now of any rose-tree roots, and empty,
too, of anything else. There was no treasure.'

Without being in the slightest moralistic, the book has the rare capacity to create
goodness, to make the decencies of life ring true.

Her effects come through her art; her negatives – 'a deep, raw hole, empty
now of any rose-tree roots' – imply her positives.

And yet there is more; already at least a pre-echo of the Philippa Pearce
music, that note of controlled poignancy that is to make *Tom's Midnight Garden*
a classic of its literature. You hear something of it with Squeak's tipsy bicycle ride
past the bewildered David:

'A voice somewhere down the drive began singing in queer, thin tones that
might have come from another world. David felt almost frightened, until
he saw that the singer was Squeak Wilson going home, the capacious basket
of his tricycle piled high, as usual. He paid no attention to David even when
he drew level with him. Now, David could hear the words of his little song:

'"Heigh-ho!

'"Heigh-ho!

'"Heigh-ho! Sweet summer!"

'All the sweet summers that David had ever known came drifting into his
mind, and last came this one – best of them all, that he had shared with Adam.
He heard the swish of the "Minnow" as they paddled her along the Say;
he saw again the moonlight silvering the water-meadows by Jonathan
Codling's bridge; he smelt – yes, he really smelt – the delicious scents that
follow in their order the summer through – only these were mixed together
all at once – hawthorn and cowslips in the meadows; in the garden, apple-
mint and clary, honeysuckle and roses. A wave of summer sweetness moved
over David as Squeak passed, singing.'

I could not imagine J. M. Barrie or Kenneth Grahame or A. A. Milne striking that note, without indulging its plangency. But here the flit of the mind backwards is given to the child – the open adult note is controlled – and the prose implies the cyclic promise of summer, not unstoppable regret for years gone by. How fine too the modulation in the next paragraph to plainer vision and quiet humour:

> 'They did not greet each other – Squeak did not seem even to see David. He appeared, as David reported later to Miss Codling, to be, if anything, more cheerful than usual. The only sign of what was to come was, perhaps, in the wavering course he steered up the drive on his tricycle. He did not seem quite in control of it; on the other hand, he certainly did not seem to care.'

Tom's Midnight Garden itself was published in 1958. A small boy at the thirteenth hour, between sleeping and waking, ventures downstairs to find that the backyard of their converted flats has slipped into its older self as a Victorian garden. Listen how clearly the characteristic music sounds now: the precision of place, the child geography, the deep-sunk sense of dream all marvellously fused together:

> 'The green of the garden was greyed over with dew; indeed, all its colours were gone until the touch of sunrise. The air was still, and the tree-shapes crouched down upon themselves. One bird spoke; and there was a movement when an awkward parcel of feathers dislodged itself from the tall fir-tree at the corner of the lawn, seemed for a second to fall and then at once was swept up and along, outspread on a wind that never blew, to another, farther tree: an owl. It wore the ruffled, dazed appearance of one who has been up all night.
>
> 'Tom began to walk round the garden, on tiptoe. At first he took the outermost paths, gravelled and box-edged, intending to map for himself their farthest extent. Then he broke away impatiently on a cross-path. It tunnelled through the gloom of yew-trees arching overhead from one side, and hazel nut stubs from the other: ahead with a grey-green triangle of light where the path must come out into the open again. Underfoot the earth was soft with the humus of last year's rotted leaves. As he slipped along, like a ghost, Tom noticed, through gaps in the yew-trees on his right, the flick of a lighter colour than the yew; dark – light – dark – light – dark ... The lighter colour, he realized was the back of the house that he was glimpsing, and he must be passing behind the line of yew-trees that faced it across the lawn.'

Again the tale has the same breathless, detective pull. The garden fills with people, and one – Hatty – can see him. 'She had made this garden a kind of kingdom' and night after night they explore it together:

'... a leafy crevice between a wall and a tree-trunk, where a small human body
could just wedge itself; a hollowed-out centre to a box-bush, and a run
leading to it – like the run made in the hedge by the meadow; a wigwam
shelter made by a rearrangement of the bean-sticks that Abel had left leaning
against the side of the heating-house; a series of hiding-holes behind the
fronds of the great ferns that grew along the side of the greenhouse; a
feathery green tunnel between the asparagus ridges. She showed Tom how
to hide from a search simply by standing behind the trunk of the big fir-tree:
you had to listen intently and move exactly – and noiselessly, of course – so
that the trunk was always between yourself and the searcher.'

But in the garden – even there – time moves too, and Hatty grows older. Who,
once having read them, can forget the chapters when boy and young woman
skate up the river to Ely?

For it is in these final sections that the art transcends itself. Through scenes
of haunting and sometimes painful beauty, Tom perceives that the old woman in
the upstairs flat was once a child like Hatty, and that age and life will make Hatty
an old woman like her: 'he began to notice, again and again, a gesture, a tone of
voice, a way of laughing that reminded him of the little girl in the garden.' It is,
if you like, one of the ordinary insights of life; but one, perhaps, we most easily
slurr over (as when politicians talk of 'old age pensioners' as if they were a separate
breed of human animal). Philippa Pearce makes you find it, feel it – and for her
child audience it is maybe the first uncovering:

'Afterwards, Aunt Gwen tried to describe to her husband that second
parting between them. "He ran up to her, and they hugged each other as if
they had known each other for years and years, instead of only having met for
the first time this morning. There was something else, too, Alan, although I
know you'll say it sounds even more absurd … Of course, Mrs. Bartholomew's
such a shrunken little old women, she's hardly bigger than Tom, anyway:
but, you know, he put his arms right round her and he hugged her good-bye
as if she were a little girl." '

In 1962 came *A Dog So Small*. Again it has the clean narrative pull, the delicious
quiet humour, an essential inwardness as it unfolds his world through a boy's eyes.
Ben Blewitt longs for a tiny dog, a chihuahua: 'a dog so small you can only see
it with your eyes shut', he says in a moment of despair as he begins to create a
fantasy dog behind his closed eyes. The chapters where boy and puppies play in
the pig sty are marvellously done:

'They went to see Tilly's puppies. She did not want them to go; but, if they

were going, she knew that her duty was to go too, and to go ahead. She
went briskly but with a waddle, being incommoded by the swinging
heaviness of the milk for her puppies.

'The sty had once belonged to some pigs, but was now perfectly clean,
with plenty of fresh straw on the concrete floor and a special lamp suspended
low from one corner of the roof to give a gentle heat. Beneath this the puppies
had all crawled and crowded together, and lay sleeping, a large, thick, sleek
blob of multiple puppy-life.'

And so too is the closing sequence as dusk falls on Hampstead Heath. It is a very
fine book, and yet – coming where it does in her work – it is something of a
pendant, a detour. So much is there, but not the music. The theme of obsession
(which of course informed the treasure hunt in *Minnow on the Say*) now dominates
and fills the gap. There is something of the psychological study about it, and –
ever so slightly – the eye slips off the child audience. Characteristically, she no
longer relies wholly on her art to do its own work, but – again, ever so slightly –
tops up the insights with glimpses of *sententiae*: 'He saw that if you didn't have the
possible things, you had nothing.' 'Granny shaded her eyes, looking after them.
"People get their heart's desire," she said, "and then they have to begin to learn
how to live with it".'

It seemed at that stage that either *Tom's Midnight Garden* had exhausted the
more elusive and precious vein, or that having hit such brilliant moments the
writer was reluctant to make the even more demanding commitment to her talents
that was perhaps required.

In the event, she felt her way out of the situation with cautious instinct.
Her next book *The Children of the House* was published in 1968. The book was
originally drafted by Brian Fairfax-Lucy, as a tale for adults. Philippa Pearce
worked on the existing draft and, as the introductory note says: 'made it one
that can be enjoyed and understood by children'. She did a good deal more than
that. She made it a classic. The setting could be that of one of the Victorian or
Edwardian writers. Four children grow up in a grand country house. Long
corridors, candles to bed, lessons in the 'schoolroom', tea in the nursery, ha-has
and pineapple houses, outlying tenant-farms and long gallops:

' "Hugh," said his father, "you will ride this morning."

' "Yes, Papa."

' "But as I shall be busy with papers, you will ride with William." The
clouds rolled back from Hugh's morning: ride with *William!*

'Their mother took over now. "This afternoon Papa and I have to attend

a meeting. I want you all to take a rice-pudding to old Mrs Higgs in the
village. You can go in the pony-trap – Laura had better drive. After that,
you may play in the garden." '

It is a grand loveless childhood, with the four children twined together in mutual
and sustaining affection. The servants bring them up, and our images of fathering
and mothering come when Elsie the maid or Walter the butler, for a moment,
tend the children. The formal parents are defined by their absence:

'After tea Walter wanted to buy some tobacco in the village, and took
Margaret with him. She held his hand all the way, and he gave her twopence
to spend on chocolate. Then he saw her back into the park, saying, "This is
my great chance for a drink and a chat in the pub, you know." Sir Robert
disapproved of his staff visiting public houses.

'Margaret ran most of the way back across the park, because she was
afraid of its getting dark and because she wanted to show Elsie her chocolate.
But when she reached the kitchen, Elsie was out; so she went up to the
schoolroom. All was quiet; there was nothing to do, nobody to talk to.
She watched out of the window until outside grew dark. Then she turned
up the lamp, and waited with the door open, for her supper. As she sat,
the schoolroom seemed to get larger and the passage outside wider and
longer, like a dark street in a town. Then the between-maid came with her
supper of soup and a cake. "And Alice says, Go to bed when you have
finished, and she will be up later." '

What takes it out of the standard Victorian mould (as it does E. Nesbit) is a
refusal to identify with the assumptions and aspirations of the upper-class home –
the sense of the house through the servants' eyes, of the eldest daughter denied a
useful education, of the old men combing the bins, or the ironic stonebreaker on
the roadside:

' "Anyway", said Laura, looking sideways at Hugh, "you're doing a very
useful job now, I suppose."

' "Oh, yes." He made the same throaty sound. "I'm glad to think that
I'm making the stones ready to fill the pot-holes in the road, so that the
carriages won't bump about so much. That's bad for the springs of the
carriages and for the coachmen and the horses and the fine gentry that ride
in the carriages." He seemed to be staring at them, but they could not see his
eyes properly behind the glasses.

' "We must be going on, I'm afraid," said Tom.'

Compared to her previous books – and perhaps because of the curious joint authorship – it takes some chapters before the vision becomes as freed from its setting as this. And it nowhere has the potent narrative thread.

But it has the music. The beautiful, piercing sense of childhood swept along – and overswept – in the stream of time. The art is superb. The ordinary incidents of childhood – boiling a moorhen's egg, a forbidden hair-clipping, finding a half-crown – lap quietly in the reader's mind: months and years imperceptibly vanish at each chapter's end.

So apt and unforced is the second half, that you may not realize how it is all building up inside you until the marvellous final section, the *adieu*. There is something almost Tchekov-like in those last dozen pages. For one splendid stretch she again meets and tops the great Victorians in their own arbour.

I do not think any age previous to ours could have so brought out Philippa Pearce's talent. Her clean, plain prose opens up her books to any child who reads at all easily. I fear that isn't at all true of many revered classics of the past. Her work brims with life, and with life decent, positive, ongoing. Again one wonders if a critical look at some of our Edwardian inheritance might find that this was precisely what some of them lacked. She writes – mostly – to and for the child: not through the child to other adults.

In many ways I feel very puzzled by the great outburst of first-class children's books this last thirty years. It is not too hard to see the social conditions that underpin it. And yet in all previous periods which have given us children's classics, there has been a sturdy adult literature. The folk and fairy tales are often that very literature, slipping, over a thousand years, from the oral world of men and women to the pages of children's books. *Gulliver's Travels* or *Robinson Crusoe* in the eighteenth century, *Treasure Island* or *Bevis* in the nineteenth are extensions of the flourishing adult novel, and Swift, Defoe, Stevenson, Jefferies, are writers for adults, accidentally or *en passant* entering the children's field. Equally, Lewis Carroll or E. Nesbit, may – if you like – be among the earlier writers who specialized with distinction in children's work. Yet there is never any doubt that they are supported by the flourishing adult novel. And at any rate, it is *there*. Yet it isn't now. At least I don't think so. And children's writing is a large and apparently self-contained genre, as it never was before. It is independent of the current adult novel. On the face of it you wouldn't therefore expect its burgeoning richness. Could it be, ironically, that precisely because the adult novel is so weak in this country, some talents have been drawn into the children's field and flourished (as others have been drawn into scientific fiction, and perished)?

It is hard to puzzle out, but a writer like Philippa Pearce quite apart from the significance of her books, indicates how fertile and accommodating this ground has been. Though it is indeed a golden age which could think of her still mint genius as silver.

From *The Use of English,* volume 21, number 3, 1970

The critic entering the author's world

Margaret Meek redefines the role of the critic when she undertakes an 'examination of the way in which a writer makes a world and invites a reader to share it with him'. The world that the novelist creates for himself has to satisfy him, and thus it may transform objective reality into a 'personal myth'. The author is, in one way, his own first reader, and his sense of audience depends on his own memories of childhood and the kinds of children he tolerates. The case of Lucy Boston is particularly interesting in this respect because she is not only author and first reader but also a principal character in her stories. Her fictional world is a conscious representation of her real-life world as described in her autobiography.

Lucy Boston
Memory in a House
Bodley Head, 1973

This leads Miss Meek to an examination of rhetoric: 'the way by which the writer makes known her vision and persuades the reader of its validity'. She shows that this also implies a system of moral values.

A private house   Margaret Meek

Some writers of children's books have a clear audience of children, or an individual child, whom they write to please. Others insist that they write to please themselves and are lucky if children read their books. In this latter group are widely acclaimed authors whose work is spoken of and judged as literature by critics who take children's books seriously, but who rarely question statements of this kind. Thus the list of prizewinners sometimes seems to be made up of those who claim to take less account of their readers and more account of themselves.

As the notion that distinctive authors for children 'really' write for themselves has more than a toehold in current evaluations, it is worth examining. It also creates an opportunity to extend the present confines of criticism, which, increasingly, substitutes the adulation of authors and implied standards of writing for the examination of the way in which a writer makes a world and invites a reader to share it with him. If an author has any idea that children are to be among his readers, he has some vision of an audience and adopts his stance accordingly. Whatever he *says*, he is always striving to make what he writes accessible to others. The self-as-author and the self-as-reader are not the same. The self-as-reader is a public self among other readers, although, usually, the first of these.

If the book is intended for children, or deals with experience from a child's viewpoint, the author-as-reader must highlight in himself that part of him which can judge his production, namely, himself as a child. Thus 'writing for oneself' for some authors implies a dialogue with the child they once were, or more intriguingly, the child they might have been. In their writing they not only recreate experience in narrative form, they create the particular illusion of childhood (Susanne Langer's 'virtual' experience), which arises out of the nature of this dialogue and which has its own rhetoric.

The opportunity to take this discussion a little further than usual is offered by the publication of L. M. Boston's autobiographical study, *Memory in a House*. Mrs Boston's first novel was published in 1954. She was sixty-two and could well claim that she had no need to do anything but please herself. She wrote *Yew Hall*, she tells us, 'to celebrate my love of the house'. As her readers know well, the house, the Norman Manor at Hemingford Grey, one of the oldest domestic buildings in England still inhabited, is the chief character in many of her books. Bought just before the Second War and restored with loving care, it is the central symbol of Mrs Boston's life and work.

The garden is remarkable for its yew trees, sweetbriar, honeysuckle, and roses. One reads about the restoration, the paths, the outhouses, the furniture and hangings with a sense of *déjà vu*, recognizing them from the descriptions in the novels, so that in the end it is difficult to sort out which are the autobiographical and which the fictive accounts. This passage is from *Yew Hall*; its counterpart is in the Green Knowe books, but it might just as easily have come from the autobiography.

> 'I have called my house a barn, an ark, a ship, a boulder, a wood ... It is a natural thing made out of the true earth. The walls are three feet thick, not of solid stone, but of quarried stone brought here by barge and laid piece over piece with the grain always lying as it lay in the cliff face but here with seams of air between the stone ... They breathe around me. Sitting here for the longest series of wordless winter nights I feel neither shut in nor shut off, but rather like the heart inside living ribs.'

In writing her autobiography Mrs Boston assumes a reader who is like a special guest, already interested in the details of the restoration of the Manor and the quality of the life inside it, to whom the choicest titbits of information are given (for example, that during the war the villagers thought she was a spy), and whose response is assumed to be conditioned by perfect taste, refined sensibility, and total sympathy for the viewpoint of the author. The invitation is to see the landscape through Mrs Boston's eyes, to admire her vistas, furniture, candlesticks, lanterns, and patchwork curtains, to validate her judgement of people, art and music. It is a tribute to the spellbinding quality of the writing that one feels oneself inside the house, in the familiar landscape of Green Knowe, so that one realizes that autobiography is simply another kind of fiction where the author borrows from life on behalf of art. The similarity between parts of *Memory in a House* and *Yew Hall* stems from the assumption that the reader will be an acolyte at the celebration of the house. If one stands outside the enchanted garden one could find the whole experience precious in the extreme and too rare to be of more than limited significance, or, more simply, irrelevant, if not odd.

After describing her friends in a circle of artists in Cambridge, Mrs Boston tells how the long peaceful postwar days alone in the house cast a spell on her:

> 'I suddenly felt that what I felt so strongly I could surely write down. This produced the novel *Yew Hall*. It was published in 1954, the same year as *The Children of Green Knowe*, written partly because I was hard up, but more to people the place for myself.'

The next sentence establishes the author-as-reader: 'I do not know how anyone can judge what they write unless they are writing for themselves.' Consequently Mrs Boston was disconcerted to find that if *The Children* was to be published with her son's illustrations, it had to go on the children's list. '...So I became a children's writer. I did not at the time realize what a step down this was.'

'A step down' clearly implies that Mrs Boston shared a view of children's books still prevalent at that time, but it is not certain if she still holds to this view. What critics have not made clear is that, for their author, *Yew Hall* and *The Children of Green Knowe* are of the same kind. The crude categories of 'adult' and 'children's' books obscure the fact they share a common *rhetoric*, that is, in terms Wayne Booth uses in *The Rhetoric of Fiction*, the way by which the writer makes known her vision to the reader and persuades the reader of its validity. The autobiography records of *Yew Hall*:

Wayne Booth *The Rhetoric of Fiction* University of Chicago Press 1961

> 'For a plot I had used the characters of my valued tenants, sometimes using their very words. I did not think my mixture of obvious truth and wicked fiction could ever be shown to them. I had immensely enjoyed writing it, and had proved to myself that I could put down what I wanted to say.'

The rhetoric of Mrs Boston's novels is the way fiction and truth are mixed in the personage who appears in all the stories – the Owner of the House. She is author–character–reader, making accessible, from whatever viewpoint she is concerned with at the time (the Green Knowe stories are set at different times of the year and the scene varies accordingly), the experiences and passions which could be, or could have been, connected with the house. The characters in *Yew Hall* are modern but the tragedy is starkly Greek or Jacobean. The most lasting impression is of the Narrator, the Owner, ostensibly withdrawn from the action, but in fact hastening on the climax by suggesting that the house acts as a judgement hall for the inhabitants.

The Owner of Green Knowe, the house in fiction, is Mrs Oldknow, whose ideal companion is her greatgrandson, Tolly. Here the author–reader relationship is embodied in the characters. The stories Mrs Oldknow tells Tolly call up children from the past – Linnet, sweet but cruel too, Toby, the mysterious one, and Alexander of the beautiful voice. They are from the days of Charles II, while Susan, who is blind, and Jacob, the noble West Indian savage, are from the end of the eighteenth century. In their story, *Chimneys*, the house is partly burned down. The stories themselves have earned well-deserved praise, but it is the passionate relationship of the Owner–Narrator to the inhabitants which ensures the readers' willingness, or confirms their reluctance, to enter into the secondary world which the house symbolizes.

In this world Mrs Oldknow is 'so old and had lived at Green Knowe for so long that she had come to accept quietly whatever curious things presented themselves and almost to think that it was the house itself that made them happen'. At first this seems like a familiar convention for getting stories to move on, but gradually we see that Tolly, Ping the Chinese boy, Jacob, and the other dream children in the portraits are not only fictional characters but other special guests. They embody the qualities which grant them access to the house and its secrets: courtesy, a grave demeanour, intelligent self-absorption, musical talent, imaginative response to symbolic forms, all the distinctions, in fact, which in her autobiography Mrs Boston demands of her flesh-and-blood friends and visitors. The notion that for special people the laws of nature are suspended or amended typifies the characters in the novels and those Mrs Boston tolerates every day. Thus the highly wrought language is as close to the author as it can be in autobiographical rhetoric:

'Tolly's thoughts were wandering.

' "When I told the boys at school that you lived in a sort of castle with ghosts, they didn't believe me."

' "Ghosts! What a thing to call them."

' "What do you call them?"

' "The others."

' "I like this house. It's like living in a book that keeps coming true".'
No wonder, then, that Mrs Boston was abashed at being classed as a writer for
children when she was, in fact, paying homage with all her artistic subtlety and
skill in the creation of a distinctive personal myth. What she presents is the
unfragmented life of childhood which depends on a vision which is partial and
egocentric. Mrs Boston may not have thought that she was writing for children,
but she chose special ones (herself, doubtless) as her allies, because they share this
vision.

This becomes clear in *The Castle of Yew* which she undoubtedly wrote for
children. In it she falls back on the rhetoric of *Gulliver's Travels*. The hero shrinks
until he is small enough to get inside a yew tree in the shape of a castle in a garden
where the yew trees are cut in the shape of chessmen. The garden belongs to an
old lady who 'can make things happen' and who tells Joseph: 'You can go anywhere you want if you really want to.' The magic depends on the boy sharing
the old lady's conviction and insight. Other aspects of this same magic crop up in
The Sea Egg and *Nothing Said*, both of which suggest that the author's powers
operate just as well outside the enchanted garden.

But the nature of the personal myth is seen best in *A Stranger at Green Knowe*
and *The Enemy at Green Knowe* where the idyllic life of the house and garden is
threatened. The Stranger is Hanno, the gorilla which escapes from London Zoo.
He would seem to be a powerful menace, but the reverse is true. He is found by
Ping in the garden wilderness at Green Knowe. Both the boy and the gorilla are
outcasts with their homes in distant lands. Ping wins his new home at Green
Knowe by befriending Hanno and concealing his presence so as not to compromise
Mrs Oldknow by telling her about him. Mrs Boston says:

> 'The subject to me was a big one. It had to contain the whole force of my
> belief that all life, not merely human, must have respect, that a man-centred
> concept of it was false and crippling, that these other lives are the great riches
> of ours. In particular I wanted to make clear my immense admiration for
> this creature so vulgarly shuddered at, and that there was no cosy answer
> to the wickedness that had been done to him.'

Here and elsewhere the myth is made out of the symbols which generate it and
which it generates. 'All life must have respect' does not include the vulgar, the

crowd at the gate. Above all it does not include the Library Association, who when they gave Mrs Boston the Carnegie Medal for this book at Llandudno, apparently subjected her to a series of personal indignities, nor the Playing Fields committee, who sought permission to build a pavilion on the edge of her moat. Mrs Boston 'took all possible defensive action' and planning permission was cancelled.

> 'The original Enemy therefore was the committee of the Playing Fields and the fight to preserve the rare from hate and contempt was against them ... Conveniently for me, there was among my acquaintances a lady of learning who served well as a model for the witch, Dr Melanie D. Powers.'

Conveniently indeed, for every myth contains its threat from the powers of darkness. In *An Enemy* they are unleashed against the innocent Owner, but the children have the necessary wisdom to come to her aid. The next generation will fight for the house against the planners and sightseers.

> ' "Green Knowe doesn't need guardians," said Tolly, showing in his face how proud he was of it. "It *can't* have any enemies."
>
> ' "It has enemies and it needs guarding all the time," said the old lady. "Over and above all the rest it seems to me to have something I can't put a name to, which always has had enemies." '

The ideal reader is also the supporter of the author even to the point of validating her obsessions.

One cannot read *Memory in a House* without feeling that Mrs Boston chafes in a particular way against the idea of being a famous *children's* author. An artist, yes, whose creation is a vision of place and time made from a personal myth in which she is herself both narrator and ideal reader. It is a complete vision, complex and utterly exclusive, within which 'writing for oneself' means 'being oneself in writing' by virtue of a rhetoric which creates, in a highly distinctive fashion, the internal dialogue of a greatly gifted writer and the unfragmented world of only some rare children.

From *The Times Literary Supplement*, 15 June 1973

Ways forward

Introduction

Children's literature has already become the subject of serious study in
universities and increasingly heavy books are being written about it. One
wonders what good will come out of all this. There seem to be four particular
dangers:

> Theoretical studies will be undertaken by people who do not themselves
> read children's books very extensively or with enjoyment.
> They will be tempted to engage in psychometric, sociometric and linguistic
> data-gathering that leads to partial but apparently authoritative views of the
> subject.
> Experimental psychologists, Eng. Lit. students, educationalists, and the
> professional connoisseurs of 'kidlit' will each pursue their enquiries in the
> light of their own specialist disciplines, with ignorance and possibly
> contempt for each other's work.
> The child curled up in an armchair with his Jennings book will be forgotten.

We have tried to avoid these pitfalls as far as possible by drawing on contributions
from novelists, journalists, philosophers, poets, and parents as well as established
academics. We believe that the view of reading and storymaking that has been
defined in Section one of this collection and has been reflected in the author's
contributions to Section two, does offer the basis for further study that can draw
on the insights of all relevant specialisms and still not lose sight of the child. We
find reassurance in the presence of D. W. Harding's article (page 379) since he has
managed to draw on his outstanding experience both as literary critic and as
theoretical psychologist to define for us the real significance of 'spectator-role
experience' for the growing child. We find equal reassurance in the final
contribution by R. L. Gregory (page 393), another psychologist, who has made
contributions to studies of the arts, since he confirms what Barbara Hardy told us
at the start of our collection, that people live by their internal 'fictions' at least as
much as by 'fact'.

Harding and Gregory offer promising ways forward for English teaching
and for the study of psychology. To these we have added contributions from a

radical publisher, a working journalist, an experienced schoolteacher, an educational researcher, and a librarian. Unless we pay attention to all of these people, discussion of children's fiction will remain narrow, élitist, and inadequate.

Testing the values in the market place

Elaine Moss is best known in England as the editor of an annual list of books for children, distinguished by the perceptiveness of its comments and the usefulness of its selection. At a meeting of the Children's Book Circle and the Youth Libraries Group, a select professional body, she was asked about the sophistication of books for children. This is her comment. She doesn't say that the book which sparked off the discussion was Alan Garner's 'Red Shift'. The main point of the argument is that if editors become too involved in teenage fiction which mirrors adult fiction, they will be in danger of neglecting the needs of the greater number of children for 'good stories'. Mrs Moss is speaking to people she knows well so that she makes her points by allusion rather than extended statement.

The adult-eration of children's books   Elaine Moss

Are children's books becoming too sophisticated? In attempting to answer this question in the ten minutes allotted to me, I shall try to look at the children's book scene as it is today with all the virtues of high standard of writing, production and, I believe, sales figures that publishers have achieved, and ask whether the moment hasn't now come, not for destroying what we have built up, but for a shift of emphasis.

By holding this meeting on this subject all of us who are concerned with children and books – all children and all their books – are demonstrating our healthy awareness that we stand on the edge of a precipice, the precipice of over-sophistication in an area where approachableness is, for the majority of children, the most important aspect of the product we have to sell. To sell, mark you! For we must face the fact that today the idea of reading for pleasure has to be sold to most children.

But let us be clear about terms. Sophistication really means the adulteration of something by the introduction of elements foreign to the original substance.

I find the use of *adulteration* in the Oxford Dictionary definition very helpful, and I propose for this discussion to use the word in a hyphenated form – ADULT-ERATION: for that, I think, is what we are really here to discuss – the ADULT-eration of children's books.

Looking at children's books over the years, the trend towards adult-eration is indeed alarming. Could the root cause be specialization, I wonder? Children's books – for better and for worse – are no longer published for fun by editors who spend four-fifths of their time in other fields and devote, perhaps, a relaxing Friday to the odd junior manuscript that may have come into the office – as Ursula Moray Williams's *Adventures of the Little Wooden Horse* came in to George Harrap's office, or Tolkien's *The Hobbit* into Allen and Unwin's in the thirties. You – the children's book editors – are professionally involved with children's books from Monday to Friday and sometimes on Saturdays and Sundays as well, and you are adults with the literary and artistic standards of adults. You – the children's librarians – are also professional, also fully involved and also fully committed; you meet children, but in the main book-orientated children. Similarly we reviewers tend to be specialist and – here we all are once again, specialists on children's books *talking to each other*. This is necessary; but it can be dangerous, because when we go out into the world – a world in which the illiteracy rate is disturbing – when we go out into the world, which is where we belong, we find that we have developed a deadly in-jargon and that we fling around ourselves a veil of quite unnecessary sophistication. The first step back from the precipice is to discard this veil. Our specialist task is to know more – much more – than the public, but to wear our knowledge so lightly, and present books to people – the right books to the right people at the right time – in so easy a manner, that no one would guess we were specialists.

Now to the adult-eration of children's books themselves. The long preamble is relevant; for, being adult, being so involved, wanting high quality in children's books, wishing (some of us) even to have children's books regarded as adult reading and reviewed on the same general critical principles as adult literature, we are all of us responsible for the adulteration – or sophistication if you like – of children's books.

The high quality of some of today's children's books and teenage books is, then, a direct result of the total involvement of dedicated publishers, librarians and reviewers who have made the path of excellence shine golden for literary authors and painterly artists. Respectable libraries stock their work (though some report that it sticks on the shelves), concerned parents know their names,

furniture designers have discovered that their books look wonderfully warm on
nursery bookshelves. (Look at the colour supplements on Sunday and you'll see
what I mean.)

We need these authors and artists; we respect their publishers; but we must
be aware that in detecting only *their* merits, in praising only *them* publicly, in
writing learned papers about just *these* books, we are merely skimming cream and
pretending that the milk is of no importance – whereas there are few children
who can digest undiluted cream and the mass of young readers will only look at
milk, and would indeed like it better if it came in coke tins. In short, *we* are
becoming élitist. But this meeting proves that we are, at least, not complacently
so. We seem to have discovered that the moment for a shift of emphasis towards
anti-adulteration is here and now.

Those of us who are middle-aged remember a childhood when we gratefully
read whatever was available – from *Rainbow*, through the densely packed columns
of *Schoolboys'* or *Schoolgirls' Own*, to pony stories, school stories or whatever.
Opening these appallingly produced books was like taking the first step into a
mysterious forest: who knew what was lurking behind those trees? Certainly our
parents didn't – which made the expedition more private and exciting. Do today's
handsomely produced books, which I confess I enjoy handling and recommending
as much as anybody, exert the same magnet-ized (forgive the pun) tug into the
unknown? I wonder.

Certainly paperback publishing is teaching us some interesting lessons.
Take *Agaton Sax*, for example (he is the Swedish private eye whose wit and verve
make him the criminal's most dreaded detective on both sides of the North Sea).
There is nothing wrong with the handsome Deutsch hardcover editions of
Agaton Sax Books – except that they are handsome (or we reviewers might have
condemned them as worthless) and hardcovered (otherwise, the libraries would
not have bought them). But in the Target paper-covered editions – bright,
accessible looking, pocket-worthy and easy to read under the bedclothes –
thousands of children are going to become Sax fans. And Sax books are wonderful
reading.

Presentation *is* important, in non-fiction as well as in fiction. We may admire
and praise in our reviews the lovely publications of the high-class publishers; and
some of our children certainly fall on them and are enthralled, so far be it from
me to condemn them. Now look at the *Hamlyn Children's History of the World*, and
you will surely see at once that it is a book to be considered seriously. But how
many reviews of it did you read last year? Hamlyn are serving – to Hamlyn

children (which is most children) – attractive, digestible, nourishing fare: an iced cake, maybe, but one made with eggs. Children are great dippers, and brightness encourages dipping.

If we mute colours, if we insist that the only worthwhile book is the one which deals with a subject in depth, we shall turn potential readers into non-readers. First steps must be sure – but easy. Trendy picture-books in which sensitive artists explore the psychological problems of childhood are beautiful to look at, fascinating for *us* to think about, and useful with special children who have particular problems; but reviews of these books tend to focus on the beautiful artwork with never a mention of the potential audience. The books we *should* devote most of our attention to are the picture-books that are on a child level throughout, like the immortal (I hope) *Rosie's Walk* – and the sadly mortal (it is now out of print) *Clever Bill*: we have moved far away from William Nicholson's unadulterated, utterly simple concept of a small child and his picture-book. The emphasis is now on the picture-book: it must return to the child.

There isn't time to examine books for the middle years in any depth; which doesn't matter particularly, since in this area adulteration is least marked – and, of course, review space given, less generous. I would like to say in passing, though, that children could do with more new straight undemanding adventure stories properly written – books that would oust for ever the Blyton series now being reissued, which Margery Fisher, in a recent number of *Growing Point*, condemns as 'slow poison'. Enid Blyton demonstrated that children are so hungry for *stories* that they will read the same story over and over, slightly disguised. If adulteration has taught us anything – and surely it has – it has taught us that children also respond to good writing. Perhaps the moment has *now* come for better stories, well written ? The success at all levels of Ted Hughes's *The Iron Man* is just one proof that we are not crying for the moon.

And so, to teenage fiction. This is the area on which there will, I am sure, be most discussion. It is the area which attracts a disproportionate amount of children's book review space – since the books reviewed are often acclaimed, rightly, as superb *adult* reading. Writers of good stories (and stories are as important in teenage reading as they are at every other stage of child development) – authors like K. M. Peyton, Barbara Willard and Leon Garfield – sit happily on children's lists and are read avidly by young and old alike. Fair enough. But when novelists who have sharpened their pens in the children's field assume – as they have every right to assume – the present-day adult novelist's techniques and ob-scurities, his psychoanalytical approaches, his obsession with the person rather than the story, I suggest that *there* the children's editor should draw the line and let the book sink or swim as adult fiction. Such books belong on the adult shelf, to be borrowed, read and revered by the exceptional teenager for whom it is not, I think, our business (since the world is already his oyster) to publish at all.

But publishing for the ordinary young teenager and for the reluctant teenage reader *is* our business, and here I would like merely to remind those who criticize the content of some teenage fiction that its readers watch television and have probably seen the film of *Clockwork Orange*. Today's teenagers know it all – superficially. Are we not therefore right to explore in some depth, in the course of a *story* for them, the topics glibly glossed over in celluloid or on the box ? Is this not a specific area in which the adulteration of children's books is not merely justified but vital ? Better surely an S. E. Hinton story than an Ian Fleming: the serious, as opposed to the glamorous treatment, in literature, of sex and violence is of paramount importance.

So, by adult-eration, we gain and we lose. That's life. Quite certainly the 'Golden Age' has been worthwhile: it has pushed back the frontiers, shown us what can be done. We must now concentrate on using our experience to provide more approachable-looking books and better written *stories* for the broader mass of young readers.

Our job, having painfully climbed up the ivory tower, is to come down again, if we dare, and test our values in the market place. It will not be easy to maintain proven standards whilst adapting them to wider horizons. But it is a challenge we face. And it is a challenge we must meet. If we do not, we shall very soon be serving only ourselves. And that would be the ultimate in adult-eration.

From *Signal,* **14,** May 1974

Ways forward for the student of popular culture

The bloodhound journalist, tracing a phenomenon to its source, inter-
viewing the people who matter, and writing it up in a style that combines
vividness with accuracy, can sometimes be a more perceptive and
informative commentator than the studious academic researcher. In this
article, Colin Smith of 'The Observer' traces the war comics to their source
in the offices of the International Publishing Corporation. What the editors
have to say about their work and their view of their readership makes a
fascinating contrast to the introspective literary contributions to Section
two of this collection. Far more attention must be given to men like
Bensberg and to their publications whose readership vastly exceeds that of
any conventional novel. Comparison might be made with George Orwell's
essay 'Boys' Weeklies', published in 1939, to see how little things change.

Himmel! The Englanders won't stop fighting   Colin Smith

It's easy to recognize the Germans. They are the ones saying 'Himmel!' and
'Donner und Blitzen' and calling each other 'Dummkopfs'. Apart from an occa-
sional reference to 'Il Glorious Duce', the Italians are limited to the craven
'Mama Mia!' The Japanese rarely get further than 'Banzai!' though they're some-
times permitted to sign off, usually seconds before extinction, with a fanatical
'By Shinto!'

By Shinto?

'Well, I'm not too sure what it means either,' says Edward Bensberg, 'but it
sounds Japanese, doesn't it?'

Bensberg, a wartime sergeant in the Royal Signals, is the editor of the
International Publishing Corporation's War Picture and Battle Picture Libraries
which publish between them sixteen 64-page comics devoted to the Second World
War every month. Their main rivals are D. C. Thomson of Dundee, with the Com-
mando series. Then there are smaller firms like Micron Publications, of Horsham,

whose Combat Picture Library is printed in Spain, and Top Sellers, of Great Portland Street, London, whose Pocket War Library is printed in Italy. Dozens of other publishers produce a war series from time to time. For, although it is twenty-seven years since VE Day and Britain is going into Europe, as far as the comics are concerned being beastly to the Germans (and not terribly polite about the Italians and the Japanese either) is, at six pence a time, a sound investment.

Bensberg says his editions are intended for children of ten to fourteen, but they also have a large adult readership. Ex-servicemen send in their own stories. The commanding officer of a British Army battalion once wrote to say how much his men enjoyed them and suggested a plot featuring his own regiment. During the rebellion in Ceylon in April last year a Sandhurst-trained Sinhalese subaltern gave me half-a-dozen well-kept old battle comics to pass the time while we were waiting for a rebel attack.

IPC seem to have recognized the potential of the comics' adult audience. Back cover advertisements in some issues offer mail-order jewellery on hire purchase with 'special arrangements for HM Forces and customers abroad'. They have fond memories about how popular the comics used to be among National Servicemen.

Edward Bensberg doesn't really think his comics are about the war as such. Nor does he regard them as particularly anti-German. They have, he says, simply replaced the unfashionable Western comics as a backcloth for strong character stories. 'I think television had an effect ... so many programmes and old films about the war.'

'We never do anything about more recent events like Vietnam or Aden (some American comics do and the South Vietnamese produce their own about the war) or even Korea. If we did that we would get involved in politics. In a sense the Second World War was the last non-political war. I know it was a struggle against fascism, but then everybody is against that so there's no controversy.'

IPC published their first war comic in September 1958 under the War Picture Library series. It was called *Fight Back to Dunkirk*. Unlike the ordinary comic, it used a semi-documentary approach. 'We try to angle our stories towards realism,' said Bensberg. 'We don't change the course of history or have super-heroes.'

A more juvenile series called *Front Line* was tried, but then closed down. All the same the Battle and War Picture Libraries are primarily for children and he is careful to allow British characters nothing stronger than a 'Cor blimey' in their dialogue. 'We have certain standards – which is more than you can say for some of the things you get on television.'

No Man's Land, first published in May 1961, and reissued in March this year, has a typical Battle Picture Library introduction. 'By Christmas of 1941 the long, punishing campaign in the western desert had swung in favour of the British Eighth Army. It was the turn of Rommel's Afrika Korps to beat a hasty retreat to defensive positions west of Benghazi. The major land battle dwindled into skirmishes and probing patrols as each side tried out the other's strength.'

The story deals with the exploits of one Lieutenant Bob Hudson, who we are rapidly given to understand is more brawn than brain, and his feud with a scholarly major from the Camouflage Corps. In the end, all is happily resolved when Lieutenant Hudson lures the Panzers up to the major's camouflaged howitzers. 'They are character stories,' says Bensberg. 'Stories of ordinary people and how they react under the stress of war. We try to show the good and bad on both sides.'

Good Germans don't necessarily have to be dead ones (though in March's *Steady the Guards* there is a discussion on that line as a wounded British general pleads for the life of a German doctor), but they do remain a fairly disreputable bunch. Even the inanimate take on national characteristics. The German machine-guns go off with 'a maniacal chatter' whereas the British, more tunefully, are like 'a synchronised symphony'.

In *The Dangerous Breed* a German officer is not only rather nasty, but also cruel to animals. He hits a dog over the head with an unprimed stick grenade. Of course, it's his undoing. The dog, now adopted by gentle British Tommies, exposes his tormentor when he's strutting around the lines in British officer uniform. (True to the earliest traditions of boys' comics, the enemy is capable of being pretty *treacherous*.)

Although some snivelling coward might appear in the British ranks from time to time, the general message is that, properly led, there is no soldier in the world quite like Tommy Atkins. The recurring themes often sound like something out of a training manual. Sergeant-majors need have no fear about the ultimate *rightness* of the war comics' philosophy: the NCO is the backbone of the British army; your best friend is your rifle and good soldiers always obey the last command.

These comics are also one of the last hiding-places for good old-fashioned chauvinism where the innate superiority of British servicemen is taken for granted. Typical is the cheery sergeant in *No Man's Land* who, about to take part in an ambush, observes: 'A ratio of three to two in their favour. Suits us, sir!'

Even so, the dialogue in the Battle Picture series is much better than in publications like Micron's American-written Combat Picture Library. In a recent issue a German officer really does say to a prisoner: 'We have methods of making men talk.'

Top Sellers' *Foe or Friend* has a more liberal, forward-looking approach. It tells the story of a British sailor who saves the life of a German submariner who, naturally, returns the compliment. The last bubble has the Briton in hospital and the German murmuring to him: 'This friendship must never die.'

IPC's war comics have a passion for technical accuracy. A whole frame will often focus on a single weapon or vehicle which is sketched with almost drawing-board perfection. Edward Bensberg's office is full of books with titles like 'Manual of Military Law 1914' and 'Ranks and Badges of the British Army'.

The technique in writing is to give the dialogue and a potted description of the sort of scene the writer imagines, usually fairly detailed: 'Picture shows an understrength section of nine infantrymen led by a young sergeant walking down a flat Dutch road towards the German border. The sergeant and the corporal are carrying Stens and the rest of the men have Lee-Enfields except for one man with a Bren in his right hand held by its carrying handle.'

This frame will then have some sort of continuity caption, usually no more than a sentence: 'September 1944 and British troops have fought their way from the Normandy beaches to the very borders of the Nazi fatherland.'

The artists often turn out to be young Italians or Spaniards who have no experience of war, let alone the arms and equipment of the various armies in the Second World War. They copy the weapons from books and old military manuals – often more accurately than British artists who imagine they know what a Sten gun looks like. The sort of mistake Bensberg is on the look out for is an American bazooka anti-tank weapon placed in the hands of British infantry instead of a proper PIAT (Projectile Infantry Anti-Tank).

Editor Bensberg frankly describes his own war story as 'a Cook's tour of the Middle East'. He was a territorial, mobilized shortly after war was declared. The nearest he got to action throughout the next six years was the tail end of some skirmishing against the Communists during the Greek Civil War. 'I tried to volunteer for various things, but they just wouldn't let me go.'

Did he regret not seeing action?

'Yes, I think I do.'

A mild-mannered fifty-two-year-old, he is the father of five children, none of whom has ever expressed the slightest interest in the comics he produces.

His writers get about £60 a story and artists, who usually have to draw around 130 frames, are paid £200. War Picture and Battle Picture have about eight regular contributors. Most of them had some experience of service life in World War II.

One exception is Miss Diana Garbutt, of Scarborough, who was twelve when the war ended. When ill health forced her to leave her job as a shorthand typist she started to write children's stories and had several accepted by D. C. Thomson. Most of them were adventure tales about Africa and animals. None of them was a war story. Three years ago Abelard-Schuman published her children's book *Black Warrior*.

She started writing picture scripts when she replied to an advertisement, under the impression that straight short-story writers were wanted. At first she thought they wouldn't take kindly to a woman writing war stories, but she has always been interested in ships and the sea so she broke into the market with a naval story. Now she writes war comics with North African and Burmese backgrounds.

Another successful war comics writer, an ex-Navy man who lives in an expensive flat near Marble Arch, preferred to remain anonymous.

'It's not something I'm particularly proud of,' he explained. 'In fact I'm sometimes rather ashamed of doing them. I suppose it does glorify war. The gruesome bits are very much played down. We never show guts spilling out or anything. If somebody gets hit by a bullet we just show him tumbling over. I don't think they're particularly *anti-German*. Well, I suppose really they're *comic* Germans. Come to think of it, I don't suppose that's such a good thing either.'

Alfred Carney Allan, who recently retired from the business on doctor's orders at sixty-eight, wrote for all kinds of comics for fifty years and certainly isn't ashamed of it. When he was working he could write a war comic in ten days.

He joined the Black Watch during the war, but didn't see any action because at thirty-five he was considered to be too old to be a frontline platoon commander. When his battalion went to Normandy he was a major, writing technical pamphlets.

He doesn't think actually seeing action would have made it impossible for him to write war comics. He regards himself as too much of a professional for that. Once he wrote a text series called *Mary Latimer – Nun* which always had to include in each serial the line, *Mary looked angelic in the candlelight*.

'I remember once meeting this ex-tank driver who had a very nasty experience. His tank had been hit and started to brew up and he could hear the other two crewmen screaming in the turret. He was unhurt, but he couldn't escape himself because the barrel of the tank gun happened to be over the hatch and he couldn't get the lid up more than a few inches. He screamed down the intercom for these two chaps who were dying, being burned alive, to move the gun and one of them must have heard or fallen on a switch or something because it did move and he escaped. I could never use a story like that.'

From *The Observer Colour Supplement*, 16 July 1972

Ways forward in publishing: transferring power to the community

Ken Worpole's initiative in setting up the Centreprise Community Publishing Project in Hackney was based on two assumptions. First, the established publishing houses are staffed by and largely cater for the middle classes and those who share the values of the present academic and economic hierarchy; they therefore have little significance for the mass of working people who remain consumers of other people's culture without the opportunity to express their own. Second, publishing is power and the majority of people in this country are deprived of power. Centreprise has given local people the opportunity to publish their own works.

Publishing is for people too   Ken Worpole

'Well, by this time the bread round was getting me down, what with the stairs and the weather and the sheer poverty I encountered. I had to pack it in. I then started a job lorry driving. I now know that driving wasn't for me – and still isn't – but that's the way of life for many people. There are thousands in the wrong job. The thought of being an artist still haunts me. I often think of taking it up but work and domestic commitments don't allow it. The things I would like to do are endless, and I'm sure that I'm not on my own in this. Painting, music, reading, writing, photography, tape recording, boating, swimming, tennis, to mention only a few. But how many people have the time, and also the energy after a week's work? And if they do have the energy, where do they get the money that most of the enjoyments cost?'

The writer is a Hackney taxi driver, Ron Barnes; the passage comes from a 30,000 word autobiography written during the last six months in his spare time. He wrote it for his teenage daughter and her generation, so that they might know what his generation had to struggle through to achieve the still limited benefits of the life they now have.

The autobiography will be published by the Centreprise Community Publishing Project, a non-profit-making project which aims to provide publishing and distribution opportunities for people in Hackney who would never think of themselves as authors within the traditional framework of commercial publishing. The project works closely with local schools, and many of the publications produced so far, which include a community-based reading book, two individual collections of poetry by local schoolchildren, a folder of historical documents about Hackney and two local autobiographies, are used quite extensively in schools.

In the preface to his book, Mr Barnes writes that what encouraged him to start writing was knowing there was a possibility of local publication and a potentially sympathetic readership, particularly in the schools. This example, taken from a growing trend in non-commercial publishing, provides a good starting-point from which to examine some of the statements made in the *TES* about the relevance to education of 'working-class culture'.

What characterizes most of the articles written on this topic is that they deal only in massive generalizations. 'The working class' is dismissed educationally, by implication, as constituting 'the less intellectually endowed members of our society' (our society?); or totally misrepresented: 'the great weakness … of working-class culture is that its aspirations are so limited'.

Presumably the writer of this last statement, Colin McInnes, is totally unread in labour history. Otherwise he might have discovered that the continuing political demands made throughout the last 200 years by working-class movements (including even the list of conference resolutions presented by constituency Labour parties each year) have encompassed possibilities for the reorganization of social life that make even the wildest manifestoes of any of the current 'alternative' groups look the piecemeal changes most of them are.

When professional commentators talk about limited aspirations, it is probably because they have spent too long looking in a mirror. Where do these generalizations about the working-class come from?

Any attempt to map out features of specific working-class cultures must begin with a look at history. Only then can one begin to see that the activities that do exist are often simply these that the ruling class have allowed to exist. At a recent meeting of young teachers in East London, Chris Searle said he had to look to Moscow to get hold of a copy of poetry written by workers involved in the nineteenth-century Chartist movement in Britain. Attempts in the nineteenth century to encourage and consolidate a literary culture, as part of a wider political culture, were met by ruthless counter measures and the imprisoning of writers, publishers and printers.

So it could be that many people do not write because they know that nobody will take any notice of what they have written. This certainly happens in schools, and one only has to look at the commercial world of publishing to realize that it is insensitive to other, much wider and deeper reasons for reading and writing. This is why some of the co-operative work now being done between parents, schoolchildren and teachers in Hackney is of considerable significance.

We hope during the next few years to build up a considerable number of publications, for use in schools and in the wider community, written by the children, parents and teachers. Two of these co-operative ventures, *A Hoxton Childhood*, written by a local cabinet maker about his early life in a specific area of Hackney, and *Vivian Usherwood; Poems*, a collection of poems written by a thirteen-year-old boy born in the West Indies, are now set books in the newly developed English CSE Mode two syllabus, the result of over a year's planning by representatives from most Hackney secondary schools.

The aim of this project is not to replace the wider literary and social culture of the better commercial publications; no teacher would want to stop using, for example, the novels of the best children's authors, or substitute local history for the larger perspectives. However, it is obvious that children and their parents can often produce much more imaginative work than the great bulk of the material on the market, and we see no reason why they should not be given the chance to do this. The one short novel by a thirteen-year-old boy that we have published – *At the cliff's edge* – has no equal commercially. (It is not irrelevant to note that last year the *TES* announced that in its information book awards competition, not one of the 125 books submitted in the junior section 'was good enough for the award'.)

In case people might think that we had a massive printing complex at our disposal, we should add that we use commercial printers. But we do have an electric typewriter so that we design and prepare everything up to the printing stage. This kind of co-operative project could be undertaken anywhere.

A culture, like a community, is not a thing, but a process. Because of this, it can change, be destroyed or strengthened. People, particularly academic educationalists who go looking for 'cultures' or 'communities', will never find them, because to do that they would have to stay for some time and become a part of them. Schools can help the growth of local communities and cultures, or they can remain separate, which is another way of destroying them.

We should agree with some of the arguments of Michael Young and Nell   q. v. bibliography
Keddie, particularly their insistence on treating children as if they had inner
worlds of their own rather than treating them as objects. But to argue for
complete cultural relativism is dangerous. Certainly any group has a culture, and
while it is interesting, for example, to look at the culture of long-term prisoners,
this should not mean that we forget to ask why there is such a thing as long-term
imprisonment. And there is such a thing as deprivation. The majority of people
in this country are deprived of power and of the means by which they can get
power. On an elementary but crucial level, it is the problem raised by Mr Barnes
at the beginning: 'The things I would like to do are endless …' There is a question
of time, money, and resources.

The project I have briefly described here shows that by making available,
in this case, access to publication (which is a form of power), many of the old
assumptions about culture and the prevailing forms of education are brought in
question. In one four-week period, with no advertising other than the existence of
our own publications, we were given: the manuscript of a 100,000 word history
of the East End written by a disabled ex-van driver; collections of poems by an
ex-prisoner, a young wife who works in a local factory, a printer; a short children's
novel by an eleven-year-old from one of the local comprehensives; a collection of
short stories about East End life by a retired electrician. We know of three autobiographies in the process of being written and we do not know yet how much
writing is being done, privately, by people who have been led to regard published
writers as something of a rare species.

The recent publication of *Elders*, the anthology of poetry by elder citizens
which Chris Searle compiled, caused quite a stir. Why ? Because, presumably,
nobody had ever asked old people what they thought, and they were surprised
when they were confronted with the sheer power of language, pride, and anger
which emerged. So, before any more people indulge in debating the relationship
between class and literature, they might first consider what chance most people
have ever been given. Teachers have a much more significant role to play in
assisting the growth of more self-confident communities, if they work as equals
with the parents and the children, using the facilities and resources at their
disposal.

From *The Times Educational Supplement*, 1 March 1974

Ways forward for the author: meeting particular needs

If it is true that children need to recognize themselves in stories – however 'recognize' is interpreted – and that children's feelings about themselves are influenced by what they read, then the coloured child in a predominantly white community tends to be seen as a special case. In fact, the case is special not because the readers are a minority, but because stories extend as well as confirm experience for all children, because they are a way of discovering the variety of life in all its forms and the common humanity of all people.

But it is true that many children's books embody racist attitudes (e.g. older books like 'Little Black Sambo') and exclusive prejudices, hence the call for 'black studies' to redress the balance. But if storying is a means for a reader to extend his experience – as we claim it to be, then children's books (in a multi-racial society) have a distinctive role which is not confined to presenting heroes who are not white.

This American article states the problems that arise and shows some of the solutions, though these solutions can only be partial.

That one's me   Liz Gant

'Once upon a time, in the ancient kingdom of Lyraland, there lived a good but lonely dragon named Harry …

' "What's buggin you, baby?" asked Mabel Mae Jones, one of the sweetest and kindest fairies in the kingdom.

' "Well," said Harry, a tear welling in his great dragon's eye, "each week, in order to win a wife, I fight the knight in shining armor. And each week I lose …"

' "I can dig where you're coming from," said Mabel Mae …'

Walter D. Myers
The Dragon Takes a Wife
Bobbs-Merrill, 1972

The quotation is from *The Dragon Takes A Wife*, one of a small but growing number of books being written with Black children in mind. Its author, Walter

Myers, who also wrote the award-winning children's book *Where Does The Day Go?*, says he became interested in writing for children after seeing his son point to an illustration of a small Black boy in a book and hearing him say, 'That one's me.'

Such identification has not always been possible. When I was a child, I remember, I wondered why there were no Black children in the stories and pictures in the books I read. The books available to us were always full of picture-perfect Sallys and Jacks in clinically uncluttered farmhouses or cottages, living neat, prescribed lives that bore little resemblance to our Black lives. Nowhere was there a portrayal of our Black and brown faces, or any suggestion of the warmth and spontaneity that filled our homes; no hint of the loving smells of sweet bread baking in the oven or the friendly and familiar scent of oilcloth-covered tables; nothing of the snap-and-dash style and wit of our language or the rhyming cadences of our voices on spring and summer evenings as we played limber-legged games that had been handed down to us for generations.

Juvenile books were seldom written for or about Black youngsters. And we may never know how many young Black minds were irrevocably damaged by these omissions.

Today Black-oriented books do exist, and Black and white teachers and parents alike are beginning to discover them. These books are being used in Head Start programmes, community day-care centres, libraries, independent Black schools and even in some public schools. In some places they are the basis for games and plays. The African Free School, in Newark, New Jersey, regularly holds a children's hour in which youngsters act out some of the stories and then take part in a question-and-answer period.

The books cover a wide range of ages and interests. And they are more than just traditional white stories with Black slang thrown in. Books such as John Steptoe's *Train Ride*, in which two boys talk about life as they ride in a subway car, allow the urban Black child to reflect on his own experiences and his view of the world. Other books like *The Children of Africa*, published by Drum and Spear Press, help answer the question 'Who am I?' And still others inform and inspire a child with the feats and facts of heroes long gone. Reading Jean Carey Bond's *A Is for Africa*, for example, is a beautiful way for the very young to learn Black history. All these books have one thing in common. They don't hurt a Black child's image of himself; instead they help clarify and strengthen it.

The circle of Black writers is widening too. Like Myers, many authors whose earlier works were written for adults are beginning now to deal with youngsters. One of these writers is the poet Sonia Sanchez, author of the books *Homecoming* and *We A Badd DDD People*. The mother of dynamic four-year-old twin boys, she is acutely aware of the needs of young people.

'Our children need positive images, and they need them now,' says Mrs Sanchez. 'Lately I've visited a lot of schools for poetry readings. The students I see have a concept of what they can be and what they don't want to be. That's why my first children's book is called *It's a New Day*. I want to give the young brothers and sisters something to think about in times of crisis, in times of stress. In my book it says:

> we can be anything we want
> for we are the young ones
> walken without footprints
> woven our bodies in tune
> to songs ...'

Sonia Sanchez' poems reflect not only that philosophy but also the use of Black English, or Blacktalk, which many Black writers are using increasingly in various ways. As she uses it, words are spelt as they are said and heard by many Blacks. For instance, in 'We're not learnen to be paper boys' she says:

Sonia Sanchez
It's a New Day
Broadside Press
1971

> we're not learnen to be paper boys
> with a one/block route.
> America is full of paper boys
> collecten dimes and quarters for
> a five/dollar a week/American
>   Dream.
> we're sellen truth
> and our route is the mind of blk
>   people ...

'Black writers today be about change,' Mrs Sanchez commented recently. 'We are not white people in blackface. Our children must have different images to grow on. I'm not opposed to their reading books about the whole world. But they need more than just the white world. I don't think you should keep things from kids. Instead you should deal with them.'

The popular books of Sharon Bell Mathis show much the same feeling. Mrs Mathis, who has three children, told me when I visited her in Washington, 'The Black child is usually portrayed as lacking street wit in books written by whites. I teach – and I see textbooks that have painted a few faces brown. But they still haven't added any facts about Blacks. Parents, teachers, and librarians primarily are responsible for the books children read. And it's their duty to inspect these books more carefully and not buy or order them just because the faces are Black.'

Mrs Mathis' latest book, *Sidewalk Story*, is a good example of the street wit that allows many Black children to master inner-city life. Ten-year-old Lilly Etta is told that her best friend, Tanya Brown, is leaving the neighbourhood. She assumes that the Browns are moving away because they want to – until her mother gently explains that they are being evicted because their money has been depleted by doctor's bills and they are unable to pay their rent. Lilly Etta then tells a few white lies, spends her last 20 cents and helps them find a new home.

Sharon Bell Mathis
Sidewalk Story
Viking Press, 1971

'She was going to Tanya's. And she would make those phone calls. Tanya is my friend, she thought, and I have to go. It was worth a spanking, even worth not getting earrings, to help a best friend. She yanked her brother down the steps.

' "Me falling, Lilly."

' "If you want to go with me you have to walk fast. I got no time for babies today." '

Although Lilly Etta's father does not appear in the story, Sharon Mathis very adequately depicts the strength and love in a home with a single parent. The language, like that in Sonia Sanchez' poems, is simple and easy to read.

The author Lorenz Graham is a rarity. He has been writing children's books with Black themes since 1946. Born in New Orleans and now living in Claremont, California, he became interested in writing in Liberia, where he had gone to teach at Monrovia College. Soon after his arrival in Africa he realized that even he, a Black man, had been affected by the stereotypes created not by facts but by the established literature – an image of Africans as 'stupid, lazy savages'.

Graham chose fiction writing as the medium through which he would seek to change those false impressions. *How God Fix Jonah*, his first collection of Bible stories written with an African slant and cadence, is now available in three small books, *Every Man Heart Lay Down*, *God Wash the World and Start Again* and *A Road Down in the Sea*.

'You have to remember,' he said as we sat in his sun-washed study, 'that

Blacks weren't in vogue in those early days.' He described to me his early two-year struggle with a publisher who wanted to water down his work. Graham, in spite of the fact that 'I was an unknown writer and a little scared,' remained firm – and continues to do so. His latest work, published by Thomas Y. Crowell Company, New York, is a dramatic trilogy. *South Town* describes the life of the Williams family in a Southern community and *North Town* tells of the changes in their life when they move North. In *Whose Town*, the third volume, teen-aged David Williams sees his school career put on the line as he defends himself against a bigot's lie.

Graham obviously doesn't believe in disguising the truth. He believes that Black children need honest preparation so that society's negative attitudes will not so dissipate their energies that they can't build on their own strengths.

This philosophy guides many new Black publishing houses as well. Broadside Press published Sanchez' *It's a New Day*, and Don Lee's Third World Press, in Chicago, has come out with its first children's book, *Jackie*, the story of a tomboy who just doesn't want to act like a girl. Joseph Okpaku's Third Press, in New York, has published *Third World Voices for Children*. Drum and Spear Press, in Washington, D.C., has published *The Children of Africa* and *Children of Ancient Egypt* – colouring books that also contain historical facts. Most of the books published by Black houses are priced under $2.

While most Black writers agree on the kinds of things their books should say, they differ quite often on how to say them. Should those books be written in Black English, or Blacktalk, the way many Blacks speak, or should 'standard' English be the guide?

Blacktalk takes basically three forms. In one of these forms the basic sentence structure is changed by omitting prepositions or conjunctions and verb forms that are used in written and spoken standard English but that wouldn't ordinarily be used in Black speech.

June Jordan, Harlem-born poet, author of the beautiful book for children called *Who Look at Me*, writes in her latest junior novel, *His Own Where*:

June Jordan
His Own Where
Thomas Y. Crowell
1970

'First time they come, he simply say, "Come on." He tell her they are going not too far away. She go along not worrying about the heel-strap pinching at her skin, but worrying about the conversation. Long walks take some talking. Otherwise it be embarrassing just side by side embarrassing …'

Sonia Sanchez, on the other hand, prefers a second Blacktalk style, altering the spelling of some words to sound more like Black speech sounds. In *It's a New Day* she writes:

dope pushers dope pushers
   git outa our parks
   we come to slide on slides
   climb the monkey bars
don't need yo/dope
   to make us git high
   the swings will take us
   way up in the sky ...

Walter Myers utilizes the third variation in *The Dragon Takes a Wife*. He intersperses Black expressions throughout the dialogue. For example:
   ' "Perhaps if you made my flame twice as hot as it is now," answered Harry. "I could win."
   ' "That ain't no big thing," said Mabel Mae. "Dig on these magic words I'm going to say ..." '
Lorenz Graham, on the other hand, uses none of these forms, but sticks to what is usually known as standard, grammatical English.

   There are arguments both for and against Blacktalk. Some of its opponents feel that Blacktalk is reminiscent of the ridiculous 'dialect' stories that whites wrote in the 'darky' days. They reinforce their arguments by saying that standard English is the tool children need to make it in school.

   On the other hand, Mrs Augusta Baker, co-ordinator of children's services for the New York Public Library, feels that there is nothing inherently wrong with Blacktalk but thinks 'it should be limited to fiction,' and that the standardized form of English should be used in instructional books 'to avoid confusion.'

   I agree, and would add that particularly with young children confusion may occur when they encounter different spellings of the same word in different books. Blacktalk is probably more successful with older readers, with whom it could well mean the difference between an uninterested and therefore slower learner and a more interested and better student.

   But the issue is really a cultural one. The Black storybooks that the average child reads are far outnumbered by his other schoolbooks, so we really can't say that they pose a serious threat to his ability to read and write.

   These new directions in children's books represent a healthy improvement and a good beginning. Black children should not be cheated and confused by having to read exclusively about a life-style that is not their own. Why should it take them years and years to discover and validate their own experience through books? As children they should have access to books whose characters become literary friends with whom they can share hopes and dreams, projects and plans.

The parents, teachers, and librarians still have a major responsibility to make these books available – and to guarantee that Little Black Sambo never lives again.

Reprinted from *Redbook Magazine,* August 1972. Copyright © 1972 by The Redbook Publishing Company.

The parent's observations: knowing all the frames of reference

The only person who can provide us with a complete account of a young child's behaviour is his watchful mother. What is generally missing from conventional research is the 'longitudinal' observation of the growing infant, in particular 'the backward and forward flow between books and life'. Dorothy White, a New Zealand librarian with a knowledge of child development as well as of literature, kept a diary of her daughter's growth which formed the basis of a fascinating study of children's interaction with stories called 'Books before five'. This is a sample extract and offers another way forward in examining the subject, though of course there cannot be any suggestion that Carol should be a model for all children.

Diary for 6 April 1948   Dorothy White

Yesterday it began to rain, which it has not done to Carol's knowledge for some three weeks. She looked out of the window and then began to talk about the *Pitter Patter* book, asking me to get the umbrella and put it up 'like the little boy'. In all the conversation which followed I could see the interweaving of three experiences, today's rain, the book, and an incident a month ago when we were caught in a sudden heavy shower of rain on our way back from Roslyn. She had been badly frightened by raindrops on her bare head and I had calmed her by a reference to *Pitter Patter*.

A Child's Good-night Book continues in favour. I was amused with Carol's comment 'sleepy carrot' as she pointed at a prone vegetable by a somnolent rabbit. The fish in this story are enjoying a boom as the aquarium fish at the museum, the breakfast fish, and these 'fish in the darkened sea' crowd to one point in her imagination. Last night for the first time she noticed the yellow bath mat and pointed gleefully 'fishy, fishy'.

The experience makes the book richer and the book enriches the personal experience even at this level. I am astonished at the early age this backward and forward flow between books and life takes place. With adults or older children one cannot observe it so easily, but here at this age when all a child's experiences are known and the books read are shared, when the voluble gabble which is her speech reveals all the associations, the interaction is seen very clearly. Now and again Carol mystifies me with a reference to life next door, or with some transposed pronunciation which defeats me, but on the whole I know her frame of reference.

The era of imaginative play has begun. This morning her doll was taken in the push-cart to the 'mus'um'. During the past week I have read Lois Lenski's *Let's Play House* to her ten or twelve times, giving a repeat performance at each sitting on the demand 'Do it again'. This is a story about three children, two dominant girls and a minor male character, who play at family life in sickness and in health. Molly and Polly feed and wash and clothe their dolls and animals, entertain guests, buy their groceries and tend the ailing.

It was noticeable a while ago that picture-books with only one thing on a page had lost their appeal for Carol. This book with its more packed style of illustration follows on well. Much of the gear that Molly and Polly use in their play (dolls feeding bottles, flour-sieves, and peg-baskets) is spread out in array as a casual border round the main subject of each picture. This, I seem to remember, is a feature of the art of some primitive people. The appeal of these borders to Ann and Carol is that they enjoy pointing out all the things not mentioned in the brief text. They label the dolls' garments with the same pleasure of an unsophisticated playgoer identifying a villain. Yet I have to admit that at first sight I thought this book was mediocre with its quite ordinary black and white pictures which do not have the aesthetic appeal of the Charlot illustrations or a book by the Petershams – I was judging it by purely adult standards.

From *Books before five*, New Zealand Council for Educational Research, 1956

Ways forward for the librarian

The traditional role of the librarian as 'the keeper of the printed word' has almost died its death. Certainly for those librarians concerned with children and young people passive industry is no longer enough. Positive involvement with other professionals and understanding of the process of reading is now beginning to be recognized as essential. Griselda Barton describes this new role.

Contexts for reading experience   Griselda Barton

The more books there are published specifically for children, the less children seem to want to read them. This paradox, investigated recently in a Schools Council Project, is a cause of major concern to many adults, not least to librarians. Over the past two decades books in children's and school libraries have improved dramatically in quality as well as in quantity. Qualities of writing, illustration, and book production are scrutinized annually and prizes are awarded for excellence. The work of people dedicated to the promotion of that excellence is also recognized by accolade; institutions and bodies exist to promote the ideal that only the best is good enough for the children. Nevertheless research continues to show that there is no appreciable narrowing of the gap between what the group of concerned adults see as desirable and what the children choose and enjoy.

Frank Whitehead
et al.
*Children's reading
interests*
Evans/Methuen
1975

There would seem to be a crucial mismatch between the adult's expectation of the impact of books upon the child and the child's actual response. One example has already been given in this area by Elaine Moss (*The Peppermint Lesson*); another anecdote that altered my focus is recounted by Nicholas Tucker:

'Like many parents I have been amused by the way my mixed infants, once in the library, have so often gone straight for those books they already possess at home. Usually I have dissuaded them, not without protest, but once when I was not looking a book was taken out which was already an established favourite on our own book-shelves. Once at home, far from any mistake being recognized, both copies were immediately compared with great interest, page by page, and then taken up to bed together, so that the characters from one page could talk to their identical counterparts in the other book. In terms of interest, therefore, this particular choice was a great success.'

Nicholas Tucker
Infant's Choice
Times Educational
Supplement
5 March 1971

Tucker goes on to describe yet another pleasure, that of having all the stories in a series (Edward Ardizzone's *Little Tim* books) open on the floor at the same time, so that the main characters could be seen in many different situations all at once.

So what at first appeared to be a meaningless choice to the adult, turned out to be important and full of meaning to the children. It makes me wonder how often we may thwart important early approaches such as these by focusing too narrowly on the intrinsic nature of the book (i.e. story or picture), thus ignoring significant extrinsic features. Nicholas Tucker's children were fortunate in that the value of their activities with their books was recognized and allowed. Too often by having too narrow a focus we ignore the very conditions that are essential for the desired interaction of books and child. The nature of this experience is elucidated by Margaret Meek:

> 'Reading is both public and private. It is public in that literacy in advanced countries is taken for granted in the organization of society, so that children are taught to read because it is useful for them to get information. It is private in that the reader makes a bond with the author in a special way which contributes to his affective growth and to the way he feels about himself. It is useful to get information: it is crucial to grow as a person ... Reading of this kind needs peace and time ...'

*British books for
school libraries*
Catalogue of an
exhibition
British Council
1974

Children and young people now spend a considerable part of their waking lives for at least eleven crucial years at school. The concern that during that time they should become not merely literate, but be enabled to enter the reading experience in the fullest sense is carried further by Ronald Morris:

> 'It is a characteristic virtue of reading on one's own that it enables the reader to make fullest use of his own association of ideas and to relate his reading as intimately as possible to his own experience of life ... But this kind of activity is a private affair, something between the book and the reader which demands quiet and privacy ... The peculiarity of the present situation, with its abundance of distractions, chaos of information, and lengthening of school life, is that more young people could profit from reading more to themselves than ever before ...

'Less time, surely, is needed for the accurate reading of merely "interesting" material and more and more time must be made available for browsing among books of quality and for the sustained quiet reading of them by those who have been made ready in school for this experience.'

Ronald Morris
Success and failure in learning to read
second edition
Penguin Books,
1973

But if reading of this nature is to be a truly private affair, then the individual needs to be able to choose when and where he wants to read. This point is clearly seen in evidence collected by Fred Inglis from questionnaires sent to fourth year pupils in seven secondary schools. In his analysis of the replies to the question 'What conditions do you most like reading in?' he concludes: 'Children would rather read in conditions of their own choosing, away from school and for long periods at a time.' (Unfortunately he makes no further comment, but continues in the pursuit of excellence without another thought about the position of the water trough and the problem of unbiddable horses!)

Fred Inglis
The Englishness of English teaching
Longman, 1969

Certainly many secondary schools are far from realizing how important it is to try to provide favourable conditions. Heads and teachers in despair about standards of reading will nevertheless cheerfully use the library as a detention centre, as a dumping ground for delinquents, the irreligious, and the non-swimmers, and as an examination room, to mention but a few mis-uses. In many ways, also, some planning of school libraries can only be called Intimidation by Furniture: serried ranks of book-shelves, and tables 'that are the enemies of knees' can all add up to a daunting and alien environment.

Edward Blishen
The school that I'd like
Penguin Books,
1969

Even in primary schools, where quiet areas, book corners, and library bays have been provided with carpet, armchairs, and cushions, children often say that they cannot settle down for a good read as there is so much activity going on around them.

This point has been made by Aidan Chambers when talking about reading at home:

'Even if books are available in the home ... the architecture of modern houses, open planned, and difficult to close off into quiet, comfortably personal areas, makes it even more difficult to engage in the activity of reading. It is not true that children need absolute silence in which to read ... but it is nevertheless true that in houses where reading must be done in the middle of a lot of family *movement*, concentration is difficult and distraction at its maximum.'

Aidan Chambers
The reluctant reader
Pergamon, 1969

Home attitudes as well inevitably affect the options of time and place open to the child to pursue his pleasure in private reading. In a small random survey of children in an inner city comprehensive school and one of its tributary primary schools, I asked the children not what they read but where they enjoyed reading. Here are four of their replies which reveal some of the constraints on their desire to read.

In the first, reading is still a favoured activity and positive encouragement seems to be the attitude:

'I like a nice book sitting on the floor. The television must be off and it must be quiet and a book I can read. I read it in my mind and on my own, no one sitting next to me with another book reading it, specially not the same book.' (*boy*, 10)

In the next, home conditions impinge but do not strongly inhibit Brenda:

My favourite place for reading
My book is on my bed
Where it's quiet and my sister
Don't jump about and shout
Or sometimes I read a bit
When the advertisement comes on. (*Brenda*, 11)

In the third, an all too familiar situation appears. Reading is no longer the favoured activity it was when the skill was new:

'My favourite place for reading is by the fire in the armchair. I am interested in my book then all of a sudden "Debbie go round to the shop". In my mind saying to myself "Oh no, not again". I've lost my interest again. Never get half an hour to read my book. So now the only time I get to read is when I'm in bed, so quiet and peaceful. No noise outside, all the children are in bed fast asleep. Then I doze off. Mum comes in and turns the light out and puts the marker in the page I'm on, then goes out. She reads in bed.' (*girl*, 12)

Finally, reading has to be carried on as a secondary activity:

'I can usually read when I'm giving milk to my youngest sister because it is quiet and also because no one is allowed in the room.' (*girl*, 14)

Pointers to the way forward

We need, then, to focus on the situation which favours reading as a satisfying activity. Elements to be considered include time, place, physical conditions, and the presence (or not) of others and their attitudes. Sociolinguists such as William Labov are paying increasing attention to the influence of such situations on language-use, and it is possible that the perspectives they provide can be applied to looking at contexts for reading when it is a private affair:

> 'It is traditional to explain a child's failure in school by his inadequacy; but when failure reaches such massive proportions, it seems to us necessary to look at the social and cultural obstacles to learning and the inability of the school to adjust to the social situation.'

William Labov 'The logic of non-standard English' in *Language and Social Context* Penguin Books, 1972

Labov has been concerned particularly with American Negro children in ghetto areas, but his observations and methods have wider implications. For example, he observes the behaviour of a Negro boy, first in the situation of a formal interview: large, friendly, white interviewer sitting behind a table; boy standing on the opposite side of the table.

> '(The child) showed defensive monosyllabic behaviour … He has learned a number of devices to avoid saying anything in this situation, and he works very hard to achieve this end … if anyone takes this interview as a measure of the verbal capacity of this child, it must be his capacity to defend himself in a hostile and threatening situation.'

Labov, op. cit.

Labov then describes the dramatic change in this child's performance when the situation is completely altered: coloured interviewer, who not only brings along the boy's best friend and a packet of potato chips, but also sits on the floor with them and encourages them to talk about anything (even taboo subjects such as sex and violence) without fear of retaliation.

Daniel Fader was working towards a similar situation in his literacy programme in penal institutions for mainly Negro boys. His policy of paperback 'saturation', and his programme *English in every classroom* has had considerable effect on the ways in which reading matter is presented in this country and in many others.

Daniel Fader and Elton B. McNeil *Hooked on books* Pergamon, 1969

However it is Elton B. McNeil, in his validation of Fader's programme, who focuses more directly on situations in which reading takes place, especially in his description of the programme in operation in a summer camp for emotionally disturbed and delinquent boys:

> '… reading is a highly idiosyncratic and personal event and … its motivation is not a mass phenomenon. Some times of day and social settings are more conducive to the act of reading than others …
>
> 'Reading appears to be an age related phenomenon whose joys are learned by practice and whose pleasures increase with greater skill. Even

these primitive children violate our expectations when the proper setting and supplies are provided for them. They don't read much from the point of view of the literate middle class child; they read an astounding amount compared with our usual stereotype of their literary interests.'

Fader and McNeil
op. cit.

All this evidence suggests that situation is a major influence in reading for pleasure. The implications for the traditionally static view of librarians and libraries scarcely needs underlining. Indeed there are enterprises in the library field now developing, aiming to break through the rigid structure of decades. One of the more striking of these in an inner city borough has been vividly described by Janet Hill, herself being at the heart of the enterprise; Believing that books should be where people are, she says:

'If we believe that librarians should be more dynamic, and should move out of libraries into the communities they serve, how can this be done? There is no one answer, and no easy answer. However, I don't see how it can happen without radically altering the way so many library services operate. It certainly cannot be done unless the *entire* library service is geared to it. It is no good for a children's librarian to decide to go it alone, and work out in the community with *children*. If there is to be real involvement, then adults cannot be left out. Children do not live in isolation. The majority live with their parents, attend clinics, schools, playgroups, youth clubs, and community centres run *by adults*. Nothing that relates to children can be tackled in isolation.'

Janet Hill
Children are people
Hamish Hamilton
1973

The way forward can never be in working in isolation. We have our particular professional skills and insights, but they are valuable only in the contribution we make in collaboration with others who are concerned with the needs of children and young people. If we truly want to promote excellence, then we need to use the insights of fellow professionals to open our minds to the dilemmas and opportunities facing the child in his search for the private world of reading for pleasure.

Telling stories: what the young writer does

The Schools Council Writing Research Project, of which Tony Burgess was
a Research Officer, undertook an investigation of the writing done by
children in school. In the course of their work the members of the Unit
proposed a classification of kinds of writing to cover the differentiated
activities which they discovered. They then set writing tasks to collect
material which would illustrate the development of the children's
awareness of the different functions of writing. This article is concerned
with first person narration: the writer writes his own story. It forms part
of 'The Development of Writing Abilities', Britton et al. q.v. Bibliography.

Story and teller   Tony Burgess

What happens when we tell a story and why do we do it? Most of us, perhaps,
tell stories of some kind daily – out of our own need, or for our own and for other
people's pleasure. Sometimes these stories are about ourselves (at their simplest
about what we have been doing), sometimes about others (for the interest of our
audience in a mutual acquaintance). What the listener is generally interested in is
how the world appears to another person. When the story illuminates that, we
are close to fiction.

But there is a dimension to our telling other than that of fiction or autobiography. For the most part we take no more trouble with our stories than the
situation demands, but from time to time something peculiarly interesting or
extravagant has happened, which requires more than usual attention to the
telling. Then we require an expanded setting. The time must be right for a
lengthier utterance; and when it is, we expect to set up substantial reverberations
in our audience in response to what we have to say. At such times utterance comes
close to *performance*; we have to hold the stage and tell the story well.

This dimension, which holds in speech, holds also in writing. Here, perhaps
because of the more extended utterance permitted by writing, we expect more

of the performer to predominate. On the other hand, it need not do so. We may in a letter, for example, take no more trouble in the telling of an incident than we would do, for normal purposes, in speech. But if we write a short *story* we are much more concerned to tell it well. The form of telling is at least as important as what we tell. Moreover, the solitary and extended context in which the writing is done invites *conscious* attention.

Behind this more ambitious kind of storytelling must lie a process of working on the raw material of experience as it presents itself to our consciousness. This paper will be concerned with that process. Teachers of English and other subjects (e.g. history) expect stories from their pupils. What kinds of achievements are they expecting? What processes lie behind them? What patterns of development are there in what our pupils do?

Two samples of narrative

In 1969–70 the Writing Research Unit set two tasks of storytelling to a junior and a senior class in five schools. The schools included two mixed comprehensives, one mixed grammar and two single-sex direct grant schools (one boys', one girls'), and the classes in them have formed our follow-up sample in a five-year project on writing from ages eleven to eighteen which we have been undertaking. We began our work with these classes in 1967 with one first-year class and one fourth-year class in each school, and have followed their work through, asking for one sample of each child's writing each term over a period of four years. These two samples, then, constitute only a small part of our work with the classes. To obtain them we asked the classes to write a first-person narrative on two occasions, with a year's interval between. It seemed to us that there was more chance of perceiving the children's development if we restricted the person of the narrator in this way. To set them going the pupils were each given a sheet of extracts from poems which they could use as freely as they liked to find a starting-point for their own story. We prepared different sets of extracts for the junior and for the senior classes, and fresh sets for both groups for the second narrative a year later.

Let me say a little now about what we expected. At the centre of our thinking was the conviction that writing is not a single but a highly differentiated activity, and differentiated most importantly according to the different purposes for which language can be used. Consequently, one of our main jobs had been to work out a scheme classifying the functions of extended discourse, and we had in mind as a

Acknowledgements are due to my colleagues in the Schools Council Writing Research Project: Professor James Britton Miss Nancy Martin Dr Harold Rosen Messrs Dennis Griffiths, Alex McLeod and Bernard Newsome. This project has now been extended by the Schools Council for a further three-year development phase to explore with schools the implications of its findings central hypothesis that we should be able to see, in what our classes wrote, a developing awareness of these functions. In these samples, then, we expected to see the movement from ordinary telling to conscious attention to it as an aspect of this overall development.

This, then, lay behind the tasks we set. The writing was done in the schools in the second term of the second and third years for the junior classes and in the second term of the fifth and sixth years for the seniors. It was supervised by the teachers in each school who had been working with us during the project. The time was standardized at forty-five minutes for each piece of writing. We received altogether some five hundred scripts achieved at four developmental points in the second, third, fifth and sixth years.

James Britton
'What's the use'
Educational Review
volume 23, 1971
University of
Birmingham
'The Context of
Language'

The narrative construct

The first point to make about the narratives concerns what was common to all of them. All, with an insignificant number of exceptions, aimed at representing 'a bit of life', as if it were actually going on. We may borrow an idea from Susanne Langer, who talks of art as aiming to present an 'illusion' of 'virtual experience'. Without pitching the account too high this was what was at work in these scripts. The pupils had to draw on their own primary and secondary experience (including fantasy) and organize it through words into what – for want of a more elegant term – we may call a construct. That construct tried to catch in its way something of the 'feel' of life.

Susanne Langer
Feeling and Form
Routledge and
Kegan Paul, 1953

The life that it caught, of course, might be something that actually happened or something that the writer invented; but the notion of a construct can be used to unify these arguably separable concerns. From the point of view of the writer what was happening was that experience was being shaped into artefact, aiming to represent either actual or possible experience.

Here, for example, is a piece of fantasy which catches the feeling of that organizing:

> 'Foxes in red jackets and yellow Rupert trousers flew across the fields singing rugby songs. I gave chase. Over field after field, from "In Mother Kelly's whoreshop" to "Down in the valley". I followed until they stopped by a door in an old oak tree.
>
> 'The masses of "Bootlegger's Daily" read on.' (*fifth-year boy*)

The narrative process

The narratives, then, had in common that they aimed for a 'construct'. To understand the different levels at which that aim was achieved I believe it is helpful to consider the narrative process in three ways, recognizing that what can be separated, for analysis, the writer must cope with in the course of a single activity.

Common to all forms of narrative is the *improvisation and sequencing of events*. It seems worth remarking that at this level narrative is not merely a public form, either written or spoken, but in touch with basic processes of the mind. We have the example of dream narrative as an indication of the form taken by the march of symbolism through our minds when we cease to control it. In written narrative the events which are improvised (or remembered) have also to be shaped in terms of some sense of the overall direction which the narrative is to take. Thus there is likely to be a tension in the writing process between the forward scanning of the shape and the improvisation of the events which are to comprise it. It seems likely, too, that competence in this will develop.

It is not merely planning which is at issue. It seems unlikely, particularly when writing is done at speed, that all the events in a narrative will be scanned and organized in advance. The sense of the overall design may be something which accumulates during the very act of writing. But it also involves more than sequencing, for the sequencing is an aspect of the evaluation which the writer puts on events as he organizes them into shape.

For many of the first-year children in our sample, clearly the process involved embarking on a voyage of discovery with little idea of their destination and minimal attention to the emerging shape of the narrative. At times the issue posed by this is merely that of *consistency*. Events arrive in the mind and arrange themselves in no consciously articulated sequence, as in the following example:

Man hunt

'I had just seen a man being chased by some horrible creatures and they were making horrible sounds he is jumping over rocks and running through trees. He must have escaped from the prison. We are on the moon and you can jump boulders about ten feet high with one leap because of the gravity. The men who are chasing the man are called gaurders which means they gaurd all the prisiners and the have horrible creatures which they set on to you they are big with claws and full of hairs. They can run quite fast but not as fast as us they are catching the man up they have got him I escaped

with him but I went the opposite way my only chance was to get to the
rocket …' (*second-year boy*)

Nevertheless, the consistency with which events are sequenced is only one of the
points that we can make about this. We can go further and discuss the *quality* with
which events are shaped in terms of the implicit or explicit evaluation of the
writer.

There is a second way of looking at narrative, which is also at issue in this
example – the maintenance and development of the narrator as a character in the
story – as a person in his world. From the writer's point of view the introduction
of the narrator into the story represents a formal element in the whole design.
His presence is an act of choice, for events could be described in other ways
without him. We, of course, in setting the task had restricted that choice, for we
had asked for a first-person narrative. By this means, in brief, a two-way focus
is set up for the writer. Events have still to be improvised and controlled, but the
narrator also has to be maintained and developed as a person in his world. A
more complex control, therefore, has to be exercised if the narrator as a person
is not to sink beneath the tide of events as a merely anonymous agent. The failure
to control this dimension is also at issue in the example above.

It is, though, a third element which I believe is most important for us. We
can compound the attention to events, and the attention to the narrator in a third
notion, and see as the central component of fully formed narrative *the way in
which the narrator is integrated with the events described*. Part of the writer's attention
will remain with the shaping of events and part with the development and
maintenance of the narrator, but it is in the way that these two are integrated
that he has the most complex possibilities for developing a shape which will
embody his own evaluation of experience. In the piece above, for example, there
is no further integration than that these events happen to this person, and the
sense of the person is largely lost; but other narratives suggested quite different
levels at which narrator and event might be integrated.

For the time being, however, let me polarize the issues and contrast two
ways of telling a story. Here is an account of a visit to a football match:

'We leave my house at 1 o'clock. Me P. Gillingwater and C. Belcher. We go
on a bus to Coldblow lane end, we go in to the ground it costs three bob.
Which I think is too dear to pay three bob to go in for a second division team.
We wait for the millwall crowd to come then we all form and stick together.
Then Kevin Kempster starts to sing mill-wall la la la. Then they stop, the
lions come out on the pitch, hooray.' (*fourth-year boy*)

In this example it is events which matter, as they happen and not as they are shaped. The 'I' is not truly a narrator in a story: he remains the boy himself; and since he is not presented as a character in the story, he could well disappear entirely as the excitement of the football game takes over. The attention to shaping is minimal, yet it is a lively and engaging piece of writing. It is so with much speech. Conversely the movement to a more formed narrative would involve the deepening of the presentation of that 'I'. Round him the writer would build a world, and he would maintain him as a reflecting and acting consciousness. The disparate happenings of this account would be simplified and shaped into a coherent pattern, and the motives and responses of the presented 'I' would be integrated with the events in an overall design. We may compare the last example with a piece of writing by a boy of the same age, and predict the manner in which each will continue:

> 'Saturday night, wandering around the lonely pavements as the park keeper closes shop for another day: two spiked green gates harpooning the night as it closes in.
>
> 'Saturday night: no shops, lousy film at the flicks, no girl, no clubs, no dance, just got my soul and the fair to the nearest party.
>
> 'Thinking why. Why did my girl have to go on holiday this week? Why did the club have to close? Why ... Why?' (*fourth-year boy*)

Clearly the second piece involves a much more conscious attention to the way of telling, and that attention yields also a more complex evaluation of experience. However, it may not simply be greater ability which underlies this difference. For the first piece may be as much shaped as it needs to be for the purposes which the writer envisages. This thought will take us away from these scripts for the moment into more general considerations.

The function of extended discourse

Let me make explicit the theory which underlies the analysis so far and enables us to link that analysis to a more general notion of development in language.

I said earlier that at the centre of our thinking has been the conviction that a writer as he undertakes a task engages not in a single global activity but one which is highly differentiated according to the purposes for which language is to be used. This has led us to try to schematize these purposes in an account of the functions of extended discourse. By function we mean something more than the writer's purposes; for we see it as something constituted in the language, which the writer selects and which, when it has been selected, connects both writer and reader in mutual agreement on the conventions and presuppositions of this particular type of discourse.

James Britton in a recent article has written a full account of this scheme. In brief, this account distinguishes three major functions of language:

James Britton
op. cit., 1971

1. *transactional* (language to inform and persuade);
2. *expressive* (language close to the self);
3. *poetic* (language which is used to shape an artistic construct).

We see the *expressive* function of language both as one capable of development in its own right and also as in an important sense the matrix of other functions of language. By expressive we pick out not merely the presence of feeling, though this may well be a component, but rather the kind of language which is close to the speaker or writer and which looks for a close and sympathetic audience. Expressive speech, for example, is typically conversation between intimates; the speaker depends on a listener who is interested in him and who will sympathize with him because of this. The speaker's utterance, therefore, is characteristically loosely structured and informal, and much of his meaning is left implicit. When the speaker becomes a writer (of a letter, for instance, or a piece of writing directed to someone with whom there is a closely shared context), he incorporates these presuppositions into his writing.

It is clear from reading expressive writing undertaken at all ages that this is a function which is capable of development in its own right, enriched by the accumulating resources in a pupil's language. We also attach considerable importance to it in education as a flexible function of language, which may operate in a first draft of important ideas. But we see it also as the matrix of the other functions of language, in that these other functions may be seen as differentiating themselves from the expressive. On the one hand, the *transactional* function of language is differentiated from the expressive for its purpose of getting things done in the world: it serves to inform and persuade, and commensurate with these purposes requires a higher degree of linguistic organization and sequencing of ideas. On the other hand, the *poetic* function is differentiated for its purpose of creating a construct in words – this function, too, therefore, requiring a higher degree of organization, though of a different kind from the transactional.

The expressive, then, constitutes in our scheme the middle of a triad of major functions, which can be represented by the following scale:
(1) Transactional (2) Expressive (3) Poetic. We consider that the writer will move

on from the expressive function either to the transactional or to the poetic under the demands of his task; also that the capacity to move on in this way may be a developmental matter. (In addition we may subdivide the transactional into informative and conative etc., but this is less important here than the notion of the dynamic relation which exists between the three main functions.)

The poetic and the transactional functions of language constitute two ends of a scale. Fully to distinguish the two we need recourse to two further ideas. The first relates to the difference in *the process by which the reader contextualizes a piece of writing* in either function. In the transactional it would seem that the process of contextualization is piecemeal: the reader takes what he needs for his purposes and jettisons what he does not need. In the poetic, the process of contextualization is *global*: the reader must perceive and contextualize the work as a whole, the whole being more than the sum of its parts. It is partly with this in mind that we speak of a poetic construct.

The second idea is more general and is part of the over-all theory which lies behind this scheme. It is that as users of language *we can orient ourselves in either of two exclusive directions* – either in the role of participant in the world's affairs or in the role of a spectator. When we use language in the role of *participant*, we record and report, theorize and classify about the world as it is. When we use language in the role of *spectator*, we shape and adjust our picture of the world, improvising upon actual or possible experience. As the issue of the one activity lie the transactional uses of language and the writings of the scientist and the philosopher; as the issue of the other lies the poetic construct and the achievements of the artist in words. It is this notion, presented here in a highly condensed form, which enables us to see the transactional and poetic functions of language as at either end of a scale.

To summarize, then, we may present our three major functions of language in the following relation to the participant–spectator dimension:

Participant .. .. .. | .. .. .. *Spectator*
Transactional   Expressive   Poetic

The writer taking up a participant role will move towards transactional language and accordingly move from the language appropriate to the expressive function. Similarly, the writer taking up a spectator's role will move towards poetic language.

It is function, then, which is the real issue behind the attention to the telling contrasted in the examples of the football match and the meditation on Saturday night. The first boy has been concerned with an expressive account; his language has remained informal; he has presupposed a reader close to his own concerns. The other boy has been concerned to deepen his narrative towards the poetic: he has worked towards a construct in which the various elements of narrative are developed and integrated.

Implications of this account of function

Before proceeding to analyse the samples it may be helpful to take further some of the implications of this account of the functions of language: first, the relation between the expressive and the transactional. We can represent a writer's task in moving from the expressive to the transactional in terms of a more highly organized sequencing of thought and a more rigorous, but also more limited, focusing of attention on specific purposes. The flexibility of the expressive, its tendency to veer between various levels of informational function, its freedom to generate speculations without the constraints of organizing them into a clearly articulated sequence, and its link finally with what is personal in the writer – all these make the expressive properly the language of thought and hence of the first draft. Transactional language is the language of formal presentation.

There are educational implications in this. We talk of the language of a subject, but there is a division to be made between the concepts which it employs and the functions of the language of which it makes use. It seems to us likely that expressive language will be of particular value in schools, for the role which language plays in learning is at least as important as the finished presentation of it. Also, if our account is correct, it is likely that it is out of the expressive uses of language that the pupil comes to discriminate the transactional functions.

Let me make clear two points about the poetic function. In our account a writer may move from the expressive function towards the poetic as readily as he may move towards the transactional; but, as I have said, we see the poetic construct as lying at the opposite end of a scale from the transactional. This is not to say that a writer using the poetic function may not wish to inform or persuade his audience. We do, however, make a distinction between the writer who mediates these purposes through a poetic construct and a writer who does not, since in practice we distinguish between propaganda and art. The second point is that a writer will move on to the poetic *via* the resources of form which he has available. Thus our allocation of a piece of writing is made more difficult by the different artistic genres used, and also by the fact that what we count as poetic for a particular writer will be moderated by what we expect of him. We are likely in practice to vary our criteria according to the level at which the analysis is being conducted.

The central implication of our account, however, is to see development as a progressive differentiation in the functions of the written language which the pupil has at his command. Let me formalize this as two hypotheses:

1.   development will involve an increasing awareness of differentiation in function;
2.   this awareness will be coupled with an increasing sophistication in the use of each function.

With this we may return from the theory to our actual samples.

A pattern of development

The principal pattern in the narratives we had before us was a growing awareness of the poetic function, which confirmed, in part at any rate, the first of our hypotheses. However, the polarity between the juniors and the seniors was more marked than the development between the first sample and the second for either group. About half the junior scripts were judged to have moved on from the expressive function sufficiently to count as poetic, whereas the proportion in the seniors was more than two thirds. But there was no significant change in either group between the two samples. This picture is not presented here, however, as a formal finding; rather as a contribution to our thinking.

What lay beneath the difference between the juniors and the seniors was a development in the way in which the narrator was integrated with the events. Many of the juniors and some of the seniors failed to move on from the expressive because they could not maintain the narrator as a person in the story or control the improvisation of events into a pattern. Though aiming at a construct, the voice remained the expressive voice of the writer. Here is a very obvious example:

'One day my boss said to me how would you like to tack a trip to the moon and I said her shore, but first you have to do a lot of training and when my boss says a lot of training he meen it. When all the training was over a was ready to go. A doctor said to me you will have to have a couple of ingection before you go to any trip after I had my ingection I met my patner I did not now that I had a patner but I got use to it.' (*second-year boy*)

This, then, was at one end of the scale. It seems worth remarking, too, that not only the quality of shaping here was at issue, but also the process of fictionalization itself. For at this level of narration we can only speak fairly tenuously of fictionalizing. There is a distinction to be drawn, certainly, between the writer writing as himself and the writer taking up the role of another person. On the other hand, the role of the other person here is only a means to the experience which the writer would like to encompass. It is the events which constitute the heart of the writing, and the writer and the narrator are their servant.

Where attention to the shape of events accompanied the maintenance of the narrator in his world, however, we can glimpse the developing achievement of the poetic:

'Alan and I had decided to play around in the house until about ten to five tomorrow. The other boys looked up at us in awe, though needless to say neither the army nor our parents new about this.

'At about two o'clock the next day we went into the house and hid on the top floor. At 2.30 a squad of soldiers came in and searched the house, though you could hardly call it searching since all they did was to have a quick look in each room and shouted a lot. They then left.

'We looked out of one of the glassless windows and saw a tight cordon of soldiers surrounding the house .. ' (*second-year boy*)

The expressive voice may still be strong, but at this point the poetic function is achieved. We can point, henceforward, to a gathering complexity in the integration of narrator and event. At the risk of forcing a distinction it seems that there is a point in the development of narrative, no doubt in the pupil's world as well, when an interest in event is replaced by an interest in the person. The job of maintaining a narrator gives way at this point to the active exploration of a person's world.

In this account of a trip to the dentist, for example, while the narrator is developed and responsive, it is still the 'feel' of events which interests the writer.

'Suddenly my thoughts rudely interrupted by a loud scream from the adjoining surgery. I must have looked as though I had seen the ghost of Hamlet as I turned to my father who was sitting next to me.

' "Oh that's nothing," he tried to reassure me, "Adults' teeth are three times as painful to extract than children's."

'I sincerely hoped that my father was right. I tried to reassure myself that all fears are unfounded.

' "Cowards die many times before their deaths. The valliant never taste of
death but once ..." ' (*third-year boy*)

However, in the following it is the world of the writer/narrator which is the central
focus and event is jettisoned entirely in favour of the symbols of that world:

'The wind in my face, spray making me damp. I feel wonderfully free with
all this natural power and beauty I feel free from school work, homework.
Each time a wave hits the wall I hear a deep thud feel the shock of impact, I
see a sheet of water rise above the green turbulent water, the swirling cross
current undercurrent and backwash of the wave as it goes out to sea again.'
(*third-year boy*)

So also in taking up the role of the other, the writer as he advances in the poetic
function may come to make the exploration of that world the centre of his
narrative. Event is now of interest as it is symptomatic of that world.

The person may be of interest because his attitudes enable moral evaluation
of areas of relatively public experience, for example, war:

'There was a thunderous crash and an array of colours smashed through the
monotonous brown and green of the woods.

'The first knight passed under me. I hesitated too late, he'd gone. I
managed to jump and unhorse the next Knight. He was at my mercy. I
pulled his helmet up, revealing a throat of human flesh, and I had to slit it.
I couldn't. Slowly I drew my arm back, dagger at the ready. I did not have
the chance to send the blade into the human flesh. A piercing blow
penetrated into my shoulder ...' (*fifth-year boy*)

Or he may embody qualities as a person which are fascinating to the writer almost
as a part of himself:

'I kicked the tennis ball hard against the wall, and watched it crawl in fear
beneath the chair. Christ! I felt sick of that peeling flat, that pock-marked
wall. Lost another tennis match, and failed another interview for a bloody
job. Bigotted old hag that benign old gentleman was. Someone more
mature in age and temperament. Huh!

'I've got to get out of this place. I'm going to drink my mutilated liver
out ...' (*fifth-year boy*)

In such scripts we may still hear the expressive voice of the writer, but transmuted
now in terms of the construct. Finally, though, there is that achieved meditation
on the otherness of another person, where the expressive origins are wholly
subsumed; and on this note we may conclude:

'Maybe today I would visit my sister, I hadn't seen her for a long time. So

I walked on, and rang the bell of her door. The door opened, and there she stood, the same as I had ever noticed.

'We sat together, drinking coffee and talking the way people do when they have nothing to talk about. Once there was a time when every break of a pattern was shared by us, and every movement of the face a secret shared. But time moved us apart, and only kept a bond by the necessity of name ...' (*fifth-year girl*)

In this example the web of narrative is completely joined.

From *Bulletin*, University of London Institute of Education, Summer 1971

Ways forward for the teacher (1): reluctant intervention

Twenty years ago, Edward Blishen wrote a semi-autobiographical account of his teaching experiences in an Islington secondary modern, entitled 'Roaring Boys'. His anecdotes about confronting children with books continue to entertain, enlighten, and often move us. He succeeded with his turbulent and capricious pupils because he invited them to engage with fiction not as a pedagogic obstacle race but in order that they should share the satisfactions of the normal unfastidious reader.

This article contains Blishen's forthright criticisms of the deadening effect of conventional literature teaching. His message, which effectively summarizes the views of the editors of this collection, is that 'in the classroom we ought never to contradict those practices that are natural to the true reader of fiction'.

Learning to love it   Edward Blishen

Walking through a train once, I was struck by the nature of the reading that was being done. Most of my fellow passengers were engrossed in paperbacks of the kind that bear on the cover two or three words of excitable promise: LUST, SAVAGERY, it might be, and perhaps (a word given a new and unlikely life in paperbacks) REALISM. And I thought that, for a great many adults, literature worth reading was perhaps defined by its being against the grain of what was commended at school.

If they read at all. And we have not begun, in the schools, to create a majority of readers. We kill the fledgling habit for so many. And we do this, I believe, by the curiously inappropriate nature of some even of the more carefully considered of our approaches to fiction in the secondary-school classroom.

At one of the Exeter conferences that have borne the thundering title, 'Contemporary Children's Fiction and Its Uses in Education', Margery Fisher said that really all a school needed to do was to provide as big and varied a collection of books as possible, together with space in which they could be read. There was much bridling and dismay among the teachers present. How on earth could that be all? The teacherly part of myself did a little back-arching, with the rest. Psst! There must be some fruitful, systematic, inspectable intervention open to the teacher!

But let us consider some types of intervention that come naturally and conscientiously to teachers even of children who come from unbookish homes, or from homes frankly hostile to books. (In Islington, where I taught for ten years, books were cheerfully blamed for a wide range of disorders – especially of the eyes, chest, and mind.) Among these interferences with the reading of fiction, tests of understanding loom large. They may be perfectly trivial and obviously inapposite, like tests of vocabulary. On the whole, we increase our command over words not by looking them up in dictionaries (though in a proper setting this can be fun), nor by any other means which involves the interruption of our engagement with a piece of fiction. Again, for most people, and certainly for most young people, fiction is not a suitable basis for formal tests of our understanding of literary devices, literary forms, characterization.

The rule, I believe, is quite simply: *We must never use fiction formally for exercises and pieces of study of this kind.* Oh, how much more liberal, more daring, how much broader we now are in the matter of fiction to be examined in the classroom. So here we are analysing Alan Sillitoe, William Golding, Barry Hines. But these feats of fundamentally anxious analysis, the writing of little essays and answering of little questions, they all, for so many young people, spell ultimately a kind of distaste, a shrinking away, for a lifetime, perhaps. Because in this way a work of fiction becomes an element in that schoolish pattern of always anxious analysis: the anxiety being that you are under test all the time. And the association with fiction of anxiety and of any kind of testing must for all but the specialists (and sometimes for them, if their specialism is imposed), be destructive of the appetite for fiction.

I saw it all at its most absurd once in a class in Canada. Eighteen-year-olds were discussing the short story. They were in fact chewing over the qualities of what the teacher described as the classic short story. It had so many characters, ideally, and dealt with (ideally), one event, or two, or one-and-a-half – I forget the arithmetic of it. Talking to the class later I discovered that most of them had never read a short story.

That is extreme. But it is an extreme that, I think, throws a light on even the best we commonly do in the classroom. Look at the way we drive young people through the study of this work of fiction or that: which may be actively disliked, or may cause complete apathy in many of the students. It may do this because that is the nature of fiction. The life of any true reader is littered with novels he picked up and could not get on with: or had to leave to some other, riper moment.

And somewhere there, I think, lies the awkward point: which is that in the classroom we ought never to contradict those practices that are natural to the true reader of fiction. And very much that we do in school amounts to a contradiction of that kind. Where is the school that looks benevolently on such natural practices as skipping, or thrusting a book away with a groan or a sigh (or even a decent sneer) after a page or a chapter ? Much of such pleasure in fiction as I acquired in school and understanding of it, came from contact with a teacher who was an avid, untidy reader of novels, who fell helplessly in love with some and was helplessly scornful of others, who made no secret of his sad inability to enjoy Laurence Sterne ('a madman with a pen') – a natural, impatient reader, obviously shaped and often shocked by his reading.

There was nothing unsystematic about that. There was, indeed, discussion. There was, indeed, now I think of it, analysis. We discussed characterization, form. But it was all in terms of a busy running commentary on what he was reading, or this boy or that was reading. Being as infectious as it is, the reading of fiction often led to us all, or nearly all, reading the same book. It was as near as anything under a school roof can come to being a natural activity. It generated its own – I think, very hard, very durable – learning. The teacher's intervention lay in his being by far the most experienced catalytic agent among us.

I don't know how else – how but in some formal informality of approach such as this: teaching the natural enjoyments of reading fiction rather than timorously toying with a reach-me-down academic approach to it – I don't know how else we overcome the fear of novels, the hostility to them, or the simple lack of experience of them that so many of our most scrupulous practices in the classroom reinforce. Or, come to that, if my railway carriage theory will stand up, the limited character of some adult reading that springs from a sense that the only good book must be one that a teacher could not afford to be seen dead with.

From 'Fiction in the classroom', *The Times Educational Supplement*, 7 July 1972

Ways forward for the teacher (2): making way for the child's own 'feeling comprehension'

This account of the value of 'response', the communication of moral values and the evolution of a child's taste, are central to the ideas contained in this collection. British and American teachers at a conference held at Dartmouth College in 1966 produced this report under the chairmanship of D. W. Harding. Their concern was to define the teacher's role as 'one who directs, or at least leads, a process by which students achieve, within the limits set by their different abilities and funded experience, feeling comprehensions of various works of literary art'. And of course 'feeling comprehension' cannot be expressed in the conventional exercises of academic study. 'It is literature, not literary criticism, that is the subject.'

Response to literature: Dartmouth seminar report
Chairman – D. W. Harding

Though central attention should be given to literature in the ordinary sense, it is impossible to separate response to literature sharply from response to other stories, films, or television plays, or from children's own personal writing or spoken narrative. In all of these the student contemplates represented events in the role of a spectator, not for the sake of active intervention. But since his response includes in some degree accepting or rejecting the values and emotional attitudes which the narration implicitly offers, it will influence, perhaps greatly influence, his future appraisals of behaviour and feeling.

> 'If we could obliterate the effects on a man of all the occasions on which he was "merely a spectator" it would be profoundly to alter his character and outlook.'

Most values are culturally derived; at their best they are the currency given to the adjustments to experience of the most sensitive members of society. Thus, in entering into the 'virtual experience' of influential works of literature, a child is offered a flow and recoil of sympathies that accords with the culture pattern in which he is growing up.

D. W. Harding
'The Role of the Onlooker'
Scrutiny
volume 6 1937, 3

If it is accepted, then, that a work of literature will embody values in the broadest sense of the term, what is the relationship between its appraisal as literature and appraisal of the moral values it embodies?

Clearly a reader cannot share in the writer's satisfaction in the organization of feelings when – all allowances having been made – he cannot share those feelings. It is this which will prevent some readers from finding satisfaction in works which other readers approve, but it would be rash to say that the judgement in either case had been made on moral as distinct from literary grounds. That one could criticize a reader for having failed to make necessary allowances is obviously true – as might happen when a pacifist reads a war novel; but there are likely to be cases where a work is universally declared bad because the values it embodies are so out of key with those of the society in which it appears that no reader is able to enter into the feelings comprising its affective organization. This would accord with a generally accepted view that moral values exercise no restraint upon an author's choice of theme or topic but are tantamount to a restraint upon what he makes of it.

The emergence of response to literature

Since young children learn literature from hearing it, classroom discussion of their responses should start from those activities that arise from listening. It seems possible, even probable, that the basic structure of these activities (i.e., of an adult response to literature) will develop by the age of eleven, given reasonable circumstances.

There appear to be four levels of response, emerging in sequence: briefly they are responses to the quality and pattern of (1) sounds, (2) events, (3) roles, and (4) worlds. A few notes follow to suggest the various dimensions of response.

Sound When children bounce on mother's knee to a song or a nursery rhyme, when they join in the chorus, when they chant 'maximum capacity' round the room, and maybe when they chuckle at special words, names, and puns, they are responding to the texture and rhythm of sounds. Such overt actions seem to be both elements of their enjoyment and signs of it.

Event Both rhythm and form involve a pattern of expectation, both for the satisfaction and the modification of the expected pattern. Stories for very young children embody a pattern of events within this rhythm or form. When a child corrects the storyteller and wants the story word perfect, he is asking for confirmation of the pattern (in one respect or the other). At a later stage he may make up topsy-turvy stories with reversals of the pattern; finally he will improvise and impose his own.

Role In free play or classroom drama, children take up the roles of characters in their stories, or perhaps continue the role playing that the story involved them in: 'I'm Jack and this is the beanstalk and you be the Giant.' Sometimes children will replay the story, sometimes reshape and improvise on it, perhaps relating the roles and events more nearly to their own wishes.

World While a story is being read aloud to a group a child may interpose: 'He's a funny boy' (about Jan in *The Silver Sword* perhaps), and the group may begin to talk about his background, his relations with the other characters, etc. A new variety of talk develops to relate and organize elements of the world of that story or to relate the world of that story to the child's own world. It will tie in all the four kinds of response, giving some a new articulation.

Any discussion of ways to foster literary response at different stages of the student's education must be qualified by the recognition that there are wide individual differences in rate of development and that in recent times the earlier onset of puberty, changed social expectations, and powerful commercial influences have modified previously accepted ideas about the stages of childhood, adolescence and early adult life. Yet some broadly defined succession of educational stages has to be assumed.

    Up to the age of about eleven the problems seem to be less formidable than they are in early adolescence. The younger child can respond directly and un-ashamedly to poems, for instance, and is less guarded in his personal responses than he becomes later. Children at this age are largely concerned with inner directed structuring of experience, not with manipulating it for socially determined ends. Perhaps we should note Melanie Klein's suggestion that 'the connections between conscious and unconscious are closer in young children than in adults, and that infantile repressions are less powerful'.

    Around nine or ten, children develop an increasingly 'extroverted' outlook; this should be allowed for in the material they are offered. At the same age greatly

Quoted in
David Holbrook
The Exploring Word
CUP, 1967 (page 134)

Quoted in
David Holbrook
The Exploring Word
CUP, 1967
(page 134)

extended private reading has to be catered for, many children exploring widely among books and devouring them at great speed.

After about eleven, children are likely to put up defences against emotional disturbances (especially those associated with heightened sexual responsiveness) and against the direct expression of emotion that may be found in literary works. Love poems become relatively unacceptable, although poems associated with friendship and generalized benevolence, to which they make stock responses, are often highly acceptable.

Some of the changes occurring after fourteen (especially for children whose schooling is soon to end) may be due less to adolescence than to the uncertainties and discords that come over children as they realize they are about to enter a world of jobs and social responsibility.

At fifteen or sixteen, problems arise from the uneasiness that young people commonly feel about expressing some range of their emotional experience, though they may have strongly sentimental responses beneath a veneer of roughness. A number of common masks for these responses are not difficult to identify: they seek the safety of conformity to mass attitudes or of participating in mass responses; they refuse to express response (not a refusal to respond, rather a refusal to express one in so many words, perhaps because of peer group pressure); they resort to adult utilitarian calculus: 'what good is all this?'; the 'better' or older students have recourse to literary criticism or explicit responses capable of more or less complete formulation, representing perhaps, an early capitulation to adult standards.

In part, of course, the behaviour of adolescents is a result of developments in internal emotional economy. But we may also guess that the barriers mentioned above are as much responses to social conditioning as they are attempts to control inner turmoil. For one thing, they may reveal a badly directed early education which has deprived the child of the opportunity to deal easily with symbolic expressions. It has been said that, in adolescence especially, education is designed 'to starve out, through silence and misrepresentation, the capacity to have genuine and strongly felt experience, and to replace it by the conventional symbols that serve as the common currency of daily life. ... It is still the spontaneous, vivid, and immediate that is most feared, and feared the more because so much desired (by adults).' Thus, in early education we may do unconsciously (or at least without overt intention) what in later education we do quite consciously (at least in the United States). It seems likely that one result of adolescence is that the child learns to repress 'meanings that are not subject to consensual validation …'

Adolescents often see the relevance of works of literature to the emotional problems of their age group and sometimes welcome the opportunity of discussing it in class or with the teacher – though they may well resent any *expectation* that they should do so. The teacher needs great tact in providing an opportunity without seeming to press an invitation. Moreover, works to be read should always be chosen both for their value as literature as well as for their possible bearing on psychological reactions of young people. Around the age of sixteen, students welcome literature centring in nature and friendship. From sixteen to eighteen, teachers expect them to tackle poetry (e.g., Hopkins) that fully extends mature adult readers, though presumably not expecting a mature response. This is probably valuable and in any case inevitable because there seems to be little good poetry below the adult but above the childhood level. In fiction, however, a choice of material for students not yet adult is necessary and possible.

At this and other points there is a need for more exact knowledge (preferably based on longitudinal studies) about changes in the literary responses of boys and girls as they grow up.

Edgar Z. Friedenberg *Dignity of Youth and Other Atavisms* Beacon Press, 1965 (pages 5 and 70) *The Vanishing Adolescent* Beacon Press, 1959 (page 20)

Modes of approach to literature

It seemed to us that good teaching at different stages depends as much on the mode of presentation, and the mode of response consequently implied, as on the selection of materials. Three such modes of presentation were distinguished:

1. The individual child with the individual book

From the teacher's view, this requires finding or assisting the child or adolescent to find 'the right book at the right time'. The approach requires availability of a wide variety of appropriate titles, teacher acquaintance with the books, and teacher understanding of the individual child. Any view of a programme in literature as emphasising the refinement of the individual's own response to literature necessarily sees guided individual reading as central to the literary education of the child, rather than as an appendage or adjunct to be relegated to book lists, 'outside' reading, or out-of-school activity. In practice, this view leads to demands for classroom book collections, better and more accessible school libraries, pupil-teacher conferences on books, class and group discussion of books which students read on their own, and similar activities.

2.   Literature as group experience

Some literature and experiences in literature are corporate possessions, and class-room approaches should recognize and respond to this fact. Such group experiences may include storytelling, folksongs and ballads, film viewing, listening to what others have written, creative dramatics, choral reading, oral interpretation, dramatic interpretation, role playing, listening to recorded literature, and related activities. In such group experiences, the child (whether five or fifteen) relates his own response to the response of other children. What the teacher strives to achieve is far more than a cosy feeling of group 'togetherness'; rather he attempts to promote a communal response which is at the same time affective and intellectual, personal and 'other directed'. Often a return to the oral reading and rereading of the same poetry selections can develop in the group a rich sensitivity to the pleasures of a shared aesthetic experience.

3.   Presentation of literary material accompanied by discussion

A common approach in the classroom is the reading of a work of literature, with assistance from the teacher, followed by informal discussion (sometimes called 'talk' in the United Kingdom) or more structured discussion. Such an approach seems most appropriate when the teacher finds it necessary to assist the reader in creating a context for the work. An alternative form of teacher presentation is oral reading by the teacher as students follow in their books, with the teacher stopping from time to time to increase personal contact and enjoyment by shaping perceptions on the work. Similarly, teachers may elect to read only the initial passages – sufficient to orient the reader and to rouse his interest – and then ask students to continue silently. With some selections and some students, teachers will ask for reading prior to discussion and then use the subsequent classroom exchange of ideas, perceptions, and articulated reactions as a way to encourage a fuller reaction.

Since the purpose of presentation by the teacher is to promote the student's understanding of and engagement with the literary work, such direct presentation should normally be reserved for selections difficult for students; works which are accessible to the individual reader should be read by students on their own. Because of its unique qualities, as well as its length, most poetry is perhaps best read aloud in the classroom at every level (often again and again), whereas literature from other genres (fiction, drama, rhetorical literature, etc.) is often best approached in other ways.

It seems likely that these modes of approach will vary from level to level in emphasis, in the ways in which they find expression in the classroom, and in their appropriateness for different kinds of literary experience.

At the primary level, as children are learning to achieve independence in reading, a programme of extensive individual reading may seem less central to the literary education of children, although even here individual selection of picture-books can stimulate personal choice. Using the stories told or dictated by a child for his own reading is related to this approach, though using such creative materials for an entire group is also closely allied with presentation (Approach No. 3). Since at this stage many children will clearly need help in the processes of reading which lead to literary experience, more reliance on teacher presentation may be appropriate. Oral reading of poems and stories by the teacher provides experience with literature which children cannot read silently; often a burst of response will follow. A question or two concerning a selection often elicits a latent response in such activities.

During late childhood or early adolescence (ages 10–15), the emphasis in classroom approaches seems to shift, but all three approaches identified here tend to be used by some teachers. As the child gains independence in reading, the teacher encourages wider and wider personal reading. To guide such reading he finds it mandatory to schedule individual conferences with each child. Because research has demonstrated that most children during this period will read more books than at any other time during their school careers, a carefully organized programme of guided individual reading seems a necessity.

A continuing obligation remains to assist the young reader to find satisfaction in selections he would not select or understand on his own. Most poetry will be introduced by the teacher (Approach 3), most often through oral reading followed by discussion. Short selections may be introduced to assist pupils with special reading problems.

At this level group experiences with literature take a somewhat different form. As children become more and more inhibited, dramatic play and story-telling become less an experience than a social threat. Puppet plays, which enable a child to express a personal response without revealing the humiliating constraints of his own body, are used effectively by some teachers. Interpretative readings and dramatic interpretations of scenes from plays can also be important. Because oral interpretation assists teachers and pupils to identify problems and differences in individual responses and can help even inarticulate students to react to individual works, more stress on oral approaches than is characteristic of teaching in many American schools seems desirable.

During the later school years (ages 15–18), the approaches continue in a somewhat different relationship. As social and personal interests of students expand, wide reading tends to occupy less of the adolescent's personal time. The child's individual interests in literary experience may be increasingly satisfied by forms other than the book – by recorded literature, for example, by films, or by theatrical experiences. The wise teacher will continue a strong programme of individual reading but will expand this programme to include discussion of other kinds of literary experience.

Group experience with the drama may tend to become more formalized, depending to a greater degree on interpretation of texts written by others, but continuing to use improvisation as an approach. Some teachers use drama to stimulate personal expression of emotion, but others caution that adolescents fear to reveal their own emotions in the group and prefer to interpret emotions of others. The problems of overcoming the self-consciousness of adolescents cause many teachers to overlook the contributions of drama in fostering an active response to literature.

As the young reader proceeds through school, teacher presentation of literature followed by discussion (in whatever form) can introduce young readers to new kinds of literature, can assist them in the problems of perception and interpretation, and thus can free them to read increasingly mature books on their own. Close reading of individual literary texts pointing toward illumination of the particular literary experience and its relationship to all human experience, rather than analysing purely external characteristics, seems to be the major method in guiding the refinement of student response. But unless the teacher stresses the processes of reading and responding to literature, rather than individual texts as ends in themselves, he is not likely to help the student reader find satisfaction in more mature literature on his own. And unless the 'presentation–discussion' approaches are carefully related to a programme of individual reading, the student will have little opportunity to apply whatever competence in analysis and response he has acquired.

A word needs to be said about issues arising from the choice of selections for presentation in a class. Clearly the teacher will need to consider the characteristics of particular children and young people based on his past experience with students of this kind, as well as his own reading of literature, and should select those literary selections to which he feels a high percentage of students may respond. Because of concern lest 'teacher presented' material dominate literary study in the secondary school, many urge that most such teaching concentrate on shorter selections – the poem, the short story or essay, even extracts from longer works. (Others would challenge heavy reliance on extracts as violating the unity of a work and preventing student readers from experiencing a work of art as art, as an organic whole.) Still, most young people will not respond fully and maturely to longer works without some help in learning the various dimensions of response. Although it seems likely that in some schools too great an emphasis is placed on repetitive teaching of certain kinds of novels, i.e. novels which tend to present similar problems in reading and response, sound planning will assure that these forms are not neglected.

Any mode of presentation, to be educationally successful, must presuppose the teacher's genuine enthusiasm for the work of literature (allowing for the limited or different appeal that works suitable for young children may have for the adult). One consequence of this is that he cannot be content to leave students to their own unguided enthusiasms, although he may be well advised to start from those. He has the responsibility of leading students towards the full range of literary experience that he himself can compass. Certain works, because of the quality of their theme and treatment, have provided rich literary experiences to readers of varied backgrounds. Such writing, for instance, by Chaucer, Shakespeare, Twain, Lawrence, Melville, or Frost, though in some sense part of a cultural heritage, is not a packet to be transmitted inert. It is alive and changing; each generation takes from it what it needs and adds to it in its turn.

In guiding the reading of young people, the teacher has an obligation to move them towards more mature literary experience. They may be ready for particular works at different times and the experience may be presented in different ways, but an education that continues until the student reaches sixteen or seventeen years should provide some introduction to imaginative literature of the highest order. 'All pupils, including those of very limited attainments, need the experience of contact with great literature, and can respond to its universality.' Whether by building on the points of contact between the book and reader, or by seizing on opportunities which emerge in the students' own responses to experience, the teacher must help young readers gain some insight

Half Our Future
HMSO ('The Newsom Report') 1963

into works which have conveyed significant experience to discriminating adults. Maybe no single literary work is so important that it must be read by all students; there are bound to be gaps in individual experiences. But any literary education should include acquaintance with Chaucer, Shakespeare, some Romantic poets, and some major fiction of the past two centuries.

The formulation of response to literature

Let us turn now to the problem, especially evident in the later years of secondary education and at the university, of the proper place of formulated critical comment and of teaching *about* literature. In the first place, 'study of literature' is an ambiguous and even deceiving term, which often deflects the energies of teachers from what many of them now consider to be their primary concern. It suggests, perhaps necessarily, that in the classroom experience with literary works, students and teachers should be seeking regularities and similarities, and treating works as the source of data for establishing general statements about classes of literary works, their parts, their authors, or the circumstances of their composition; or that they should be composing rather closed formulations of the probable causes in works of assorted effects in readers. However useful, these are activities more appropriate to historians and critics than to young people whose sensibilities or powers of imaginative sympathy are as yet unpractised and untrained. Without undervaluing or disregarding cognitive analyses of literary works or conceptual schemes for analysing 'literature', many teachers would say that in the classroom the chief concern should be for extending the student's disciplined acquaintance with and response to a certain number of literary works.

Achieving such an acquaintance is different from the study of a body of knowledge, because the student's affective response is an integral part of the experience with the work. That he likes or dislikes his exercises in geology may be a pedagogical help or hindrance, but the essential task is completed if he learns and understands the facts. In literature, however, it is the knowledge of facts which may be a help or hindrance; the essential task is not done without his affective involvement. In its ideal form, comprehension of a literary work should involve the response of a whole, organized person; and it should be consistent with a framework created, first, by an intellectual grasp of the work, its parts, and its principles of organization, and second, by knowledge of the world the work refers to, its connection with the student's own world and experience, and its relation to other works.

The ideas of 'response' and 'involvement' are emphasized here to counter the consequences of too rigid application of the otherwise valuable notion of the work of art as a thing in itself. As the term is often used, *work of art* suggests the existence of something quite and wholly outside the perceiver, existing in ineluctable perfection and subject to only the most partial and inadequate approach. The phraseology used here hopefully suggests that works of art are by no means so separate; rather they exist always through their moment-by-moment experiencing by one or several perceivers. In a significant sense, works of art exist as perceived, or as a constantly growing and developing body of perceptions.

Of course there is something 'out there' which is, or can be, an object of some kind of attention and which provides a referent to test the fidelity of the perceiver's responses. Hence there ought to be no suggestion that 'response' in our usage refers to anything, free-floating or merely emotional. To clarify this point, it may be prudent to indicate the various activities that may be subsumed under the term 'response'. The primary centre of the whole activity of reading is some sort of state in our feelings that we can call, for lack of a better word, enjoyment. How enjoyment comes about is never very clear, but it seems to depend in some fashion on various kinds of activities that lead to understanding. It may also be supported by those typical, though maybe not essential, activities that form a kind of intelligent scanning and internalized comment (perhaps preverbal) on the work as it is being experienced.

Finally there is the activity that we are stimulated to or prepared for by all our other contacts with a book. When we have put a good deal into reading a book, there is, as it were, a reverberation of the work in our minds, which leads us to return (sometimes again and again) to elements of that experience. Perhaps the process is similar to that of a discussion where we sympathetically entertain the frame of reference of our fellow participant, following through its implications into realms of novelty hitherto unsuspected, and then recoil momentarily as we set this new frame and its implications against the context of our own beliefs and assumptions. A successive scanning and reorganization follows, as we move between the novelties we have entertained and our accepted tenets. Just so, perhaps, the partial world of any work of art questions and confirms elements of our existing representational world, making us look for a new order that assimilates both. This, too, is our 'response'.

In the optimum situation, the teacher is seen as one who directs, or at least leads, a process by which students achieve, within the limits set by their different

abilities and funded experience, feeling comprehensions of various works of
literary art. This process should be seen as a continuing one (only part of which
can occur in the classroom) under the direction of the teacher. Of less importance,
therefore, is what is often seen as the one valid form and test of classroom
reading; that is, the formulation of descriptive statements about responses, interpretations, or structures.

It is likely that a demand for more analysis, judgement, interpretation, will
inhibit proper affective response. This would certainly be true for younger readers
and probably for undergraduates too. (Results of premature formulation are hor-
ridly visible even in graduate students, but these are perhaps the most accessible
group for the teacher trying to erode formulation and get back to response.)
James Britton suggests in his discussion that 'the responses of most adult readers
are sharpened (and perhaps more fully integrated with their previous experiences)
if they are in some measure formulated.' 'In some measure' needs a long hard look.
We often suppose, encouraged by schematic literary criticism and the demands of
examinations, that formulation should be explicit, broad, and objectified. As
teachers we should remember how long it takes even to respond to poems of our
own choice, how often we are quite naturally numb to parts or wholes as we
encounter literature, and not expect too much from the students. First encounters
in the classroom should deliberately hold back formulation, should back away
from everything that isn't tentative and partial. We need to encourage, very
warmly, verifications from personal experience, not frown on the 'That's me'
identification with a character.

People who need to use the concept of 'discipline' in talking about response
will be uneasy about the freedom of 'That's me', but it can perhaps be accommo-
dated even to a literary respect for the work of art. 'That's me' has two
components, and our aim is to move dynamically from the 'me' of personal
identification to the 'that' of the poem or the object in the poem. The discipline
lies in the attentiveness to the 'that', and it should be made plain that there is no
real dichotomy here, but a natural movement from subject to object and back
again. The 'That's me' may well reveal a very partial and too selective selection
from the work, but the teacher will get nowhere in the attempt to make the work
meaningful as experience if he does not begin with the 'me'. And this kind of
identifying is often more interesting than it looks. A middle-aged schoolmaster
who said 'I am Bobadil' was not just being confessional, for he proceeded to
look around and say that everyone else was too. The discussion of the 'that' was a
discussion of the humanness of Jonson which moved miles away from auto-

biographical chat. But the particularized responses should be primary. There will be movement round the many people in the class, and a restrained and thoughtful sharing of personal, incomplete, and implicit response which can lead back to the particular work, and to repeated sensitive readings. The reference to life is not purely illustrative but confirms the affective experience of literature, and is of course its foundation.

The teacher should aim at the teacher's, not the scholar's best, dropping the possessiveness and awed respect we all seem to feel so readily for works of literature. The teacher reporting the 'low level' exclamatory response, or 'the autobiographical bit', or the 'extreme' selection betrays an unholy preference for poems rather than persons. If the implicit or partial or wrong response is stamped on by these literature lovers, there will be little chance that the student can be taken back from the 'me' to the 'that' in an extended exploration of the work's properties.

Some properties will be more easily explored than others. In some circumstances early or broad formulation is particularly inappropriate. When should the teacher try especially hard to sit back, relax, and shut up, to expose fragments, elicit fragments, pass on, be superficial? When the student is responding to something very distant in time and convention, say Spenser or eighteenth-century verse or Scott, then formulation should wait – empathy is not going to come easily (if at all) and students should not be made to feel that they are aesthetic cripples if they simply do not respond. A toleration of the selective or superficial response may really be a way in. Recognizing the response implicit in an emphasis that looks odd or hostile is an important action of the teacher's sensibility. It may be hard to move from the 'that' to the 'me' in reading Scott, but there are those other cases in which it is hard to separate the subject and object, as in an emotionally or sensationally confusing first encounter with something very raw or unaesthetic or powerful (or all three), say James Baldwin or Donne or Lawrence. And there are those works to which we have an over-acculturated response which keeps the 'me' miles away from the 'that'. How hard it is to take in the fantasy in *Jane Eyre* or Paul Dombey, inhibited as we may be at various ages by current attitudes to 'objectivity', 'maturity', 'sentimentality', and dramatic conventions of narrative.

Response is a word that reminds the teacher that the experience of art is a thing of our making, an activity in which we are our own interpretative artist. The dryness of schematic analysis of imagery, symbols, myth, structural relations, *et al.* should be avoided passionately at school and often at college. *It is literature, not literary criticism, that is the subject*. At the present time, there is too much learning about literature in place of discriminating enjoyment, and many students arrive at and leave universities with an unprofitable distrust of their personal responses to literature. At the university, as in the secondary school, the explicit analysis of literature should be limited to the *least* required to get an understanding of the work, within the student's limits, and the aim should be to return as soon as possible to a direct response to the text. Of course, one must also realize that with the present forms of school and university examinations, this is impossible in the United Kingdom and often difficult in the United States.

From *Response to Literature*, J. Squire (editor), NCTE, Champaign, Illinois, 1968

Ways forward for the psychologist: alternative fictions

In this article, R. L. Gregory, Professor of Neuro-Psychology in the University of Bristol, collects together a number of ideas that seem to point the way forward for psychology. He brings together the contributions of anthropologists, sociologists, linguists, educationalists, and philosophers of art to illuminate 'the internal fiction that is, for the organism, reality'. The core of his argument, that intelligence might be defined as 'the generation of appropriate novelty' leads us back to the initial statement made by Barbara Hardy. This suggests that cognitive psychology and a poetics of children's stories might offer mutual support.

Psychology: towards a science of fiction   R. L. Gregory

Psychology, it must sadly be admitted, is a somewhat suspect Cinderella, in spite of its status in some universities as a natural science. Physiology and biochemistry are no older, as areas of speculation and experiment, than psychology, and molecular biology is much younger: yet these and other biological sciences command greater respect. They have higher standing as being truly 'scientific'. Why is psychology suspect as a science? Its methodology has been a spur to developing statistical methods; some of its experimental techniques have flair and elegance; and its questions are both intellectually exciting and of unrivalled practical importance. Like physics, it has respectable roots in classical philosophy; but it has not taken off in the same way as a science. One suspects that part of the trouble is lack of a paradigm, in Kuhn's sense – lack of a general viewpoint and set of linking concepts to give point to data and purpose to theoretical research.

Much current experimental psychology is largely dominated by physiology, sometimes to the extent that we seem to be waiting to be taken over by, or to have psychology 'reduced' to, the concepts of physiology. Though physiology has made enormous contributions, and co-operation is wholly welcome, psychology is in principle a science in its own right and should not be afraid of going its own way. It is, however, a very odd science. So odd, indeed, that it needs a paradigm which may at first sight look un- or even anti-scientific. The step I am advocating for developing a paradigm for psychology is to *take fiction seriously*: to consider behaviour as being largely controlled by fiction. What we need, on this view, is a science of fiction. This would make psychology something of an unnatural science: but this may be its true relation to physics.

It is significant that in many public libraries more space is devoted to 'fiction' than to 'fact'. There is surely a deep biological reason for the importance of fiction: that it states and considers alternative possible realities – allowing escape from the prison of current fact. There is more to this than the pleasures of 'escapism': for it is only by considering what might be that we can change effectively what is, or predict what is likely to be. Fiction has the immense biological significance of allowing behaviour to follow plans removed from, though related sometimes in subtle ways to, worldly events. Fiction frees the nervous system from the tyranny of reflexes triggered by events, so that we respond not merely to what happens, but also to what might happen. 'Brain fiction' thus frees us somewhat from the world of physics, though actions are limited by the restraints of physiological processes and anatomical structures. Fiction in art (including science fiction) gives – in forms to be shared – the essential need of all intelligent organisms: alternative views and courses of possible action.

Fiction is defined in the *Shorter Oxford Dictionary* as, among other things: 'The action or product of fashioning or imitating', and as: 'The action of feigning or inventing imaginary existences, events, states, and things'. It would be wrong to think of works of fiction as wholly, or even largely, false. Novels describe recognizable people, with the usual number of heads and arms, living in ways which are broadly familiar. Even in science fiction, probably most of the propositions accord with our world. It would be an interesting exercise to count up the number of 'true' and 'false' statements in a work of fiction. It would be interesting also to estimate how much would have to be changed to convert novels into history. I suspect that the gap is not large – a few names and dates changed, and a novel would be a history with more or less just comment. By neither being tied to fact nor quite separate, fiction is a tool, necessary for thought and intelligence, and for considering and planning possibilities. Fiction is vitally important – indeed we may live more by fiction than by fact. It is living by fiction which makes the higher organisms special. By recognizing the importance of 'brain fiction' for perception and intelligent behaviour, we might make psychology a science.

This notion of the perception and behaviour of higher organisms as being given by a kind of running internal fiction, rather than from stimuli directly related to events, has been suggested in various forms by many psychologists – William James, Sir Frederic Bartlett, Kenneth Craik, Jean Piaget, Jerome Bruner. But it meets general opposition from physiologists. This conflict is not of merely historical interest: it is currently an issue too hot to be handled safely. If, indeed, much of behaviour is given from internal, largely inaccessible 'brain fiction', then the hope of finding simple relations (transfer functions) between inputs and outputs, or stimuli and responses is destroyed (except for special cases such as startle responses to unpredictable events), and the foundation of the behaviourist school of psychology collapses. On the other hand, the notion of behaviour and perception as depending on internal fiction – based on the past but deviating in many ways from fact, and freeing much of behaviour from reflexes – provides a take-off platform for psychology as a science in its own right. This commits us to theories of behaviour very different from stimulus-response accounts – theories which are difficult to test or develop because observable data are indirectly related to what matters most. To make this move requires an act of faith that adequate scientific methods can be devised for discovering and describing the fiction that controls organisms – and is their perception of the world. Physics developed to describe objects which are not predictive, do not plan their futures or act upon assessed probabilities, but are affected immediately according to surrounding events. Even delayed effects such as metal fatigue, (which leaves a kind of memory in the metal) are rare in physics and are difficult to handle. So it is not surprising that this notion of organisms being not so much pushed around by the world as following internal fictions, challenges the power of scientific method, keeping cognitive psychology largely outside the harbour of the natural sciences.

Physics, chemistry, physiology, and so on are concerned with facts of the physical world. There are undoubtedly facts of this kind associated with the function of the nervous system. Such facts are established by electrical recording from nerve and brain. Many experiments in physiology are thus similar to experiments in physics; but physicists do not *talk* to their experimental material, or try to discover the secrets of the Universe by asking the Universe questions. This technique is limited to theology, psychology, and perhaps also sociology. Our ability to communicate with other people, and to a limited extent with other animals, gives a *prima facie* case for thinking that organisms are essentially different from other lumps of matter. There is a particularly interesting mixture of talking-to, hearing-from, and experiment in anthropology. Extreme behaviourists may deny that speech is more than sound, or writing more than patterns; but behaviourist psychologists write books, and apparently expect them to be understood, so they are on the edge here of paradox.

Language gives the most immediate access to part of the internal fiction of other people. (From what one hears, some of this is fiction in the pejorative sense of the word: 'Supposition known to be at variance with fact, but conventionally accepted.' This is not, however, the sense which concerns us here.) What we are concerned with is organisms 'fashioning and imitating'; and 'inventing imaginary existences, events, and things'. The use of deliberate falsehood is, however, of great interest – it is an attempt to distort another's fiction, so that his (or her) understanding and prediction are at variance with what we accept as fact, or predict will happen. So falsehood becomes a weapon not of a physical kind, such as a fist which may deflect or prevent action according to the principles obeyed by other physical objects: it is a weapon working within the logic and rules of the 'brain fiction' by which we see and understand.

It is not only communication and language which provide evidence that organisms are controlled by fictions rather than stimuli. Consider any skill, such as a ball game. What stands out in games and skills is the importance of prediction. It has been known at least since Hermann von Helmholtz a century ago, that neural signals take nearly half a second to travel the nerve fibres and cross the synapses linking receptors to limbs – and yet skills run in 'real time'. Skilled behaviour is not delayed by the delay-time of the nervous system, when prediction is possible. We respond without delay to regularly repeated flashes or other predicted sensed events. On the other hand, if the regularity changes, or the light does not flash, then we may 'respond' to what *should* have happened. So we are responding to predictions of events. This is shown by absence of delay-time in skills, and by errors occurring when the expected does not happen. It follows that the notion of stimuli as triggers for action is, at least in these cases, mistaken.

One attempt to save stimulus-response theories, is to admit that much of behaviour is predictive, but to hold that *predictions are a kind of stimuli*. Will this work to save the stimulus-response paradigm? I think that it will not; for stimuli are essentially patterns of energy at receptors (the eyes, ears, skin, and so on) which can be detected and measured with the kinds of instruments and techniques familiar and accepted in physics. But behaviour based on prediction cannot be like this, because the events to which behaviour may be appropriate have not yet happened – and so cannot be stimuli or be detected. Physiological techniques of recording from the nervous system may make it possible to record the neural processes carrying out prediction; but this does not take us back to stimuli. Prediction requires data, assumptions and generalizations based on the past; but these are very different from stimuli as triggers of action. They are so different that we cannot hope to find direct relations (transfer functions) between sensory stimulation and behaviour or perception. We must discover the selected internal fiction to see what lies between sensory signals and behaviour. This is surely the central problem for academic psychology – but the answer will not be 'merely academic'. It is our reality. It is the springboard of our actions; and society is created by, and in turn largely creates, the fiction by which each of us lives.

The internal fiction controlling behaviour may go wrong – in some situations to generate errors which may be disastrous, like when driving in fog. It may produce all manner of illusions, from distorting shapes to making us see motives incorrectly. It may go drastically wrong in some individuals – to become living horror fiction.

If it were true that we were controlled directly by stimuli, it would be difficult to see how originality or intelligence would be possible. We would surely be tyrannized by reflexes, so that we would be no more than complicated marionettes, dancing to the pulls and pushes of stimuli. Unfortunately, however, the alternative notion of behaviour given by 'brain fiction' does not easily let us off this philosophical hook. The problem of autonomy remains. For what is it that writes and reads and selects from the internal fiction that is, for the organism, reality? We do not know how to think about this. Our philosophical fiction is not yet adequate. We might, however, be able to say something here about intelligence.

What is intelligence? Many definitions have been suggested, perhaps the most popular among psychologists being 'the ability to see relations'. Undoubtedly this is important, but does it get near the heart of the matter? What is an intelligent solution to a problem? Certainly, it may require the seeing of relations to arrive at an intelligent solution; but this hardly tells us what it is about the solution which demonstrated intelligence. Putting the emphasis on the kinds of solution which seem to show intelligence, I think we see two characteristics. Intelligent solutions must be *appropriate*, and they must be *novel*. Novelty generated through randomness, without selection, will not generate intelligent solutions beyond a chance level of success. A solution must be appropriate to have any kind of success. If we consider a perfect historical account, or a xerox copy, these are not intelligent for they are not novel, and are immediately inappropriate in a slightly changed situation. So we might suggest as a definition of intelligence:

F. C. Bartlett
Remembering
CUP, 1932

J. S. Bruner
Beyond the Information Given
Allen and Unwin
1974

K. J. W. Craik
The Nature of Explanation
CUP, 1943

M. Douglas
'Self-evidence'
Proceedings of the Anthropological Institute, 1972

R. L. Gregory
The Intelligent Eye
Weidenfeld and Nicolson, 1970

R. L. Gregory and E. H. Gombrich (editors)
Illusion in Nature and Art
Duckworth, 1973

W. James
The Principles of Psychology
Holt, 1890

U. Neisser
Cognitive Psychology
New York
Appleton-Century-Crofts, 1967

W. U. Quine
Word and Object
MIT Press, 1960

'the generation of appropriate novelty'. Now what can generate appropriate novelty? Hypotheses in science have the power to generate predictions and inventions: showing the intelligence of appropriate novelty. Even untutored brain fiction could be rather like the predictive hypotheses of science.

The fiction of human brains is only partly available to consciousness or introspection, so it must be discovered by experimental means. This requires techniques which may differ somewhat from the techniques of the natural sciences. Could it be, though, that cognitive procedures are similar in important ways to the *methods* of science? This would be so if perceptions are structurally like scientific hypotheses of objects and causes and situations. This would not be too surprising, since both science and organisms have to make effective use of limited data, to predict and control and understand. The success of science shows the power of hypotheses as fictions of limited truth. The methods of science demonstrate several extremely effective ways for generating and testing fictional accounts of possible realities, and applying them to win over the environment.

This may suggest that cognitive psychology might learn even more from the methods and philosophy of science than from what science has discovered about objects. Objects are different from us, because they are all fact: we are works of fiction.

From *New Society*, 23 May 1974

Bibliography

Introduction

The first part of the list has a selection of specialist studies which contribute to the general theory of this book. They are related, either directly or by association, to Storying or narrative or fiction. The notes are not definitive statements. In most cases they are simply intended as links between the themes in the essays and other writings where the relevance might not be inferred. As the well-trodden path into the study of books for children is the historical route, we hope to show other ways of approaching the topic.

In the second part we have listed some of the readily available studies of children's literature which follow in the wake of F. J. Harvey Darton's classic, *Children's books in England; five centuries of social life*. As Virginia Haviland's *Children's literature, a Guide to Reference Sources* and its *First Supplement* are also available, there seems no need to reduplicate references but simply to direct readers to them and to other authors whose work anticipated or inspired our own. A book such as J. Rowe Townsend's *Written for Children* in its second edition (Kestrel, 1974) includes not only an exemplary survey of the field, but also a list of books for children and about books for children from which any student could profit.

There are many omissions. We have not included a list of the reviewing media nor of journals devoted to reviewing children's literature. This should not be allowed to obscure the fact that both the writing and the production of fiction for children have been kept at a high standard by the seriousness of the accompanying criticism. Journals such as *Signal*, *The Use of English*, *Horn Book*, *Children's Literature in Education*, *Children's Book Review*, *Books for your Children*, *Growing Point*, and *The School Librarian*, have contributed much to this book and to the promotion of children's literature in general.

Specialist studies

Aarne, Antti *The Types of the Folktale*, revised by Stith Thompson, Helsinki, 1961.
A standard classification and numbering of themes and variants of traditional
tales from all sources. Accompanies Stith Thompson, 1955–8 (q.v. below).
See also Briggs, 1970–1.

Alderson, Brian *Looking at Picture Books 1973*, National Book League, 1973.
Introduction to a catalogue for an exhibition of picture books. Presents
a critical exposition of the 'permanence of traditional values in book
illustration'. The compiler's fervour and hortatory style support the
exclusiveness of his acute judgements.

Alderson, Connie *Magazines Teenagers Read: With Special Reference to Trend,
Jackie, and Valentine*, Pergamon, 1968.
This special study, with introduction by Basil Bernstein, deals not only
with the magazines but the 'pop scene' as it was then. Much of the evidence
is relevant now. Mrs Alderson writes as an angry sociologist about the
manipulation by the big-time operators, and the precarious variability of
the world they have created. This one would not dispute.
What does stand out is the hunger for story recognized by the 'manipulators'
and expressed by the schoolgirls; and the need to daydream.

Applebee, A. N. *The Spectator Role*, Unpublished Ph.D. Thesis, University
of London, 1974.
Encyclopaedic research documentation of theoretical and developmental
studies of responses to literature, based on empirical studies of children's
storytelling and reading. Compare Harding and Britton.

Auden, W. H. *The Dyer's Hand*, Faber, 1963. *Forewords and Afterwords*, Faber,
1973.
Endlessly haunted by the fascination of writing about reading and writing,
Auden has left some gnomic phrases in these two collections of essays.
The Dyer's Hand contains 'Making, Knowing and Judging', his auto-
biographical Oxford lecture; *Forewords and Afterwords* also has pieces on
Grimm, Andersen, Lewis Carroll and Walter de la Mare.

Avery, Gillian *Childhood's Pattern: a study of the heroes and heroines of children's fiction 1770–1950*, Hodder and Stoughton, 1975.
A critical survey of stories for children in the light of adult preoccupations and values. The author's focus is chiefly on the middle years of the period when the social orders and mores were reflected in the heroes and heroines. It is useful to compare it with Philippe Ariès' *Centuries of Childhood* (1962).

Bardgett, Keith ' "Skinhead" in the Classroom' in *Children's Literature in Education*, July, 1972.
A probationer teacher discovers his dilemma in the face of his pupils' devotion to Richard Allen's novels.

Blishen, Edward *This Right Soft Lot*, Thames and Hudson, 1969.
A sequel to *Roaring Boys* (1955), episodes from four or five years teaching at 'Stonehill Secondary Modern' are presented in the form of fiction. The effects of storying, their own and other people's, on pupils who are ' ... largely reluctant, baffled, and unhopeful' are described with moving perception, together with other aspects of a desperate but often grimly humorous experience.

Bolt, Sydney *The Right Response*, Hutchinson, 1966.
A follower of F. R. Leavis discusses how he trains his Further Education pupils to make particular critical appraisals of major works chosen by himself.

Bolt, Sydney and Gard, Roger *Teaching Fiction in Schools*, Hutchinson, 1970.
Argues that 'understanding involves criticism' and makes a plea for teachers 'to develop skill in reading fiction *as such*'. Unfortunately the book fails to make clear what fiction 'as such' really is and what happens in the mind of the pupil.

Booth, Wayne *The Rhetoric of Fiction*, University of Chicago, 1961.
Detailed examination of means whereby the novelist makes known his vision and attitudes to the reader and persuades him of their validity. 'In short, the author's judgement is always present, always evident to anyone who knows how to look for it.' Very applicable to children's literature.
cf. J. R. Townsend on modern didacticism in Egoff, 1969.

Briggs, Katharine M. *A Dictionary of British Folk-tales*, 4 volumes, Routledge and Kegan Paul, 1970–1.
The standard collection of British fairy tales, local legends, original myths, jocular tales, and historical traditions, complete with regional variants.

They have been classified according to the Stith Thompson Motif-Index (cf. below) with elaborate cross-referencing and a full bibliography. Apart from its importance as a great work of scholarship, it is an entertaining collection in which to browse – as the titles of the first two sections of Part B, Volume 1, 'Black Dogs' and 'Bogies', suggest.

Britton, J. N. et al. *The Development of Writing Abilities 11–18*, Schools Council Research Series, Macmillan, 1975.
The first detailed report of the Schools Council writing research project. Challenges traditional categories of rhetoric as a means of classifying what writers actually do; sets out and tests a more realistic set of categories. Tony Burgess's essay on page 363 stems from this research.

Britton, J. N. *Language and Learning*, Allen Lane, 1970.
A very important account of the language development of the child, drawing on the writings of philosophers (notably Langer, 1953, and Michael Polanyi), psychologists (notably Kelly, 1955, Piaget, and Bruner) and psycholinguists (notably Vigotsky, 1962). Of particular relevance to reading is Chapter 3 which distinguishes between language used in 'the spectator role' and in 'the participant role' (cf. Harding, 1937 and 1962). His account, based on Kelly, of comprehension as 'modification of expectations' is also crucial (compare Smith, 1971, and Sartre, 1947).

Burgess, A. et al. *Understanding Children Writing*, Penguin, 1973.
Examples of the process and development of the writing done by children under the aegis of their teachers. Real writing by real children.

Cameron, Eleanor *The Green and Burning Tree*, Little, Brown, 1969.
A collection of critical essays on a wide range of children's authors.

Chambers, Aidan *Introducing Books to Children*, Heinemann Educational, 1973.
Carries by means of commitment and conviction the argument that 'wide, voracious, indiscriminate reading is the base soil from which discrimination and taste eventually grow'.
The Reluctant Reader, Pergamon, 1969.
Examines reasons why the 'submerged 60 per cent' of the literate population never reads books. The author, an experienced teacher, places much of the responsibility on publishers, teachers, and authors for not catering for children's real needs.

Chukovsky, Kornei *From Two to Five*, translated and edited by Miriam Morton, University of California Press, 1963 (first edition, Moscow, 1925).
Chukovsky, Soviet scholar and children's poet, first published this fascinating

study of children's language and literature in 1925. In 1934 he added the
account of the reinstatement of fairy tales at the First All-Union Congress
of Soviet Writers and in the 1956 edition could finally say that 'Now it is
regarded as a generally recognized truth that the fairy tale develops, enriches,
and humanizes the child's psyche ...' An extract is reprinted on page 48
above.

Clark, Margaret M. *Young Fluent Readers: what can they teach us?* Heinemann
Educational, 1976.
The writer, a psychologist, examined the case histories of thirty-two
children who read at an early age without formal instruction. The role
of the interested adult and the part played by the library are examined
in detail.

Cook, Elizabeth *The Ordinary and the Fabulous*, CUP, 1969.
A beautifully written account of the place of myth, legend, and fairy tale
in the education of the child. She discusses the main areas for study and
examines in detail the currently available versions. Of great practical help
to the teacher. A section from the Appendix is reprinted on page 272 above.

D'Arcy, Pat *Reading for Meaning:* Volume 1 *Learning to Read*; Volume 2 *The
Reader's Response*, Hutchinson, 1973.
Reports of research and surveys up to 1969. Volume 2 contains summaries
of Jenkinson (q.v.), Fader (q.v.), and techniques for the analysis and
assessment of 'comprehension', 'literary appreciation', 'response'.

Dixon, J. *Growth Through English*, 3rd edition, OUP, 1975.
Defines its aims as 'personal growth', as opposed to 'skills' and 'cultural
heritage'. Seeks to give meaning to phrases such as 'intellectual organizing of
experience' and 'ordering of the feelings' through the use of language. In its
reaction against older elitist views, it does not adequately redefine the role of
literature in the new curriculum.

Egoff, Sheila et al. (editors) *Only Connect: Readings on Children's Literature*,
Edited by Sheila Egoff, G. T. Stubbs, and L. F. Ashley, OUP, Toronto,
1969.
'Our aim has been to find selections that deal with children's literature as an
essential part of the whole realm of literary activity, to be discussed in the
same terms and judged by the same standards that would apply to any other
branch of writing.'
A diverse collection, including major essays by C. S. Lewis, T. S. Eliot,
Edmund Leach, and J. R. R. Tolkien, representing a change of critical stance

and opening up new possibilities for undertaking enterprises such as ours. Sheila Egoff's dissatisfaction with the traditional mode of treating children's books is expressed in her *Republic of Childhood: a critical guide to Canadian Children's Literature in English* (1967).

Fader, Daniel N. and McNeil, Elton B. *Hooked on Books*, Pergamon, 1969. In Part 1, Dr Fader describes the highly controversial approach to the reading programme at a school for delinquent boys in Michigan. He flooded the school to saturation point with paperback books. In Part 2 Dr McNeil evaluates the programme. However the most telling section of the book is the postlude 'What I done last summer' in which McNeil describes a similar experiment in a summer camp for emotionally disturbed/delinquent boys.

Farmer, Penelope ' "Jorinda and Jorindel" and other stories' in *Children's Literature in Education*, 7, March 1972. Describes herself as an 'introvert' writer interested in an audience responsive to 'fantasy' (individual subconscious). Shows impressive insight into the process of her own composition of novels for children, which include *The Summer Birds* (1962), *Charlotte Sometimes* (1969), *A Castle of Bone* (1971), and *William and Mary* (1974).

Feiffer, Jules *The Great Comic Book Heroes*, Dial, New York, 1965. Reviewed by Mordecai Richler on page 299 above.

Field, C. and Hamley, D. C. *Fiction in the Middle School*, Batsford, 1975. Presents the argument for stories as offering 'a wide range of insights into human behaviour' and preparing the reader for 'experiences yet to come'.

Fisher, Margery *Intent upon Reading*, Brockhampton, revised edition, 1964. A refreshing and perceptive survey; an important landmark in viewing books for children as part of the mainstream of literature.
Who's Who in Children's Books: a treasury of the familiar characters of childhood, Weidenfeld and Nicolson, 1975. Not a reference book so much as a gallery of old friends, intended to bring back memories or to suggest new reading.

Freud, Sigmund 'Writers and Day-Dreaming' (1908) in *Collected Works*, editor Strachey, volume IX, Hogarth, 1959. A lecture to a group of booksellers on the relationship of literary to private fantasy. ' ... a piece of creative writing, like a daydream, is a continuation of, and a substitute for, what was once the play of childhood'. Compare Britton page 40 above and Winnicott, 1972.

Froebel, Friedrich *The Education of Man*, Appleton Century Croft, 1887.
Contains a defence of fiction as a means of developing a child's personality
on the grounds that 'the story concerns other men, other circumstances,
other times and places, nay, wholly different forms; yet the hearer seeks his
own image, he beholds it, and no one knows that he sees it'.

Frye, Northrop *Anatomy of Criticism: Four Essays*, Princeton, 1957.
A massive neo-Aristotelian critical system. Classifies plots according to the
hero's power of action and bases the whole on a Jungian theory of
archetypes. His model might usefully be adapted for children's literature.
The Stubborn Structure, Methuen, 1970.
'As for the teaching of literature, it is obvious that a good deal of it
should consist in reading and listening to stories ... Myths represent
the structural principles of literature; they are to literature what
geometry is to painting.'

Goodman, Kenneth S. *Analysis of Oral Reading Miscues: Applied Psycholinguistics*,
Reading Research Quarterly, Fall, 1969.
A theoretical account of reading as a psycholinguistic activity. Compares
unexpected responses in oral reading with expected responses, and
produces a taxonomy of cues and miscues with which to analyse the oral
reading process. (cf. Smith, 1971).

Greene, Graham *The Lost Childhood and Other Essays*, Eyre and Spottiswoode,
1951, Penguin, 1960.
Called 'A Personal Prologue', the first essay in this collection asserts that
'it is only in childhood that books have any deep influence on our lives'
and demonstrates with high particularity the links of fact and feeling
between Greene's early reading, his later experience, and his own writing.

Harding, D. W. *Experience into Words*, Chatto, 1963; Penguin, 1974.
Essays developing the theme that 'the understanding of a poem is an
experience quite distinct from any other experiences on which its creation
may depend', yet the author or reader should be able to relate the poem to
the same kind of other experiences. Examines the relevance of some
psychological studies to the relationship between author's symbolizing of
experience and reader's response.

Harding, D. W. 'The Role of the Onlooker' in *Scrutiny*, volume VI, 1937.
Describes the evaluative response of the reader of fiction in the same terms
as that of the spectator of real events. Important argument against use of
terms 'identification' and 'vicarious experience'.

Hardy, Barbara *Storytellers and Listeners*, Athlone Press, 1975.
Extends into a full study the first essay in this collection.

Haviland, Virginia *Children and Literature*, Scott, Foresman, 1973; Bodley
Head, 1974.
A collection of essays about books for children; probably the most
convenient source of the classical pieces, well annotated.

Hazard, Paul *Books, Children and Men*, Horn Book Incorporated, 4th edition 1960.
One of the first pleas for 'children's rights' passionately written by a
French academician in 1933. The rights to read for pleasure and to read what
they want to read, not material foisted upon them by oppressive adults.
All is written from the heart and is a delight to read. It is also important
because of its influence on other writers such as Lillian Smith (q.v.) and
much American comment on children's books.

Hewitt, Douglas *The Approach to Fiction: Good and Bad Readings of Novels*,
Longman, 1972.
'The relationship between a novel and life is akin to that between the two
parts of a metaphor.' Considers how different types of metaphor make
different types of demand on the reader, and describes the problems of
the critic.

Hill, Janet (editor) *Books for Children: The Homelands of Immigrants in Britain:
Africa, Cyprus, India and Pakistan, Ireland, Italy, Poland, Turkey, the West
Indies*. The Institute of Race Relations, London, 1971.
Attempts a critical assessment of children's books both fiction and non-
fiction 'about countries from which people have come here to settle'. Not a
list of recommended titles; indeed, the survey shows that many children's
books about other countries are 'biased, prejudiced, inaccurate or just
plain dull'. How much actual experience or information the compilers
obtained from experts about each country is not stated.

Hill, Janet *Children are People: The Librarian in the Community*, Hamish Hamilton,
1973.
Outstanding in an otherwise uneven book are the two chapters 'Working
through the community' and 'Introducing and publicizing books'. In the
first Miss Hill shows how a public library service in an inner city area
radically altered its nature to meet the particular needs of the community.
In the second there is a vivid account of taking books and stories out into
the community.

Hindle, Alan *Literature for Children*, Open University Press, 1973.
Unit 2 for the Reading Development Course of the Open University
emphasizes reading for the private satisfaction of the child. It includes
Hindle's own good paper on 'The Literature Under the Desk', and Barbara
Hardy on why English teaching should not be just a 'critical discipline'.

Hoffman, Miriam and Samuels, Eva *Authors and Illustrators of Children's
Books: writings of their lives and works*, Bowker, New York and London, 1972.
Devotes ten papers to mainly US writers. Includes an excellent essay on
Sendak linked with George MacDonald, and a useful survey of C. S.
Lewis's Narnia books.

Holland, N. N. *The Dynamics of Literary Response*, OUP, New York, 1968.
A full but very readable account of the reading process by an orthodox
Freudian; literature is examined as it 'transforms the unconscious fantasy
at its heart into intellectual terms'.

Hughes, Ted 'Myth and Education' in *Children's Literature in Education*, 1,
March, 1970.
Suggests reasons why myth is important to children and explains some of
the ideas behind the composition of *The Iron Man*.

Inglis, Fred *The Englishness of English Teaching*, Longman, 1969.
Inglis argues with passion and eloquence (following F. R. Leavis) that
'adpop' culture has left our children with a language of values that is
'irreparably partial, incomplete, diseased'. He bravely declares his hatred of
contemporaneity and his vision of the English teacher as 'at once critic and
creator of his society'. But the design of his survey of the taste of
fifteen-year-olds on which the book is based is open to criticism.

Jenkinson, A. J. *What do Boys and Girls Read?* Methuen, 1940.
An obviously very dated survey of the reading habits of three thousand
children but still the most thorough and thoughtful. 'Children's reading
matter can be classified into three sorts according to its significance for the
individual: some of it is residual and derives from stages outgrown; most
of it refers to the actual situation, to the stage in which the child finds
himself; some of it indicates potentialities … The teacher's task is to satisfy
the actual, to promote the potential, and to tolerate the residual, remembering … that adults also live at many levels'. Compare Whitehead 1974 and
the other surveys cited therein.

Jones, Anthony and Buttrey, June *Children and Stories*, Blackwell, 1970.
Many insights that marry well with the main theme of this book, and a

wealth of practical examples and help to all who believe that children should *enjoy* storying, both their own and other people's.

Jones, Richard *Fantasy and Feeling in Education*, New York University Press and University of London Press, 1968; Penguin, 1972.
Rejects the notion that cognitive growth is the only concern of education and reasserts that play, dreams, and storytelling are crucial to development of mature adults. Compare Singer 1973.

Kelly, George A. *A Theory of Personality*, Norton, New York, 1963.
A concise summary of Kelly's Theory of Personal Constructs: 'A person's processes are psychologically channellized by the ways in which he anticipates events.' The implications for learning theory, personal growth, and the 'construing' of experience (both real and imagined) are discussed by Britton (1970). *Inquiring Man* by D. Bannister and F. Fransella (Penguin, 1971) reviews some of the research based on construct theory.

Kermode, Frank *The Sense of an Ending: Studies in the Theory of Fiction*, OUP, 1966.
Drawing on theology, anthropology, and philosophy, Kermode examines the notions of *time* and *apocalypse* in literature. 'This, I take it, will provide clues to the ways in which fictions, whose ends are consonant with origins, and in concord, however unexpected, with their precedents, satisfy our needs.' Compare Tolkien's *Christian* view of 'eucatastrophe' (1964).

Labov, William and Waletsky, Joshua 'Narrative Analysis: Oral Versions of Personal Experience' in Helm, J. *Essays on Visual and Aural Narrations*, University of Washington Press, Seattle and London, 1970.
Fundamental narrative structures are said to be oral versions of personal experience. An analytical framework based on recurrent patterns is applied to fourteen examples and the results described. Offered as alternative to techniques developed from studies of folk tale, this report makes clear the basic forms and their development.

Laing, R. D. *The Politics of Experience*, Penguin, 1967.
An expressive and, at times, incoherent exposition of the ex-psychoanalyst's view of the alienated individual and his inability to share experience except at the level of extreme subjectivity. ' … perception, imagination, phantasie, reverie, dreams, memory, are simply *modalities of experience*, none more "inner" or "outer" than others'. Compare Barbara Hardy on page 12 above and Britton on pages 40 and 106.

Langer, Susanne *Feeling and Form*, Routledge and Kegan Paul, 1953.
Elaborates the theory of art first set out in *Philosophy in a New Key* (Harvard

University Press, Boston, 1944) and based on a theory of symbolic transformation derived from Cassirer's *Logic of Symbolic Forms*. From these works we take our notions of literature as 'virtual experience'. The theory is also embodied in *Mind: an Essay on Human Feeling* (John Hopkins Press, Baltimore, 1967). Britton (1971) discusses Langer's theories in relation to the child's language development.

Langman, F. H. 'The Idea of the Reader in Literary Criticism' *British Journal of Aesthetics*, **7**, January, 1967.
'We shall fail to see the work correctly unless we see to whom it is addressed ... the work itself implies the kind of reader to whom it is addressed and this may or may not coincide with the author's private view of his audience.' His distinction between the actual reader and the reader that is implied by the work leads to a discussion of the 'ideal reader' and the difference between 'reader' and 'critic'. Highly relevant to the problem of 'children's literature'.

Lewis, C. S. 'On Three Ways of Writing for Children' reprinted in Egoff, *Only Connect*, 1969 (q.v.)
Classic statement of position 'that a children's story which is enjoyed only by children is a bad children's story'. Should be set in context of author's autobiography, *Surprised by Joy* (Bles, 1955), where it is clear that his first audience for his own stories is himself as a child.

Library Association: Crouch, Marcus *Chosen for Children: An Account of the Books which have been awarded the Library Association Carnegie Medal 1936–65*, Library Association, revised edition, 1967.
Of considerable interest because of the extraordinary variety of ways in which 'an outstanding book for children' has been interpreted. The title tells its own tale: these are the books that librarians would like the children to choose – but have they ?

Lüthi, Max *Once upon a Time: on the Nature of Fairy Tales* trans. Lee Chadeayne and Paul Gottwald, with additions by the author. Introduction and reference notes by Francis Lee Utley. Frederick Ungar, New York, 1970.
A collection of broadcast lectures by the Professor of European Folk Literature in Zurich. By their readability and clear definition of fairy tale, local legend, and Saint's legend, they provide access to a wide field of folklore study.

McKellar, Peter *Imagination and Thinking: a Psychological Analysis*, Cohen and West, 1957.

The theme of the book is the relationship of autistic (dream, hallucination) to rational thought. Enid Blyton's contribution is in the chapter 'Works of art as thought products'. The book brings together the testimony of poets, artists, philosophers, and psychologists in an interesting synthesis.

Maranda, Pierre (editor) *Mythology*, Penguin, 1972.

A selection of writings by anthropologists mostly sharing Lévi-Strauss's view that metaphor, myth, language, and social structures share certain structural characteristics. Fascinating extract from Vladimir Propp on 'Transformations in Fairy Tales'. One cannot examine folk tales and myth without an awareness of the theories expounded in this book, however obscure they may appear.

Marshak, M. D. 'A Psychological Approach to Mythology' in *Didaskalos* volume 2, no. 1, 1966.

A contemporary Jungian view of myth. The first essay offers a theory of archetypes based on the genetic transmission of 'innate schemata'. The second discusses the 'numinous world of subjective experience' and the third relates the theory to the child's psychological development. Her dismissal of alternative theories may alienate uncommitted readers.

Melnik, Amelia and Merritt, John (editor) *Reading Today and Tomorrow* and *The Reading Curriculum*, University of London, 1972.

The Open University has published these two collections of papers for its Reading Development Course. They give a clear picture of the research that is going on, for better or worse, in America and Britain. This inevitably emphasizes the quantifiable aspects of reading (acquisition of skills, testing, etc.) rather than questions such as what children need and why – though the first volume includes a fascinating extract from Sartre's *Words* (1964). Smith (1971) must also be read for a clearer view of what reading *is*. The second volume emphasizes reading across the total school curriculum but pays little attention to the most important reading that takes place outside school for the child's own satisfaction. See also Hindle (1973).

Moffett, James *Teaching the Universe of Discourse*, Houghton Mifflin, 1968.

Offers a rationale for the teaching of the mother tongue based on a study of its use in all forms of 'discourse'. Narrative is central, as children must 'make it do for all' until formal thinking and abstractive categorizing develop. Moffett examines a sequence of narrative types on the basis of the author's stance towards his reader.

Montessori, Maria *The Advanced Montessori Method*, Heinemann, 1917.
Distinction made between *creative* imaginative activity based on truth – the
reconstruction of data given by past experience, and *illusory* imagination such
as playing with toys and hearing stories – which is compensating for lack
of real experience. We might accept her distinction but not her rejection of
illusory imagination. She condemns stories that 'exploit a child's credulity'.
Her strangely narrow view is still influential, even among modern English
teachers. The tendency to press children to 'write from their own
experience' rather than to explore alternative lives reflects this approach.

Morris, Joyce *Standards and Progress in Reading: Studies of Children's Reading.
Standards and Progress in Relation to their Individual Attributes, Home
Circumstances and Primary School Conditions*, National Foundation for
Educational Research, 1966.
Report of a survey undertaken in a sample of Kent primary schools bringing
up some interesting and disturbing data, especially concerning Heads' and
teachers' attitudes towards 'reading books' and 'library books'. Of particular
interest: Chapter VI (especially sections on 'Reading environment', 'School
and class libraries'), Chapter VII (especially 'Reading by the teacher') and
Appendix D ('Books recommended by teachers for junior classes').

Moseley, David *Special Provision for Reading: when will they ever learn*, National
Foundation for Educational Research, Windsor, 1975.
A survey of reading research which leads the author to claim that a
community must underwrite the resources necessary to produce universal
literacy.

Moss, Elaine *Children's Books of the Year 1970*, Hamish Hamilton, 1971; and
annual sequels.
Brief but singularly penetrating reviews of a year's output of books for
children and adolescents by a wise critic with an appraising eye for the whole
scene.

Opie, Iona and Peter *The Classic Fairy Tales*, OUP, 1974.
This lavish edition contains the earliest English texts of 24 of the best-known
tales with a historical commentary. The illustrations show the range of
visual interpretations of the stories through the ages. The volume is an
excellent starting-point for a study of the subject; Cook (1969), Lüthi (1970),
and Maranda (1972) will then open up the wider issues.

Paffard, Michael *Inglorious Wordsworths*, Hodder and Stoughton, 1974.
Subtitled 'A study of some transcendental experiences in childhood and

adolescence'. Deals with dimensions of experience called 'the numinous'
and the particular qualities of vividness, significance, and elation attached
to it by young adults who provided the evidence. Important, hitherto
unresearched area related to all other studies of *response*.

Philips, Robert (editor) *Aspects of Alice: Lewis Carroll's Dreamchild as seen
through the Critic's Looking-Glass 1865–1971*, Gollancz, 1972.
This collection of writings about Carroll ranges from Auden ('today's
Wonder-world needs Alice'), Empson ('a shift on to the child of the obscure
tradition of pastoral') and Virginia Woolf ('the Reverend C. L. Dodgson
had no life') to some rather odd psychedelic theories by modern Americans.
An intriguing sampler of critical approaches.

Piaget, Jean *The Child's Conception of the World*, Routledge and Kegan
Paul, 1929; Paladin paperback, 1973.
An early but unsuperseded study of the child's developing notions of: the
distinction between the external and the internal subjective world, 'thought',
'nominal realism', 'dreams', 'child animism', 'moral necessity', 'physical
determinism', and 'artificialism'.
All this is central to any consideration of fairy tales and myth because these
are the structures that the child shares with folklore. This study, if
combined with an anthropological approach to sympathetic magic etc., will
form a most fruitful basis for an investigation of a young child's narrative
experience.

Piaget, Jean *Play, Dreams and Imitation in Childhood*, Heinemann, 1951,
Routledge and Kegan Paul, 1962.
If we accept that storytelling and the reading of fiction is 'improvising on
reality' and a development from play and daydream (cf. Freud, 1908,
Winnicott, 1972, and Britton, 1971), then our attention must turn to the
child's acquisition of the powers of imitation, play, 'secondary symbolism'
and 'the assimilation of reality to the ego without the need for accommodation'.
This book, based on three detailed case histories, is essential to our understanding of 'deliberate illusion' and fiction-making, which in turn are central
to the problem of reading.

Richards, I. A. *Practical Criticism*, Routledge and Kegan Paul, 1929.
An account of what the author regards as very unsatisfactory evaluative
responses to pieces of literature by his Cambridge students, and a classification of their difficulties and sources of deviation. 'Indeed, the more we study

this matter the more we shall find 'a love for poetry' accompanied by an incapacity to understand or construe it.'
Maintains that reading literature 'is a craft, in the sense that mathematics, cooking, and shoemaking are crafts. It can be taught.' Its influence on examinations and classroom teaching has been enormous and, in general, disastrous. See also *How to Read a Page* (Routledge and Kegan Paul, 1943).

Rosen, Connie and Harold *The Language of Primary School Children*, Penguin, 1973. *Language, Thought and Comprehension*, Routledge and Kegan Paul, 1965. Based on a Schools Council project on language development in British primary schools, this book documents broadly and in depth descriptive and critical accounts of the relations of language to learning. The comments on reading are of exceptional value, criticizing those who 'deal with fiction' for 'a deep lack of confidence in the power of literature to do its work and a profound conviction that unless literature can be converted into the hard currency of familiar school learning, it has not earned its keep'.

Sartre, J.-P. *What is Literature?* Methuen, 1947.
Examines the role of reader and *engagé* writer. Chapter 2, 'Why write?' describes reading as a dialectical synthesis of perception and creation. ' ... the literary object has no other substance than the reader's subjectivity; Raskolnikov's waiting is *my* waiting which I lend him.' Compare Smith (1971) on 'what the reader brings to the text'.
Words (*Les Mots*), Gallimard, Paris, 1964; Hamish Hamilton, 1964.
Compare Graham Greene's acceptance of the relation of his early reading and his late writing with Sartre's handling of the same theme, treating as 'illusion' his early experiences of the world he now interprets as the sage of his generation.

Singer, Jerome L. *The Child's World of Make Believe*, Academic Press, 1973. The author's chief concern is 'to relate symbolic play (cf. Piaget) to the development of imagery in the child'. In doing this he touches on many things related to reading, notably the necessity for private fantasy in the lives of over-socialized children. Cf. Winnicott.

Smith, Frank *Understanding Reading*, Holt, Rinehart and Winston, 1971. Description of the 'cognitive' skill of reading drawing on psycholinguistics. An essential corrective to the Skinnerian accounts of reading as conditioned behaviour that still dominate most theoretical studies. Unusually, it bases its account on what the normal fluent reader rather than the novice does. It shows that 'comprehension of meaning normally *precedes* word identification':

it 'is *not* decoding to spoken language'.

Its sequel *Psycholinguistics and Reading* (1972) contains papers which link the theory to the teaching of reading, and a third book, *Comprehension and Learning* (1975) offers, 'a conceptual framework' while reading with other studies of language development.

Smith, Lillian H. *The Unreluctant Years: A Critical Approach to Children's Literature*, American Library Association, 1953.

Acknowledges the influence of Paul Hazard (q.v.) and C. S. Lewis (q.v. in Egoff *Only Connect*) in her demand that we examine children's books by 'the same standards of criticism as any other form of literature'. We must attempt 'critical analysis of each book in relation to the fundamental principles of good writing as found in literary classics'.

Squire, James R. (editor) *Response to Literature*, National Council of Teachers of English, Illinois, 1968.

A collection of conference papers by leading British and American teachers of English including Britton (reprinted on page 106 above) and Harding (page 379 above).

Steiner, George *Language and Silence*, Faber, 1967. *Extraterritorial: papers on literature and the language revolution*, Faber, 1972.

The work of this critic is a constant challenge to conventional literary attitudes. It would be interesting to extend their implications to children's books and reading. 'Unlike Matthew Arnold and unlike Dr Leavis, I find myself unable to assert confidently that the humanities humanize. Indeed, I would go farther: it is at least conceivable that the focusing of consciousness on a written text, which is the substance of our training and pursuit, diminishes the sharpness and readiness of our actual moral response.'

Storr, Catherine 'Fear and Evil in Children's Books', in *Children's Literature in Education*, 1, March, 1970.

Examines the possible effects of horror and 'sick fear' in children's response. The discussion that follows this conference paper is specially relevant to Alix Pirani's essay, page 294.

Thompson, Stith *Motif-Index of Folk Literature*, 2nd edition, 6 volumes, Bloomington, Indiana, 1955–58.

An encyclopaedic reference work subtitled 'A Classification of Narrative Elements in Folktales, Ballads, Myths, Fables, Medieval Romances, Exempla, Fabliaux, Jest-Books, and Local Legends'. Mostly used by

anthropologists. Each motif (i.e. the smallest element of folk narrative) is
numbered.

Tolkien, J. R. R. *Tree and Leaf*, Allen and Unwin, 1964.
First published in *Essays presented to Charles Williams* (OUP, 1947), 'On
Fairy Stories' is issued in this volume with 'Leaf by Niggle' which was also
written at the time when *The Lord of the Rings* was being planned. Dealing
with the art of 'sub-creation', Tolkien rescues the fairy story from the anthropologists and the philologists on behalf of children for whom it is the
archetype of experience.

Townsend, John Rowe *A Sense of Story*, Longman, 1971.
Sub-titled 'Essays on contemporary writers for children' these are depth
studies of 19 British, American, and Australian authors in the traditional
manner, amplified by biographical and bibliographical details with some
personal testimony added by the writers themselves.

Tucker, Nicholas 'How Children Respond to Fiction' in *Children's Literature in
Education*, 9, 1972.
Analysis on Piagetian model to explain 'response' in terms of young readers.
Books and the Child: A psychological exploration, forthcoming CUP, 1977.
A study of children's intellectual and affective development and the
reading that matches it.

Vigotsky, L. S. *Thought and Language*, Moscow, 1934; MIT Press, Boston, 1962.
The implications of the theories in this seminal book are now being extended
to all studies of language and thought. While they seem chiefly relevant to
concept formation, they have also much for the student of children's stories
and reading. Claiming that thought and language have different genetic roots,
Vigotsky shows how thought becomes verbal and speech intellectual.
Drawing on illustrations from Tolstoy, Dostoevsky, and Stanislavsky, he
describes the linear surface nature of discourse and how an understanding of
an author's thought depends on our contact with its 'affective and volitional
basis'. See also *The Psychology of Art* (1971) 'The analysis of the fable',
where he describes reading as a 'state of voluntary hallucination'.

White, Dorothy *Books Before Five*, New Zealand Council for Educational
Research, 1956.
A children's librarian's diary about her own child's first book experiences
from her second birthday. Of particular importance because of the clear
observation of the interaction of books and life in these early years. The author
is also honest about the toppling of some of her own preconceived ideas.

Whitehead, F., Capey, A. C., and Maddren, W. *Children's Reading Interests,*
(Schools Council Working Paper 52) Evans/Methuen Educational, 1975.
An interim report from the Schools Council research project into
children's reading habits, 10–15. A broad survey by questionnaire of 8000
school children in a stratified random sample. Considers that narrative forms
the bulk of children's reading, that the 'informed enthusiasm' of teachers is a
significant factor, that a 'disturbingly high proportion of boys and girls' do
not read 'enough'. Nevertheless, says the report, 'experience shows that there
are very few children, if indeed any, who cannot be "hooked" on books if the
right ones are put in their way.' Leaves many assumptions unexamined and
could probably be compared with an earlier survey – Yarlott, G. and
Harpin, W. S. *1000 Responses to English Literature* (Educational
Research, **13,** 1 and 2, November, 1970 and February, 1971) which examined
the basic reading tastes of examination candidates and their attitudes to
set texts. Compare also Jenkinson, 1940.

Wicker, Brian *The Story-Shaped World*, Athlone Press, 1975.
Drawing on linguistics and theology, Wicker explores the notion that the
relationship between real life and fiction is based on a 'metaphysical pact'.

Williams, Raymond 'The English Language and the English Tripos' in *Times
Literary Supplement*, November, 1974.
Trenchant survey of English literary studies at Cambridge University since
1918. Suggests some areas unillumined by significant study of language
need reconsideration, and of these writing for children is one.

Winnicott, D. W. *Playing and Reality*, Tavistock, 1971.
Explores the nature of the intermediate area between internal and external
reality and the use made of it by the individual, first in play and shared
playing, and then as the realm of the creation and transmission of culture.

Young, Michael (editor) *Knowledge and Control*, Collier-Macmillan, 1971.
A collection of papers by educational sociologists who share the view that
a society selects, classifies, distributes, evaluates educational knowledge and,
in doing so, reflects the distribution of power and principles of social control
in that society. The contributions of Keddie and Bourdieu are important.
Such an approach has immense implications for literature: *Who* determines
which art forms shall be promoted in the 'competition for cultured
legitimacy?' See Worpole's article on page 344 above.

Studies and surveys of children's literature

Alderson, Brian *Catalogue of an Exhibition of Pictures by Maurice Sendak,* Bodley Head, 1976.

Bechtel, Louise Seaman *Books in Search of Children;* selected and introduced by Virginia Haviland. Hamish Hamilton, 1970.

Binding, Paul *Robert Louis Stevenson,* OUP, 1974.

Boston, L. M. *Memory in a House,* Bodley Head, 1972.

Cass, Joan E. *Literature and the Young Child,* Longman, 1967.

Crouch, Marcus *The Nesbit Tradition,* Benn, 1972.
Treasure Seekers and Borrowers, Library Association, 1962.

Darton, F. J. Harvey *Children's Books in England, Five Centuries of Social Life* 2nd edition, CUP, 1958.

Elkin, Judith *Books for the Multi-racial Classroom,* Library Association Youth Libraries Group, 1971.

Ellis, Alec *A History of Children's Reading and Literature,* Pergamon, 1968.
How to Find Out about Children's Literature, Pergamon, 1973.

Ellis, Anne W. *The Family Story in the 1960s,* Bingley, 1970.

Eyre, Frank *British Children's Books in the Twentieth Century,* Longman, 1971.

Fenwick, S. I. (editor) *A Critical Approach to Children's Literature,* Chicago University Press, 1967.

Fisher, Margery *Matters of Fact: Aspects of Non-fiction for Children,* Brockhampton, 1972.

Gifford, Denis 'The Evolution of the British Comic', *History Today,* May, 1971.

Green, Roger Lancelyn *Tellers of Tales,* new edition, Ward, 1969.

Haviland, Virginia (editor) *Children's Literature: a Guide to Reference Sources,* Library of Congress, 1966; First Supplement, 1972.

Hildick, E. W. *Children and Fiction,* Evans, 1970.

Hollindale, Peter *Choosing Books for Children,* Paul Elek, 1974.

Hürlimann, Bettina *Three Centuries of Children's Books in Europe,* OUP, 1967.
Picture-Book World, OUP, 1968.

Jan, Isabelle *On Children's Literature,* Allen Lane, 1973.

Laski, Marghanita *Mrs Ewing, Mrs Molesworth and Mrs Hodgson Burnett*, Barker, 1950.

Lewis, Naomi *Fantasy Books for Children*, National Book League, London, 1975.

Marshall, Margaret R. *Libraries and Literature for Teenagers*, André Deutsch, 1975.

Marshall, Sybil, Gagg, J. C., Glynn, D., Cass, J. E. *Beginning with Books*, Blackwell, 1971.

Martin, Nancy 'Children and Stories: Their Own and Other People's' in *English in Education*, **6**, 2, Summer, 1972.

Meek, Margaret *Geoffrey Trease*, Bodley Head, 1960. *Rosemary Sutcliff*, (in the Monograph Series), Bodley Head, 1962.

Meigs, Cornelia (editor) *A Critical History of Children's Literature: A Survey of Children's Books in English From Earliest Time to the Present*, Macmillan, New York, 1953. Revised edition, 1969.

Miller, B. M. and Field, E. W. (editors) *Caldecott Medal Books: 1938–1957*, Horn Book Incorporated, 1957.

Moorman, Charles *Arthurian Triptych: Mythic Materials in Charles Williams, C. S. Lewis and T. S. Eliot*, CUP, 1960.

Muir, Percy *English Children's Books 1600–1900*, Batsford, 1954.

Pickard, P. M. *I Could a Tale Unfold*, Tavistock, 1961.

Thwaite, Ann *Waiting for the Party: the life of Frances Hodgson Burnett*, Secker and Warburg, 1974.

Thwaite, M. F. *From Primer to Pleasure in Reading*, Library Association, revised edition, 1973.

Townsend, J. R. *Written for Children: An Outline of English-Language Children's Literature*, revised edition, Kestrel Books, 1974.

Trease, Geoffrey *Tales Out of School*, 2nd edition, Heinemann, 1964.
A Whiff of Burnt-Boats, Macmillan, 1972.
Laughter at the Door, Macmillan, 1974.

Viguers, Ruth Hill *Margin for Surprise: about books, children and libraries*, Little, Brown, 1964.

Acknowledgements

The editors wish to thank authors, periodicals, and editors for permission to reprint the following Copyright material:

Joan Aiken: 'Purely for love' from *Books*, 2, Winter 1970. Reprinted by permission of the National Book League.

Arthur Applebee: 'Where does Cinderella live ?' from *Use of English*, **25**, (2), Winter 1973. Reprinted by permission of Chatto and Windus Educational, Ltd.

W. H. Auden: 'George MacDonald' from *Forewords and Afterwords* by W. H. Auden. Reprinted by permission of Faber and Faber Limited. Also by permission of Farrar, Straus, & Giroux, Inc. from *The Visionary Novels of George MacDonald*, edited by Anne Fremantle. Copyright © 1967 by W. H. Auden.

Betty Bacon: 'From now to 1984' from the *Wilson Library Bulletin*, October 1970. Copyright © 1970 by the H. W. Wilson Company. Reprinted by permission of the editors.

Georgina Battiscombe: 'Exile from the Golden City' from *The Times Literary Supplement*, 13 March 1959. Reprinted by permission of the editors.

Edward Blishen: 'Learning to love it' from *The Times Educational Supplement*, 7 July 1972. Reprinted by permission of the editors.

Lucy Boston: 'A message from Green Knowe' from *Horn Book Magazine*, June 1963. Reprinted by permission of The Horn Book, Incorporated, Boston.

James Britton: 'The role of fantasy' from *English in Education*, **5**, (3), Winter 1971. Reprinted by permission of the author. 'Response to Literature' from *Response to Literature*: National Council of Teachers of English (publisher). Reprinted by permission of the author.

T. Burgess: 'Story and teller' Copyright © Schools Council. Reprinted by permission of J. N. Britton.

Frances Hodgson Burnett: 'Literature and the Doll' from *The One I Knew the Best of All* (published by Warne and Company Limited 1893 and 1975). Reprinted by permission of Frederick Warne and Company Limited.

Hester Burton: 'The writing of historical novels' from *Horn Book Magazine*, June 1969. Reprinted by permission of The Horn Book, Incorporated, Boston.

Dick Cate: 'Uses of narrative' from *English in Education*, **5**, (3), 1971. Reprinted by permission of the author.

Kornei Chukovsky: 'There is no such thing as a shark' originally published in *From two to five* by the University of California Press, 1963. Reprinted by permission of the Regents of the University of California.

Elizabeth Cook: 'Cinderella's sisters get ready for a ball' from *The Ordinary and the Fabulous*. Reprinted by permission of Cambridge University Press.

Liz Gant: 'That One's Me' from *Redbook Magazine*, 1972.

Alan Garner: 'A bit more practice' from *The Times Literary Supplement*, 6 June 1968. Reprinted by permission of the author.

William Golding: 'Fable'. Reprinted by permission of Faber and Faber Limited. Also © 1965 by William Golding; Reprinted from his volume *The Hot Gates and other Occasional Pieces* by permission of Harcourt Brace Jovanovich, Incorporated.

Robert Graves: 'The Cool Web' from *Collected Poems 1965* by Robert Graves. Reprinted by permission of Robert Graves.

R. L. Gregory: 'Psychology: towards a science of fiction'. This article first appeared in *New Society*, London, 23 May 1974, and is reprinted by permission of the editors.

D. W. Harding: 'The bond with the author' from *Use of English*, **22**, (4), Summer 1971. Reprinted by permission of the author.
'Psychological processes in the reading of fiction' from the *British Journal of Aesthetics*, **2**, (2), 1962. Reprinted by permission of the author.

Barbara Hardy: 'Towards a poetics of fiction' from *Novel: A forum on fiction*, Brown University, Fall 1968. Reprinted by permission of the editors.

Janet Hill: 'A minority view' from *Children's Book News*, May 1967. Reprinted by permission of the publishers, Children's Book Centre Limited, London.

Brian Jackson: 'Philippa Pearce' from *Use of English*, **21**, (3), Spring 1970. Reprinted by permission of the author.

Randall Jarrell: 'Children selecting books in a library' from *Collected Poems* by Randall Jarrell. Reprinted by permission of Faber and Faber Limited. Also reprinted by permission of Farrar, Straus, and Giroux Incorporated, from *The Complete Poems* by Randall Jarrell, Copyright 1941 by Randall Jarrell, Copyright renewed 1969 by Mary von Schrader Jarrell.

C. S. Lewis: 'On stories' from *Essays presented to Charles Williams*. Reprinted by permission of Oxford University Press.

'A letter from C. S. Lewis' from *Horn Book Magazine*, October 1966, Reprinted by permission of The Horn Book, Incorporated, Boston.

John McCreesh: 'Children's ideas of horror and tragedy' from *Catholic Education Today*, September 1970. Reprinted by permission of the editor.

Peter McKellar: pp. 136–9 from Chapter IX, 'Works of art as thought products' in *Imagination and Thinking: A Psychological Analysis*. Reprinted by permission of Basic Books, Incorporated. First published in Great Britain by Cohen and West Limited 1957. Also reprinted by permission of Routledge and Kegan Paul Limited.

Margaret Meek: 'A private house' from *The Times Literary Supplement*, 15 June 1973. Reprinted by permission of the author.

Joan Bodger Mercer: 'Innocence is a cop-out' from the *Wilson Library Bulletin*, October 1971. Copyright © 1971 by the H. W. Wilson Company. Reprinted by permission of the editors.

Elaine Moss: 'The adult-eration of children's books' from *Signal*, **14**, May 1974. Reprinted by permission of Signal, The Thimble Press, Lockwood, South Woodchester, Gloucestershire. '*The "Peppermint" Lesson*' from *Books*, 2, Winter 1970. Reprinted by permission of the National Book League.

National Council of Teachers of English: 'The Study Group Report: Response to literature'. Copyright © 1968 by the National Council of Teachers of English. Reprinted by permission of the publishers.

Philippa Pearce: 'Writing a Book' in *Horn Book Magazine*, June 1967. Reprinted by permission of The Horn Book, Incorporated, Boston. Review of *The Owl Service* from *Children's Book News*, 1967. Reprinted by permission of Children's Book Centre Limited, London.

Alix Pirani: 'Writers for Children: Ivan Southall' from *Use of English*, **22**, (3), Spring 1971. Reprinted by permission of the author.

Beatrix Potter: ' "Roots" of the Peter Rabbit tales' from *Horn Book Magazine*, **5**, (2), 1929 pages 69–72. Reprinted by permission of The Horn Book, Incorporated, Boston.

Mordecai Richler: 'The great comic book heroes' from *Encounter*, May 1967. Reprinted by permission of the author.

Wolfgang Schlegelmilch: 'From fairy tale to children's novel' from *Bookbird*, **4**, 1970. Reprinted by permission of *Bookbird*, Vienna.

Maurice Sendak: 'Questions to an artist who is also an author' from *The Quarterly Journal of the Library of Congress*. Reprinted by permission of the editor.

Colin Smith: 'Himmel! The Englanders won't stop fighting' from *The Observer*, *Colour Supplement*, 16 July 1972. Reprinted by permission of the editor.

Catherine Storr: 'How to earn a dollar every four words' from *The Guardian*, 1974. Reprinted by permission of the author.
'Things that go bump in the night' from *The Sunday Times Magazine*, 7 March 1971. Reprinted by permission of A. D. Peters and Company.
A discussion with Julia MacRae on *Finn's Folly*, first published in *Children's Literature in Education*, March 1970. Reprinted by permission of the editors.

Geoffrey Trease: 'Old writers and young readers' from *Essays and Studies*, 1973, edited by John Lawlor. Reprinted by permission of the author.

Jill Paton Walsh: 'The rainbow surface' from *The Times Literary Supplement*, 3 December 1971. Reprinted by permission of the author.

Ken Worpole: 'Publishing is for people too' from *The Times Educational Supplement*, 1 March 1974. Reprinted by permission of the editors.

Dorothy White: 'Diary for 6 April 1948' from *Books before five*, page 13. Reprinted by permission of the New Zealand Council for Educational Research.

INDEX